THE
SLAMMER

ABOUT THE BOOK

The American prison system has gone off the rails. Originally started in the country by King George III, the pre-American Revolutionary prisons were inhuman and savage petri houses of filth and diseases. The first post-Revolutionary prisons were not much better; in fact, the Civil War prisons rivaled the inhumanity of pre-Revolutionary ones. It was not until Reconstruction when the stark realities of American prisons were viewed by highly educated overseers as shameful and repugnant. A new language referenced the need to view conceptually a new type of prison: a reformative one that would prepare the prisoner for post- incarceration life. However, throughout the near century and a half, the politicians in charge of legislation have done little to change the culture of prison warehousing.

This story will concentrate on the facts that keep the unfortunate in miserable sardine cans without any provable consideration for change. Our politicians are the nation's lifeline for change, and yet many should be switching places with the incarcerated. If there is ever going to be a sincere change in the warehousing of human beings, there has to be a will for compassion and the election of politicians who do more than mouth false promises.

A country is only as good as its least fortunate. Providing an atmosphere to allow for self-actualization rather than big government handouts starts with health, the family unit, and especially education. Recidivism is the default issue. Only a minority get out with a sense of pride and the ability to reconstruct a decent life, and there is often a latent prejudice against former prisoners. Finding a "second chance" vocational opportunity or an avenue back to school for youth is an absolute must. Prisons provide training in some areas, but nowhere meeting the needs of the large prison populations. This is a generational issue which has never been fully remediated. The book takes on the central issues underpinning the ever continuum of prison expansion.

THE SLAMMER

A CRITIQUE OF PRISON OVERPOPULATION, A MENACING

FLAW IN AMERICAN CULTURE

ROBERT ALLYN GOLDMAN

ISBN: 978-1-7361100-1-0 (sc)
ISBN: 978-1-7361100-0-3 (hc)
ISBN: 978-1-7361100-5-8 (e)

Library of Congress Control Number: 2020925546

Print information available on the last page.

This book is dedicated to all my sons with
love and affection:

Anthony Robert Goldman
Nicholas Allyn Goldman
Timothy Brett Goldman
Christopher Scott Goldman

And

Enduring fond memory and love for my daughter
Stephanie Beth Goldman
(September 4, 1972-September 6, 2002)

CONTENTS

Section 6:
Turmoil...345

Section 7:
Blowback...399

Section 8:

Afterthoughts

Epilogue:

Some very important conclusions in line-by-line presentation.

"Beauty is truth, truth beauty, that is all Ye know on earth, and all ye need to know."[1]

SECTION 1

Beginning Thoughts

Prologue
Introduction

PROLOGUE

Our social behaviors dictate how we interact, how we mature, how we comport ourselves in relation to laws, and, most of all, how we learn personal respect for the environment around us. Civility and collegiality enhance the positive elements of relationships while incivility and being contrary are effectively antisocial. Why do people act the way they do? Well, this has been studied for many years in every manner through the hard work of professional researchers and clinicians. We are delivered lengthy scientific papers, elaborate studies, and even intuitive explanations which ring a bell in us that says: hey, I knew that, why so much money and time into findings that support what "I" already know? That is the sixty-four-thousand-dollar question! Nevertheless, the clarion call has drawn attention to the fragile fault line running right through the American prison system. The crucible of ardent reportage decrying "mass incarceration" is polarizing, but not as one might immediately assume. The polarity is not right versus wrong. It is far more serious because right versus wrong assumes prior knowledge of the subject matter. The current divide separates people who are "invested" versus "the unaware". It pits a minority who have a serious background and understanding against the backdrop of an overwhelming majority who are completely unfamiliar with anything that may or may not be controversial about the prison system. To the mainstream the rejoinder to the suggestion of trouble would be "what trouble"? The cynosure is a prison, so what? In actuality, the average citizen is detached because of what I label as "expected enduring nonchalance."

Expected enduring nonchalance is the emotional vacuum which rightfully justifies the feeling: "If it does not affect my everyday life, why should I care"? The answer is that "the invested" made up of scholars, bloggers, and the wealth of fiction and nonfiction writers clearly demonstrate how intimate a relationship exists between the prisons of the United States and their surrounding communities. In fact, they conspicuously point out how much more history shows numerous parallels between prison life and normative living. The back-loaded information gathered from a long review of all these materials will be woven throughout the forthcoming story.

Central to the prison system is how families related to prisoners and victims of crime cope. Fear and coping mechanisms of these people are at the heart of how the criminal justice system ultimately determines their fate. The victims and their families retain profound emotional burdens. The perpetrators suddenly are placed into an environment they suddenly realize is an emotional reality far beyond their fears. The unexpected nexus for both sides is as explosive as it is a bureaucratic nightmare, to wit a legal cottage industry has grown year by year dealing with complaints and prisoner rights.

I include a great deal of information regarding the relevance of psychopathic behavior, evil, and violence. Expected behaviors do not always follow what people expect out of friends or family members. The reality is that violence springs up very unexpectedly, and often from the most unexpected individual. The fact is that prisons are loaded with very complex and deceptive characters. Only denial or being totally unaware can step in the way of reality. Evil does exist, but it wears many disguises. Many people deny evil, and I quote individuals from different belief systems. I interpret what I believe reflects common sense and what intelligent thinking might reflect.

The world is full of stories of "bad seeds" who pass through adolescence unidentified only to suddenly explode into a tsunami of serial killings or of carefully planned murders like the Las Vegas concert slaughter, the Ft. Lauderdale airport murders, or the Orlando Gay Night Club massacre, etc. Criminality extends from having a wallet stolen to the serial killer. Criminal justice experts, scientists of all stripes, and behaviorists are all wrestling these misfortunes. The fact is that learned people are desperately trying to reason these behaviors and conjure up predictable protective measures. However, spending time interrelating with both non-violent and violent criminals define the illogic deduction that patterns of behavior are predictable. They are not clearly predictive behaviors which may be graphed to demonstrate under certain conditions a certain level of crime may result. In general, as I stated above, disguised behaviors can throttle one's imagination. We cannot predict the human slide into evil. It's usually shrewdly veiled or purposefully camouflaged.

In the following pages I am going to open up and express a great number of thoughts I developed about the American prison system. How did I get to this point? For years I worked as a professional playing amateur psychiatrist to people with bottled up fears cast in my direction unintentionally, and simply as a human response to deeply rooted dark fears. Because I was in a surgical specialty, I often unraveled cobwebs of deeply unrelated apprehension. Yet, I had to accept this to sort out how I would do what I had to do while dealing with their subliminal agitation. Getting to know prisoners offered me the good fortune to experience interactions which made my research so vividly relevant.

Over the years I felt I had learned about the human condition until I took a job in a mixed population prison. Then within two months I found myself in a maximum-security prison which had recently been converted from an HIV/AIDS prison to a center for the "worst of the worst." That is, a population composed of pederasts, kidnappers, molesters, and drug addicts/ traffickers, backyard drug formulary gang bangers, child traffickers, pimps with victimized prostitutes, and, of course, the HIV/AIDS individuals unceremoniously convicted for any of these crimes. They all had one common "distinction": they were murderers as well!

As I progressed daily through this maze, I refocused my attention to a different kind of world no one really understands. I was a witness every day to some of the most unsettling violence imaginable. In fact, I realized the total uncertainty of certainty! Prisons are houses of horror spiced up with interludes of riots and clandestine murders in the night!

The cost realities also stood out prominently for anyone who might understand cost-benefit ratios, or simply overhead without productivity. Or, in the case of prisons, redeeming some positive sign from the vast taxpayers' expense. The expense of managing a prison system, whether state, federal or private, is like a swollen river out of control. It is a deluge of an unfathomable reality, a system which offers very little except growth. If it continues in its current direction, the country's population growth alone will make it untenable. The gangs alone are seemingly running the asylum(s).

As stated, I talked with many of the prisoners over the years. With some, I came to know everything about their lives, including what became the impetus for their criminality. I could perceive the need for a complete restructuring. The prison was like a clipper ship lost at sea with defiant killers who had completely lost their humanity. I saw the young hellions and the mellowed specters of once proud and robust souls. They were like Orwellian creatures, wayward and detached. However, I knew from my experience at a mixed institution that not all prisons house these violent types on the fringe of life. Most prisons house non-violent prisoners, and that is when a light bulb went off in my brain. The real world of prisons is one where a mix of corruption and the helpless reality of sentencing is out of control and blatantly ignored.

Ultimately, I thought it would be prudent to quit my job as the temperature of the environment was rising to a threatening level for me. The cellblock housing the most unpredictable (the psychopaths) had begun to mutter some convincing threats my way whenever I walked the yard. I knew from other prisoner contacts that it had nothing to do with me. But I had to deal with the real and imminent. One of the associate wardens with whom I developed a special relationship tried to deter me, but I knew inside my time was up. All the kind personal attributions for my commitment would have been irrelevant to family and friends lowering me into the ground. I knew that for a certainty.

The insight I shall bring will support many of the authoritative literature which attempts to bring reason to such a vast array of human personalities. My personal commentary is not without severe criticism for pitfalls which have lingered far too long. Many people have pointed them out as well, but none have seen them play out daily, every day. I have tried to bring a little bit of humor and authoritative commentary so the reading would not be sterile, dull and tedious. I was fortunate to interact with some of the most delightful, hardworking and well-meaning people in my life. They were a major reason why I felt compelled to write this book.

The American prison system is a reflection of the culture within the United States. It is the centerpiece for the confinement of empty, forgotten souls in an environment where time has stopped and only imaginary dreams linger. To understand and appreciate our freedoms it is vital to understand how prisoners are so adrift with only a lifeless sense of hope buried deeply within a soul which dies a little more each passing day. Safety requires "mouse traps", but the present ones are vestigial and broken. Hopefully, the ensuing story will separate the legitimate facts from mixed messaging about the enduring issue of "mass incarceration."

INTRODUCTION

"Nothing is at last sacred but the integrity of your own mind"
Ralph Waldo Emerson[2]

"There is a time in every man's education when he arrives at the
conviction that envy is ignorance; that imitation is suicide; that
he must take himself for better or worse ... The power which resides in him is new
in nature, and none but he knows what that
is which he can do, nor does he know until he has tried."
Ralph Waldo Emerson.[3]

During my life I have been fortunate to experience everything from teaching complicated science to post-doctoral residents to diving off rock cliffs and ski jumping off escarpment ledges as a post- pubescent youth in the states of Maine and New Hampshire respectively. I distinctly remember the rebounding thoughts in my brain at the time like they were yesterday. The sheer fear was held concealed out of youthful bravado, a character trait of such ignorance that can only be excused by immaturity and consequently bold ignorance. I broke my nasal septum coming off a jump in a whiteout blizzard and hitting a giant oak tree I could not see as I landed. I had surgery for a severely deviated nasal septum by a renowned surgeon, Dr. George H. Shedd.[4] I "shudder" to remember this day: As I lay on a surgical table just outside Mt. Cranmore in North Conway, New Hampshire fully clothed in my ski outfit I still hear the bellow sound of his voice: "Son, this will only hurt for a moment" as a lengthy surgical hook went up my left nostril as he braced my head to yank my blood gushing nasal septum to the right!

"Well son, how do you feel" to which I awakened to his sonorous voice ten hours later in the night? I survived without brain injury because I laughed torture-like to my mother days later: Her reply: "No brains, no injury"! Typically mother-like: "Don't you ever be so stupid again!" Wow, many, many years later I still recall the stupidity of flying birdlike over trees in a blizzard. Such unacceptable behavior is benign, but it rang loudly in my head as I met so many youngmurders!

Youth is forgiven, adulthood cannot without consequence. A price has to be paid before forgiveness and second chance. Somewhere along the line a barrier is jumped, and learning from juvenile mistakes can no longer be accepted and brushed aside. And nowhere did I find this more pertinent than during my experience in a state prison system. However, and this is an important caveat, it is about time the American prison system turned a purely punitive system (no matter what is propagated) into a rehabilitative one. To accomplish this American culture must be reconfigured.

This is long overdue. Therefore, an overriding theme throughout will be dedicated to how this can come about. Because through time immemorial "prison reform" is all that blares with futility, and yet with continuous political bluster and self-flagellating. Nothing gets done because legislators do not understand the issue, and the issue becomes tagged like the forgotten stepsister to a number of other legislative bills. I intend to delve into this controversial subject as society cannot depend on karma. Otherwise, the system will continue to ebb and flow with the statistics constituting fluctuating prison populations. Effective reform is chancy just as Brown v. Board of Education Supreme Court decision of 1954 or The Civil Rights Act of 1964[5] came about only when the politics were ripe.

One thing is for certain: how little is known about prisons and their grim reality. It is an ongoing cultural war with survival tenuous at best. Viability for those locked up due to criminal violations is predicated on the crime committed, the sentence, behavior while locked up, and the ability to keep productive. Very few "reform" because of the prison culture.

The prison experience is irrational and tragically miserable. In many ways the consequence is a loss of identity and a return to a primal existence. Boredom is watching paint dry; tragedy is the imprisonment of a human being wasting away. I have watched and talked to the exuberant youth so blind to what a life sentence represents, and, likewise with the wizened, moribund aged just awaiting the Lord's calling. The general population is an admixture of hellions and the repentant, born again souls desperately hoping to get out. Their conversions to religion are desperate and sad. The punishment for a period of marauding and gratuitous depravity does not properly assuage grieving families, especially the lifer's own.

So many commentaries argue against over-crowded prisons, poor conditions, harsh sentences, early pardons or release, onerous sentencing guidelines, etc. My feelings from on- site experience tells me this kind of reasoning may be valid to some extent; but it is also very overboard in its totality while leapfrogging many important considerations. There has to be far wider latitude in making and justifying cases which are tendentious in scope. The prison system is the sole means of holding the criminal at bay. It is all society has. Its importance cannot be minimized and shredded by academics posturing when its very being is so difficult to run. It is imperfect in its day-to-day headache provoking incidents. Somewhere there is a very reasonable solution. But, unfortunately this lies at its nexus with the fluctuating political climate from one generation to the next. I will discuss this later because I do wholeheartedly believe prisons are holding far, far too many prisoners. And I feel it has a lot to do with tendentious politicians and the dull-minded bureaucrats

People living everyday normal lives believe they understand prison life through movies, television documentaries and, in some cases, books of fiction. However, the truth is that the majority of thoughtful, family-oriented people do not have a clue what goes on behind the razor wires. So much of today's television news renders a highly distorted impression. Viewpoints are highly narrow and biased. Simply stated, prison life is like a block of frozen ice on a steamy summer day, a diaphanous identity melting away. The psychological misery is directly proportional to the type of criminality and the level of lockup.

But it should never be misunderstood, prison life is a walk back in time. I have used a simple mathematical equation to quantify "the hell." The misery index delivers a sense of proportionality. Fear of physical paybacks intensifies the misery. Obviously, prisoners in maximum security prisons have a greater chance of living in misery than in minimum security ones for many reasons, but the obvious one is that the environment is less stable and prone to very explosive flashpoints.

The optics can be very disturbing, but it is what it is. Assuredly, however, seeing it daily is more than an enlightening experience. It reshapes a person's tolerance for how pathetically lives are wasted. Recidivism, being expectedly high for violent criminals, is a major concern for the non-violent. It is a societal albatross. Records from the International Prison Commission shows it was 40 per cent in the late 19th century. It now waivers higher than the 50th percentile. This is tantamount to a discussion of the realities of the family unit in the United States. Truancy and loss of family connection results in the poor, the neglected and forgotten waywardly finding criminality. The absolutes of prison statistics point to the most glaring consideration: loss of the father influence in matriarchal families eventuating in criminal behavior. There are a number of very interesting books written which document the history of the American prison system in very impactful detail. In addition, there are stories by ex-prisoners who, for one reason or another, have put them to writing. Two very excellent books reflect a lot of time and perseverance exercised in bringing to light statistics supporting topical issues of a political nature. One very active website pretty much covers all facets of prison system topics which highlight overall state-by-state differences. I will bring them to light as I analyze fundamental prison issues. The facts are somewhat paradoxical because they define the reason for the most complex social system in the country: protecting the citizenry from all levels of criminals. Without prisons people would live in a perpetual state of turmoil. And yet, as this story evolves it will become apparent how the system has gone overboard in its protection raison d'etre!

I worked within a state maximum security prison that housed the most dangerous, anti-social criminal individuals I have ever met. worked as the prison dentist, but it was obvious to me during the first week that it had very little to do with the quality of dentistry I practiced for many years. It was triage for pain, violence or both. What is more important is how close I came to meeting my maker on a daily basis. My story is going to be fashioned by my daily interactions with some of the most violent criminals I got to know. Before I arrived at this prison, I was told it housed primarily HIV and AIDS inmates. However, when I came on board there was a rearrangement within the state and all the violent criminals were assembled and reprocessed. These miscreants I came to know were violent murderers: child predators, rapists and killers; kidnappers, rapists and killers; robbers and killers; or killers related to heavy drug activity through manufacture, distribution, trafficking, or all.

When I first arrived, I had no idea what to expect. I was a highly-educated person and exposed to all types of people through my entire adult life. Years ago, I met one of the great clock makers in the country, Elmer O. Stennes[6], from Weymouth, Massachusetts. He was incarcerated at the Massachusetts Correctional Institution in Plymouth, Massachusetts. He and his second wife, Eva, had a daughter, also named Eva. After an altercation with his daughter he shot her with one bullet to her head from his .357 magnum derringer. He was sentenced to 8-10 years, but only served 4 years. Subsequently, he remarried and was shot dead while sleeping in bed. Supposedly his third wife, who was also shot (but lived) identified the assailant as a son by his second wife. Having talked to Elmer, I always thought it was so difficult to connect such a talented man with such a mental/emotional reservoir of violent behavior buried deep within. His case was never prosecuted. Stennes was a gifted man, self-taught with a strangely detached personality. When I met him while he was serving his prison term, I found him incredibly well- spoken but with inscrutably poor social graces. I had one of his miniature Simon Willard look-alike clocks which broke so I visited him at the Massachusetts Correctional Institution in Plymouth, Massachusetts. He brilliantly repaired it with very few improvised tools. As I watched it gave me insight into how criminality can coexist with quite normal behaviors. Stunning! It was a very unique experience for me as I recall because I did not reflect at all on the nature of incarceration at all. "Wow" was all I could think as I left the prison. Although a very bizarre man, he was impassioned and certainly did not outwardly present the deportment of a cold- blooded killer. Later in time all I could do was shake my head when reading of his murder. I developed an interest in criminal behavior from this experience as well from the seedy criminals of Boston fame: Whitey Bulger[7,8], head of the notorious Winter Hill Gang in South Boston (who personally murdered one of my very young patients, never realizing she was attached to his righthand man, Stephen "the rifleman" Flemmi, and knew too much), and Specs O'Keefe[9] of the great Boston Brinks Robbery of 1954. He became known for a very quick sense of wit. When asked by a local Boston reporter why he stole a million dollars from a large known Boston Bank his rejoinder snapped out snarky: "Because that's where the money is!" This retort lingered throughout my whole youth. I also knew I had a distant uncle who went to prison for white-collar crimes; i.e., bank fraud, theft and bribery. I never knew him, but my parents told me he was loosely bound, calculating, and very slippery and crafty. Yet, through these experiences, I was never impacted at all by the meaning nor social consequences of crime until the Stennes incident. I gravitated to material written about the country's penal system, particularly as it related to societal issues: poverty, education and the family unit. Finally, I also remember having a very close childhood friend who went to a reform school at about 14 years old before he embarked on a lifetime of crime. He was the product of a badly broken home, and his arrest one day (while we were playing around with his Lionel trains) really impacted me, even to this day. I have always wondered what became of him. He was not fortunate to experience any kind of normalcy except when he was with me at my house. He was precocious and very alert, particularly as he repaired his broken trains attached to a very convoluted set of tracks he designed himself.

When I went to work at a maximum-security prison my mind was quietly flooded with all the thoughts I carried from not only these experiences but from so many others I vicariously came to know from one of my dearest marathon buddies who happened to be the Commandant of the Massachusetts State Police (aka "Staties") at the time. Even then, while at work, it took a while to let all my experiences settle in before a heavy cloud definitely settled down over my mind with my exposure to some very irrational and savage prisoners.

The histories on the American penal system are fascinating, but the books concerning facets of the law which get caught up in various debated political issues like sentencing, early release, non-violent and violent crimes, rehabilitation, parole, recidivism, etc., are very doctrinaire and partisan in their philosophical stance. The carceral state and death penalty (capital punishment) engender unending debates, and statistics are refreshed continuously to vindicate opinions and belief systems. If I had not spent so much time inside the prison system witnessing the pitfalls so ingrained within the system, the litany of statistics would have provided very little contextual value. My experience vindicated the importance of the back-story of comparative statistical evaluations. Perhaps not always, I feel true meaning is often lost in numbers alone. A very funny, but telling quote once impacted me convincingly in this regard by Aaron Levenstein[10], former Business Professor at Baruch College: "Statistics are like bikinis. What they reveal is suggestive, but what they conceal is vital". My mission will be to unearth the hidden and unknown about prison life. It certainly has more than an undesirable energy and vitality, but, nevertheless certain and irrepressible. These are thoughts I carried internally as I witnessed and talked to prisoners on an everyday basis. I did learn enough to know that there are very cause-and-effect reasons why prisoners are beaten up, shivved or shanked, sexually victimized, randomly abused, and aggressively assault guards. There are certainly defensible arguments for sentences, and the levels of confinement are structured according to the degree of criminality.

When I first entered the prison, I walked quite blithely and nonchalantly through the yard. I did not pay much attention to my body alarm, and I engaged many of the prisoners far too casually. When I think back on this, I realize now how naïve this was. Movies like "Shawshank Redemption" patently lowball how dangerous a maximum-security prison is. The truth of the matter is that vigilance and awareness are foundational for survival. Prison is no joke, and particularly in a Level 3. The most significant feeling I had is how naïve I was about the inside atmosphere, the stark prisoner personalities, and the way so many fractious ones sauntered around the yard unsupervised. And lack of supervision is a reality I shall discuss. Occasionally, I would just stop and gaze around to see how such activity in the various cell block mini-yards seemed so out-of-control and raucous. It seemed to hold together, but there was always a violent altercation which put the yard (or, various cell blocks) in lockdown. The daily experience eventually made an unforgettable impact. The prison held together, but with a significantly high level of fragility and vulnerability.

A prevailing feeling I always had was the high degree of political correctness which obstructed what could be a far greater semblance of certainty and control within the prison. I could not understand that of everything necessary in such a massive complex the one most important feature was obstructed: resolute compliance. When I was a teenager, I used to ride on a lake in Maine on a Higgins craft, the very same the allies used to ferry the American troops onto the beachhead from the LST's in the Normandy invasion on June 6, 1944. Riding in it there was a restrictor feeling as if the engine wanted to power away but could not. Well, there was a device connected to the intake of the engine called a "Governor" which prevented the engine from exceeding a power level to speed up. Well, this is exactly the feeling I had about the prison. There were so many "this and that's" regulating the free flow of control mechanisms within the prison that it provided for a contrarian polar opposite effect: a prevailing dangerous environment. It was so far beyond the pale that it will take a chapter or two to describe it.

The most important function for a prison is to protect people in both local and extended communities from the harm which might prevail if prisoners were to escape. And subsumed within is the protection of the guards and other personnel employed to ensure their safety and maintain calm. However, life is most often painted with different outcomes, which is to say that oft-times expectations do not go according to Hoyle. And this is the defining quality of prison life. For all the intangibles that can turn a prison upside down very suddenly prisoners across the country are kept in tow exceedingly well. Yes, escapees get their mugs on television and in newspapers, and it shows to what extent the most desperate will go to break out.

The greatest complications the system faces arise where political/legal controversies hover over everyday prison management. To me the most glaring example is the perpetual back-and-forth regarding life sentences versus the death penalty (capital punishment) in cases of murder. It's one thing to see thinking and legal decisions evolve over time. But having talked to a lot of prisoners faced with life sentences in a state where the death sentence was more common than it is today, their emotional state is palpable. Lifers' personalities are like looking into a kaleidoscope, rapidly in flux as the days twist and turn within the yard. The complexities are extreme, and prisoners with limitless time on their hands become acutely aware of outside issues which impact them. This is the challenge of the prison system (especially in a maximum-security complex): to keep the everyday challenges separate from bureaucratic influence. That will always be a fact of life, but the daily grind within the prison is very fragile and sensitive to impacting demands of the government. And, not to forget, it ages the employees physically and emotionally.

With this in mind, my footprint will be where the most tangible issues are so poorly understood because blogs, magazine articles and books do not reflect light on the emotional tenor challenging personnel to their wit's end. Prison is a place where calm can turn suddenly without expected provocation and upend the most robust and stalwart.

My view is that prison life is recondite and yet is an ever- present entity that pokes its presence every now and then into the public square. What the public hears and knows from newspaper and television spillage is what the prison bureaucracy wants to reveal and not necessarily what prevails. For the lifers the vigor of life is lost both tangibly and, for the most part, to the people who become their surrogate caretakers. It is the epitome of helplessness and subsistence survival. The most difficult story to tell is in fact a balancing act, and very profound. On the one hand there are people convicted of some of the most heinous acts and vicious murders conceivable. And yet they are so clever in their ability to shroud their evil. As they age, they mellow and assume very normative composure. Their testosterone is drained, and once uncontrolled and eager defiance is replaced by a quiet and friendly demeanor. It can be shocking to observe, particularly after reading a personal history replete with nothing but murder and mayhem. They vainly attempt to hold secret the details of their crimes for psychological reasons, I am sure. But, their personal histories on the prison website reads like a time warp. Even the most violent clearly reveal their shame and regret many years later. Statistical analysis cannot frame this visual. It took me time to accept the categorical difference of the hellion youths from the subdued middle-aged individuals. Even the most educated and perceptive individual can be fooled. No doubt, it is a profound intellectual challenge. Prison system's life and existence through time is indeed a riddle. Much time and energy is expended to pierce the invisible shield which hides its understanding. It is a conundrum which will remain inexplicable throughout time because at its core are the eternal complexities of human behavior. Reading "The Reformatory System in the United States. Reports Prepared for the International Prison Commission" (printed in Washington, D.C. in 1900)[11] is rendered so clearly like a time warp because the only change is technological development, the people as prisoners are timeless. Written in 1800 matters not. The places may change, but crime remains eternal! It vindicates the expression that "what changes over time is that nothing changes!" Perhaps it tweaks now and then, but substantive change in the prison system remains quantitative, not qualitative. Maximum-security prisoners are people who acted in ways that more fortunate people avoid by chance.

I hope that the ideas I bring will fill in the gaps where other books do not. I do not want to conflict with tell-it-all stories of individuals who met destinies wrapped around their crimes. This I do not want to touch. Such are for the interest of very specific events, misfortunes and poor life decisions and how they played out. People will become aware of what a horrible and tense environment it is, and then gaze into space occasionally wondering why anyone of sound mind would want to wind up "in stir". Then, at the conclusion, be able to contemplate where society has possibly failed these people, and, to ruminate what a dirty business politics is as political ambitions are always at play.

SECTION 2

Reflections

Chapter 1: The Prison System a/k/a the Big House.

This is a very elaborate discussion of what it's like to walk into a maximum-security prison in the dark of the early morning hours in a very austere, remote location. Follow me through and feel the anxiety.

Chapter 2: The Misery Index.

Prisons are miserable. This chapter renders a very realistic picture of how miserable. And I offer a very real mathematical formula (in a simplistic manner) to quantify how so, particularly as the different levels reflect the prisoners' classifications.

CHAPTER 1

The Prison a/k/a The Big House

What is our understanding of discipline in the home or in the school?
We understand it to be that course of treatment best suited to
educate, to whom we call disciples or learners…[12] This will make
prison discipline what it should be, a process of teaching and training,
not mainly to make obedient prisoners, but rather
to make them good citizens when they shall cease to be prisoners.[13]
Mrs. Ellen C. Johnson
Late Superintendent of the Massachusetts
Reformatory Prison for Women, 1877.

Mrs. Ellen Cheney Johnson was a pioneer do-gooder in mid-nineteenth century Boston as a spokesperson for women on welfare. She transformed many of her welfare improvements into the early changes she brought to bear for changes in women's prisons (during the period women were housed with men). Her extreme efforts were materially responsible for separating the women out and improving their living conditions. She was responsible for the founding and building of the Massachusetts Reformatory Prison for Women in Sherborn, Massachusetts which opened in 1877 as a result of her considerable effort and empathy for mistreated incarcerated women. Her life was consumed with ideals which, for the most part, spoke volumes for the practical yet rooted in idyllic behavior modification. She markedly gave thrust to major educational programs to make women self-resourceful and thus more equipped to readjust to life outside prison.

However, even today, prison life for both the majority of men and women has resulted in greater survival barriers. The effect of this has long term profound consequences. Of course, this factors into Level 3 being significantly more of a physical danger than Levels 1 and 2. So, let's take a real look at what many do not understand about a system where this is endemic, but certainly where most people's minds never drift. Ideals are important for any society as they serve as tangible objectives, but, on a practical basis, realities may suffocate them when life and death dominate the environment.

The Urban dictionary defines "The Big House"[14] as a maximum-security prison. Coincidentally, it was also a 1930 Hollywood Metro Goldwyn Mayer movie starring Chester Morris, Wallace Beery, Lewis Stone and Robert Montgomery, and was based on the 1926 original story by Lennox Robinson. The story gave the whole idea of prison flare and a sense of early Hollywood romanticism, a very typically antithetical look at prison life even if by 1930's crime interpretation. However, the lingo gave it a verve and suddenly tweaked established thinking so it stuck. And when said it softens the thought with comic relief a smile or a smirk prevails. In the real world, though, many people I grew up with thought The Big House was no more enchanting than an outhouse. So, whatever anyone thinks, the moniker does nothing more than to engender a rather light-hearted reference for perhaps a casual smile. And there are others to foster a softness to the eternal juggernaut: slammer, hoosegow, stoney-lonesome, joint, crowbar hotel, and many others. Let's be clear, there is nothing pleasant about prison. It is composed of a cross-section of both non-violent and violent offenders. In a "politically correct statement at the end of his book, John F. Pfaff makes a very personal belief statement:

> Still, there are a host of strategies we should be pursuing. Some appear straight forward enough, like changing how we talk about people who are in prison ("people convicted of violent crimes", not "violent offenders").[15] I am of a very different opinion, however. Although Mr. Pfaff is convinced

that the language will somehow change the reality of why a prisoner is confined, begin to explain sentencing guidelines, and somehow believe it will whitewash the depth of a crime, I believe it is the beginning of an altered reality as in "It depends on what is is" (to draw language from former President William Jefferson Clinton's personal format for word processing). Yet to a more serious extent the system seems to noticeably live in a typical altered reality when prisoners can fall through the cracks and be victimized by excessive sentencing as a result of "the classification process", or, more importantly, the political slant of any given parole board.

Attributions which refrain from what is real actually hurt more than it helps. It is a stark reflection of "political correctness" which does not help any venture to make the prison system function better nor help the prisoner trying to improve his reality (which is ultimately trying to show redemption and be paroled). But I shall address this in a later chapter. For now, it suffices to say that it is just one example of a system poisoned by "political correctness." I am of the belief that extremes are injurious in all contexts, but evasiveness, living in an "altered reality," and "plausible deniability" are very damaging. And the prison system is a very fragile one, to wit every politician has her/his two cents for improvement!

I started out working in a Level 2 for a couple of months and then moved to a Level 3. The Level 2 was a mixed group, but mostly people who were incarcerated for offenses related to robbery and drugs. However, it had its share of violent individuals who murdered for any number of reasons. They committed murder, however, in the act of robbery, dealing in drugs, rape or kidnapping (or both), or gang violence. At the time I transferred to a Level 3, the prison was transformed into a different kind of prisoner. It was pretty much an institution where HIV and AIDS prisoners were housed. But this changed just before I arrived. When I started it had just produced a central location for the most aggressive male prisoners in the state. They were the twenties and thirties testosterone jacked types in for kidnaping, rape, distribution and use of heavy drugs, and psychological issues which made them a risk to themselves and everyone around them.

One thing is very clear: the prison system is a temporal, yet where spirituality is a very big deal. It seems incongruous, but after spending just a bit of time there it is easy to see its place. Running a prison is uniquely a very complex day-to-day issue because no one day is the same. Surprise is more common than ho-hum! There is no convenient time in the day to lack focus and be inattentive because something unforeseen is always happening. The unpredictable always ruins quietude. The explosive nature of fragile personality types always poses a dangerous threat to the surroundings. For this reason, procedure plays a dominant role. The ingredient which can make everything flow is an "IQ!" I found there were a very large number of low-level employees who were not very intelligent (and, I am not talking about education as much as common sense), and this got in the way of making very basic judgment calls.

Another point I want to make before proceeding is that the true leaders in the prison system are the wardens and associate wardens. They are extremely intelligent, immensely focused on maintaining order by keying on and integrating the units within the prison into a continuous flow and communication. They often make order from disorder, quiet from sudden pandemonium when a body alarm would go off due a prisoner going off on a guard either yelling obscene language, getting physical, or interceding very quickly during a fight. The ones I got to know worked long hours, were physically worn most of the time, but always presented a smile and a lending hand when needed. Their biggest difficulty from an administrative point of view is the prison yard and cellblock. Issues aside, bureaucratic indifference from central headquarters is real. It was often a very obvious convenient disregard. Unsettling day-to-day "internal tension" made efficiency trying because daily uprisings, fights, or even murder compromised and endangered the entire prison. Civil society cannot imagine the explosive nature of a maximum-security prison.

Walking into work in the very wee hours of the morning was often an experience rather than an automatic happening. As my stomach acids started churning in response to my sympathetic nervous system as I approached the first gate, the sight of the first gate from the main drag grew to be a daily emotional experience to which I never fully adapted. It was this first gate where I stopped while the attendant "swiped" my credentials identification card through a magnetic strip. This never portended anything of concern, and often I would take a couple of minutes to chat with the guard who came out of the office. The small cabin, with an ingress-egress on either side, usually had two overnight guards who were very nice and extremely cordial. The light chatter was pleasant, but it never assuaged the pit in my stomach as I gazed ahead through my windshield to the mile and a half ride to the prison entrance. It was real country farm land, a patch of rolling hills serving countryside cows and deer wandering free and easy aside of this deep-south city.

The ride was bumpy through uneasy terrain and saddled with fences on both sides to contain the cows from the farm abutting the prison. On the left side I made my way through there were also other prisons within the complex as well as a teaching and housing complex. I grew very resentful of the "mental torture" which went for required teaching within, merely a politically correct prerequisite of bureaucratic mind- streaming. It served as the central training unit for the several prisons within the complex as well as all the other statewide institutions within the prison system. (Headquarters was the main administrative building by the main entrance gate). As I became familiar with the area, it was obvious that its out-of- the-way location constituted reasons for the prison's vulnerability to both aerial and ground contraband thrown over the razor wire fences. If it were not for the austere nature of the buildings, the rolling hills and beautiful scenery would have been more comforting. But the uniquely fabricated synergy of the dangerous undertones with the emotionally draining atmosphere completely rained feelings of misery into the experience. Simply put, I never met anyone within the system who enjoyed the destabilizing working conditions. It is no exaggeration at all to say that the atmosphere is overly charged on a daily basis.

As I made my way through the night, I had to drive with care and extreme caution as deer were very common running through the grounds. And, somehow, they got around and over the fences with incredible speed and alacrity. I often saw them in groups as I approached the prison entrance. When I first started my employment, I traveled nightly through the state to one of the prisons in very rough and fallow countryside. It was dark for most of the ride and I learned very early that it was not uncommon to be hit by a deer crossing the road. The speed limit was 50 and 60 mph in various portions of the ride, but it was obvious that the most pristine areas had never been protected with safety highway guards or proper lighting. I was almost killed twice: once by a deer I swerved to avoid and almost toppled (I do not know how I did not turn over into the water under the wooden bridge I had just crossed. I guess as the saying goes that "It was not my time!"). The second time was avoiding an "18 wheeler USPS mail delivery truck" speeding by me in a pouring, wind-swept rain out of control over a very high mountainous zone. I saved myself as I swerved away from going off to the side and down a very steep escarpment. With my heart in my throat both times I somehow survived. Each time I was left like a speechless zombie-like witness staring through the windshield as my heart beat out of control. Feeling my heart in my throat, I hyperventilated and oozed with sweat seeing my life before my eyes. Somehow in the dark of night I got my car back in control thinking "There but for the grace of God go I!" When I moved to this maximum-security prison within the city limits, my cautionary memories and feelings accompanied my other concerns, chief of which was: Why am I doing this? I have never been able to reason a realistic answer except to say to myself in a ludicrous manner: "the educational experience!" What insane sophistry! So twice my life being challenged by the dark of night, I approached this country road in the capital city tinged with bad memories.

I thought for a very long time that something was wrong with me, that I would feel internally empty and just generally "sick". It was not a buyer's remorse; it was a flagrant, uncertain sense that I refused to show externally as I proceededthrough the day. The feeling grew old and burdensome with each passing day. I had, up to that point in my life, been to many dangerous places in the world, and subjected myself to danger zones I still do not like to remember (like the Tangier Casbah in Morocco at night). But this was a slow grade in the daily journey that seemed to feel more dangerous with each passing day. Night time always seems to accentuate anything that is largely tenable in the light of day! Perhaps it was related to the fact that with each passing day more and more prisoners knew who I was and now an invisible target was "etch a sketched" on my back. Word travels very quickly through a prison yard so I gathered very soon that reputation meant everything. As the days proceeded, I got to know fellow employees very well, and, I was somewhat encouraged by their universally and freely expressed feelings that "yes", misery does like company! The one thought that never stopped rippling through my brain was how high the "misery index" grew during my employment stay. The people in the suits at headquarters did not care to ever address this for the lower level employees and feigned concern whenever and wherever possible to keep peace. It was really Orwellian[16] in nature!

At the beginning I had to fulfill administrative policy obligations, like take basic tutorials on the prison computer. I would soon learn for myself that this was just a beginning to what was a mere facet of a giant bureaucratic maze. The prison was under the control of a weighted state bureaucracy, onerously overbearing, ill-conceived and demoralizing without any careful thought behind it. In time I came to recognize how off-the-cuff it was run. Having been a professional for many years, I had commonly confronted the irrational power puppeteering of midlevel automatons working in a system just to collect a paycheck. This was a little different however. This was a prison system staffed with highly disgruntled people who couched their anger because they supported someentity: a family, a living need, an expensive health requirement, or even a basic car loan. It was, plain and simple, just one job of a two or three-tiered job lifestyle necessary to support overall survival for others besides themselves. Administrative employees who would barrage the statewide computers reminding everyone to stay current with tedious and mercilessly repetitive obligatory courses were grating and objectionable. It was quite apparent that the training program followed compulsory standards of employment, but with an incredibly token, unsophisticated format with very low-level standards. The atmosphere reflected a *Weltschmerz* I had never witnessed so intrinsically and pervasively entrenched. It was systemic.

Stepping back from the "Big House" tentacles which daily seemed to lurch out unmercifully to taunt already unhappy employees, I want to colorize and give substance to the reality of an acolyte seeing a maximum-security prison for the first time. The entrance to the prison itself was a screening process managed by highly somnambulant individuals who were always sullen, angry and resentful. They hated and resented the overnight duty in such a grim and cold "hell hole" (as told to me quite often). There were very strict policies about what could or could not be brought into the prison. But the physical "pat-downs" were performed by some highly contentious and frustrated employees. Almost anything, without exaggeration, was considered contraband. They were usually very nasty officers who so carefully patted down body surfaces that it relentlessly tested one's patience for its indiscreet taunting. As for myself, I never wanted to make trouble so I let them have their fun. In addition, there were restrictions on how things could be packaged. This was an area where childishness exceeded need with clear astonishment and exasperation. The combative, defiant people who exacted their small amount of power were covetous of their control. As insignificant as this may sound it was a paradigm structured into the system which resulted in anger, frustration and premature loss of disgusted employees. At times it was excessively degrading. It was my considered opinion that the bureaucracy glossed over these issues with the childish attitude of "hear no evil, speak no evil!" The programs set up for marketing to the public domain rendered a very false sense of job security, promotion and long-term self- satisfaction. Low level awards, brunches, lunches, music recitals, and other ritualistic blessings of appreciation were publicized to over-embellish a very pretentious sense of caring while shrugging off the more significant need for wage increases and less burdensome hours. Prisons' high employee turnover reflect this glaring failure to remedy. Administrations put on a surface image which is only accepted by a minority who are able to tolerate the nonsense with maturity, but internalized disgust. Needless to say that the bureaucracy diminishes enthusiasm and caring. The general employee attitude progressively languishes to an intolerable boiling point when she/he finally terminates with disdain. The few who survive to progress up the ladder of promotion are people with unique skills to surmount the pettiness in the wake of danger and fatigue. This does not paint a pretty picture, but the reality is that a prison is a dangerous, desultory environment with few benefits and very rare gratification. The endgame for those that thrive is a state retirement benefits and health care support program, and, in synch with the blasé bureaucracy a notation of gratitude on the prison website and maybe a gratuitous "thank you" awards luncheon party with fellow employees. All the bridges these survivors have crossed deserve so very much more, over and above the cursory sanctimony and priggish words of praise. In my life I have never witnessed so many disgruntled, disheartened people, and people I admired for their hard work and very pleasant friendships.

Getting out and leaving the sanity of my car for the daily purging of one's soul to manage the exploits of the forthcoming day was a feat unto itself. Putting normalcy aside for whatever would enrage my internal spirit and ramp up my blood pressure was no doubt an unhealthy start. I remember a Caribbean nurse with whom I worked, who often shared her daily remorse, was the most clever and hilarious person I had ever met. I remember one Friday afternoon when I was on my way out after a particularly horrible day of stabbings, alarms going off, lockdowns, and just generalized turmoil of all kinds, we stopped in the parking lot after the last gate and door out to continue our banter. We were just chatting small talk when she started to do her thing about the prison system and its lack of sensibility for hard working employees. It was as good as some of the great repartees that ever came out of Robin Williams. It was so hysterical that in spite of my anxious desire to go home she had me bellied over and effusively teary-eyed with uncontrollable laughter. It was cathartic beyond understanding. Her ability to capsulize the nonsense and failings of the system just brilliantly exposed it for why it is amazing that it survives at all as a functional entity! It reminded me of the talk when I was much younger that there was more insanity outside a prison than inside! It did not, however, take me long to realize that concept is reversed, no matter how quippish! If bureaucrats who complain about employee retention, they have no further distance to travel than the nearest mirror. I learned during my stay that prison management is a major disaster. This is no exaggeration.

The real problems today with "the Big House" mismanagement are overcome and held together by the most noble of prison staff, the tireless working wardens. They are constrained by a "political correctness" so weighty and irksome that effective management is overwhelmed daily by policy constraints and the legal rights of the prisoners. The very people whose thoughtless behavior results in perfidious violence in total disregard of the basic human rights of their victims are flooded with legal rights that torture any normal thinking mind! The prison system exhibits a political correctness on steroids, dangerously and frivolously opening up to control issues in the yard. There is no doubt that this consideration is a political football kicked all over the bureaucratic ladder right up to the Director of Prisons.

However, I believe that a distinction has to be made between prisoners who have committed non-violent crimes and those whose violence may or may not have led to a victims' death. And it seems appropriate and wise to put bias of thought and prejudicial feelings aside to look at crime through the prism of common sense. What stood out was the daily conduct of wardens and associate wardens as "exhibit

A", a managed code of behavior conditioned by imbecilic bureaucratic demands and not their learned leadership thinking. The result: all day long prison management exhausted themselves falling over backwards to make nice to prisoners. It was (and remains) "P.C." run amok! Their proper and necessary leadership skills came through only when pressed to their wits' end. Then, and only then, was the marshalling of force applied to keep them in their place. Salty and thoroughly undisciplined prisoner behavior was a daily head-shaker that was draining and intolerable for all prison employees. Some could absorb it better than others just to get by the day and go home to sanity. Bur, let it be very clear, the wardens I knew were some of the finest people I have ever known, and they had their daily feast of mental beat-downs with expected regularity. This is all tantamount to a deeper conversation later in the book.

When I got to the initial check-in in the wee hours of the morning, I was very apprehensive every single day. There was never any sense of mutual respect for the on-duty officers. They were, for the most part, emotionally tortured individuals, a profound display to observe. For the most part, the lowest level guards were overworked and so severely underpaid that they had one (or sometimes two) other job(s) to pay the bills. Very young single mothers were in the vast majority because of boyfriend/husband abandonment. Therefore, when I got to the check-in area, I witnessed the overnight guard(s) understandably asleep. Usually, by rapping hard on the window I got them out of their slumber to check me in. This involved going through the X-ray walk to ensure I was not sneaking in contraband of any kind, and especially for any particular prisoner. (And, this, believe it or not, is a daily experience). Some were very nice, but most were unfriendly, exhausted and thoroughly in a bad mood. When I first passed through in the initial days of my employment I was stopped for taking in a radio for my office or other alike items with the warden's written permission. If I took this route, I had to carry his letter through the check-in. And, often a big deal was made, to the point that calls back and forth to the control room make it seem like I was a convicted smuggler. The major problem simply was illiteracy, and I reasonably refrained from shaming them for their social circumstances. Sinfully, most were so resentful and angry that I absorbed their frustrations because I was impassioned by their misery. However, it became very old very quickly. After the X-ray walk-through, I was patted down with a thoroughness that was more often than naught an unnecessary, nasty experience. I never made a bid to deal about it because of the "intangibles" at that hour of night fraught with potential danger.

I would redress from the ritual disrobing of exterior appurtenances like my belt, shoes, car keys held in my pants, and any other potentially radiolucent items. They were all put through in advance. This five-minute process extended to thirty minutes of nonsense. I arrived at about 3AM when it would be customary to encounter no more than the yard cats desperately in search of food. Most employees entered about 5AM, and that was followed by "the ladies and gentlemen" of the 8AM wave. The delay was always due to acquired survival skills: nonchalance and oblivion. And I sincerely understood this. When I fully redressed and collected my senses I was buzzed into the central office where I gave up my ID card for swiping (which most often than naught was out of order and delayed my entry sometimes as much as a half hour until calls to the control room got it fixed, or someone would come all the way down to mechanically remediate the computer glitch). Picture this in the damp, cold, sometimes windswept rain of the early morning. Moreover, I have to add that frequently I would have to await the guard who was on night guard patrol in a beat-up truck doing her rounds around the entire perimeter of the razor wires surrounding the grounds. When all this was completed to some degree of certainty, I passed through the swipe in office and was buzzed out to the breezeway to the control room, about a football field entry to the main door. I felt very often that the expenditure of emotional energy was so depleting that I had to regather and toss all my thoughts to the heavens and just proceed on. There was always tension in the air! All this just to nursemaid some of the most vile and violent individuals I have ever met! The rapid walk through the breezeway was the habitual low of my day.

The most humbling feeling was the complete lack of respect. I was in some form of private practice for about forty- five years. I was a professional, and this was in complete disregard. I cannot emphasize enough how churlish these guards were. I always kept my cool, but the general tenor of the prison was as inhospitable as it could be. The warden and officers did not care one iota. If I had not been determined to understand the workings of a maximum security prison, I would have quit. I rationalized that I was in a hell-hole, and the staff reflected it!

Before I continue it is necessary to reflect on a few thoughts. Prisons are not on any priority list for any citizen. It is also true that they are important for community protection. The spillover from within remains limited and controlled for the sake of safety. Locals do not feel obligated to tolerate movement in and out of prison grounds. Prisoners are moved constantly for health or relocation considerations. Everyday people do not feel their lives should be interrupted by prison activities. Strict controls are followed as guards are in constant control of movement through either highly populated city streets or uninhabited countryside. Lapses of attentiveness can be a disaster.

I was often struck how casual this was taken in contrast to the checking-in process. In any massive organization such as a prison system (a publicly managed facility) its obligation is the protection of the public sector as well as employee harmony/discipline. However, I gathered very early on that the administrative leadership was passively aggressive in daily management. Tension was constantly in the air, and I attributed this to very poor leadership.

One other very significant point. A Level 3 prison is a brutal place so I expected more professionalism. In general, the atmosphere was so tense that guards felt tremendous pressure from all areas. Not a single day went by without a crisis. The bleak reality is not comforting for a hardworking guard. I often witnessed guards being physically assaulted. This added to cold, drab feeling. And, piling on with constant computer obligations in addition to self-defense classes with gun range obligations made it confounding why the bureaucrats could not understand the employment turnover. Such prisons are not correctional. They are purely protective institutions.

Why is this important? The prison system was at one time in its early days structured physically and intellectually to prepare prisoners for their release post-incarceration. The objective has always been to prepare prisoners to become employable public citizens with a newly invested sense of social responsibility. For many reasons this was a dream and an unreality reminiscent of a song with universal words by Dusty Springfield[17] in 1964: *Wishing and Hoping*, adopted her with a different intuit but similar meaning. I certainly understood the sense of idealism, but the leadership mentality defied this objective. The institutional Achilles heel prevents this lofty expectation. It is important to show how certain prisoners are showing character development, but it's not right to look away from the reality of a very dangerous and desperate atmosphere. Self-flagellating about lofty accomplishments for public consumption is terribly misleading. This neatly fits under the heading of "political correctness", the oxygen of the public domain. It would be encouraging to validate euphemistic language with concrete results.

As that piercing sound from the buzzer thwacked my mind as I entered the breezeway there was no uncertainty in my spirit. I was always a "half-cup-full" kind of person so William Safire's[18] expression, "Don't let the bastards grind you down", echoed through my mind every morning as I expected the unexpected. It was a universally accepted feeling of "function for dysfunction"! I grappled mentally and emotionally, as everyone else around me, to do the job for which I was hired with a smile and a "stiff upper lip". In a way the breezeway was a momentary suspension of my thoughts as I gazed upon my surroundings: the prison cats so skittishly running through the grounds, the "death house," the amount of razor wires around the enclosure so stark, the prison nursery, and the plantings right and left so beautifully, but distinctly, out of place with the very harsh backdrop.

At the beginning, my impressions were instructive, like I was a "goody-two-shoes" here for a noble mission. But as the days passed on this feeling evaporated into the sheer reality of its very disdainful unpleasantness. As I approached the main control room door there was a very large and lavish sign against the wall in front of me denoting this rather unembellished place as "correctional". Then, as I turned to the right for the control room to acknowledge my presence with another ear shattering buzzer to pull open the screeching iron door, I entered to another sign of one word, overstated and pretentiously displayed clichés: character, respect, humility, brotherhood, caring, etc. In my mind I knew it was very robust "P.C." and very much over the top. Were they meaningful and instructive? Hardly, most likely due to the daily overreach of propagandized expressions to uplift already depressed feelings. I never counted them, but there must have been about fifty words which seemed to be very anachronistic and quite pretentious. It is quite Hobbesian[19] in its governmental, authoritarian and determinist manner for mind-streaming and thought control. I was always warned against making an exaggerated show to make a point. I used to think to myself: a little late for some of the very, very few! It was a very pretentious attempt to convey the importance of ethical and moral rectitude while instilling a universal feeling for virtue and leadership qualities. This obvious and very glaring self- righteousness was only exceeded by its thorough hypocrisy delivered with an unavoidable daily reminder for the employees spending their shifts in conflict, never experiencing lighthearted banter and realizing high-sounding moral standards of behavior. Such was the out-of-place, gratuitous administration sanctimony. My fellow employees did not know whether to go wild with anger, quit, or complain. They did none because they were poor and needed the work!

The big iron door clanked and squealed as it slowly passed to the left. I slivered through sideways as soon as I could fit. There I would be met by the overnight woman guard at the central prison control room with more than a dozen television screens focusing everywhere along all facilities. As she gave me keys to the infirmary as well as a body alarm we chatted. She and I developed a friendship over time because of our mutual love history with cats. She was a typical rural, indigent, hard-working, very intelligent (with no formal education) woman who thoroughly despised her job. She confided to me that without this overnight position she and her husband could not survive. The dangerous environment and the understated important concerns versus the overstated compliance to trivia rattled her patience. Her feelings spoke volumes about state bureaucracies which unabashedly and wastefully allowed talent to languish while the supporting tax money was squandered in the rueful pursuit of sententious public acclaim.

My eyes would automatically look to the numerous TV screens above the desk of phones and other screening paraphernalia which cast numerous views of the prison yard and individual cell blocks. I typically viewed some early rising prisoners passing through the yard. She would then give me her daily warning to be careful as well as a listing of which cell blocks were in lockdown due to some form of violence, contraband event or escape in the late-night hours before I arrived. Being a maximum-security prison with very young prisoners (a great number being very psychologically challenged), this became a nightly occurrence. I would then make my way to the second iron gate diagonally behind my right shoulder as she wished me a safe day. The initial clank and release squeal gave me a pit in my stomach. As it slowly opened, I usually saw duffel bags along the right wall opposite the temporary retaining cells for prisoners in abeyance awaiting transfer to another of the state facilities, or, for others being held as arrivals for administrative protocol in the morning. Some slumbered on the uninviting cement benches affixed to the walls while occasionally some would make a racket yelling obscenities or meaningless, mostly unintelligible commentary as I passed through. I always looked to the right where the windows revealed multiple computers for the overnight control guard (usually an attending Lieutenant or Corporal). I knew them all well.

When the Corporal met me at the next fence gate, she would gather the correct key while she bantered warnings and very kind words of appreciation for my presence. She was a very diminutive black woman who would hug me while we talked. She would always give me a breakdown for a future she was relishing at her retirement (after 25 years). She was such a breath of fresh air, an absolute sense of calm, joyful thought and comfort in this house of utter insanity. Being one of the two final gates to the yard, she would warn me to exercise extreme caution as there were no guards on duty. Knowing I had to walk about the length of a football field to the final locked steel door to the infirmary, I listened carefully as it was a very dark walk. Admittedly, as I proceeded through, I would feel for the proper key with my left hand while I properly arranged my body alarm for easy reach. But, as I left the Corporal, I always ruminated how she was immensely undervalued for her inspiration and sense of humor.

My inner thoughts sped hastily from the reality of "same old, same old" to visceral infuriation that government can fail so miserably. I realized two things: (1) government-controlled institutions like prisons cannot realize increased employment numbers due to internal systemic corruption, and (2) that all the bombastic, puffed-up, genteel euphemisms do not fool nor assuage the deep resentment held by the majority of employees. I referenced in my mind the long forgotten "The Peter Principle" by Laurence J. Peter[20] in 1969: how people rise up in business to the level of their incompetence. Prisons bleed this principle, but their failures bleed from the top of the administration!

I made my way through a garden area to the yard gate, left unlocked because the yard was supposed to be empty. But prison recklessness being what it is, there were enough times to make my heart pound as I saw prisoners wandering in the shadows unbeknownst and unsupervised. A few times I was accosted in a not-so-friendly back-and-forth. Some of my colleagues (especially one Nurse Practitioner) would give me an earnest, friendly dress-down about not using my body alarm. I was hardly cavalier. I was just downright ignorant. This prison was primarily for young, headstrong killers without any respect for life. The proper remediation for ignorance is knowledge, but this is dreaming! I quickly grew into the starkness of the environment as I assumed a much more cautionary awareness (for my own survival). Plain and simple, the prison atmosphere is not a place for relaxed behavior.

The dangers of the night hit home why grades Levels I, 2 and 3 are so pronouncedly different.

When I finally got to my destination, I would unlock the door as occasional prisoners would accost me with questions which were covers for some ulterior contentious motive. I learned to be terse and abrupt as it became the norm for a guard to be assaulted in this area. The "pill room" was within feet of my entrance so prisoners would linger at this gathering point. The more rural Level 2 prison where I started was more relaxed. I still had to pass through a gaggle of prisoners before reaching a guard. As uncomfortable as that was, it was nothing like the Level 3 maximum security waiting room in the infirmary where fighting was more common and sometimes very dangerous. This area was nothing more than a steel-iron cage simulating a circus of safely enclosed animals. This was simply for safety, and employment taught me why. The prisoners were treated in these types of enclosures with due respect, but without this type of waiting room, all hell would break out.

The "Big House" concept is one of many euphemisms for referencing a prison, a necessary comedic understatement for how criminals are housed. It is essential for public protection, not only for their conceivable endangerment as well from each other. The major issues I saw as fundamental for the wardens are contraband issues, vicious gang conflicts resulting in stabbings and deaths, assaults on guards, guard- prisoner secretive sexual and contraband collaborations, and drug paraphernalia being secreted in through the entry points or thrown over the razor wires.

Unfortunately, the "Big House" gets bigger when necessary resources are not properly apportioned by the state to pay a proper way to both secure and retain adequately trained guards. But, as I stated, there were grievously underpaid and highly overworked employees who were always discouraged and exhausted from the lengthy hours. It is extremely important to realize that for an institution whose primary obligation and credo being safety, the hypocrisy of such a necessary steadfast compliance to this reality being subverted by overt oversight is stark. Laughable to a greater extent is to hear the media advertising on radio and television for the potential financial growth in "correctional institution" employment. Staggering is the reality when ambitious young guards revolve in and out of employment owing to low pay, long hours and a complete lack of administrative concern. Institutional focus is "keeping the peace". Yet, beyond this one wonders why administrative concerns concentrate on what looks right rather than what is right! The problems the wardens face are their efforts to make their institutions function in spite of administrative higher-ups allowing politics to derail measures that would make employment more desirable. The institutions are held together by many dedicated leaders who honorably maintain stability in spite of the flagrant oversight by politicians whose bureaucratic devotion to their own pockets sets up the institutions to daily risks. And yet, the politically correct measures taken with righteous indignation is to publicize very limited images of "the good deeds" and religious/educational reformations being advanced at some of the Level 1 and 2 institutions. It almost seems like a cruel cover-up for the violence that is really much more significant than the public will ever realize.

Stunning is how old and really filthy are all the facilities. The infirmary is an OSHA disgrace, a rather clarion call to the leadership that willfully condones such an environment. It is "hear no evil, speak no evil" conduct of behavior, an unforgivable "razzle-dazzle." Anyone with basic medical training quickly realizes a complete lack of sterility and sterilization procedures. The equipment is old, the instruments are ill-suited for the prisoners' needs, and the core of capital investment virtually non-existent. Cleaning up from a knife fight (after which the prisoners enter the infirmary with blood falling pretty much in their wake) involves a mop, water, alcohol and some Clorox. The beds are so dated that a modern-day cot would look advanced. And the heating/AC system is overly antiquated and always dysfunctional. It is important to just mention this because so much lip service is paid to emphasize how the prisoners are well served. Yet, they are coddled and unrealistically pampered in spite of some of the most heinous and disturbingly violent crimes. The people employed to carry out the medical/dental procedures necessary to maintain a basic level of care are asked to administer in both a disturbingly dangerous and "unsterile" (to be gentle) environment! This is very reminiscent of Angola Prison in Louisiana prior to the Civil War where prisoners occupied areas where their roommates were all kinds of vermin. After all my training during my lifetime, particularly paying homage to advances in and the practice of proper sterilization procedures, it was certainly an eye-opener. My conclusions are put in the context that I know that the accepted science is definitely slighted by money and convenience when left to the druthers of government as well as the choke-hold and expediency of bureaucracy. A final consideration which I shall illustrate is the continuous "plausible deniability" which runs rampant throughout the entire system. It is like a drug that has addicted the business and operations control as an extension of "political correctness." It seems that the behavior is so endemic that the "quality assurance" (which is feigned) is really the ultimate disguise, much to the chagrin of the very aware employees. I shall touch on this in a later chapter.

Leadership is a quality that is reflected from the inside of people who comport themselves according to the highest ethical standards. Sensing the necessity to be the ultimate example of moral rectitude, leadership in the prison system is special because of its concentrated risks and teeter-tottering emotional demands on a daily basis. Up and down the ladder of employees, the atmosphere was poisoned because of the very out-of-place glorious talk that did not translate to their satisfaction. The daily charge could not be implemented under the stress and strain felt by the majority of people. There was a pervasive feeling that leadership was an act, not a meaningful concern. The boiling point was always reached when the prison became suddenly overwhelmed by a fatality, an extremely bloody fight, or a guard being tragically assaulted. The palpable anxiety and high degree of emotional distress permeated throughout the entire system. Distrust of the leadership made a good number feel all was naught and frightfully unarguable. The facial reflections were ones of disgust and hopelessness. It was awful to see on such nice and hardworking people. But I feel that the wanton cover-up with smiles, ebullient behavior and false bravado made the administrative leadership appear malevolent. The political correctness and plausible deniability are the scourge running havoc throughout the prisons. It was obvious to me that sanctimony from above crushed the plea for honesty from below.

The panoramic view behind the razor wire is pretty much generic. That is, a very cookie-cutter layout that is common to the state prison system. If you have seen one, you have pretty much seen them all. The grounds are very similarly arranged, differing only by size. Some have more cell blocks; some are resplendent with gardens and an occasional pool surrounded by exquisitely verdant plantings. Most, however, have a sterile, very bland appearance. It really depends on the prisoners, and certainly where their energies are expressed. Everything of a maintenance need is generally handled by a prisoner with prior training and experience. Otherwise, more specialized problems necessitate bringing a private repair person into the facility. I can personally attest to the fact that some of the prisoners exhibited pretty fancy technical knowledge, especially dealing with some very complicated plumbing and electrical repairs. I still find it incongruous that these prisoners I came to know quite well were really hardcore, very vicious criminals. It could then be extrapolated that if the key word: is "was," then early release /mitigation should be seriously considered. I have important thoughts on this issue based on my experience and exposure (which I shall get into in later chapters). Suffice it to say that this is a topic which will always be promoted, rejected, and promoted ad nauseam.

Today when I hear or see written "The Big House," I no longer find it as amusing as I once did. I'd like to consider myself as intelligent and understanding enough to have seen the humor, but spending so much time muddled in the heart of hard time my outlook has demonstrably changed. Walking through the yard is an interesting experience. At times it was a very surreal, an out-of-body feeling: the sublime fused with the absurd!

The yard is an interesting experience. At times it was a very surreal, an out-of-body feeling: the sublime fused with the absurd! For the people who have been working there for years it has never changed. It is a very dangerous place, and, it took a while for me to accept this because it is easy to get complacent and forget where you are. And, worse yet, as any person growing up and living very distant to heavy survival crime locations of the country, it takes a while for the whole effect to settle in. I worked with a professional lady who always reprimanded me in a motherly way for my naïve trust. In time, my perception and feeling for the danger really hit me. I was extremely friendly with one of the guards who was always looking out for me, and, he was always warning me to watch myself. He sensed and knew everything about every prisoner. And, boy, was he right on!

Prisoners very quickly learn survival techniques (for many reasons that are obvious). I came to learn about some of their hidden fears because of the times I would spend talking to them. My other colleagues within the infirmary warned me early on not to talk to them because word flitters around the yard very rapidly, and, at some later time, I could be the object of an untoward assault. I can confirm that I took the advice with a serious appreciation but continued with selective judgment. I would watch other employees interact with prisoners, and this was a very educational experience. It was hard to detect what high-level officers (up to the warden himself) were really thinking. This conversation was not taboo so I went back-and-forth with everyone who would listen. It was very informational.

The prisoner mindset was always in motion because of in-house gang violence. Out of sheer self-protection, it was stark how fast their eyes surveilled their surroundings to ensure no one would suddenly appear with a shivv or a shank. They did not hide anything because their uniforms would not allow it. They wore light brown khaki sleeveless shirts with long-legged khaki, string-tightened, very fluffy pants. They all wore Crocs or athletic shoes.

It never ceased to amaze me how nice their running shoes/cross-trainers were (gifts from family). In the winter they wore a wool-lined dark greenish brown overcoat (without pockets). In spite of this, the dangerous wannabes found the right timing and appropriate garb to hide a shivv or shank. The violence was planned, but the immediate action, spontaneous. I had just come in early one day when I witnessed (and, then administered treatment to) a guard crying terribly because a prisoner tried to rearrange the anatomy of his face. He was in shock and very hysterical. It appeared one of the prisoners was out in the yard wandering before light (against rules, but this night guards were hard to find). Because guards are always in markedly short numbers the prisoners very quickly become aware. So, when he was turned away at the infirmary for being too early for "the insulin line", he responded with his one-man revolt. He took it out on the first person he found.

Oh, yes, he got his insulin, but then he was locked up in "a special housing unit." Pardon me, I mean "solitary confinement!" Which brings me to my head turning experience, or, what I reference as my personal learning experience: the use of politically correct language in a prison. Well, prisoners have their own slang, but the prison has its own identifying language. So, I quickly digress to expose "the idiocy" of prison culture. I believe in not dancing around the use of terms and language.

As a new and unschooled employee, I was brought up to speed very quickly about a lot of cautionary matters of conduct while moving around in the prison. Along with this I learned very early on that the guards do not carry guns. They are left with their rather soft means of self-protection: pepper spray and a walkie-talkie type telephone. Try to imagine for a minute what good would either do if a number of prisoners jumped a single guard. Well, it happens all the time! This was the ultimate insult in an environment of recurrent periods of ungodly terror. The number of times the prison went into total lockdown for serious attacks involved guards as well as prisoners. It always made me repeat in my head the sardonic warning that "you can't bring a knife to a gunfight!" I saw very young women commonly brought to tears. The result was their quitting, leaving the system vulnerable and dangerously short on key personnel. It is the "theater of the absurd!" Some would call this classic kabuki theater.

There is no doubt that I was witness to strange events and people. But the "political correctness" just ran rampant through a system which had no business not rejecting. Like wandering through some vacuous dream, I couldn't mentally condone such a significantly misplaced value system. In this respect, the responsibility for the mayhem which prevails with impunity on a daily basis rests solely with legal bureaucrats who subject wardens and their officer corps to the dangers embedded in unstable, unsafe areas. Highly risk-taking actions unsupported by proper armamentarium is painfully unreasonable. Surely, the elite guards (Elite Special Operational Guards come equipped with M-15 Vindicator with Disruptor Ammo) enter (after the fact) with guns and chemicals, but, by then, great damage to life and structure has already been done. The "Big House" is not a "backwater outhouse," it is the last and only refuge for human beings (convicted of very violent crimes) confined, for the most part, for their natural lives. Language, behavior and self-protective mechanisms cannot be made up as if the prison is a fairyland where everything is "soft" and "so, so" such that all is superficially proper and justifiably broad-based. There is no place for this kind of thinking where so many lives are at stake. It always made me wonder how could violent offenders (who are incarcerated for murdering in ways a clean mind could not fathom on a bad day) be sequestered in an environment they know could erupt in a riot spontaneously!" I could never reconcile this in my mind!

The infirmary is a very well-built concrete structure with a holding cell for all prisoners who await pre-authorized appointments. It reminded me of a New York subway stop of unkempt, loud ruffians. At best it holds 20 people, sometimes more for standing aside. The clinics are facsimiles of makeshift "Doctors Without Borders" backwater fabrications. One guard is at attention to keep order, but without a weapon and limited to a walkie-talkie phone as well as the usual pepper spray.

To my thinking this was ridiculous, just baffling! I was present in very untoward, calamitous disturbances. When very volatile prisoners start yelling, fighting and generally upsetting the general atmosphere the boiling point is reached very quickly. It is often prevented in "the nick of time". The treatment rooms are close by only feet away from the holding cell and on the exterior of the emergency area. The corridors are very narrow and with hidden zones despite specifically placed wall-ceiling mirrors. When there are emergencies with prisoners either lying down or sitting so that personnel can attend their bleeding wounds while EMS (Emergency Medical Services) is on route from the local hospital, the environment is generally emotionally hyperbolic and strained.

I have seen it at its best and its worst. The fear I always had was the sudden reach for sharp instruments (of which there were many) to be used as a lethal weapon. No doubt that the incredible limitations on proper control always made me askance as to the "geniuses" who allowed so many people to be so vulnerable. These are the same individuals whose training courses for personnel are so over-the-top detailed beyond need, and to boot taught by some of the most power hungry and unskilled individuals possible. I have never encountered such self-centered and self-flagellating ne'er do wells in my life.

Teaching officers possessed degrading deportment which was only exceeded by their weak-minded presentation(s)! In teaching for many decades, it is a travesty to see a burlesque-like mentality that is the prison's excuse for a teaching platform (replete with two overly burly individuals with backwoods-level intelligence). The continuous loss of discouraged, recently hired guards was striking. I witnessed in the teaching center individuals who left permanently in a huff. In a distinctly depressed economy the finding of acceptable employment is treasured. Yet, the eventual drop off from the approximately sixty adult employees was close to 75%.

A time must come whereby sufficient employee retention numbers should override the burdens which are currently too weighty and emotionally taxing. The time- consuming educational format for all employees does not conflate with the job descriptions.

Simply put, they reflect compliance with regulatory controls which make for a uniquely high employee misery index. Between the six-week basic training that guards undergo at the very beginning of their employment, the yearly continuation courses, the shooting range compliance exercises, and the self-defense updates would all fulfill the "necessary and sufficient" mathematical standard if there would not be such a psychological drubbing in pursuit of the daily demands. It is also fundamentally senseless. The guards are the most friendly and highly personable people who have invested tedious and demanding training so that their safety and appreciation demands far greater investment in their safety. A Level III is not a walk in the park atmosphere!

Walking amidst the buildings of the yard there was always an elevated spirit. There is no question that I always felt a mutual respect and good humor like no other place I had ever worked. It did not make any difference whether employees were from human resources, certification, the arboretum, the cafeteria, wood-working, etc. There was a generalized feeling of mutual understanding and respect. Their sense of dedication was lost to the long hours and very low pay. Within the state prison system across the country this translates to internal violence which can take a life or lives any day of the week. The longer an employee stays within the system for the carrot at the end of the stick (the insurance and retirement benefits) the more noticeable is the gloom which bleeds into every conversation. The older guards always reflected a sense of glee when their retirement was imminent, never afraid to come forth with how much they hated what they did and will never, ever look back. And such was that common denominator that always made me so deeply reflective. The prison computer always exhibited a fawning note that splashed praise to recognize them for years of dedication. Or, there was the proverbial "dog and pony show" which excited a pseudo-sense of mirth as the retiring employee was exalted with an obsequious social glee and delight. In the end it would clearly misrepresent the true mixed emotions prison employees share regarding their many years, never realizing their true financial worth.

Every business, be it in the public or private sector, demands leadership and accountability. The state prison system being within the public sector is stymied up and down by bureaucracy and corruption. The "Big House" is its very life force that has not changed since its early beginnings, and most likely will never change. Its management is trying, and it is afflicted with profound inertia. The corruption I shall touch on later, but, for now, it is presently noteworthy to understand that political correctness is the scaffold on which the system rests. The following is known.

1. The language of communication has been watered down "to please" and "to appease". For example: convicts or prisoners are referenced as inmates. Cell blocks are called dormitories, or, dorms for short. Guards are not guards. They are officers. Solitary confinement is called a Special Housing Unit.

2. Incident reports are for documentation of negative events which require administrative review and reconciliation. They are basically impact statements. However, they are abused overwhelmingly so that a simple animus for another employee can be used as an abusive cudgel. It only rarely conveys value to what is an already laborious procedure weighed down by reams of paper trails (that generally get lost in the system, or that take so much time to investigate that their value is lost).

3. The prison system has its employees reduced to "robots in a tiered system". They are very congenial, intelligent people, but so undereducated and ill- informed that they do not think nor intelligently communicate. It is purposefullyrun
this way so there is bureaucratic control over the system.

4. The employees who travel between the different in- state institutions are in more stable positions as they are not present long enough in the Level 3 institutions

to feel the daily tension: the people working in classification, some psychologists, and outside delivery personnel.

5. For the most part, the majority of the prisoners are flagrantly pampered and given costly access channels not even available outside to people in need. This will be discussed later as the most politically correct gratuity making a mockery of legitimacy and equity.

6. There are prisoners inside who should be released, others whose sentences are too long due to ridiculous sentencing guidelines, others who are released way prematurely, and those who should die in prison for the horrific nature of their crimes.

7. Inaction, failure of action, and, methodically evasive action by prison bureaucracy enables a level of bureaucratic corruption so systemic that it is sadly inviolate.

8. The prison system cannot ever change as is because its lifeblood is the "business as usual" mentality. Its existence is defined by decades of misappropriated history and "good-ole-boy" political coddling. Its Achilles heel redounds to issues intimately connected to education in the country. As it remains, visceral wounds in the system are patched as if Merthiolate tincture would suffice where reconstructive surgery is indicated.

9. The training center for prospective employees must be turned upside down on its head, re-evaluated, and then reshaped to attract and keep ambitious, worthy, and dedicated people. Perfunctory complacency is a losing proposition.

10.   Each state needs organizational fealty at the Governors' level to be a watchdog on the conduct and channeling of money for its prudent disposition. Left to its druthers, the correctional institutions require close surveillance for what is "run-amok", self-serving power and failure to address the needs of its employees.

11.   The general policies of the prison system are written in typical legalese, and they are on the website

for every employee's scrutiny. Its stream of consciousness is every bit politically correct and, as absurd as it might sound, is written with the expectation of "plausible deniability". The administrative bureaucracy would never accept responsibility for misgivings. It would be the misfortune of a more appropriately selected lower level employee. I chose to name the policies as "selective adjudication!"

The primary obligation of the prison system is to protect citizenry against exploitation by those people who would willfully break the law committing either violent or non-violent crimes. It is as simple as that. Oh that it would be so easy and possible! Perhaps in Shangri-La, but certainly nowhere else. Shangri-La is James Hilton's [21] *Lost Horizon* utopia, and, in some sense a prison is conversely a dystopia where "correctional" is not applicable beyond what it really is: a lockup. That is the cold reality. For some who prevail and truly make the most of their detention in a positive direction it is different. It is important to understand that the tiered nature of a prison makes true separation of prisoners important. As in life, when people of like mind assemble for the same purpose, there is a greater chance that positive energies are channeled for those that want to improve their station in life and create a purpose for themselves. Prisons housing violent people are generally devoid of soul, and hollow to the core. This would never be the covenant of a religious prelate, a priest or even a committed religious devotee. But I am observing strictly as an educated, observing and practical individual who has witnessed a prison system lost in time.

Reflecting carefully on opinion blogs and books, I do not believe there is enough of a clear distinction made between prisoners convicted of non-violent versus violent crimes. If these individuals are separated out, then I feel an argument exists supporting differences of opinion regarding sentencing, parole issues, parole boards, prisoner rights, bureaucratic corruption, "three strikes and you're out" sentencing, life sentencing, etc. There are so many inherent wrongs which may never be properly addressed and redressed, but at least discussions can be more sensible and less emotional. There should be room for "truth without prejudice."

There are so many tenable issues raised by both Gottschalk[22] and Pfaff[23]. However, in my estimation, their philosophies and arguments made in support of and against certain laws and regulations are statistically significant but practically refutable. Their arguments and statistical breakdowns lack substantive appreciation of the daily burdens. Non-violent offenders demand sensible re-evaluation of overboard sentencing. Violent offenders are "cats" of a different breed. There is no reason to let them out without serious scrutiny and evaluation year to year. There is no doubt that careful evaluation will determine some should be released at some point. In this regard, this consideration demands watchful analysis over time. Grouping them together in one institution further hardens their being if that is the prisoner's inclination. For both groups, life stops upon imprisonment, and, as they are inured to their surroundings, some become resentful and ossified. It is important to separate the resentful from the resilient. To the falsely incarcerated the advent of DNA identification and other chemical/ biologic markers can liberate falsely incriminated prisoners. And, a district attorney who prosecutes with an ax to grind can ruin lives (later I relate such an officious case in New Orleans). The importuning of an innocent "violent offender" by dint of personal foibles is such an unfortunate happenstance. Personal vendettas as well are beneath any forgiveness! The blur between non-violent and violent offenders is quite clear, but this does not excuse following strict investigation, honorable trials, proper defense, honest prosecution, and reasonable sentencing devoid of political intent. Overcrowded jails and prisons with non-violent offenders have to be dealt with in a serious manner or mass incarceration will never get the serious reduction it demands. In this regard, I fully acknowledge that much more has to be done to clear out the fog and bureaucratic corruption to realize what prisons are and are not: they are warehouses of humanity, and, they are not sufficiently what they purport to be: correctional institutions. In general, they are shrouded with timid advocacy and support groups of all types, grasping for reality, and yet just turning within the same wheel from generation to generation like laboratory rats.

reality, and yet just turning within the same wheel from generation to generation like laboratory rats.

Unless there is an acknowledgement that the laws require reconfiguration in the way state prosecution handles non-violent offenders all the words and writing will be empty and feckless. It is a sine qua non that most prisons realistically reflect extreme racial imbalance and this redounds to domestic upbringing and inferior education. Saddle this with high unemployment, failure to remedy drug addiction and the insidious exposure to drug trafficking, and especially murder rates associated with gangs and extreme religious fanaticism, the future looks quite dim for delimiting the rates of incarceration. I do not want to embellish here, but to even begin thinking about how to remedy the way the country (really the individual states as noted above) develops a consensus and gets serious will be delimited by typical political bargaining. The problem is too serious to be eternally run amok. Between prison bureaucracy and continuous political attention this issue will continue for years.

Being in the "Big House" does leave a social stain. Generally, it reflects back very painfully on family with profound disruption and the subtleties of unspoken pain. I walked through the yard every day and frequently stood outside of the infirmary door glancing around the individual cell blocks. And the prisoners would stroll by me without giving me a stare or even saying hello. A great number would come over and start a conversation. I was friendly but extremely cautious because of their interest where I live. Very cleverly, most would attempt to pry into my personal life, but I would quickly shut this down. They have easy access to family and friends on the outside who would do their bidding should they wish to seek revenge on an employee. One such episode about which I was numerously warned was the murder of a person who came to his door and was shot in the face. This was a revenge killing on behalf of a prisoner who was angry over disciplinary punishment for a prison violation. I cannot vouch for this, but I was repeatedly told by a reliable source early on in my employment to keep me aware of the inherent exposure to any suspicious motive(s). At first, I disabused myself of such extreme apprehension. But as time passed, I realized how accurate the warnings were. My learning curve was rapidly accelerated as I witnessed extreme behavior play out. The prisoners were like chameleons, adopting behaviors which advanced their personal agendas. It is amazing how fast information travels in a prison yard.

Survival is generally their number one priority. And, they take to the extreme, some with subtlety, but the majority with overtly extreme passion. In his book, *The Survivors Club: The Secrets and Science that Could Save Your Life*, Ben Sherwood[24] reduces the survivor's profile to five types: The Fighter, The Believer, The Connector, The Thinker, and, The Realist. All five characteristics define whether the survivor will fight physically and mentally, never deter from his/her internal belief system, develop personal connections with others for aid and comfort, will act predominantly thinking actions through in advance, and will accept that there will be ups and downs (and, things will not always work out as desired). My observations as I came to know many and watching them from a distance convinced me that they manifest profiles which are a product of some or all such characteristics. Most were "gut-checkers" with very evident instinctive behaviors, but occasionally I met a very overriding cerebral personality. By every measure they were all desperate survivor types. Because they are severely educationally challenged the cerebration qualities Ben Sherwood describes are almost universally deficient, but grousing to any extent was non-existent.

I made contact with individuals of all ages. Both the middle-aged and the more wizened had substantially mellowed. They stood out amidst so many arrogant and brazen "Young Turks." The youths were flashy, know-it-all types with gang affiliations, and covered head to toe with tattoos of every conceivable gang affiliation. Some were so prideful they would stop me to illustrate the meaning (as they pointed) of each different one. Even as they were laden with ink the configurations were as stark as they hideously shrouded a prior pubescent life. It was bizarre in its simulation to a living totem pole. In my conversations with many I would point out an older, calm prisoner and point out that this would be their change in a number of years. Some would come back at me: never, in defiance! Once in a while I got to one of the young ones, leaving him totally silent (seemingly trying to consider my shared thoughts).

As I recount all these conversations, I am still imbued with the distinct feeling how even the most heinous murderer will, for the most part, become the people they defiantly rejected as a young hellion. This is eerily alarming in considering the need for guidance and education opportunities during the most vulnerable years of development. Molding clay by a talented artist speaks volumes of the importance of family and education in the development of America's youth. It was obvious to understand how gang affiliation became a surrogate need for even the most odious criminal. The spiritual needs and feelings surface even within the wicked.

As I walked through the yard, each cell block had its own side yard with a basketball net, a mini track, a calisthenics workout area with weights and lifting bars, and an area just to pass time. Some would just lean against the fence, but groups were quite evident. I always thought that "bugs" may be placed strategically to listen in and monitor. But that was probably my suspicious mind wandering as I hastily walked so as to avoid prisoners yelling at me from the fences. Thank the Lord for the advent of razor wire! The prodigious effort to leave the prison was in many ways worse that my nightly entry, even though the light of day was certainly cathartic!

The one time I could keenly observe, be accosted, and talk was during my exit because I came in the dark of night (when I was met by deer, feral cats and the occasional snake). I was always amazed by the relaxed atmosphere, seeing the randomness of prisoners hanging alone or in groups. Where were the guards I thought? Most of the time, nowhere! So, there I was alone with the Level 3 "worst of the worst!" I slowly got to know a great number of them quite well from having treated them repeatedly for some of the worst acute oral infections. And, when they saw me they were inscrutably demanding, overbearing and bossy.

A few of the older prisoners were a breath of fresh air. When I went back to my computer to observe their criminal histories I recoiled with amazement. The person then was hardly the person today. This, for my thinking, is and should be the wakeup call to anyone in the field of criminal justice trying to make a mark dealing with the issues of mass incarceration, for social workers, or governmental operatives (inclusive of politicians) dealing with inner city crime. They were crafty and clever, mostly out of the self-defense and survival personality mindset developed over time. The youngest recent arrivals were just simply "in-your-face aggressive" borne of their "street upbringing." However, at some point in time, there is a transition, a wakeup call, a "come to Jesus" moment that blossoms, and a new person is really alive with a sense of passion for life itself.

Regrets are so evident that as I left the prison grounds in my car I could not help but think that change must come, and that the repetition of the criminal mind generation after generation cannot continue! I also thought that with my seventeen years in school and professional development I could read and research everything printed on criminal justice, but truly "seeing is believing!" Scholastic experience is very defining, but it is empty without observational training day in- day out! Always attentive to my daily exit strategy I always avoided eye contact (unless I was called out by name, which was often), never lingering at a gate, and, when possible, holding my head down. This was an imperative to avoid sudden attack. I understood it was no joke. It was akin to walking through a bread factory without awareness of its intensely pungent aroma sedating one's soul with a serotonin surge! At times I felt that I was really in trouble because there wasn't one guard in sight should I be "grouped" by some of the young ne'er-do-wells. When I was accosted, often I could not understand their very garbled speech. I have never forgotten the contrast so apparent between the splendor of the rustic surroundings and my body swelling with inner glee as it was shattered by numerous encounters. Most were conventional, but one day it was just one of these encounters that contributed to my self-imposed termination, suspecting that at any point I may not see a tomorrow. There was no doubt in my mind. As I said, word travels through the yard with incalculable speed so it is impossible to detect even a flashpoint. I was always alert. One Friday, a couple of weeks before my leaving a prisoner hanging around the "pill room" outside the window next to the infirmary door told me he was going to "f" me up. Did I get under someone's skin? I do not think so because I had a stellar reputation (so I was told by many of the prisoners). But, I understood that at any minute anything can happen. This had to be a basic understanding!

I had never even seen him before. So as my joking mind would do, I tried to apply sensible thought with the very mathematical computations for my demise. Ridiculous. I never thought I would react with such dark humor. I very quickly squirreled that thought away. I always tried to dispel the unbelievable with a blend of the pragmatic. I also had such a growing sense of the administrative corruption which was so drowned in political correctness that I realized how difficult it must have been for the wardens to handle the daily outbursts of violence. And I know the administration put on a great dog and pony show to camouflage the very clear-cut, striking realities of everyday encounters (some savage, some mild). The public was definitely kept in the dark with occasional newsworthy platitudes. When encounters made the news it was due to parents of prisoners leaking to the press or media.

So, my daily exit was never a "rite of passage." From the cavalier initiate I became the undeterred realist. Having witnessed the incorrigible ferocity amidst "God-fearing prisoners," I became committed to the belief that the prisoner domain is so complex that the outside-inside perceptions of its grim actualities are upside down.

I have read many blogs and books reporting statistical defenses for critiques of endemic prison failings and shortcomings. Or, ones that weave incongruent commentary about the prison system paralleling historical periods and movements; e.g. the women's movement, the civil rights movement, the underground railroad-slavery movement, etc. The social-economic consequences impacting issues which outline percentage ups and downs of prison numbers, sentencing guidelines, state issues with excessive sentencing ("three strikes" life sentences), parole boards and paroling, early release, natural versus life sentences, false convictions, etc., are too complex to draw summary opinions without seeing and measuring intellectually the realities of prison life from the inside out! I cannot make petty or unnecessary objections to scholarly efforts based on statistical scrutiny. There are in fact sociological points to be made, but such efforts might render a false sense of the everyday prison system. Statistical analysis is important, but blind to the reality of prison life. This is where the story of mass incarceration begins and ends. Not with statistical analysis. Statistics are markers, not indicators. This is hard for analytics to accept. Statistics have very definite limitations as noted by this comical, but profound, thought:

> Statistics are like a bikini. What they reveal is interesting. But what they conceal is vital.[25]

Statistical analysis in and of itself renders a pure black and white picture without understanding causation. In order to capture meaning for what statistics depict the facts on the ground paint the true picture. Whether they are skewed or meaningful can only be judged over time as viewed with intention. Whether incarceration rates for non-violent offenders have increased from the millennium change to now, and by how much, is pertinent, but its significance lies in the circumstances which contributed to that. For example, it might be the demographic changes relating to census changes, migration patterns, influx of immigrants, increased violence within the inner cities, etc. Statistics make concepts interesting, but their meaning (their vitality) lies in the whys and wherefores. Even my favorite author, Mark Twain[26], never couched his feelings. He offered up this famous line in his autobiography from the wisdom of the Conservative British Prime Minister, Benjamin Disraeli: "There are three kinds of lies: lies, more lies, damned lies, and statistics".

My observations during my employment led me to believe that prisons are to some degree a microcosm of society's underbelly, that area which expands with its hard luck individuals. White collar crime and non-violent "soft" offenders do not fit this category. The gang populations and extreme zealots who would just as soon fillet your body with a razor- sharp hunting knife as say hello are people who compose the bottom of the food chain. They are the "somewhere people" who for any number of reasons watched as life passed them by. The most dangerous prison gang, Mexicana, is a perfect example of "crime for crime's sake!" Their violent nature cannot be seen buried in a statistical page. Statistical numbers are analytic numbers for their long-term understanding. Seeing and understanding events in real time convey true meaning. The shifting numbers vary over time, and this has meaning. Onsite events colorize the value and meaning of statistics. Social movements and judicial refining of laws will reorient the statistical basis of how prisons will shift in population, but the more important issue is why prisons have never changed. Why are they frozen in time and remain a constant thorn in the side of the justice system. Time stands still inside a prison. Correction is relegated to the "born again" to some degree in Level I and Level II facilities, but only sparingly in Level III. Level III is generally a dead-end.

I would suggest that the "Big House" is other-worldly and run by a two-tier system defined as a "correctional institution". One of the reasons I took the job was to learn about the system which seems to live in its own unique twilight zone. It is a world which can only subsist from day-to-day, an eternal entity frozen in time. Its personality is unambiguously one-dimensional, defined by the ill-humored, ill-tempered and peevishly embittered. There is no other way it can be, or ever will be. Bloggers and books written (except for ex-convicts who write tell all books) seem to be formulaic in subject matter. Viewing it in motion daily is educational as well as emotionally redefining. The emotional pulse is thoroughly mercurial, each day giving up the unexpected with an excitement that sometimes is tragically jaw-dropping. Being there left me with an incredible respect and love for the wardens I came to know. Their dedication to the spirit and demands of their jobs is unwavering. The guards, subjected daily to the unpredictable and harsh physical interactions with prisoners, went way beyond the call of their duties. Seeing is believing, but it is also riveting to witness such devotion. And the danger zones are omnipresent. They are compelled to expect the unexpected. The torrent of emotion I witnessed from them on a daily basis would capture the admiration and gratitude of most outside employers. In the prison, it was gratuitous and expected. The bureaucracy plays its employees with cunning and hubristic pride. It was put on to engender group think and commandeer allegiance in lemming-like solidarity.

One day I was in the operational room talking to the head nurse when I heard this bellowing howl. So, I went out to the call center of the infirmary where the attending guard was telling a prisoner to shut up. The call center was flooded with prisoners to the brim. He was trying to shut him up so as to foment a riot. The prisoner did not care. That type of incident is one that can result in the worst type of event. And, because this prison was so understaffed there was no easy way out of this event. Inevitably something would happen, it had to, either explode or calm down. Well, neither. The prison got away lucky this time because a few of the extra-large prisoners took over and subdued him. This was a unique circumstance because most events like this do not end so cleanly. For example, the prisoner who was rushed into the infirmary on a holiday day with a "slicing and dicing" to his left cheek and lip while in the cafeteria. He almost bled out!

The Bureau of Justice Statistics[27] in 2014 documents 1,561,500 prisoners in state facilities, a 1% decrease. Federal Prisons held 5,300 prisoners, a 2.5% decrease. In the last United States 2010 census[28,] the population tallied 308.7 million, a 9.7% increase from the 2000 census. Of this number
125.9 million were adult males, and 119.4 females. At age 85 and older women outnumbered men about 2:1 (4 million to 2.1 million). John Pfaff notes that there were a total of 2.2 million federal and state prisoners in 2014[29]. But my experience tells me the numbers are only significant if a case is being made where numbers are used to make a meaningful argument. And the story he relates is spot on, but its black and white picture has to be colorized to really understand what he relates. But, in general, his message holds true. "The Standard Story" theme makes a lot of sense and is indubitably well documented, but I

want to add one very delimiting essential area of differentiation: offenders involved in very violent crime. I do not want to diminish his arguments because he is totally correct in areas of non-violent offenses. In a like stream of thought, Marie Gottschalk's[30] book, *The Prison and the Gallows*, argues in a like manner for a constructive reduction in prison numbers in tracing various historical movements: the welfare state; feminists' groups, the anti-rape movement, and, the battered women's movement. She traces capital punishment, court decisions and related arguments. A very detailed and powerfully scripted analysis, she relates very bold statistics illuminating where the penal system has failed various elements of society. Like my supplemental thought for Phaff's "The Standard Story" argument, I likewise add this distinction to Gottschalk's thoughts about mass incarceration. Non-violent and violent offenders must be viewed differently in consideration of prison reform. This is so important and cannot be truly appreciated without being witness for an extended period of time. They are "apples and oranges" in view of the level of criminality and general depraved behavior.

Prison numbers as large swaths of the criminal population have decreased into the late 1990's. However, viewing the problems today with gangs, criminal illegal aliens, and radical Islamic terrorist incidents, I see the numbers always on the rise. It is thus imperative to be declarative and peremptory about comprehensive prison reform. This argument I shall lay out later. Otherwise, prisons will become ungainly to manage at any level of safety and administration.

Prisons have evolved as a clear-cut reflection of many real social problems in the country: drugs and disease in particular. Criminal behavior is not a hot button issue without understanding the demographics of American society. Education, employment opportunity, retention of the family unit, religious participation, political reform, media reform, corruption control, and ending the country's divisiveness must arouse serious concern and provoke reasonable accommodation and change by thoughtful and concerned leadership. Throwing money alone at these problems will never suffice. Contentious living is out of control in the country, and the inexplicable lack of control will not only destroy generations in the future, but the prisons will expand in number and kind. They are national "cancers" for which universal attention is long overdue, or the country will pay a potentially irreversible price. It's an inside-out conundrum of huge proportions!

The penal system and the carceral state, as I see it, is never changing in this country. It is both the byproduct and embodiment of bureaucratic neglect and corruption at all levels of government. It is also a reflection of egos and pride, the self-flagellation and power hungry at both local, regional, state and federal levels of government. The will of our political leaders is too soiled to think virtue is going to suddenly ride into our cities and states on a white horse in the guise of limitless integrity to affirm and make good on their demagogic pledges for change. For people who believe in their false promises, just read (even in a cursory manner) just the historical record going back to 1776. Greed for power and position will never allow our prisons to suddenly separate out the people who should be allowed a new found freedom, and those who should be imprisoned while throwing the keys away. Just the insanely low approval rating of Congress is hugely appalling (wavering around 12%, up and down, sometimes as low as 7%)[31]. On the one hand, this all serves as fodder for those who write books, critical blogs, magazine articles, etc. And, in my opinion, it ends there.

Therefore, when examining the statistics cited above, that's what they are: just statistics! They do not in any measure have enough impact to think that things will change for the better. Out of approximately 330 million people (in total; about 245 million adults) there are slightly over 2.2 million in our prisons. It is more significant to examine why the carceral state continues to expand despite periods of slight decline. The "Big House" will always be with us. What can be done to bring down these glaring numbers is the magical question! It might take some form of alchemy to wake up the country that change is necessary! The outside is deaf and blind to the inside, only important to the families who play a support role for those fighting for a second chance at freedom and those who grope at very frail vestiges of hope as the vestiges of human life decay year to year without a wit of horror and concern for the person without a stake in the issue. However, is this not the reason for the political class? The "Big House" is so different from everyman's house that maybe the important reasons for its salty state of existence should be examined, even if subjectively, through the prism of social circumstances which seem to provide gasoline for the fire that burns from one generation to the next. And to some degree it is why candor slides where real reporting is obscured and facts hidden from public scrutiny. So, let's proceed.

> We are so biased in our own favor that often what we take for
> virtues are only vices disguised by self-love.[32]

In the ensuing chapters I am going to clarify what I consider some of the most considered reasons for what has turned our culture upside down, so divisive (which is really not new), and seriously on the wrong track in dealing with poignant deficiencies in the management of the prison system. But, at the same time, I want to clearly point out that it is also all we have to keep civil society protected. Level 1 and 2 prisons do not reform, and they should. The prison industry is a self- sufficient cottage industry. This is not the fault of its employees. It is the fault of federal and state politicians who know they can "go along to get along" without having to answer for their continued empty talk and sinful banter. It is sufficient to keep them under control (especially the maximum-security Level 3 institutions) and out of the news. For them no news is good news. Liberty provides us freedoms seen in no other country, but it does not relinquish society from its responsibility to those held in confinement. It's not enough that custodial care and support continue from one generation to the next. There are no elegiac memories for the wasted lives. Though it is hard to digest, they are human beings and history shows that their numbers will continue to increase. This thought raises the uneasy reality that prisons will have to readjust and become truly correctional. I am going to try to measure up to the challenge and demonstrate how this is possible. I hope my reasoning will echo and create a national conversation so that individuals far better than I will rise up from their stagnant thresholds and enter the fray where they may be creative and productive. However, the specter of the past also suggests this may be illusory in hope and impractical in reality. I hope not, at least for the sake of future generations.

CHAPTER 2

The Misery Index

"The misery of man proceeds not from any single crush
of overwhelming evil, but from small vexations
continually repeated."[33]
Johnson: Pope (Lives of the Poets)

Misery is serial in nature and the consequence of repeated and profound negative emotions, experiences and events. At some point the misery is the consequence and misery arises from profound negative emotions that are evil, but from small vexations continually repeated the consequence of repeated and human spirit is so broken that all hope is lost. And if all hope is lost over time, the will to live and thrive disappears. The "small vexations continually repeated" as Samuel Johnson bespeaks become targeted threats to survival and eats away at the very foundation which supports the human misery and soul.

Misery is also antithetical to a human's constitution. A psychiatric issue aside, people tend to rebound from adversity because of natural survival instincts. It takes a constant beat down in life to undo and unravel the network of self-protective mechanisms which bind the human spirit. There is no more an exemplary environment where humanity is lost than a prison. Whatever individualism is left before incarceration seemingly bottoms out in most cases. Group think and reaction takes over and intensifies in direct relation to the austerity, instability and peril of the facility. Like termites gathering in dark, woody foundations burrowing and destroying the tedium, danger and despair slowly eats away at the prisoner day-to-day. Fear and anxiety are ever present except for the steely-eyed, hollow individuals who lost their souls somewhere along the way. The hardcore ones are so vacant that they possess a threatening style of inestimable hostility. Levels I, II and III facilities reflect a definite "misery gradient" of danger and despair with the latter housing the most imposing, bold and belligerent.

Some prisons have a literal "come to Jesus" loss of hope. To escape the woe and melancholy that overtakes their will to live and survive suicide often grabs and destroys whatever spirit remains. Witnessing this personally is very hard, and it defines the reason why the employees of the prison system are at least trained to see and recognize suicidal tendencies. This is no joke, and, in many cases, prisoners feign their inward feelings and do in fact commit suicide. Even some of the most unruly and bad-tempered individuals can occasionally deceive. Sometimes and despite stepping up monitor schedules, when the prisoner is fixated sufficiently to deceive and elude a "suicide watch," the individual successfully takes her/his life. It is disquieting and emotionally unhinging for guards, and far worse for the young and newly trained. The word gets around the prison with alacrity because the event strikes right at the core of every attentive employee.

Depending on the prison environment the levels of danger (threats and outright violence) all vary tremendously. Generally speaking, prisons today are endangered by the presence of competing lethal gangs. This will be subject to a more detailed discussion in an ensuing chapter. But, for purposes of the present considerations, the evolution of gangs in the prison system over the last fifty years (and particularly within the last fifteen years) has negatively impacted the security of all prisoners and employees with great daily concern. It is in this regard that the tension of a Level III maximum security prison arises from gangs which mutually settle differences or precipitate severe blood curdling violence. Or, they may act as go-betweens and peace makers. The situations are determined by improvised, spontaneous reactions. It is naïve to believe in inter-gang harmony because hormones roar, and, worse yet, sudden change of heart can result in bedlam. The prison is a self-contained entity where the quietude can be breached with a sudden burst for any reason no matter how trifling. To say a keg of dynamite is more controlled is not an exaggeration. Hyperbole never loses its defining basis, especially for a Level III.

Difficulties in responding to prisoner demands are tenuous at best. Employees consequently must be ready at any time for unbridled, spontaneous mayhem. To emphasize a familiar thought: an idle mind is the devil's workshop. And though the system attempts to keep prisoners' minds focused and busy, the Level III is an alternate universe where quiet is rare, and channeling energy in a creative direction nearly impossible. Boredom is the sugar that feeds the violent criminal's mind and abets his malicious inclinations. Gang rivalries overtake the prison population psychologically too often, seemingly with a magnetic-like impulse, polarizing their responses to the will of their group leaders. Seeing their day-to- day shuffling about, slight tensions can instantly precipitate a breach of trust with such disturbing abandon. It usually results in a stabbing or a deathly violent putdown. This is not so common in a Level II where violence is still a consideration, but certainly not to the extent of a maximum-security prison. Prison is prison, and whether common or not, guards must always be alert to the possibility of extreme behaviors as violent and as high pitched as the crackling sound of lightning in a tropical storm.

What makes all this a horror show on a daily basis is its stifling, unsettling unpredictability! Permeating what can be lovely, peaceful weather, a lazy, hazy summer day, or a brutally relentless cold winter, one with subzero temperatures, can be the sudden outburst which suddenly shakes up a humdrum, steady calm. The atmosphere can pan the extremes from a clearly methodical, almost clinical response by the emergency riot teams to an all-out "cri de Coeur" emanating from different areas of the yard and infirmary. But in all cases the wardens and associate wardens are usually all present along with an assortment of other officers and guards. And, mind you (for later consideration), the only guns are with the critical response teams or ones sanctioned by and distributed from the lockup quarters at the entrance gate. No question, there is a sudden gravity which permeates the entire prison, sometimes silent, sometimes a fervent commotion of serious concern written all over every face! And, at times, solemnity, disgust, indifference, fear, or other ranges of emotional reactions are part of every array imaginable because the atmosphere elicits so many possible elements of prison agitation. If guards were allowed to be armed, most disturbances and violent uprisings could be put down with more meaning and immediate efficiency. The guards are open to so many uncertainties and threats that it is inconceivable that, in spite of their training, guns are "NOT" part of their everyday protection. Ask the magic question: why have gun ranges and require practice/performance requisites? This is just one element of the strange bureaucratic tangled web of "Policy" nonsense! Why train? The brain requires repetition to retain skill level, but, in this case, for what? Walking through the prison as I left every day it was to the distant cracking of shots at the gun range. I grew up learning how to shoot pistols and rifles so this was a head-shaker for me!

Denial of the best defense system is a manifestation of the "politically correct" thinking in the nation today. The environment of a maximum-security prison can be maintained by pepper spray, but ultimately pushback with force is the best iodine! However, the arrogance of power is arrogant and loathsome. There is no virtue in a detached, "politically correct" dissent over policies which put so many lives at risk. On most days there is some incident that so heightens the stress load that it defies common sense. It makes tedium and worry so appalling that employees are miserable. I have witnessed level- headed adults cry from frustration.

As I reflected on this daily psychological beat-down for so many people, one day I thought that it would be comical to consider misery as part of a negotiable standard for salary negotiation if it were not so pathetic. People who never consider misery as part of their daily job description have no idea what it would be like to go to work with the expectation that something so outlandish might happen that they might never know where or when the level of forbearance might be no longer worthwhile. If it sounds like foolishness, it is not. It simply is one of those human emotions that has its limits. It does not enter advertising or marketing as well. Yet, in all truth, it is a serious cause of prison upheaval and one of certain reasons for employee turnover.

Thus, in consideration of my daily ruminations, I came up with what I thought would render a sensible mathematical formula to frame "The Misery Index" into a fixed frame of reference. It is simple mathematics that links the causes for gnawing distress. It is easy to understand as well as it holds true to form. There is nothing complex about the formula, and it directs the mind to appreciate how much daily change in the prison environment affects the general malaise. It was also my concerned feeling that a prison is a necessary evil. Without somewhere to house people who are a viable threat to humanity society, it cannot thrive. Ambitions might be broken and squandered by out-of-control danger (as in many other areas of the world like Venezuela, Mexico, Argentina, Brazil, Somali, Zimbabwe, etc.) The United States has a prison system which cannot satisfy a lot of people, but it is the best we have and comparatively the most humanitarian in the world. And yet it is a system constantly struggling to hold it together in spite of the barrage of its daily challenges. The bizarre struggles are so inflammatory at times that without total lockdown to bring things under control rioting might spark the indwelling misery and fire up sensational gang violence. Therefore, "The Misery Index" offers a tangible reference for how vulnerable the prison system is by relating the mutually related factors. So, let's take a look at it and try to make sense of it:

$$M = \frac{cSEC}{n1/n2/n3}$$

where M: refers to the general all-around sense of Weltschmerz (melancholy, weariness, or outright fear).

c: a constant which reflects the factors which influence the durability, survivability and longevity of the American prison system in face of the ever-present threats, alarming prison riots, and persistent political considerations.

S: refers to sentencing and how it directly impacts all aspects of prison life; how sentencing guidelines are structured and modified throughout time; sentencing is intimately related to parole and how Parole Boards all govern, the stability and health of the prisons being directly impacted as its determinations preserve the safety of a civil society; and, once again, politics extending its lively tentacles
overbearingly so as to disable meaningful resolution.

E: refers to the expected/unexpected dangers which are both fickle and variable with unfortunate spontaneity: for example, the appropriate classification of prisoners which governs the facility's threshold of harmony and safety.

C: the degree of bureaucratic corruption as it impacts the overall governance and health of all institutions; the standards and policies and their judicious effectuation in the face of viable administrative missteps, or, even calculated and/or devious misbehavior (a reality of politics interceding in, and at times controlling, prison life).

n1: the number of violent prisoners.

n2: the number of non-violent prisoners.

n3: a mixed population of violent and non-violent prisoners which would be common to Level 2 and Level 3 prisons depending on the state.

Prisons are complexes of formidable need. Yet, they are also houses of profound anxiety. Prisoners are living under difficult conditions and must be able to adapt to "on call," which is to say from moment to moment. They tend to put on a good face, but the environment is always in flux. The formula above is an indicator of the emotional highs and lows. For example, if the "constant" (the prison remains durable) prevails over time, but any of the variables changes in the numerator or denominator, then there will be a change to the "good" or the "bad". Sentencing (the "S") is a variable, but does not experience as much flux as the others. The expected/unexpected dangers (the "E") is elusive, uncontrollable and the sudden spark for adversity all day and night, every day. "E" reflects spontaneity. "C" has more of a long term or slowly progressive effect that inches into notice and impact. And, the "n's" (1, 2 and 3) change all the time. Therefore, with all the daily changes being made, a good hypothetical example (simply to understand the measure of misery), would be a 10-year sentence for a non-violent prisoner in a Level II mixed population prison housing 1,200 individuals. If all the prisoners presented the same length of term for the same crime, the homogeneity would create a safe environment with guards having less anxiety trying to keep the peace. This is, however, very unrealistic. If you decrease the prison population, control increases. If the population doubles, the demands for control increase. If the quality of prisoners change (the numerator) so that there are now violent prisoners with lengthy or life sentences now present, the "Misery Index" suddenly turns for the worse as the "S" and "E" factors per unit differences in quality of prisoners (by the quantifiable differences in crimes committed) increases (and in complexity). Subsets of the "n" factors (such as 2a-infinity) can (and do) vary. This can all be factored in, but to keep it all simple, the mixed population can be a miserable place to be for a bank robber placed into a prison with rapists-pederasts- murderers. And if there is an understaffed prison (which is very common today), the danger-flashpoint for one prisoner to an entire prison can erupt automatically. It is interesting to see how the prison yard reflects this index.

This is where quantifiers regulate the immediate quality of all aspects of prison life. Anyone who ponders any of the above variables can appreciate how the system can be upended with devastating impact. Classification, sentencing and parole considerations are intertwined so meaningfully that causative effects on prison life, individuals whose hopes and prayers are inherently juggled, and families with daily

emotional strain all factor in to precipitate a wide range of reactions which cannot be anticipated, and certainly should not be under-considered. These variables are extremely difficult to control, but examined
within the context of a formulaic relationship is very stark. The people who are vested with the control of agencies withinthe prison system are so mutually dependent that their responsibilities at no time should wander. Their decisions are so vital as to be tantamount to the justice meted out by their decision making. Too often the right hand may forget the left hand so to speak, and to the detriment of so many. The scales of justice should be equal and devoid of the politics (which would be overly intrusive). Finally, people within the prison system should have proper training and experience. However, this is whimsy because this is not stable and predictable. Insufficient pay and long hours make it almost impossible to retain adequate employees. This is unfortunate, but it broadens the harsh reality of attracting necessary talent through proper compensation.

It is very clear that in a confined space like a prison every person has a breaking point, even more so than most people in private life. The adrenal gland more than likely pumps out more than its complement of reactive body chemicals (epinephrine and cortisol) which react to urgency and long-term stress respectively. These are mother-nature's slow death sentences. A reasonable medical study would be to trace the aging of the human body due to the persistent hyperbolic chemical responses. The habitual misfortunes occurring with such wild abandon within every maximum- security prison in the United States are well-established. The inability to control the haphazard nature of violent occurrences results in a misery of unparalleled consequences in a civil society. PTSD (Post Traumatic Stress Disorder) is very real ina Level III prison. War is not part of this discussion, but it certainly has its own well-documented state of soldier desperation. And history defines other societal hells like the German sponsored holocaust death camps or the Russian gulags during WWII. Certainly, hell may present a chameleon-like effect, but hell is still hell and the end result is human suffering.

Human misery is nothing new. Even the Greeks in their heyday B.C. clutched their souls directly to a mythology that either cushioned their daily problems or vindicated their experiences. Nevertheless, misery played a major role in their lives. An example from Edith Hamilton's[34] book on mythology beautifully captures this. Tartarus is a region below Hades (Hell: defined as a bottomless pit, an abyss) where mythological figures like Tantalus (who killed his son), the Titan Cronus (who overthrew his god-father Uranus and tried to eradicate his brothers before being saved by Zeus), and Sisyphus (a deceiver who tried to outthink Hades and spent his eternal life pushing a rock up an unreachable hill). Hamilton relates in descriptive passages how misery can "tantalize" (taken from the mythological man, Tantalus) man for coldhearted and disdainful behavior. To be willfully and imperiously cruel is to be cast to a forever world of suffering and acute anguish in Greek Mythology! Perhaps if education was more prevalent in areas of the country where high crime rates lead individuals down an unrepentant path to incarceration, eyes might be opened and informed against brazen criminal behavior. Mythology is not where the rubber hits the road so to speak, but it codifies cause and effect where miscreant deeds can only lead to loss of the freedoms that this country affords people in so many ways. The loss of liberty this way is real and tangible, and the misery is not mythological!

The impressions I drew from the prototypical maximum-security prison were sensorial and quite disturbing because there was a universal feeling of "I do not want to be here". This was quite evident from the employees as well as the prisoners. Yes, the number of prisoners who could only be described as contemptible and shabby at best certainly outnumbered the numbers who evoked contrition. I learned very early on not to be deceived by any well-wishing, congeniality from any because I was told it was a defense mechanism rooted in survival. And boy this proved to be so true. I became quite observant of every word, movement and reaction for my own protection because danger jumped out without any warning and around any corner. The suddenness and severity was astounding when it occurred. I still remember good friends mopping up the blood on the floors to restore the normalcy so difficult to maintain, be it somewhat of a sham or not. For many, it was at least a relief in spite of the visuals left behind in memory.

Therefore, I did not want to impose mathematics to define "The Misery Index" as a vague or a confusing measure of the prison environment. I found it illustrates very simple variables which are interrelated and measurable with consistency, and do not change. I wish they would, and for the positive. However, the way life goes today does not seem to forecast any tangible change for the good in the near future. As La Rochefoucauld so brilliantly said: "Quarrels would not last long if the fault were on one side only."[35] The intensity which is felt throughout a prison day is a reflection of both sides: the lay-about prisoner and the full-throttled. Both meet each other daily like prize-fighters feeling each other out with cautious tenacity.

Let's examine the parameters. The "c" in the formulaic analysis represents the prison system as a permanent fixture in our culture. It certainly has manifested in every culture since recorded time. There is no distinction between the federal, state or private systems in this viewpoint. (The private system came into being for two main reasons. Firstly, there has been a forever feeling that the state system is a failure and the people who brought the private prison system into being did so as entrepreneurs wanting to capture the almighty dollar. They felt that a government run system had no chance to flourish for the same reasons as many believe government stultifies instead of enhancing the business of any cultural need. And secondly, the private prison system was thought as an eventual replacement for a failing governmental one bereft of ineptitude. But this has not turned out to be the case. In fact, the private system may make money, but it is a failed system as well. Yet, there is no doubt that in any shape or fashion the prisons will remain as permanent fixtures in American culture.

Therefore, the "c" is cemented in American life (no pun intended). It might be chameleon-like as it changes through the years to satisfy governmental impulses, but it is here to stay. The "c" will always be 1 (unless heaven and earth turn upside down on humanity).

The "S" is for sentencing. Unfortunately, this is always a highly contested variable. The arguments, pro and con, are the underpinnings of the left and right of politicos who exercise their wills in defense of personal belief systems that may not always be practical nor reflective of "what is" versus personal fantasy and prejudicial thinking. It is impossible to bring the two political wills together to reconcile what is best for society. Classification as an instrument of placement in the prison system is the by-product of sentencing to place prisoners in correct cell blocks to preserve "tranquility" and functional harmony. In other words: to keep the prison safe. But the "S" is too variable. To delimit appropriately predictable placement as the consequence of such "subjective decision making from objective criteria" is inherently weak. This requires later discussion, but for now accept that sentencing is a variable from state to state.

The "E" is a measurement of the prison environment. Yes, its danger zones! There is so much flux within the system that with certainty the temperature governed by danger from day to day will impart unpredictability just as assuredly as day and night come and go. When there is quiet and laughter at any given time danger can suddenly raise its ugly head! It seems that fate rains holy hell in spite of conscientious preparation. The lifeblood of the prison system is the support staff, and it can be easily upended very suddenly.

The "S" and "E" are much more significant for the Level III prisons, though Level II prisons can vary depending on the admixture of prisoners and personality types at any specific time. Some Level II prisons can experience very fragile periods of excitement and danger, but with certainty the Level III will always expect the unexpected. Movement of prisoners from one facility to another is a measure taken without certainty that such action will abort a riot or improve the daily life where threats of danger may be imminent. There is nothing scientific about this, though a measure of common sense often prevents flare-ups.

The "C" references the degree(s) of corruption spread within the prison system or within a single facility. The prison system, be it state, federal or private is bound by administrative regulatory controls and policies. More times than naught they appear to be for show. The reality is that corruption is a disease of any massive administrative system, and prisons are no different. But corruption is an untenable variable. "God forbid" this claim is made, but the truth is that it can be so wanton that the job of a warden can become a stress-laden exercise to circumnavigate daily events just to get by. Problems are naturally going to occur in a system that gets by trying to hold the status quo. However, it becomes untenable when corruption puts the squeeze on everyone from top to bottom. So much of this is unnecessary, but it prevails just as sure as day will appear from the night. Large administrations get wobbly as if in a drunken stupor. Inject a few bad apples into the system, be it at the top or anywhere where the net effect is blatantly felt, and the throttle unleashes a very unhealthy state of frustration.

The "n's" reflect the quality of the prisoner. The 1, 2 or 3 are subsets of the "n" to characterize the prisoner as violent or non-violent. The number 3 will define the most passive character type in the system, a prisoner who may be placed for release, home bound for a period of time after parole, etc. The $n1$ is the most dangerous threat while the $n2$ can meld peacefully or evolve to extreme danger. The $n1$ or $n2$ may be mixed in a Level II prison. Therefore, the "n's" in the denominator will be a unit measurement of the numerator variables. Thus, in simple terms, taken together to create a multiplier effect (numerator) per population type and mixture (denominator) where the constant of "1" is a certainty and will never change. Thus, where $n1$ is a non-violent Level 1 facility, the sentencing ("S"), facility level of vulnerability in terms of danger ("E"), and how the corruption within the system impacts a particular facility ("C") all multiplied together will render a per unit facility degree of misery. And the variables as they change will impart degrees of differences from facility to facility.

Is this fanciful? Maybe. But, as I ruminated daily, I found a direct connection within the context of these variables. They presented to me an expression of the sullenness, brooding and resentment I saw every day. It was an expression of "normal" people asserting their maximum effort to keep the "abnormal" under wraps. "The Misery Index" is certainly a discernible element that is an expression of facilities reflecting levels of extreme danger that everyday people outside the system could not fathom nor endure unless inured to high levels of comparable challenges within their own lives.

The prison system is the most profound threat to a human being who cannot endure the constancy of burden and threatening encounters. And the outside world requires protection from those who impart danger willy-nilly due to mindless acts or sickness. It's a balancing issue. The net effect on society is the same. And so the prison system evolved for civil protection. But when it is infected by contagions like greed, power and control, then an institutional misery evolves which blankets everyone burdened with the responsibilities to keep the facilities tethered to a temperate status quo.

And, in this vein, chapters will ensue to take measure of its depth and variability. So much is reported on websites, in a few books regarding statistical quantifiers of changing societal norms, in blogs that argue weaknesses by statistical comparisons changing over time, individuals who write tell-all stories of their time in "The Big House", and even by professorial types to render historical views as statistics change over time as politics challenge the system. But I prefer to encapsulate perhaps some of everything of the above as a witness up close and personal. I think that all perceptions are worth evaluating. The prison is a necessary megalithic institution of Americana with unimaginable tentacles extending so pervasively into many societal agendas. It has also become as fragile as I have perceived it. In my mind, it'll never improve. It will always falter because it is so vulnerable, fragmented and politically influenced.

Before proceeding one more important point has to be made in wading into a deeper and expanded exposure of what the prison system is in its uncertain state of being. In such a multi-faceted world, crime, for the majority of people, is not studied to any extent except for those whose professions (Criminologists, Psychiatrists, Neuroscientists, Neurologists, etc.) draw them into this mutable area of study, research and clinical treatment. Within the prison system nationwide individuals are imprisoned for many reasons and levels of criminal behavior. Whether for theft or murder there is a compelling reason for incivility. If researchers and/or clinicians could figure out the whys and wherefores, then jails and prisons would be out of business and the world would be one big Shangri La. But the truth of the matter is the opposite is true to a very unpleasant extreme. Cadres of professionals have studied the human condition which hardens individuals to perfidious lifestyles at all levels. And here is where a very important point is to be made.

Most of the time, prisons are not deterrents. Recidivism is hard to contain and eliminate. So, why crime and why varying degrees of criminality? In this regard, the study of various areas of the brain through Computerized Axial Tomography, aka CAT Scans (specialized X-rays used to detect disease or abnormalities) have been used. Articles and books written on this subject have shown definite anatomical changes to various locations of the brain where increased heat to areas correspond to increased brain activity. The heat corresponds to increased blood to the areas with increased blood pressure, reflecting activity. To see where human emotion and decision making as well tissue changes in disease (tumors, strokes, depression, Alzheimer's, etc.) CAT Scans have contributed immensely.[36, 37, 38] However, despite research and clinical therapies for treatment of neurological dysfunction and disease, science cannot as yet provide answers necessary to offset all levels of crime. Sure, it may be straightforward to recognize deviant behaviors for which prisons become the responsible agencies to manage. Nothing could be more trying and extreme for all within the criminal justice system. And the professionals responsible to diagnose and treat prisoners are for the most part base level clinicians. Yudhijit Bhattacharjee's article has many examples of studied brains in an attempt to reconcile neurological changes to differentiate good and evil behaviors. In an example of psychopathy, he points to a neuroscientist who found the right Amygdala (the area of the brain responsible for emotions, memory and survival instincts) increased in size in a study of 4,000 prisoners. Thus, in spite of having this information, on a daily routine basis it does not contribute to any amelioration of "The Misery Index". And at a very mundane level, any guard would say "so what?"

As Rudyard Kipling[39] intoned in "The Ballad of East and West": "Oh East is East and West is West and never the twain shall meet". (The "twain" is an archaic term for "two"). What prison professional personnel confront on a daily basis is light years away from the very level of sophistication involved in studying why psychopathic (or even neurotic) behaviors give rise to very cruel and heinous behavior. The guards and professionals, nor the leadership (wardens and officers), though burdened to keep a controlled environment, are subjected to the very unreasonable neurological changes as well. They are human, subject to the high tension every day. They deal with everything from low level impudent behavior to murderous violence daily. This consideration is of immense importance in an environment that would prefer to attribute "reform" as the essential and primary reason for a prison's reason for being (as noted in my introduction). In an ideal world this would be a wonderful reason for being, but in all practicality the ever-present issues of financial pressures to manage a prison and prison life does not permit such a luxury.

Keeping in mind the above narrative, it is important to emphasize what Samuel Johnson meant when he stated at the beginning of this chapter: "The misery of man proceeds not from any single crush of overwhelming evil, but from small vexations continually repeated."[40] To me this is why "The Misery Index" colorizes what might otherwise be taken as overly simplistic or black-and-white. Misery, as previously stated, is a double-edged sword in the prison system. The repeated evil prisoners bring to bear on others results in "repeated vexations" brought to bear on the personnel responsible for them while incarcerated. At a Level III prison the general disharmony never lets up and the guards become the victims of their chicanery and outright audacity. It all boils over when the threshold of the boiling point builds beyond containment, and a riot ensues. It is repetitive incidents of deceit and evil ongoing that makes the concept of reform almost inconceivable. Of course, every rule has an exception, and there are a plethora of exceptions. But they are so low in number that it makes the thought of general redemption quite laughable in a very sardonic manner.

The chemistry of "Love" is a very interesting consideration that equates quite readily to the mellowing effect of aging[41]. In tempestuous love the dopamine effect within the brain is so strong that it overwhelms all other behaviors. But gradually the dissipation of the physicality in early love experiences results in a mellowing effect whereby there is an almost complete drop in the dopamine effect and oxytocin takes over the chemical effect on the relationship. The result is a "more mature" and calming effect in the chemistry of love. Why is this important? Because love is a mood (a sense of one's being), and the chemistry of violence and deceit (and other behaviors seen in prisons) are also regulated by these and other indwelling body chemicals. Moods manifest in a myriad of ways. This is seen in the prison system whereby young hellions gradually lose the "vim and vigor" that got them into their trouble(s). They mellow out and lose the edgy, brazen, hate-laden behavior of their youth. There is no doubt that the chemistry of "Love" and "violence/evildoing" is similar in nature.

In addition, brain chemistry altering behavior in so many ways is very difficult to fully account for the myriad of reasons why prisoners say what they say and do what they do. Sweeping generalizations are also dangerous, but it is important to realize that making excuses for criminal behavior is improper as well. There is a difference for individuals who but for a better chance at life might have overcome and acceded to a far more productive life. Just as the love potions of dopamine and oxytocin can have a true effect in relationships, Slater[42] significantly points out examples of antidepressants (which are part of treatment modalities for prisoners) changing the balance of the brain chemistry to alter behavior. In such a way, when psychiatric antidepressants are given to aggressive, depressed prisoners, the neurotransmitter serotonin displaces (through inhibition) the "love bearing chemicals" (dopamine and oxytocin) as it enhances negative results while treating principal needs. She points out that when serotonin floods the neuron-neuron juncture OCD (obsessive- compulsive disorder) results as dopamine and oxytocin are blocked in their natural behavioral pathways. I take this out of the article not as a pretext to alter the meaning of her article where she investigates love relationship changes as a result of the natural changes in brain chemistry. There is an evolution in the natural sexual relationship between men and women through these chemical modifiers. But key to this is a mood modification that is seen so significantly with the majority of prisoners that I saw.

I observed mood alteration at all age groups, be it the over-sexed violent youths to the mellowed-out "wizened warriors of the yard!" When violence and suicide become so much of the conversation in the training of guards and the daily governance of the prisons brain chemistry influences are the catalysts of the dangerous violence erupting daily. I did not see this taken seriously on a universal basis at all. Psychologists and Psychiatrists serve as a battery of professional guidance and treatment, but only on a prescriptive basis. I am not making an argument for the chemical dulling of prisoners' minds to effectuate environment modification, but I witnessed the prisoners whose histories paralleled flashpoints. I always thought that the foxes were truly running the henhouse. The quiet, unobtrusive prisoners were always at the mercy of the brazen hellions insensitive to the challenge of any kind of punishment. It was amazing to witness the persistent observation of a youth returning to a Secured Housing Unit (Solitary Confinement). The misery level was elevated drastically because such dangerous individuals were far in the majority, and it took repetitive punishment to keep them under wraps. In such an environment where guards do not carry guns and are themselves open to forcible violence the obvious question is: why? Sheer understanding of the basic brain chemistry, the natural setting of prisons (and particularly Level III institutions), insufficient training where far more meaningful insight is needed, and an institutional inability to make guards more commanding in their perception and outright presence are the factors so obviously overlooked because of politically correct leaders. The social concept of "correctional" as it perceived by the public is more important for "show" than living forthrightly to its message. Just as brain chemistry applies to "mood qualities" affecting day-to-day governance, the true misery so apparent within a prison is the result of true evil. Yes folks, the old debate: "Good versus Evil." This has been discussed thoroughly in books, religious organizations and institutions, by theologians, philosophers, etc. Why? Because the written word delineated in the Bible contextually presents both a spiritual and secular record of the word of God in view of men's flaws and actions from the Book of Genesis of the Old Testament through the New Testament. They are the written record of man's travails as a litany of historical peoples contest the will of God by testing his "Grace" through recorded historical events that reflect both goodness and the malicious intent to violate his glory. This is the very basis of so much written about man's journey to lead a just life or follow the path of dishonor and wrongdoing. John Bunyan's *Pilgrim's Progress*[43] and Dante Alighieri's *Divine Comedy*[44] (composed of three sections: *The Inferno*, *The Purgatorio*, and *The Paradiso*) are just two classic examples of man's continuous struggle with good and evil.

It has been my experience that "evil" is very hard for many people to conceive. Be it through denial or lackluster people it is frankly not interesting to many. However, "evil" like "love" is brain-centric and has been studied[45, 46, 47]. Why do people grow into the people they become? There are no sure answers, but academic luminaries in specific areas of study (as noted) have provided some brilliant answers which go way beyond just pure speculation thanks to the advances in technology.

Why do people kill without empathy nor any consideration for the consequences of their actions? When I grew up this was known as the sixty-four-thousand-dollar question.

However, brain scan differences between cold-blooded killers snd reasonably normal, well-adjusted people. The locations of the brain may reveal different changes on brain scans, but the changes are evident and there is no guesswork. Jeff Wise delineates this in a wonderfully crafted book on fear (Wise, 2009)[48]. Subjected to varying degrees of threats to our physiologic homeostasis, he details the affected areas of the brain and the manner by which our brains command our organs through convoluted nerve transmissions to respond as means of self-protection. And as Lauren Slater (Slater)[49] documents patterns of changes in the way people evolve in love relationships, the brain chemistry responds via brain locations to produce chemicals that govern our behavior. The manner in which a loose-minded juvenile reprobate or cold-blooded killer behaves is likewise governed by the brain chemistry and dictates of nerve transmission from the oldest ancestral areas of their brains (spinal cord and brainstem) to the more advanced and developed frontal cortex locations via the areas denoted as relay stations like the Amygdala, Thalamus and Hypothalamus. I am convinced there are no definitive answers because neuroscientists do make the well-studied conclusion that programmed violence can be modified by the love of a family environment. This falls under the heading of the age old "nature versus nurture" discussion. Why an inherently evil person totally loses empathy and will kill without a scintilla of compassion or regret cannot be predicted, but it has been shown (Bhattacharjee[50]) that on a brain scan there are no "hot" areas of the frontal cortex where normal people display neurological communication. The researcher who studied this used 400 Level III violent offenders to make this contrast. I shall get into this later because it warrants a more thorough discussion.

The substance of all the writings of such erudite delineations is the clear acknowledgement that there is an evil which threatens man's existence. It must be a full awakening for any sensible individual passing through life. There is no place with as realistic display of evil as in any Level III prison anywhere in the world. And it is the obligation of prison staff to safeguard the welfare of the citizenry by managing the passionate violators of the public safety so peace is held in reasonable sway. This is the first rule of government: to protect its people and preserve the public safety. However, this certainly is not inviolate. And this is where the rubber hits the road: where the threat of crime is not controlled properly due to corruption and willful neglect of political leaders. This is why it is important to come to grips with the unending stream of the "good and evil" challenge confronting man (Bhattacharjee[51]).

The point to be emphasized is that the environmental/cultural pressures which bring youth to crime are not one dimensional. Poverty, lack of education, single parent families, individuals who grow up in foster care, lack of guidance and all the other societal factors which bring them to crime are in force when the latent chemistry of development are in play. And, more often than naught, the negative influences that may be otherwise contained by proper parenting and educational role models are not present. In fact, the "dopamine effect" would tend to increase aggressive behavior in the absence of mentoring. That is not to say many parents see this play out anyway when there is a "normal household," but the gift of strong parenting and mentoring is a strong deterrent.

Prisons at all levels are sterile and confining. Non- violent offenders should endeavor for pardon and release without recidivism under a watchful eye and helpful guidance while in prison. Prison reform is required for this to come to fruition. But remanded to politicians the feasibility is questionable. Unfortunately, platitudes supplant real time results. This has also been argued for violent offenders whose mellowing brings softening and sensitivity.

This leads into a different discussion which ushers in so many other considerations of incarceration. I shall touch on this later, but for now it suffices to conclude that the concept of misery must take into consideration not only the environmental factors which lead to crime but also those that deal with the chemistry that makes some individuals prone to overreact to societal stress. And it is also important to remember that people need people, even the worst kind of people, even prisoners. This opens up the whole discussion of gangs in prison which serve to bring like-minded individualsto fill a void for the same fears anyone would possess: the need for protection and brotherhood. This may seem treacly, perhaps a tiny bit. But despite the commission of crimes at all levels, most prisoners retain different levels of humanity which, by all accounts, serve to build on and enhance their errant pasts. The emergence of violent gangs over the last thirty years has provided "a different kind of family" from lost souls who need an emotional connection, maybe a sense of identification. However, a prison has become a cauldron for feverish battles and furious infighting daily for those who are entrusted with the high-risk authority to deter deadly cell block fighting or outright rioting. For those who do not understand the true influence of gangs on prison life it is important to identify them and reveal their entrenched resolve.

SECTION 3

The Core

Chapter 3: Prison Gangs: The Hard-Cold Facts

This chapter statistically quantifies the numbers as they reflect on the dangers they bear on "the outside" from "the inside".
Gangs are treacherous and they have a direct effect on our living realities.

Chapter 4: Prison Gangs: The Reality Check

Take the objective numbers and view the impact on society. The "wow, I did not realize that," factor is detailed.

Chapter 5: Islam and the Radicalization of the American Prison System Political Islam is the terrorist arm of Religious Islam, and the former is overtaking our prisons and inner cities. It is a reality most want to deny

CHAPTER 3

Prison Gangs – The Hard-Cold Facts

You don't have to do anything to become a victim, and, there's no one man who is strong enough to come against a group of five or six. And if someone gets a wild idea in their mind that they want to do something obscene or what-have-you, there's nothing I can do if they catch me in the wrong spot at the wrong time.[52]

One inmate at Kern Valley State Prison summarizes incarceration simply as "predatory. Prison is predatory".[53]

In 2011, of the male inmates in California's prisons, 64 percent had been convicted of violent crimes, such as rape, assault, and murder; 16 percent had committed property crimes, such as burglary and theft. Many of these men are experts at deception and guile, and some are capable of monstrous acts of brutality and violence...In 2012, about 57 percent of inmates in the California system were either Level III or Level IV inmates...[54]

A maximum-security prison is a stand-alone study in survival. In the time I spent working in one and talking to so many and getting to know them as well as anybody can truly know someone, I came to one very certain conclusion. Never in my life have I met such cunning, clever and elusive people. The behavior is manifest for survival. Desperation compels desperate behavior as a survival instinct. Bravado suddenly changes into a defensive attitude. No one, even a hardened killer, ever anticipates such a sordid environment. It breaks down the most bullheaded. I saw many sides of such diverse individuals, and yet, the most signal trait was a sense of profound fear for their lives. Talking long enough always triggered this emotion.

The way each prisoner is awakened to the sudden reality that this grungy, dismal place is home for life is stark and frightening. Some talk freely, some clam up and some react with fervor and hate. Whatever be the reaction one thing is certain: I have never witnessed so much evil congregated in one place where distress resulted in such violent bloodshed so often. In talking to officers and primary entry guards, I was always warned that I should keep aware and alert to any prisoner while at work, and all the time. This is so counterintuitive to anyone used to the spirit and exercise of free living that I had to learn from this significant advice and act accordingly. Prisoners likewise learn compulsive reactions which result in a sudden physical rush to a violent attack anytime. They are primal and very hormonal. In fact, the warden finally cut down all the beautiful trees and bushes lining the breezeway central yard because prisoners were always sexually relieving themselves under cover. It became offensive to all the women employees. Being a friendly, engaging sort, there was a seasoned major who would chide me with a laugh that if I am not careful, she'd be visiting me in the morgue. Then she would smile while admonishing me with serious intent. I finally learned my lesson, but such detective- like instincts were not natural.

As I stated, these individuals' bodies were artistically carpeted from head to toe with gang related tattoos as reminders all day long of their immediate bearing: cajole, calculate, and create all designs common to their gang allegiance. Their craftiness created a constant flurry of incident reports, dental and medical issues just to compel workforce turmoil. It certainly did, and as part of it so many times the prisoners persisted in this kind of craziness to no resistance. Incident reports against employees flowed like an open spigot. They filed formal legal complaints with unbridled and frivolous arrogance just to be troublesome. It was exhaustive for employees because they had to then endure a rigorous investigation through the chain of command. Often, they would leave employment because of the nonsense and extremely unreasonable nature of the administrative genuflection to "political correctness". Such provocations dispelled any feeling of respect for the system even as the most hard working and very poor employees were trying to eke out a living. It was simply irrational.

The prison environment is very clearly "predatory", and evil permeates like smoke from a fire. Danger is a natural circumstance. And prison gangs are the conduit for all the frenzied events. Evil can be a convenient way to describe perpetrators whose empty souls think nothing to shed blood at the drop of a hat, without feeling and with a heated intent that only such destroyed bodies can reveal. The big question is how gang life can be an emotional attachment for such bestial individuals. It points out that "need" in the form of alliance is the expression of a "fear" for survival that was never accorded the victims whose demise brought them the outrage they now had to embrace. Gangs are inherently outrageous, but they are a fact of prison life so I think it is necessary to examine what some consider "evil" and others "a lack of empathy". Baumeister summarizes this thought this way:

> Evil usually enters the world unrecognized by the people who open the door and let it in. Most people who perpetrate evil, do not see what they are doing as evil. Evil exists primarily in the eye of the beholder, especially in the eye of the victim. If there were no victims, there would be no evil.[55]

Later in this chapter I shall make a key differentiation between brutal, vacant violent killers with severe mental deficiencies and devoid of any compassion for human life. And then I'll make a case how certain criminals are so profligate and dangerous that they will always be a danger to society.

They are individuals Baron-Cohen classifies as Zero negative Psychopaths (Type P)[56]. Society never wants to permit these people on the streets of our country. A model case for this kind of individual is Herman Bell, a Black Liberation Army gang member (part of the Black Panther Party) whose cop murders in San Francisco, California and New York City, New York in the early 1970's were unspeakable. He did not murder, he perpetrated gun mayhem of such ghastly determination that it can only reflect such a level of evil that just makes any human being wonder how anyone could think he should ever be trusted in society again. To pump so many bullets into human flesh with such cold indifference and disregard for humanity can only make one sick (NYPD News)[57]. And yet the direct opposite is an example of an individual who is in prison for an invalid probation violation concerning a crime he never committed. Yet a judge, so sanguine and headstrong, prepared a 48-page opinion supporting her stance for the man's 2-4 year sentence as well his probation violation that countered the defense of his probation officer (Boston.com)[58].

Many people believe fervently that all criminal behavior, whether rape, kidnapping, drug smuggling, pederasty, or robbery all leading to violent murder can be rehabilitated. For people who cannot render forgiveness and support rehabilitation it is unacceptable thinking. But this dichotomy is real and fervent. This approach is capsulized very well by Sydney Smith, an English cleric:

> Never try to reason the prejudice out of man. It was not
> reasoned into him, and cannot be reasoned out[59].

Trying to reason with such a belief system is futile because it is impossible to reason with a subjective emotional determination. Therefore, it is better treated as a difference of opinion. As human beings, there is nothing wrong with a difference of opinion if anger and vitriol do not permanently destabilize communication. In addition, I have witnessed people reason based strictly on the need to satisfy or vindicate oneself for no other reason than intuition or instinct. Some people would label this sophistry. I view it as an emotion pre- empting reason. I have often been privy to mothers forever crying because an adolescent or child was violently raped and murdered by a profoundly narcissistic sluggard. One thing is for sure in the case of the serial cop killer, he deprived two children from growing up with a father, as well a wife left in total despair. This is the modus operandi which very few living in the world of total, inarguable rehabilitation understand about wastrels, and especially the ones aligned in the vast array of prison and street gangs. The blanket killer is a separate consideration, and prison is the sole safety net for society.

I do agree with Baumeister when he resolves that self- control is the cause of crimes, not poverty[60]. I additionally feel that extreme poverty is so impactful that profound despair and a sense of urgency will lead to crime (the degree of which will reflect the level of anguish). That is not to say that people from a comfortable middle-class neighborhood will not lose self- control and violate the law. But I am certain from what I have seen that poverty is so discouraging that over time the spark that makes one turn to crime is more odds-on likely.

Gangs have a dichotomous reason for being. They serve the survival of the criminal mind. They cripple deterrence and play a very distinct role in the lives of violent criminals. Given the above examples it is hard to believe that some deny the reality of "evil" and feel that virulent murderers, rapists, and kidnappers deserve better. I believe it is imperative that society must be protected from them. These type prisoners are empty vessels and will kill for the sake of killing. Comparatively, "the worst of the worst" are a very low percentage, about 7-8 %. Murder, however, is not always the by-product of "evil." It can be quite circumstantial, and does not fit the extreme category above. However, those who commit non-violent crimes should have a second chance. They should not languish forever in a lockup state of existence forever. It becomes a burden to the system as well as to the taxpayer. This is where reformative contingencies are imperative to stop warehousing prisoners and, instead, educate/train for a viable future. This is the proper context for arguing rationally for "reform", not the continued oversaturation of the prison system.

The first definition of "gang," as the term refers to people, in the Merriam Webster dictionary is twofold: "a: a group of persons working to unlawful or antisocial ends; especially: a band of antisocial adolescents; b: a group of persons working together" (Merriam-Webster Dictionary[61]).

The United States Department of Justice is far more detailed and descriptive, but this is the idea it is trying to convey: "A. An association of three or more individuals; B.

Whose members collectively identify themselves by adopting a group identity...C. Whose purpose in part is to engage in criminal activity..." (U.S. Department of Justice, Office of Justice Programs, National Institute of Justice[62].)

The gist of this is to understand that a gang is an assemblage or group of people with a common purpose. Its collective nature is tribal, and by nature it is tribalism at its core. But it is selective, not uniform tribalism. Isolation, desperation, and, most of all, group identification compel prisoners because of survival instincts. Without an allegiance to a protective group isolation would vastly shorten the lifespan of the average Level III (IV) individual.

It is certain that hardened criminals fall into groups that must be protected because their instincts are so primal that an early death is close to a de facto certainty. The irony is their strong, self-protective and very natural impulse to survive. The dangers in the prison so exceed the ability to be independent that social alignments are necessary more for survival than friendship. The "forced grouping" is ironically more dangerous because of the extremely whimsical and spontaneous infighting which explodes without notice. A "kill or be killed" understanding is so prevalent that planned conflicts arise as gangs deal in so much contraband that they automatically come into conflict because of rivalry and control. As a result, retribution evolves spontaneously or through collaborative planning. In any case, it is bold and devastating. The cold but passionate display of bloodshed is meted out with enough shock and trauma so as to send a defiant message. It is a copycat form of what the military calls "MAD" (Mutual Assured Destruction) (Getting MAD: Nuclear Mutual Assured Destruction[63]). Gabriel Morales (Morales 2015a; 4th Edition[64]) writes about the vindictive attitudes and the blood curdling in the CDC (California Department of Corrections). The history depicts a wanton view of human life so savagely rippling through the system that it can only be described as amoral and animalistic. Individuals seek out group attachment out of fear, and ironically wind up cinching the probability for an accelerated demise in a bloody mess over drugs and money. It makes a mockery of true tribalism where the cast is hardened against an opponent. The burden in a maximum-security prison is to recognize that danger lurks everywhere, gang-to- gang, and, gang- to-guards. It is a volatile, unstable survival predicament. But, make no mistake, it is an out-of-control, warped reality foreign to the general public (even most people who have written on the prison system). Looking at Gabriel's many pictures casts a voyeuristic sense of the ultimate in the macabre. They are all real, and makes one wonder how humanity can completely lose its self-awareness and connection to one's fellow man. It represents the spiritless, hollowing out of mankind leaving animals to a wretched debauchery shedding blood in the most horrific, unimaginable manner. In my prolonged research I have never uncovered such a bleak reality. Morales spent many years as a guard in the California prison system and was given carte blanche to record murdering, related cavorting, and leaving the reader a chilling disgust. If anyone ever wonders how a human being can drop to the lowest part of the food chain, his documentation is exemplary. After reading his book there is no other choice but to realize that these people are irredeemable and they should never be allowed out to terrorize the outside world.

Because the Department of Justice deals with crime, criminals, jails and prisons, the very important classification system addresses detailed and specific characterizations. The common thread is the prisoner: his/her identification is used to define proper housing where conflict is potentially minimized. This is, in practicality, is laden with fault mines because it is very subjective despite all the planning through personality investigation and prior histories (medical, social and criminal). Physical and psychological observations impart important housing information, and yet may prove inaccurate. It is a safety net which certainly may go awry, and often does as measured by the numbing amount of violence. Episodic gang violence is disproportional to the time taken to prevent it. But that is the nature of prison. Reading Morales' book offers an objective view of how dangerous a Level III (IV) maximum security prison is despite inexhaustible efforts by personnel to maintain safety. It is frankly impossible. The bloodshed visuals

he presents (noted above), I have to repeat, render vivid depictions which continue to be very unpleasant no matter how many times they are viewed. I am always in disbelief how a person can do what he/she does to a fellow human being. In many ways these prison gangs make the worst of the mafia's "Murder Incorporated" of the twentieth century look like softies (if that is possible)! Having been part of this experience I can attest to the gruesome mess that defies anyone's imagination. I have recognized that there is an intimate relationship between the prison system and the people whose responsibilities are to have oversight for their rule and governance. Over time good intentions may dwindle with the turnover of personnel. It is just a fact common to large bureaucracies that lack of consistency in leadership leads to
confusion and disorder.

Corruption, on the other hand, is real and makes daily life unmanageable. The administrative food chain is rife with ambitious people loaded with a disdainful sense for control and a hunger for power. At its best, wardens are still beset by tension. At its worst, wardens are stifled. I witnessed some wonderful and hard-working wardens. But, in over a year, I saw wardens change three times (once at Level II, twice at Level III). Let's just say they are the scrutiny and pressure from the administrative level (the seat of corruption). I labeled prisons as "complex complexities" (a double entendre). They are large and amorphous, and rife with disturbing mismanagement at every corner at the administrative level). I was a super-trained multi-specialist who practiced and taught in three states (with a rank of full Professor). I thought academia was rife with corruption, but the prison system puts medical centers to shame.

The leadership positions are filled with people who game the bureaucracy for financial advantage. It is counterintuitive because most power-hungry risk takers who skate along making the right contacts up the promotion pole are the most self-centered and ambitious. Most often they trip over unanticipated warning signs and get caught in their own greed. Bureaucracy is loaded with such types, and the prison system is a government entity so massive that such people are easily camouflaged until their zeal is exposed. Unfortunately, government workers are impossible to fire so they are generally moved laterally or retired when they get in the way. All up and down the administration of the prison system there is flagrant misbehavior, but the system is so thickened with policies and procedures that it is impossible to clean it out. And this is the Achilles heel of government. I always likened this predicament to a failing "universal joint" in a car or truck. When it is not properly oiled the car freezes and cannot be driven. And, if someone tries to drive with a failed universal joint it causes such a high-pitched sound it is intolerable! A prison infected with corruption is unmanageable, and its daily problems have a disturbing reach into the entire system.

The suggestion or appearance of "corruption" is virtually impossible to eradicate so it ossifies over time and becomes part of the weave that threads through the day-to-day management and operational performance of personnel. It is defined simply in the Merriam Webster Dictionary (Merriam- Webster Dictionary[65]). Its first definition is: "dishonest or illegal behavior especially by powerful people (such as government officials or police officers): DEPRAVITY". We all live our lives with temptations. Low hanging fruit can be an accepted part of "doing business", though still loathsome in its reality. This leads to some important points which are consequences of mismanagement and corruption in the prison system:

*Short of a magical disappearance gangs are going to be a permanent fixture within the prison system(s): state, federal, or private;
*Overcrowding and mass incarceration are enduring: both are factual, shameful, and cause for splintered opinions; the prison system is corrupt because there is no incentive for politicians to initiate reform. There may be a permanent, fragile relationship bordering on the unethical, the immoral, and perhaps even the illegal underpinning its governance. Politics will never allow a panacea for society's benefit. The conclusion (at least for now) is that all the arguments swirling about the

minds of highly educated critics will descend into a perpetual maelstrom.

*Solutions will be hard pressed to be forthcoming since there is no "magic bullet." Short of a polar shift in human behavior correcting the seemingly uncorrectable would be like trying to pick up mercury with one's fingers.

*Every opinion really counts for something, but, realistically, opinions mixed with facts is a brew that only makes the intellect drunk with personal convictions. And these are more often like repelling magnets.

*Politicians are inexorably linked to the bureaucrats charged with prison system administration so the wrongs which spill over into society are sadly inured.

*Reflexive arguments, complaints and unfulfilled promises in behalf of refining, or wishfully "correcting" the "correctional system" have been so ubiquitously voiced and documented in writing that they are now boomeranging onto totally deaf ears.

*Therefore, the real question is: If human nature will never fully resolve the inequities built into the prison system, how can improvements be even marginally attained, even when society will be the beneficiary at all levels of need: safety, financial, educational, and yes, even political.

*Finally, the money savings through sentencing reduction, early release and probation, reorganization of parole boards (perhaps through election rather than political appointment), and election of directors and wardens (would extract some degree of corruption of "the good ole boy" network) would be a great initiative toward prison reform.

The gangs are to a very large extent the result of this societal impasse to refine the system realistically and honestly, understanding that like in a biochemistry laboratory different chemicals can be separated out and define to refine. Many more prisoners could have sentences shortened, but there doesn't seem to be interest for this. I have seen individuals at both ends of the spectrum: those without hope due to very corrosive parole boards, and those who have relinquished all hope. The prospect for reform appears bleak due to general disinterest. The prison system is old and stodgy. Its bureaucratic ladder of principals at all levels are bot-like without creativethoughts.

From Level I to Level III the mix of prisoners is comparatively soft, compliant and mindful of good behavior during the duration of their sentences. Most in Level III appear way off into a different world with such a vivid detachment that it almost seems inexplicable how they arrived at such a low point, even knowing forthrightly the truth. They battle within themselves, with other prisoners, and with guards. Their world is like an open blister.

The face of a Level III (IV) prisoner is the face of "evil". And evil is like a chameleon, changing appearance with its surroundings. Hollow, vacant eyes stare with an indefinable quality that is so beyond anyone's "normal" comfort zone that there is no doubt, face-to-face, this is the force of evil ready to pounce with a sense of hell-bent, decisive destruction. This is the stare of a merciless killer. This is the edge of life where there is no mercy, no forgiveness. A person who can assault without remorse and a blatant intent to kill is not rehabilitative. I cannot quibble with specific language to define whether she/he is a person who committed a violent crime or is a "violent offender". In my viewpoint the meaning trumps the language. In fact, Simon Baron-Cohen prefers the word "empathy" (or, lack thereof) for evil. (Baron-Cohen, *The Science of Evil: On Empathy and the Origins of Cruelty* September 4, 2012[66]) I happen to think Baron-Cohen presents a very detailed neuroscience-based explanation which I'll broach later because of its relevance. To me, word games are linguistic "avoidance coping" to neutralize a tragic prison reality as the following conveys. Real identification simply avoids "useless idealism":

Another appeal of the gradual approach is that it can be used
to educate the public about what is perhaps
the biggest and most important misperception of violence: that
it is not a state, but phase. Our rhetoric does
not reflect reality. We call people "violent offenders" instead
of saying that they committed violent crimes. An attitude shift
is essential, but it is very difficult to achieve. Proposing some
sort of "let's just educate the public" campaign is the worst
sort of useless idealism[67].

"Quo Vadis" ("Where do you go")[68] is fanciful in a period of time
when violence was rampant. And, though I disagree with Pfaff in the
choice of this well-known expression, I agree to a greater extent with
the message he delivers. I know Pfaff even disagrees with the use of
the following wording: "violent offender", as he denotes in his book
(Pfaff 2017[69]). But, to repeat, contention with semantics/phraseology
are individual choices. I do not want to argue because a personal belief
system for expression should not cloud the reality. However, I support
conceptually "The Standard Story" argument he presents as well as
"locked in" verbal framing for essentially seeing nothing get done
about the shameful overpopulation of the American prison system. He
presents a very convincing argument which I know to be very true to
the facts. I shall add to this discussion later in this chapter.

Aaron T. Beck, M.D. expresses the most important detail of the
"violent offender" with this thought:

> Given this profile of the violent offender, it seems plausible
> for an authority to punish him severely enough that he
> learns that "crime does not pay".
> Thus, the
> management of the offender generally focuses control and
> deterrence. However, this group is highly variable;
> understanding the workings of the mind of the specific
> offender is crucial for appropriate intervention as well as
> prevention[70].

If interventional therapy can search to understand the mind of the "violent offender" for the purpose of rehabilitation, such consideration is admirable. In an ideal world reintegration into society would be a meaningful goal. However, based on the preponderance of evidence, I feel it might be too risky for the protection of society against victimization. The dream or hope argued on paper cannot supplant a real-life possibility.

In essence the prison system has the facilities for psychologists to work with prisoners in need, but it is far too insufficient. It was apparent to me that it was haphazard in scheduling, and more often than not the psychologists were inattentive and lackadaisical. It is hard to disparage what I saw on a daily basis, but I concluded early on that the energy and commitment to the prisoner was very much lacking. The system certainly allows for a "correctional" environment, but it is ill-equipped to follow through on such a commitment. The result is that prisons are realistically much more punitive than "correctional". To rehabilitate the prisons must commit to high caliber trained professionals whose
compensation matches the private sector. However, the general prison malaise and dangers are a deterrent. Administrative leadership, however, consists of facilitators, not difference makers where quality professionals are carefully searched and hired.

Because my upfront experience with the face(s) of violence is saturated with long memories, I'll allow others to argue the proper wording for however they feel. I simply feel, cutting to the chase, that there is too much bureaucratic corruption to initiate real "reform" programs. It appears to be unsettling for "politicos" to expend the energy and redirect the resources. The political "ne'er-do-wells" and the hell-bent prosecutorial overreach is easier. It is exploitive and willful disregard for measures to truly do something about "prison reform". What the prison system excuses as prison reform the facilities set up for dental, medical, psychological, and religious counseling to countenance the legal system"s obligation is vastly deficient. But, the perception of light, fluffy social events and programs serve as favorable advertising when, in fact, specific long-term educational programs linked tightly to psychotherapy would condition the prisoner's mind to the benefits of real learning. The learning process can be a tangible benefit as well as a feeling of well-being which most prisoners have never experienced.

The former Governor of Massachusetts, Michael Dukakis, once said very emphatically: "The fish rots from the head first!"[71] This pretty much describes why American prisons are not decreasing in numbers.

The case Phaff makes to address the "The Standard Story" and point out the numbers. To reverse the trend in overcrowding, however, is a daunting task the country has never accomplished because leadership does not have the political will. The Dukakis quote captures the issue facing prison reform. It is not enough to boast political platforms which do not change from generation to generation because political leaders will say anything to get elected. Somehow the words are empty, and most people have very short memories.

All the problems relating to mass incarceration arise from the "Board Rooms" of bureaucracy: Directors, Government Bureaucrats, and State and Federal Politicians. The inaction continues to linger right up the bureaucratic ladder where the problem should be unearthed, debated and solved. But, conveniently, bureaucracy is like a hoarder's home. After a while nothing can be found. Somewhere in the mass of paperwork are fanciful plans, but it would require a massive "cleaning" to find out where to begin! Such is the woe unmercifully scripted by "The Peter Principle."[72] History clearly shows that "The Complex (Prison) Story" will not change without going to the source. What does change are the faces on both sides of the complex. Michael Dukakis as Governor of Massachusetts and purveyor of the rich idealism of John F. Kennedy politics recognized the bitter reality of trying to fight city hall to effect legislation in the manner and style he viewed governance. In his stallion efforts the only recognition he could muster were dishonorable sobriquets: Michael "Du-kaka" and "Michael Du-tax-us"! This is his legacy from unwitting and thankless voters. However, at least the electorate and legislature allowed him to construct the first statewide long bicycle lane through Massachusetts to protect bicyclists. Even the famous "1978 Nor'easter"[73] (snowstorm which is rated one of the most devastating in U.S. History by some meteorological groups) which closed the state for three weeks was used to pillory his new colored sweaters. He used each one on his television advisories each day so it was hard for "the Fourth Estate" to overlook his appearance in their coverage labeling him "The Sweater Governor". So, with examples of

drivel, in search of concrete reform and legislation, "here ye here ye" we have examples of the bunkum which makes effective leadership seemingly impossible. Dukakis will always be remembered for his sharp quote, but isn't it interesting that politicians ever since continue to reflect the rot which is generated from the top! This is the reason for the statistics in Pfaff's "Standard Story"! There is no will! Dream hard, dream hard! Politics dictates change, and politics is the worst kind of dirty!

Maybe then all writing and discussion should be stifled. No. The problem is there is too much invested by bureaucrats who stifle the will to truly govern where prison reform would demand real leadership. But, with constant literary and verbal attention to the subject over time the long, tall, wall of disregard will never crumble. As I have stated, Phaff[74] makes a cogent, well-substantiated argument to support the fact that mass incarceration suddenly ballooned from 1979 on (and keeps pace without long overdue serious government retooling), only to fall and go up again. This was at a time when the sociology of the problem was very different. There are other facets of this failing system which are frozen in massive administrative complexities. Politicians do not want to factor reform into all their hidden, fattened conspicuous agendas. Political activism is plainly supercilious for any honest change. The prison system waddles like an overweight drunk trying to sober up and find a non-staggering path to change instead of belching out vague promises.

It is easy to be churlish or overly casual in dealing with such a serious subject. And, it is too simplistic to find quick answers to an old problem. Being in a maximum-security prison everyday does one thing (if nothing else): it drives home the feeling for how awful a place it is. I worked with a lady who would shake her right index finger at me while informing me that we were all just one bad mistake from "a life in the hole!" Every day I received the same reminder. She made me laugh. But, she was so correct! It was funny but scary!

Face it, most prisons are grievously dirty and barren. I used to retort to my co-worker with this characterization: "Coupled with the depressing, fitful environment are low-level employees who are responsible for all the hard management, many mid-level administrators who are punch drunk with the very limited power they relish and flaunt, and then the true upper tier leaders who are not afraid to conduct their business with an elevated swagger far beyond their accomplishments". The prisons are simply frozen in time and the culture is not conducive to change in spite of the seriousness of the problem.

"Tell all" books written by former prisoners, books which paint a historical picture or simply opine on its stagnant culture, or blogs which offer constant reality checks on political issues, just simply do not move the needle for modification or innovation. I do believe that in the years to come there will be a ground swell for reform. In the meantime, the newspapers will cover the escapes, riots, corruption, and maybe the dirty politics. It will not take an act of God for change, there will be a "deus ex machina"-like event which will make the time ready and exploitable.

Anyone who has worked "the yard" for any extended period of time can "separate the wheat from the chaff". David Skarbek[75] speaks in plain language clearly defining the indisputable nature of violence and violent offenders. The violence is so rapacious and unspeakable that to pettifog is other worldly, an unreality and rather misleading. All one has to do is look at a mother, a wife, a father, or a sibling of a prepubescent child who has been raped and killed unimaginably and nothing more has to be said. Morales' vivid pictures of California and

Texas prisons reinforce the disgrace of it all. The brutality is attention-grabbing, often sufficiently jaw-dropping enough to wonder how human beings can fall so low that raw, primitive behavior runs amok! This is the very essence of out-of-control tribalism. It makes pre-historic man look cerebral beyond considered historic development.

Prison gangs are a very disturbing lot with their one-way agenda. They comprise the most violent individuals being held away from a citizenry so blindly trusting in such a fragile system. In today's culture people have a distorted television sense of its reality (which hardly captures the emotionally desperate ethos running through, and very deeply). The "short" truth is that the court system and prisons must do a better job to get non-violent offenders back into society prepared for job opportunities while able to handle the stigma they carry. They must be able to handle dissonant language and possible mockery. Resources and commitment to augment remedial efforts are needed to encourage their ambitions toward a far more productive lifestyle. Without this, sense and awareness recidivism will remain high. The effort today is listless and mechanical. It lacks energy and day-to-day desire.

The "correctional" in "correctional institution" is truly a word for the non-violent. It is the only reality for dealing with mass incarceration. Will it work? From what I saw I do not believe it is plausible (maybe possible), particularly when I see the concentrated efforts being accented toward the frivolous: as in social gatherings, holiday parties, band presentations, etc. Yes, this has its time and place, but the serious minded would look to education (vocational or higher; reboot the effort to deal with prosecutors over-charging and over-sentencing; legislate out the three strike guidelines in sentencing; and, make political efforts to set guidelines where there is conflict between counties and states for the money to support prisoner incarceration, etc.) The pipeline for change is blocked, and a "plumber-like" reaming internally is needed to free up the flow of coordinated policy changes. Hapless defines the prison system as it is the victim of rancid politics. It seems like politicians quietly relish an overpopulated prison system. It is a source to generate power and control. And, let's not forget that it's a money tree (on the backs of taxpayers). Generations down the line leading voices will lament sardonically why no one took up the mantle to make sense of such a monstrosity!

Prison gangs are composed of prisoners of like-minded background. Group-identification is essential. The result: each individual gang embrace like-minded individuals. Thus, Mexican gangs, Aryan white gangs, black gangs, Latino gangs, etc. There is no doubt that there is a higher number of Mexican and Latino populations in west coast prisons, but, along this thought line, there is a higher black population in east coast prisons. During my time working in both Level II and III institutions there was, no doubt, a disproportion of black males. I spent many hours talking to them, and I was convinced these were people whose lives would have been very different had better fortune and opportunity come their way. In her book Michelle Alexander says the following:

> Black crime cripples the black community and does no
> favors to the individual offender. So herein lies the
> paradox and the predicament of young black men labeled
> criminals. A war has been declared on them, and
> they have been rounded up for engaging in precisely the
> same crimes that go largely ignored in middle- and
> upper-class white communities—possession and sale
> of illegal drugs. For those residing in ghetto communities,
> employment is scarce—often nonexistent. Schools
> located in ghetto communities more closely resemble
> prisons than places of learning, creativity, or moral
> development. And because the drug war has been raging
> for decades now, the parents of children coming of age

today were targets of the drug war as well. As a result,
many fathers are in prison, and those who are "free" bear the
prison label. They are often unable to provide
for, or meaningfully contribute to, a family....[76]

How can this be argued. It cannot. I found this to be glaringly
true. Her statement does not do enough justice to its accuracy. I worked
primarily with black guards and prisoners. It was simply pathetic how
victimized the prisoners were, both by circumstances that got them
incarcerated and the pressure inside to survive by gang affiliation. I
spent hours talking to so many about what got them there, what their
home lives were all about, etc. Simply put, the system let them down,
and their survival instincts led them to crime (often unspeakable and
usually centered on drugs, drug trafficking, and frequently resulting in
murder). The majority were friendly, nice people. I was working where
severe mental disturbances were part of the murder profile as well.
Michelle Alexander aptly discusses the cultural circumstances which
made crime inevitable (misfortune driven by necessity). In addition, in
another facility with a mixed population where there were primarily non-
violent offenders, more often than not I was at a loss to understand the
lengthy sentences for non-violent crimes. If the costs of incarceration
were redirected to support rehabilitation, a reparative cultural would be
a societal enhancement over time. But, in this regard, the criminal
justice system is burying such people in a wasteful disregard of time,
repetitively throwing away lives which (again, over time) could divert
their energies productively and not simply in a languishing,
deteriorating state (marking time)! What a pity, and what government
neglect!

The gang replaces in many ways what life could not provide
violent criminals: a safety net and identification. The Kumi African
Nation Organization (Kumi 415), like the Black Guerilla Family and
the Black Panthers, had a California identity. Kumi in Swahili means
ten, and, 415 was the Bay Area Code (in and around San Francisco,
narrowing to just the city

as the population expanded). Also, as Morales points out: 4+1+5=10 or KUMI. Although their vulnerability increased with gang affiliation, they had no choice. Survival depended on group protection and support. And prison gangs are intimately linked with street gangs where drugs, money and control are everything. Their ethos is their pathos. And that is a tragedy.

The courts are the heart and soul of the prison system for their inviolable control of lives. They breathe hope into the accused as much as they send them off to the unimaginable places of danger, despair and delinquency. These are three realities which chase them until they leave, or free to progress, or regress and die. Prison is not just a fortress to enclose the physical body, it is much more. It is a stronghold where the mind is subjected to inescapable pressures which subvert hope because there is no place to go, escape or hide from bad influences. Prisoners become the helpless prey of peers who further increase the depth of trouble, anxiety and misfortune they may find. To incarcerate and open these susceptible individuals to chancy decisions is blind and ignorant. It is the formula for no good. It is the recipe for all the bad that happens inside prisons as well as the bad rap prison bureaucrats deservedly suffer. And, by bureaucrats I do not mean low level guards or the leadership ladder up to the warden. I mean the directors and politicians who mix not caring with lack of directed leadership.

From Level I right through to the bottomless pit of the most villainous killers there must be "organized schooling" of some order. Aside of the vocational, religious and social programs, there must be order to the lives of prisoners who do not seek venues for productive usage of their time. Walking a prison yard while watching groups self-engaged whether in their mini-workout areas or just ambling around without purpose is counterproductive by any standard of analysis. Yes, "an idle mind is the devil's workshop," and particularly in a maximum-security prison this is where trouble brews. For all the dog-and-pony self-flagellating ceremonies directors produce for public consumption, no attention is paid to "the passage of time" for all prisoners. Oh yes, they'll deny this common sense thought, but forced programming will avert so many flashpoints and truly reinforce the "correction" in "correctional." The continuum of feathering the same environment standards has never worked. Left to the bureaucrats' generational habits continue with clear disregard of the obvious! Most prisoners come from very marginal homes and circumstances so that their opportunities have been limited for lack of guidance and direction. A committed mentor has allowed the average prisoner to become fastened to a neighborhood "buddy system" which led to criminal activity. The prisoners I came to know very well would laugh when I would say opportunity is not a given, that people make their own opportunities through hard work and desire. The mere fact that not one could understand this discouraged me, always aware of the continued wasted time prison was sanctioning.

The way this is handled is more legislative, or administrative staffers meet to thrash around "novelty" ideas and schemes to satisfy themselves, and not deal with the endemic problems. This is the pure definition of bureaucracy, and at its quintessential best. Everything comes full circle as the courts living their reputations to the fullest extent send more to do time in one of the many "shrines of crimes."

Just as newspapers and news services love to bellow the latest in the "sin and grin," there are individuals who get lost in the system and are put away for many years. Before the advent of DNA identification, many were imprisoned for long terms or natural life. In the Bell case mentioned prior, he was a multiple "cop killer" incarcerated in New York (whose family is now trying to override the Governor who just signed his release). This is a case where the burden placed on a family for years further deepens their stress and misery to see the system support for an individual whose unholy execution of cops in two cities so wantonly becomes the beneficiary of a political choice. This does not qualify for "prison reform" in any sense of the discussion. To those who favor this because they have never looked into the eyes of pure evil, I at least say think of the family. Freeing this man into society after many years is a societal risk of monumental proportions. Predicting how this will play out is anyone's guess. Playing the roulette wheel at a Las Vegas casino might be more Las

Vegas casino might be more predictable. Conversely, the Mill case mentioned also worked out well for a man falsely convicted only to be further harassed by an obviously emotionally bothered judged fixated on throwing his parole officer to the dogs so as to further criminalize him over a false parole violation. Fortunately, the judge was overruled and he was freed. So here are two very glaring cases of mixed judgements. This is unfortunately common today, and whatever judge rules the roost (pending the political orientation) will determine how cases are adjudicated. This kind of justice is for "just us!"

From The National Registry of Exoneration[77] two cases on its website that are further evidence for how the court system can be so wrong. Two prisoners on death row for many years were hours before "the hour of death" when lawyering finally proved misidentification in one case and a headstrong District Attorney who used the legal system to bring a judgment for political reasons. One Gordon Steidl was given a death sentence at 35 years old in 1987 for the brutal stabbing of a married couple. He suffered from a very egocentric, careless legal defense, was falsely accused, and finally incarcerated for 17 years. He served on death row for so long that DNA identification came into being as the "Gold Standard" and was finally released. In a civil law suit he won 3.5 million dollars. But what were the years really worth? (The National Registry of Exonerations[78]). Finally, the case of John Thompson who, at 22, was misidentified as a perpetrator of a carjacking resulting in robbery and murder. An overzealous District Attorney (the father of the acclaimed singer, songwriter and actor, Harry Connick, Jr.) failed to present exculpatory evidence at trial. He proved he was an "activist" not a "lawyer!" Because of legal procedure he was turned down for appeal and the District Attorney (Harry Connick, Sr.) remained recalcitrant in his political jockeying as he adjudicated the matter. Consequently, Thompson served on death row for 18 years. Fortunately, two out-of-state attorneys picked up the case and after lengthy legal haggling the court finally offered a new trial which Mr. Thompson turned down because he felt his innocence was being victimized by the system. The two attorneys ultimately got his sentence reversed on appeal even as his appeal litigation was only offered within hours of his sentence being carried out. The appeal resulted in his exoneration after years of "Holy Hell!" After his release, he sued the state in civil court and won 14 million dollars. Once again, was it worth the years of his life given up? The pity was his death very early on after his release. Cases like this are quite disturbing. And, what Harry Connick, Sr. put this man through was unforgiveable (The National Registry of Exonerations[79]).

I presented examples of four cases to illustrate how unfair life is, the difficulties getting caught up in legal contrivances being just mere issues of the greater complexities man faces without falling victim to it one way or another. The prison system is swimming with varying horror stories the majority of which do not play out with a storybook ending. Furthermore, both served in maximum security prisons where it is almost impossible to negotiate through the legal entanglements common to the very one-way thinking, myopic prison system. The National Registry of Exonerations[80] reveals a statistic to think on: 2,203 exonerations representing cumulatively 19,350 years of "living!" OMG! In addition, think again of the prisoner I previously mentioned who has been serving for many years and numerously told me he was not guilty of the murder for which he was given "natural life" and subsequently denied twice by the parole board. Now after 25 years and in his early fifties, very kindly and wizened beyond his years from emotional stress, he languishes without hope! The "youngsters" newly acclimated to the gangs will eventually mellow. The young turks are so naïve and young that they cannot comprehend the seriousness of their sentences! It is very sad. On the one hand they are monsters. On the other hand, they are so incredibly "stupid"! Whatever they have done, talking to them can make one bleed inside with pity! Beating the system is not in the cards for these young hellions. Someday, if they live "in stir" long enough, they too will mellow. For now, I leave you with this thought: what would you say and how do you feel about this issue? Give it thought, even though you have never seen what I have (and hopefully never will). Ultimately, a sentence is, for the prisoner, the reality! Yet, eventually, they all lose their high-flying bravado! Yes, they do!

Are there people whose violence may be incidental, defensible and arguable? Yes, as I have tried to show, absolutely! I do not consider such individuals "life-enders." To this extent, I do not consider such offenders whose actions- reactions which incur serious violence to be all incapable of redemption. In addition, where state laws are overly punitive resources should be channeled for offenders whose personal histories show a potential for resolve. Separately, there are those individuals whose lives succumb to the "three strikes and you're out" laws which result in lengthy sentencing for non- violent and petty crimes. This is as offensive as it is unspeakable. No doubt it is the most painful example of padding the prison population. It is effrontery for any sound thinking human being not to stand back and say "why?" Perhaps it can be considered the king of legislative shenanigans. States with the "three strike law" (Arizona, Arkansas, California, Colorado, etc.) underscore examples why the United States has the highest incarceration rate in the world. This should be a must change through legislation, but I will not hold my breath.

As I got into the writing of this book, I found that most of the research supported my observations. My day-to-day talking to and meeting prisoners of all kinds substantiated a lot of the research. Most of what I concluded through my daily slog around a maximum-security prison comes down to this: prisoners do not want to be there and wake up to "regrets" when it is too late. I would never play the role of "Mr. Obvious," but from everyday discussion I was taken back by some of what I distilled. As bold and deeply bitter most prisoners were, I always detected anxiety and fear in their body language. Thus, one of the reasons for gangs (which are surrogate families)! Strange, but true. They are the refuge for survival. However, let it be clear, these gangs are other worldly to anyone who leads a quiet, busy, unimposing lifestyle.

That being said, I still think about the Morales book every day. It is the one book out of my bibliography which gets my most continued attention. It is not erudite, but it is incredibly detailed and earth-shattering! In fact, I suggest the book as a must read for anyone interested in the "real" breakdown of prison gangs: (Morales 2015a; 4th Edition[81]). I give kudos to Gabriel C. Morales for the incredibly factual delineation of gangs which, though nationwide, have a tight hold on the west coast prisons where they arose and have flourished in their spread across the country. As I get ready to publish this book, President Trump is dealing with MS-13, a horrendous group of thugs and killers, but, believe it or not, are nowhere near the worst of the worst! Let's first list the most significant: Nuestra Familia, The Mexican Mafia, The Aryan Brotherhood, The Black Guerrilla Family, The Texas Syndicate, The Mexikanemi, The Barrios Aztecas, The Border Brothers & Paisas, The Netas, The UBN and other Prison Gangs (for example, MS-13, etc.). Yes the country is obsessing with MS- 13, and rightfully so, but the principle gangs listed above are the most treacherous in their dealings. MS-13 is receiving all the press right now for their ravaging indefensible young people. Their degree of violence is rapacious and depraved. Should the reader want a more in-depth discussion of issues governing their hidden agendas then read Morales's book (Morales 2015; 4th Edition). The information is stifling and overwhelmingly impressive. As I previously stated, he paints a uniquely vivid, "living" history of California prison gangs (where they were born, festered and spread). For me, it is "the bible" of prison gangs in the Americas. It has served to validate my thoughts about the heinous violence I personally witnessed in the prison system.

Morales does such a wonderful job in uncovering the origins and growth of the most active prison gangs. His writing is difficult at times, but his coverage is a wealth of minutia. He bears out what seems logical, but the horrific disregard for human life is nevertheless hard to digest. The irony is the perception that gangs are "family" for these marginalized human beings. It is a final refuge where death is a hiccup away. The gang remains the last vestige of group identification and protection for the average prisoner.

The perception of most people is that there are a few, but the truth is that there are so many that it would be futile to list. Suffice it to say, there are thousands (statistics coming up), many being breakaways or offshoots of the larger well-known ones. For example, the Border Brothers are undocumented Mexican Nationals who wind up in American Prisons and are identifiable by their very specific tattoos (as are most gangs). The Border Brothers are very low on the totem pole, but they serve as key runners for the Drug Cartels. Gangs interrelate when it involves drugs and situations arise whereby rival gangs, which normally will go toe-to-toe with each other, do business when money and drugs are involved: for example, the Asian gangs linking with the Border Brothers to smuggle and sell drugs. Gambling as well is frequently involved, and gangs which normally would kill each other at the drop of a hat do business in peace. Just to mention one other group which caught my eye because of the way they mongrelized is the group called the Barrio Azteca which absorbed a street gang called X14 and fought wars with the gang TS, the Texas Syndicate. As Morales describes, most are heroin junkies and are desperate survivalists at any cost. His book is a real head-spinning read. Very few books dealing with any part of the prison system ever talk about the gangs, but they are the prime integral unit of all prisons in the United States.

Starting on the west coast the gangs emerged as protective families, places for the abandoned, fearful and frightened. They became shelters for the displaced, the lonesome, and the confused. Does this sound a bit hokey? Maybe. But I found that underneath the false bravado of very young rapists, vicious killers, and pathetically uneducated, very strident, but street savvy criminals, there lingered a sense of fear (even bewilderment) which I could uncover in most. Whether they were in for very long-life sentences or "natural" life (never to be paroled), there was, for the most part, a common denominator: they were afraid of dying in prison at the business end of a shiv or a shank! This is hardly the sense of a conjugal family, merely an attachment where security was never guaranteed, but where a sense of "home" offered day-to- day, and mutual defense against another gang. Defiance at any level translated into a very bloody death.

To this end, gangs became "family." As Morales depicts, Nuestra Familia was one of the first, if not the very first in this country in the California Department of Corrections (be it Folsom, Soledad, Kern, San Quentin, etc., just to pick out a few of the more dangerous ones). These gangs served as protective shelters where loyalty conveyed brotherhood and trust. Whether a prisoner was killed in the stealth of the night or in an outright riot did not matter. That was not the point. For the long-term, the gang was safely in the prison jungle. In California in the 1960's and 1970's prisons were violent, dangerous and so vicious that life expectancy was very low. Today, the only difference is the size (by numbers) of the gangs.

Street gangs started on the streets, prison gangs started in prison, but Morales notes that the prison gangs eventually held sway and controlled the streets. He refers to prison gangs as "Security Threat Groups" or "Disruptive Groups" because they were a constant threat to guards and wardens trying to keep the yards under control. Morales quotes Leo Duarte, a retired California prison gang expert:

> They (had) three things in common: Control, Drugs, and Power. All of them (had) a blood oath. Once you're in, you're in "till death!" Once prison gang members return to the street, they are expected to collect taxes for the gang and kickback money or drugs to their brothers behind bars. If they do not, they may be "checked", or killed."[82]

The bare minimum facts are stark. Yes, gangs served as a refuge, but the code of conduct was written in stone. As Leo Duarte notes above, a prisoner is in a very fragile position. To repeat, survival in prison is all about control, drugs and power. If the prisoner kept his mouth shut, did his job unceremoniously, then there was a greater likelihood that he would endure (translation: live to see the next day, maybe not the one after!). Another common unwritten understanding as Morales discusses: "Blood In" and "Blood Out." A prisoner kills as a "rite of passage" so to speak, but gets killed as the only way out! Where and how does this abject suffering begin? And why? A short digression is in order to make a few extremely relevant points. (The bane of my research and writing).

GANGS: As a research source for the Bureau of Justice is a website, the National Gang Center (National Gang Center 2012[83]), which captures a very frightening statistic. However, the latest gang threat assessment was done in 2011 by the Federal Bureau of Investigation.[84] (2011 National Gang Threat Assessment 2011). In 1996 there were Americans, 22%; Hispanic Americans, 19%; foreign born non-citizens, 20%; all children, 18%; single fathers, 13%; and, married couples, 5%.
(Census Bureau 2017[85])

POVERTY and EDUCATION: When poverty is linked to education, the contrast between those above and below the poverty level is stark. The 2017 population was estimated at 325,719,178 people. The median household income was
$55,322. The percentage of high school graduates or higher was 87%. The number of people without health insurance was 11.7%. The median housing value was $184,700. Against this was a population below the poverty level: 12.7% (Census Bureau 2017[86]).

EDUCATION: When considering education, it is important to consider that there is disparity between big city and suburban graduation rates. Sam Dillon in the New York Times noted that in the nation's 50 largest cities the graduation rate was 53% compared with 71% in suburban high schools. Whitney Wright notes in a research article for a presentation at The National Conference on Undergraduate Research in 2012 that only 19% of students from urban school districts seek higher education compared to 70% in suburban high schools[87, 88, 89]. Therefore, with this in mind consider the following for inner city schools: above poverty level, in the demographic of education for all races, in the 18-24 age group,

8,658 had completed high school. In the 25 and older category the number is 62,512 Americans. For whites 18-24, 6,358 were high school graduates. For whites 25 and older the number is 49,209. For blacks alone 18-24, 1,527 were high school graduates. For blacks 25 and older, the number is 8,722. Hispanics (of any race) in the 18-24 age group 2,165 were high school graduates. In the same group 25 years and older, the number of high school graduates was 10,126[90].The point I am delineating: these figures show that even at the above poverty level, the number of high school graduates in the inner cities is low compared to suburban areas of the country. And for blacks, the numbers are the lowest. This synchs with poverty statistics.

DRUGS: From the Drug Enforcement Administration[91] there were 63,632 drug overdose deaths in the United States in 2016. This translates to 174 deaths per day, or, one death every 8.28 minutes; 42,249 (66.4%) of those deaths were from opioids. This is more than from firearms, homicide, suicide, and motor vehicle accidents. However, many opioid related deaths are too frequently associated with them. In addition, this does not account for alcohol. In addition, heroin, fentanyl, carfentanil and krokodil are killing in horrific numbers. Currently, opiates have overtaken the news with its venal onslaught at all levels of the population. From the youth who fancy it with a very blind and ignorant bravado (until it results in death to very horrified and devastated parents), to inner city youth, and even the well-heeled mother who gets hooked using them for post-surgical pain. They are most addicting as they take lives and leave the United States population with an unexpected anathema. Of the many, but oxycodone and oxycontin are the villains! dilaudid and hydrocodone do not get the press, but they are commonly used for post-surgical pain and are common to the addicted. Fentanyl (a synthetic heroin) is 50-100 times more powerful than morphine (IMF, or Intravenous Morphine Infusion). In one report concerning fentanyl usage in Florida during the years 2013-2014 for persons aged 23-34 this group had the highest death rates (3.2 per 100,000). Correspondingly, in Ohio the figure was 10.5 per

100,000 for the 25-34 age group. And, without getting overly detailed, deaths were even involved in the over 50 years age group. In addition, heroin addiction and deaths kept pace with opioids and fentanyl at alarming rates. Fentanyl is gaining favor simply because of its strength. If this breakdown isn't bad enough, a unit of carfentanil (another synthetic that is used to sedate elephants) is 5,000 times stronger than a unit of heroin, and 0.2mg can kill a user. A unit of carfentanil is also 100 times more powerful than a unit of fentanyl, and 10,000 times more than a unit of morphine. Overdose and deaths from overdose have become epidemic and destructive to families even in rural areas (New Hampshire, for example). Its usage has never gravitated from urban and suburban cities, but it has expanded countrywide. It is no longer sectional or regional, it is a national plague. The important consideration is that drugs have become an insidious curse that is tearing at the very fabric of this country. They are breaking families apart.

It is no longer sufficient to consider the inner cities the only focal points of reference. The drug epidemic has no discretion. It is a pandemic national curse. The CDC presents a necessary bleak picture, but it hits home with impactful justification. Among prisoners that I encountered the most flagrant drug abuses dealt with usage and trafficking in methamphetamine (because meth labs arise in rural areas like dandelions in grass). Drugs are a scourge that has captured and been embraced by criminals involved in gun trafficking, sex trafficking, prostitution, illegal gambling..., and associated with the misery of the impoverished as well as the well-to-do! It is an indiscreet societal nightmare![92, 93]

GUNS: To draw this statistical analysis to a suitable conclusion here are some notable facts about guns associated with violence: firearm suicides claim more lives than any other type of gun violence. And having a gun in the home increases suicide risks owing to its physical presence. But the inclination for danger depends on improper storage or an overzealous mindset[94]. Most homicides are committed with guns. Gun- related homicides are most common to gangs (seemingly common sense, but backed up by facts). In 2011, crimes committed with guns comprised 8% of all violent crimes. This has remained consistent from 1993 through 2011[95]. Three million citizens in the U.S. carry loaded guns every day. Right- to-carry laws are directly related to a 10.6 percent increase in a state's handgun homicide rate. The year 2016 saw stolen firearms higher than in any previous period. And more than 135,000 students in the U.S.A. have endured school shootings! One study claims 43% of gun owners have no formal training. (The Trace-A Nonprofit Newsroom Covering Gun Violence in America n.d.[96]) Finally, one third of all gun-causing hospitalizations cost the taxpayer $242 million per year. The numbers of stolen guns over a ten-year period was higher in 2016 than in any previous year. $622 million dollars a year are spent on hospital bills just for gun injuries (which included records for hospitalization for the typical firearm injury averaging $20,000 dollars, double the cost of a typical hospital stay)[97, 98]. Finally, I must add that guns (gun carry) consume the public argument and divisiveness more than perhaps any other statistical issue (even abortion). However, unless and until there is a change/amendment to the Constitution (Article 2), the right to bear arms will prevail. I will leave it at that.

PRISON POPULATIONS BREAKDOWN AND FACTS:

Before proceeding, it is important to put in perspective what all the categories mean as I summarized in the preceding breakdown. They are not just numbers because ultimately society is how children grow up and assume the reigns of leadership from their parents' generation. When children go against the grain and break the law, they pay a price. However, that should not mean they should be locked up and the keys thrown away. People should be offered a second chance, even a third in some cases. The categories above represent the most influential statistics affecting factors which, when not properly channeled for accepted growth and development by societal standards, result in crimes of both non-violent and violent behavior. In this regard, it cannot be emphasized enough that there must be separation of those who commit the most heinous crimes and those who do not. This is a conscious mindset which has to translate into a practical awareness, or, society becomes one dimensional and blindly prejudiced. There is almost no reference specifically laid out in the literature or books where this carries authoritatively and incontrovertible answers. Why? It is a common sense issue based on insight, open-mindedness and thoughtful consideration. Some might say this is basic thinking. It is the nexus for prison reform. Prison reform must come through legislative channels. One would hope that as functionally egocentric their behavior, egotistic their thinking, and how corrupt their historically documented history, perhaps one day politicians may rise above their greed and legislate necessary reforms for the common good. If violent offenders are treated as a separate category prison reform may establish sufficient consensus to provide change in the way prisons do business.

The Prison Policy Initiative[99] breaks down all the detailed facts regarding current prison populations. The United States holds 2.3 million prisoners in varying levels of confinement. (I am only going to touch on the most significant items, keeping in mind that the most violent account for the lowest numbers). What does this mean? It signifies that the United States condones the overpopulated prison mess for which a lot is written, and only lip-service continuously paid. Data for drug offenses (including trafficking) are included in murder rates. Of the 1,316,000 in state prisons 718,000 are violent, 364,000 are the most violent and 182,000 are held for homicide. This translates to 13.8% of all state prisoners held for homicide. As to jails: there are 731,000 in our jails, of which 2.3% are in for homicide. As to private prisons, they hold state and federal prisoners in 29 states. According to the U.S. Department of Statistics these prisoners account for 8.4% of the overall prison population or approximately 126,000 prisoners. And of that number 3.3% are in for murder[100]. The Bureau of Prisons & the U.S. Marshals Service hold 225,000 prisoners of which 1.3% are in for murder. And ICE (The Immigration and Customs Enforcement) holds 34,000 prisoners contracted out to private prisons, and a much lower number to local jails. Thus, the percentage of homicides would be listed under the private prison heading for murder. Finally, the

Juvenile Justice System houses 53,000 of which 770 or 1.4% are in for murder. It is important to take into consideration that there are other categories for violence: namely human and drug trafficking, assault, robbery, rape-sexual assault, manslaughter and a mix of such criminal activity. This is not the place to review the details from all reporting sites, but to take one very important category (murder) and show that of the 2.3 million prisoners in the United States jails and prisons a very low percentage are in for the most heinous crime: murder. What does this mean? It should convey the idea that prison reform has a great deal of wiggle room for politicians should they decide to adopt prison reform as a principal concern for the country. Segregation of this most violent group rebuffs the attitude that scrupulous planning for a remaking with strategic modifications is very possible. All the taxpayer money routinely squandered year after year could be reallocated for elements of consequential reform: drug treatment, education, etc. Also, there are other acts of violence that are repugnant, but legislative reform has to start somewhere, not everywhere. And I firmly believe that murder is the one category where families will remain defiant against any remorse by the courts or legislatures. I have seen blogs, books and articles take varying positions regarding prison reform, but I am convinced that very, very few have sat back to look at the broad picture in order to fashion a sensible argument for reform. And as I said previously (but, important enough to repeat) politicians will say anything just to get re- elected (such as constructing a bill in Congress merely to reflect positively for their constituents, or, tagging a ludicrous demand to a bill to satisfy a constituency, but often will prevent a logical bill from passing; e.g., padding). Often follow-up soon evaporates like melting ice on a hot summer day. If all politicians could spend time like I have in a maximum-security prison, they would understand how this kind of behavior (so common) is very detrimental. It's common sense when looking at the numbers. Voltaire, the great French philosopher and writer uttered so tersely in a somewhat testy put-down: "Common sense is not so common."[101]

Well, what does all this mean? It is one thing to harbor facts, it is another thing to translate the meaning and underlying issues which swirl around people with agendas to foster prejudices to support their beliefs. Most of all, to get lost in the weeds and not see the larger picture or to deceive with bill padding is disquieting and frivolous!

The bleak picture paints not only misfortune for the large urban cities of the United States, but there is a very close correlation of poverty, lack of education, unemployment, and drugs[102]. When guns are inserted into the mix all hell breaks loose over constitutional rights. This proceeds into a visceral uprooting of contentious arguments over whether guns lift shoot by themselves (paranormally) or the political alignments drive the murder and mayhem. Adult discussion evaporates and tribal behavior stultifies the arguments and prevents consensus. Nothing but divisiveness and insults prevail. The societal cancers will never be eliminated, but surely there is a reasonable expectation for urgency in addressing the country's concerns. Facts can be distorted, but reasonable reflection of what they represent should be debated, not bedevil! Implicit within the data is the reality of the troubles and troublemakers which is cause for our prisons exploding in numbers.

Here are some significantconclusions:

> ***From the U.S. Department of Education: the U.S. High School graduation rate from the latest comparative data of 2013-2014 (the 3 year change from 2010) is up for all ethnic groups: American Indian/Alaska Native, Asian/Pacific Islander, Hispanic, Black, White as well as low income and English learning groups; and, from a low of 3.2% for whites to a high of 5.3%, 5.5%, and 5.6% for Hispanic, Black, and English Learners respectively[103].**
> ***Reported from the FBI, tracing homicides in the ten largest cities, there was an all-time spike in homicides from the last years reported: 2015-2016**

with a low of 4.5% for New York City to a high of 10.3% for Chicago[104].

*More than 210,000 students have experienced gun violence at school since Columbine, and, after Sandy Hook more than 400 people have been shot in over 200 school shootings[105].

(Do not forget these are pre-COVID-19 statistics. Comparatively, NYC above is 4.5%; as of today it is 29.3% due to the BLM (Black Lives Matter) and AntiFa riots. Personally, I feel statistics are more significant in more balanced times, and I do not feel this disruption will last after the November 3, 2020 elections. I am counting on sobriety and cooler heads returning to reality. And, the country getting back to a more common sense reality).

For discussion's sake, I found it very significant that in spite of prison overpopulation, inner city gang violence exploding, and some devastating social ills (drug addiction, gun and human trafficking, etc. the usually mentioned culprits), and school gun violence with shootings like the country has never experienced, high school graduation rates are increasing to the extent one would think contradictory. It demonstrates a shining star through the clouds hanging over the country. If listening to the news is like daily Armageddon, the facts demonstrate there is hope and positivity.

The negative impact of crime, however, seems to run parallel with everyday people who awaken each day to face the challenge of just making a living and supporting families with jobs. When the people are watching the news they are sobered and chilled by the litany of local and world insanity. As I stated previously, if it leads, it bleeds on television, on iPads, computers and phone apps: the constant barrage of crime. To wit, I say the data presented must be taken into context because the numbers make it seem like the final curtain is coming down on the country. Such acrimony reflects the crime statistics from the U.S, Department of Justice which shows very clearly that between 1960 and 2014, as a percentage of population growth from 179,323,175 to 318,857,056, violent crime as reflected in the rates for (1) murder and non-negligent manslaughter, (2) legacy rape, (3) robbery, and (4) aggravated assault all significantly lowered (Uniform Crime Reporting

Statistics[106]). Some tomfoolery because one would think I was going to go in sync with my prison description.

As I said in Chapter One, I am not a big fan of data (the land of endless statistics) because carefully placed in any writing they can support an argument with "truth" to the numbers. Even as he has written with an honest belief in the data he presents, Pfaff does not contextualize his numbers when he presents his argument for overpopulation of American prisons. As I said, I do agree with him concerning putting people away with heavy sentences (and, no doubt, over-prosecution) for non-violent crimes (example: "three strikes" sentencing, which is beyond the pale)[107]. But, the numbers do not tell the entire picture. Sure, the 2.4 million plus people in federal and state prisons looks tawdry compared to other countries, but there are social mores which have to be presented that steely statistics do not convey. For example, a lot of countries have a pass-through conveyance of prisoners to labor camps, death squads, etc. which are not only inhumane, but swift and harsh. Other countries do not factor into our statistical records. This is for a later discussion, but most people are aware of third world countries which do not waste time with court trials, and an appeal system that can make people forget the crimes by the time appeals are played out. Some countries will render a "dog and pony"-like show trial only to take the prisoner to a private setting to be shot or hung.

Simon Baron-Cohen (to whom I previously referred) is officially a Professor of Developmental Psychopathology in the Department of Psychology and Psychiatry at the University of Cambridge in Cambridge, England, UK[108]. He is a very lucid and descriptive writer extraordinaire, and a philosopher who does not make his argument from data-based research, but from his own very concrete research studies, formulating conclusions which I find extremely relevant and constructive. His overall presentation of "empathy" (both the issues underlying the Zero-positive and Zero-negative people) really cuts to the understanding of human behavior. He draws from studies which clearly show and analyze human reaction to societal challenges as a manifestation of areas of the brain which directly play into the

"Empathy Circuit" (the guide to brain locations and chemistry which dictate human behavior under different emotional challenges). I shall get into this later, but suffice it to say that I found it an incisive discussion on human behavior (especially discussion on "the science of evil") because of his mastery of eloquence and style. I mention it here because I contrast his book to that of Phaff's. I am not a numbers person so I feel Baron-Cohen's delineations are far more meaningful if one wants to understand all forms of human behavior. He gave me extraordinary insight to what I saw every day!

Piercing the qualities of human behavior from a very incisive writer like Baron-Cohen conveys a broader, more in-depth sense of understanding rather than frame observations against numbers alone. I only know that when confronted head-on in the prison yard in the face of perceptible danger the immediate sensation is to make for safety in any way possible. One has no way to tell in a prison yard what can, does and might happen at any minute! As a result, I have to discuss ideas about natural life sentencing and the death penalty from a psychological context. To a very large extent, the question should be asked: Where does "empathy" morph into "super-empathy" in the face of such "evil," homicidal maniacs. That being said, his book delivers insight into the most offensive, dangerous minds. Where are the limits to be drawn, how does punishment versus reform enter into picture, and how does the law break it all down? Mass incarceration and prison reform are the two most dynamic issues of much controversy, lingering up front and in the back-drop of every discussion and opinion.

Amen, Baron-Cohen, Baumeister, Beck, Gilligan, Kiehl and Samenow lend their authoritative opinions, often very different on very subtle, but undeniable neurological behaviors. As far as this discussion is concerned, where can the line be drawn to separate the reformative non-violent versus the over-the-top, non-reformative violent individuals for the sake of "prison reform." It is surprising how this never enters the national discussion, being strictly limited to the limited few authority books. Occasionally national and local reports pop up in news, newspapers, or blogs. It is very difficult to listen to non-authoritative individuals rendering very bold opinions. They are challenging, but mostly vague and uninformed. When violent murderers make up the smaller percentage of incarceration, it is inconceivable that there is not a meaningful and serious pursuit of "prison reform". The huge numbers of prisoners weakening and enfeebling over time is comparable to "government hoarding" of humanity. Like a "Russian (Soviet) gulag" or a Chinese "re-education center", this continued mass incarceration is headed in that direction. Social policy at the local/state/federal levels should prioritize change in the sequestering of non-violent prisoners for such long periods of time. As the population changes and expands, crime will be more pervasive (with the present national circumstances hardly illusory), and prison numbers will continue to expand (in spite of a relative cutback since the "great expansion" from the late 70's into the late 90's). The pages ahead will address the real problems and how to frame the discussion.

CHAPTER 4

Prison Gangs-The Reality Check

"Denmark is another European nation with a
"philosophy of humanization…"
Prisoners are required to either work or attend classes every
day from 7:30 A.M. until 3:00 P.M…
Those who prefer to work have several choices…
Living normally, or what the Danes call normalization, is
fundamental to the Danish approach to punishment and to
prisons. They believe life in prison should resemble life outside
prison as much as possible…
And it apparently works. About half of the inmates in the
United States and Great Britain return to prison after their
release. In Denmark, that rate is 27 percent."[109]

The long-storied history of United States prisons is one of punishment, not restitution, reformation, or rehabilitation, though it is feint as evidenced by a continuous, platitudinous public celebration by their directors of the very limited social and limited educational programs. From the way they are fronted so often in the media, it would seem this so common with accomplished support and results. True, to a very limited extent. By far, the surely far greater majority of prisoners just lollygag listlessly all day long just passing time. The result is that trouble finds so many of them. The amount of daily brutish behavior confirms the saying: an idle mind is the workshop of the devil. In Level I and Level II prisons there is a greater effort to afford the prisoners productive learning experiences to condition them for their release when job opportunities will (not "might") require familiarity, if not experience, with hiring questions demanding specific answers. The inability to be prepared for life outside is at the grassroots of high recidivism rates.

As daunting as the challenges of prison are, release into the "real-world" again is more so, even cruel because life is not a walk in the park. Level III (IV) prisons are occupied with just keeping a sense of order so that occupational or basic education programs are offered, but they require the prisoners to be compliant and without behavioral issues. So, right out of the gate this is very chancy and limited due to the environment in which gangs dominate 24/7 with a sad preoccupation for "business operations" which inevitably lead to some violent conclusion.

In order for prison reform to become a reality someday there has to be a political will in sync with rehabilitative programs as in Denmark "for all", not "some". There has to be a complete retooling of the thinking by those who run prisons without concentrating on policy paperwork, constant course work for employees which are totally overbearing and unnecessary, a coordinated approach by people who are familiar with occupational and educational course design for specific grade levels, and concentration on bringing the prisoners closer to real-world conditioning to schedules and trustworthiness. To return to life as it is, and not as it may be in any prison environment, prisoners must learn responsibility. The only way to reduce recidivism is to restore confidence and provide the prisoners with a defined ability and self-confidence that they can readapt to the challenges of the real world.

In this regard, none of this will have an effect if gangs and gang life are not isolated away from prisoners who will eventually qualify for release because gang-bangers are in a different world and are non-rehabilitative. This is an assessment that must be accepted. The reproducibility of violence is a severe hindrance to change as well as a stifled mentality.

Of course, there may be "some" diamonds in the rough, but they are limited. If a change to the existing reality is not accepted mixing hardcore killers into any environment is a losing proposition. A willingness to fashion a new way of thinking will ultimately establish positive returns, but it takes revolutionary changes. Reverse thinking is necessary to make a difference because the system is a bureaucratic mess. Languor and laziness in the way prisons are run today reflect a total lack of openness for change and a determination to effect change.

The greatest influence on the way prisons are organized and administered redounds in every way to politicians and political influences. This is where all problems start and where they proceed. And, this is the reason why every state has to have the kind of enlightened leadership "to start" on a new course. It would be naïve to think that euphemistic language and frothy promises will be effective. No they will not. However, change requires a brave adjustment in the way state governments do business with regard to prison organization. A great awakening is the only solution because the way the United States population is expanding with a major ethnic expansion which carries language and cultural adjustments.

I want to bring into focus a number of thoughts which make gangs both inside and outside such a growing and disturbing impediment to both law enforcement and prison containment. They are the bane of those whose lifeblood is the protection of society, and "living" evidence of Simon Baron-Cohen's[110] description of Zero-negative Psychopath (Type P) individuals. Poverty, lack of education, unemployment and drugs lead to behaviors that result in questionable associations, delinquent juvenile actions which grow into criminality and eventual problems with the law. How far each individual distances herself/himself from the mainstream and to what degree of crime evolves will determine a future that goes downhill into a mindset where like-minded individuals accelerate negative outcomes. Prison and street gangs are the results of people who follow a road of crime for lack of no other alternatives.

While gangs become their safe harbor, they lead them further and further into darkness and danger. How do such individuals get there?

I have to reference a thought which really hits home:

> ...it is almost a truism that poverty breeds crime, and poor people are certainly more likely than rich people to commit crimes. But poor people do not commit crimes. So there is a serious flaw in the theory that poverty causes crime. Usually poverty doesn't cause crime...Evil or violent tendencies are usually met with strong restraining forces, most of which can be conveniently categorized as self-control...The immediate proximal cause of violence is the collapse of these inner restraining forces...All that is necessary to stop restraining or preventing it. Once the restraints are removed, there are plenty of reasons for people to strike out at each other[111].

Now that is a fascinating viewpoint from a very credible source. I would agree except when individuals find themselves in prison and refusal to find a group (gang) for protection will lead downhill. At this point self-control loses out to survival. And, this is the difference between scientific analysis and practical considerations that most never see (and therefore do not understand). The most important reason for gang alliance is survival. The more dangerous the prison environment the greater the need for "group" associations; e.g. gangs.

Murder and non-violent crimes are in the crosshairs of the demographics noted previously. Prison and street gangs pump and circulate its poisons throughout every major United States city (and today, though not the core area, rural America). The perilous, disruptive, socially upheaving drugs: methamphetamine, cocaine, heroin (and now fentanyl and carfentanil) as well as all the synthetic opioids (oxycodone, OxyContin (the extended release form of oxycodone, etc.). But because it is the most abused among prisoners, marijuana is in the mix, and, to a lot of professional thinking, a gateway drug. Crimes, whether they involve homicide, drugs, gun trafficking, human trafficking for prostitution, etc. are the life force of incarceration. Eliminate them and prisons would essentially disappear. (Maybe not totally because human beings would probably find some other deleterious behavior, but the above point is important). Believing they shall be is unrealistic, and maybe even romantic.

Incarceration is a containment process, not an event. For this reason, it is imperative to know and understand it. Before I formulate a few judgments let's examine some pertinent facts. They can be distorted according to different personal viewpoints and what they want to emphasize. That does not concern me as long as they are put in proper perspective. (And, I am using pre-COVID-19 statistics because I feel they are more realistic. At some point, society will return to a settling normality. The environment today is an aberration and cannot continue).

The national homicide rate in the United States has risen 11% in 2015 after falling for twenty-five years. In the cities of Chicago, Philadelphia, Houston, Los Angeles and New York, homicide rates showed the greatest alarming increase, and particularly the percentage of gun murders. (The statistics for the COVID-19 environment are inflated due to BLM, Antifa, and other radical anarchical right and left wing gangs overtaking major cities). The most dramatic change was in the city of Chicago where in 2016 the number of killings rose from 485 to 764[112]. One report (Federal Bureau of Investigation 2012[113]) reviewed murder, forcible rape, robbery and aggravated assault throughout the United States in 2012. The country witnessed a steady rise in all four categories (murder: an increase of 1.1% in 2012 from 2011; and, 0.2% increase for rape, a decrease of 0.8% for robbery, and an increase of 1.1% for aggravated assault, all for the same time period (2011-2012). In general, though not wanting to diminish the significance of any increase in such a throttling of human-to-human level of crime, these remained fairly constant for the years 2011 to 2012 when contrasted to the horrific increase over the years through the 1980's and 1990's from lows during the 1970's (Bureau of Justice n.d.). However, in an FBI report (FBI National Press Office 2016) comparing the same crimes, the increases were dramatic going from 2014 to 2015. In that period violent crime rose 3.1%, rape 6.3%, robbery 4.6%, and murder and non- negligent manslaughter was up 10.8 %. Why? The association with the pandemic of drug trafficking. A statistic that is of considerable relevance reveals that from 2002 to 2011 the average homicide rate for blacks was 6.3 times higher than the rate for whites[114].

On the other hand, nonviolent offenders appear like lost souls on a roller coaster at an "amusement park", the speed is exhilarating but short-lived. From the Bureau of Justice Statistics[115], a statistic jumps right off the page: 7 of 10 nonviolent offenders were rearrested within 3 years of release, only this time for a new crime. About one half were reconvicted and over a quarter were returned to prison. 1 in 5 of them committed a violent crime. One other not so less significant factoid: 80% of those released have a prior conviction history. This captures a very important consideration: without proper direction, there is a gradual deterioration in the lifestyle of a nonviolent prisoner. She/he needs guidance and direction or there will be a price to pay: a continuous downslide as well as physical deterioration. Purpose and "coaching" are needed to end the regression, as well as the need for a support team. To forestall a continuous slide, coaching should be universally mandated. The most morbid statistics, and surely the most eye-catching and disturbing, are from a vice.com website and the United Nations[116], both reaching very deeply into statistical depths that makes one wonder if there is any possibility that drug trafficking and usage will ever be eliminated, or even diminished. Looking at the detailed maps and correlating them with facts does not make the evidence appear at all optimistic for positive change. The pervasive reach and largesse of money and associated businesses (prostitution and kidnapping of children) make for an octopus-like, multidirectional extension into the underbelly of an industry and way of life that has a vice-grip seemingly too strong and emboldened to loosen.

The U.N. report shows that North America accounts for 40% of global cocaine consumption. In 2008 the global cocaine market was estimated at 88 billion dollars for just the European Union countries and the United States. Cannabis is the most commonly used drug in prison. Injectable drugs (especially heroin) are associated with HIV, AIDS and Hepatitis C because of associated sexual promiscuity. The use of methamphetamines, opioids, the Ecstasy group, and heroin are not diminishing. Their usage in fact is growing. Back in the 1960's Librium and Valium made all women (especially suburban married women) addicted. In the 1970's Quaalude ("ludes") became a common street drug, and into the 1980's Oxycodone became the over prescribed pain killer that addicted both men and women. And that lasted until OxyContin (as stated, the time-release version of Oxycodone which makes it so overwhelming and insidious) came on the market. But through these times, Heroin (aka "The Horse") was always present. As the United Nations report underscores, it is the reach into every continent. The permanent attention of international law enforcement is necessary to monitor, interdict and capture both the drugs and money, let alonethe almost impossible hunt for the purveyors. Reaching into the drug strongholds around the world is life-threatening and almost impossible to eliminate (with the capture, interrogation and murder of many agents). It is a recurring scourge, and linked to government corruption at the highest levels in many third world countries.

The concatenation of these facts with all the other social issues brings into clear focus the almost insurmountable challenge to diminish the power and control of the prison- street nexus. The problems are pressing to the extent that the costs at local, state and federal levels are ballooning budgets (and in mismanaged ways). Public resources for educational needs, health policies, the war against crime associated with drugs and sex trafficking, etc. are draining and diversionary. Throughout the prison system there is an organic slow-walking to all administrative policies and decisions. This is a major problem with all government agencies, and particularly within the prison system.

Every time I read another blog, article or book supporting release for some of the most heinous and insidious crimes known to man, I pick up Gabriel C. Morales's authoritative review of all the "Blood In, Blood Out"[117] gangs. Then, knowing their past histories and quite certain loss of respect for human life, and remembering my own months spent working in a maximum-security prison, I regard all the statistics quoted an almost insurmountable effort. And, it is at this juncture that I separate myself from those making the argument for the release of a murderer without defined and fastidious reasoning[118].

The willful disregard for life may be debated in a spiritual, psychological context, but tell that to a crying mother whose 5- year-old daughter has been kidnapped, raped and murdered. The over-zealous pursuit of conviction for non-violent crimes is where definite inroads can be made to shrink mass incarceration, the Achilles heel of state, federal and private prisons. Nowhere do I read or sense this important distinction made.

The "Blood In, Blood Out" characterization is nowhere more pertinent in today's life than the open borders of the United States. I know the average citizen cannot understand this. It has nothing to do with xenophobia and everything to do with inordinate pressure on everything related to the law of the land (and right down to its last refuge: the American prison. There is an increased chance of violence and predatory incidents. The American citizenry is very much more vulnerable than at any time in our history. With the changing patterns of ethnic population migratory patterns the country is in flux and learning how to adapt. Safety and crime are the underlying issues. It is more important than ever to stave off political considerations in being vigilant and open to all immigrants coming through proper legal channels.

The country has a crime control problem more than any time in its history, and it is for this reason that double-speak and slanderous back-and-forth between political parties should end. There is no redeeming value to this behavior. Along with the good comes the bad. I cannot imagine politicians acting tendentiously for open borders without careful scrutiny of evildoers expanding what is already an overly swelling prison population.

There are very willful killers in the population mix, and the gangs are a very discernible reflection. Like the miasma of a longstanding landfill, the pungent smell of death might re-order thinking and make everyone stand up and realistically take notice. This is the scourge of a maximum-security prison.

The nexus of violent crime and immigration demands more ethical balance to political thinking and action. This should be the most important consideration of law enforcement because "the bad" cannot obscure "the good," the immigrant who will assimilate and proudly enhance the beauty of American life. If I learned one thing from a maximum-security prison, the evil that prevails could easily chill the feeling for the needy and hardworking immigrants. The gangs run the streets in a very threatening, robust way, and immigrants are mired in that cauldron of daily fire. The news of late is pounding the daily concern for MS-13. But, and unfortunately, this is only one of many more lethal gangs living and murdering with wholesale abandon in our city streets. Crime statistics from the FBI for preliminary figures for 2017 reveal murder and non-negligent manslaughter increased by 1.5 percent. And the overall number of violent crimes in cities with populations of a half to a million citizens had the largest increase, 1.2 percent. In cities with populations of one million and over there was a decrease of 3.3 percent. Non-metropolitan counties and metropolitan counties fell 6.1 and 1.5 percent respectively. Property crime and arson were up and down depending on the section of the country. Rape is no longer reported using the Uniform Crime Reporting (UCR) Statistics. These are the preliminary data for 2017, but I wanted to point out that they reveal a pattern for the small cities where street gangs are the most active on behalf of their incarcerated counterparts from where the orders spring[119, 120] (These statistics and all subsequent ones are pre-COVID-19). Gangs marginally grew in the 1960's, having been common to prisons around the world to some extent since their origin, but began to flourish with wild abandon in the 1970's. Prison administrators were very aware, but, like their other frustrations with political bureaucrats, were helpless to

contain them. Therefore, two major concerns undermine any hope for containment: (1) the speed of their growth, and (2) the expansion of the American prison system in synch. Rather than reason, evaluate, and source an intelligent plan to purge this growth,
the centralization of government power being thick with inaction as it is, gangs just grew like insidious weeds taking over cultivable land. Unfortunately, bureaucracy is institutional quicksand where good ideas and creative thinking become buried and irretrievable.

Reconciling policies for adaptation to need at this point are impossible because bureaucrats will not respond until exposed. If one is digging oneself into a hole, stop digging! It's brutal to know that they know but do not care. "The Peter Principle,"[121] which postulates that in a hierarchy people tend to rise to "their level of incompetence." And, this is everywhere at all levels of politics. This principle speaks volumes to large, wobbly corporations unable to win the battle of performance, growing expenses faster than profits on the way to failure. Well, multifold is the bane, headache and frustration for the unfettered growth of government. The political solution to government failure is more government, more waste, more money thrown perilously at taxpayer expense, and more of the same circular, habit forming thinking from one generation to the next. This about quantifies and qualifies the American prison system. The very thriving "Peter Principle!" So, at this point, restructure and rethinking is "a political Christmas wish!" And over time cottage industries grow into the mix to make it an institutional mess.

Prisoners have cultivated obvious, full-throttled behaviors during this time which have further paralyzed the prison system. They have cultivated a trait which is called "jobbing the system." In these times where "political correctness" has pushed common sense aside, prisoners have been allowed to go hog wild in pursuit of "their civil rights!" Well, between mobilizing prison staff for the imponderable, head shaking legal opportunities, trips to hospitals, outside dental care, etc., they have immobilized staff to accommodate their every wish. Be it filing incident reports to run the chain of evaluation or demands for intra-prison opportunity of all sorts, the entirety of prison staff have become strange hamster types running a treadmill. This policy has destabilized a system and disabled progress. No one should interfere with human rights, but the prison system is off the charts in a disillusioned world where prisoners are afforded so much more than needy homeless individuals. In a world of low pay, extended hours, and not able to carry guns for politically partisan and irrational reasons, the gangs prosper because they are well aware that their numbers and organization can foment disorder and bedlam at will. The prison policies will never allow prisons to decompress because they are the grease that advance free-wheeling by prisoners' sense of what the system owes them. The outside has no feel for this inside conundrum. The Rubicon[122] has been crossed long ago and gangsrule!

In the time I worked at the maximum-security prison I became very friendly with a guard 36 years in the system, a man well into his late 70's and laden with fear of his cancer issues. He was a wonderful mentor, a wonderful man, and spoke openly about the failure of prisons. He was neither resentful nor argumentative, just frustrated by their failings. He was so close to the prisoners that he always knew (very privately) when a riot was planned and programmed into their minds.He would always tell me: "They rule, we don't"! He knew the system was a wreck and totally in free-fall. We wouldtalk about prison reform, and he would roll his eyeballs as he intoned: "Ya! Never!"

The interplay between prison and street gangs is a thriving business. It has no end in sight, and the cat and mouse game that is played with contraband continues and will sustain. There is no will for change, only a public display in the form of a pretense for change. I often wondered why the sheer pretext for "the dog and pony show" was not more apparent. As I grew into a different state of awareness it was quite clear that the lack of pride and self-esteem made employees silent and despondent. Most came from such poverty that nothing mattered besides collecting a paycheck. They were very much aware of their circumstances, but they were also acutely aware that the atmosphere is very fragile.

Passing through the prison gates at any time of day clearly imparted the brazen behaviors of prisoners. Their temerity was baffling. I would stop and take the time to speak personally to a great number of the prisoners who viewed the proposition as a "who cares?" scenario when "I have nothing to lose!" One in particular (a staunch gangbanger) would jawbone so continuously I could not get a word in edgewise. He had a disturbingly savage background; but, when he saw me coming, he knew I would stop for his venting. He would hang around the entry lockup by the control room gate (officially there to collect and move laundry), but he was freelancing because of the lack of supervision. He would tell me in an unruly way how he and "his friends" were in control and to "watch my ass!" The system is whipsawed by the prisoners. I do not have the expertise to pass judgment on what can contain this unbridled trend. It made me aware of how explosive the atmosphere was. The foxes do run the henhouse, I would drive home at the end of a day ruminating over a system locked in time. If anything impacted me, it was the sameness, day-in, day-out, perennial madness in its own orbit!

Gun trafficking is the main staple intertwined with drugs and all other crimes which put the gang offenders into prison. The flow of guns in and out of this country is disturbing to say the least. All the other considerations related to both non- violent and violent crimes committed are directly related to the easy manner with which guns may (and can, and are) obtained both directly (store and internet purchased) and indirectly (the black market). The distinction must be made that I am not arguing against second amendment rights. I am pointing out how deeply ingrained is the smuggling of black market guns into the United States. As supported by documentation,[123,124,] [125] the ease with which handguns, rifles of all kinds, and military types find their way to inner city gangs. Serial numbers are rubbed out and they somehow get to young gang-bangers! This makes the criminal mind and offender very much more imposing and threatening to neighborhoods as well the defenders of law and order (which has never been more threatened and consequently more defensive than ever). The seemingly once natural state of orderly life is long in the rear-view mirror. Marie Gottschalk[126] writes forthrightly about the cost for local and state governments as well as the epidemic of HIV/AIDS and Hepatitis C in prisons across the United States. She says: "Numbers alone do not fully convey the distinctiveness of the U.S. carceral state. In short, "American punishment is comparatively harsh, comparatively degrading, comparatively slow to show mercy."[127, 128] Firstly, I say that I agree, but I would add that the punitive nature has a lot to do with both the physical housing and overcrowding. The harsh and drab surroundings make for built up tension. The guards are left to watch their every move, and, in time, most are ready for excitement. This leads to trouble-making and inevitable punishment. The buildup of inner frustration and disgust ultimately leads to very regrettable violations and transgressions which bring punishment. This becomes an endless loop of misery. Health care is another issue. The basic care is very basic. More advanced care is farmed out to private offices and hospitals because prisons do not have advanced facilities. But, the existing facilities are not sterile, and is another source of stress for acute wounds! But, maybe, Gottschalk[129] is too ladylike in tone, though right on the money. I could not believe how the system made such a big deal about medical/dental care, but, in fact, it was degrading. Just as a side, I have been in infirmaries where bleeding wounds from shanks and shivs have run off onto the floors and walls. These wounds are from HIV, Hepatitis C infected prisoners. Watching the lack of sterility and how the surroundings are cleaned post- operatively is anathema and astoundingly accepted as passable. I'll clearly say that after many years in health care, the health care delivery to prisoners is about a 2 to 3 on a 10 scale. I realize that in a Level III the prisoners are some of the most vile human beings anybody could encounter, but that still does not excuse such neglect. I used to say when I was in private practice that the way to a healthy mind is a healthy body. There is no resolve for change because the administrative bureaucrats do not care. The politics is indifferent to at least reaching minimum health standards. It is a stark reality which just adds to the daily concerns and feeling of tension, especially the prisoners. (Bureau of Justice n.d.).

Why is the prison a throwaway environment?

Consider this: statistics cited speak volumes for how the cycle of repetitive crime-to-prison is an endless loop from one generation to another. And yet warehousing of prisons and detention centers are more endemic than ever. One facet of "prison reform" would be to end this cycle. The political disgrace of "prison reform" has transmuted from generational insult to a complete vacuum in Washington, D.C.. Each state is responsible for its own prison complex, but the overall political will is highly insufficient. President Trump started with the First Step Act for non-violent federal prisoners. However, this is a small number compared to all the state prisons. It is surprising how the House of Representatives and Senate in Washington,
D.C. set bleak standards for state prisons which ungainly overcrowded. The inattention to real prison reform is an out of sight-out of mind circumstance. "Those who do not remember the past are condemned to repeat it."[130] It is bewildering how man can perpetuate errors of deep generational concerns without the type of self-reflection and guilt that would finally override political malarkey. Day after day as I walked through a maximum security "yard" it was always a saunter into the past. Shaking my head so many times probably instilled this foray into prison analysis. The best way to put it is that all considerations relating to "prison reform" rest in a vacuum where nothing moves.

Daily management of a prison is a feat, keeping the peace against the potential for a sudden incident at any moment. Minute-to-minute disturbances are events. At the beginning of my tenure, I always heard the horror stories of total prison lockdowns, particularly not being able to leave and being sequestered for any length of time that is required to re- establish control. When there is a prolonged lull the tension is still as high as prisoners move about through the yard going to various buildings, on-site jobs, or marched to vans for outside visits. It is expensive financially and emotionally as it ratchets up the anxiety for the guards involved. My mind always drifted to Morales's descriptions. They do not reflect literary skill, but they are so telling that they were in my mind all the time while I walked to various locations during the day.

Violent deaths leave too many vivid memories to people who work such a complex day-to-day. The impressions are both mind-bending as well as personality effectors over time. Street gangs are responsive to the commands of the prison gang leaders who possess a very strange sense of power. To me it was quite eerie! Civil society is abjectly affected in ways they do not know, and that is a good thing. It is an awful and awesome task that is impossible to contain. Metaphorically, the gangs create a buoyancy which is ready to explode at any time with levels of piercing brutality so very foreign to even the most educated minds. It is conceptually very hard to grasp, even for people who watch the prison television shows because it is far worse in real life.Identification with a gang is key to survival[131]. Loyalty must be unwavering or sooner than later nothing shy of a bloody death is certain. Today there are so many prison gangs that it would take volumes of writing to describe their origins, idiosyncrasies and how they all interrelate. However, there is no such thing as flourishing in a Level III (or, Level IV, for the California prisons). Today, prisons all over the United States are filled with these gangs, and the most violent in nature battle for turf: like EME (the Mexican Mafia) and The Aryan Brotherhood. Dereliction of allegiance will get a street gang member bludgeoned without notice or second chance.

In today's political arena, there is a "big tattoo deal" being made of MS-13. Its very vocal destructive presence should never be minimized, but to be fair, there are so many dangerous gangs in the United States that to "exalt" one is almost derelict because of the prevalent damage left by the others. The others are just as violent, and more so in many cases. MS-13 is composed of very young hellions to whom sworn allegiance is more important than life itself. MS-13 arose in the state of California in the 1980's so it is not recent, though this is not discussed enough by the American press. Since moving to San Salvador its numbers have swelled. Member identification is to the extreme MS, or Mara and Trucha. This is a San Salvadoran identity: Mara means gang in San Salvadoran Caliche, a type of slang in reference to Marabunta, the name of a savage type of ant. Trucha is also Caliche slang for being "alert", and Trucha is often referenced as

Salvatrucha because Trucha is often combined with Salvadoran. The Salvadoran peasants became assassin-like guerilla fighters as part of the "Farabundo Marti National Liberation Front." But, to be clear, the MS-13 gang is no longer keyed into warfare for survival in San Salvador. Its reason for being changed because the fighters had nowhere to go. Pillage, rape, gun running, drugs, and other high crimes became their only resource for survival. Today it is a bloodthirsty group of young troublemakers bent on the violence evident now in the United States. Their members are known for being tattooed from head to toe! The 13 in MS-13 represents the thirteen seconds of violent initiation a member must endure to become an active member. These youths will never be confused with nice, smiley Guatemalan landscaping workers seen all over south Florida! Their call of the wild is violent destruction in anything or anybody who steps in their way or threatens their existence. This is disturbing for our city streets, but, unfortunately, they are only one of many threatening gangs. Media does not report on the others because of their "hear no evil, see no evil" mindset. The biggest challenge to America's state prisons are these gangs that live and breathe a lifestyle almost impossible to understand because it is so foreign to human nature. Yet, be clear, it is the most dangerous threat to our safety.

As sinister and menacing as daily life is for "the worst of worst," I am always reminded by this inscrutable thought: this human being was once cradled in the arms of her/his mother. Babies are like clay and will mold to behaviors with the mentoring of loving parents. Gangs are composed of young boys and girls who, for the most part, never benefited from the loving attention of parenting. Gangs unfortunately are diabolical. To think otherwise is dangerous. That would be like playing with fire.

Reading through the Morales book is an encyclopedia of the most dangerous gangs. I always kept in mind his writing as I walked through the yard. After a while I knew the personal histories fairly well so I developed a very cautionary resolve. My initial naivete transitioned in time to a circumspect attitude, especially early in the morning walking in the dark. When I would talk to a gangbanger, I would think: good grief, what happened? I have no answer, but trite as it may be: it is what it is. I can only relate a very real observation I saw repeated and repeated. As foul mouthed and abusive as a violent killer may be, I noted by talking to many that there was always a concern for family and a spiritual connection to either the gang per se or a fellow prisoner. The whole scenario was warped! Some would say: "see, there is hope for rehabilitation!" Maybe. Not all. Emphatically not all! Because in the same breath they'd eviscerate you in a nanosecond. As much as I believe in prison reform it is warped thinking to believe wholesale reform should replace discretionary judgment. I suggest that resources and time be devoted to individuals whose attitudes and prison behavior reach contrite and positive reversal.

That is where the gang takes on a dangerous role. As much as the prisoner joins needing a sense of identification no useful purpose other than wanton gangbanging is the outcome. The gang becomes the mothership for the long journey ahead "in stir". It is the vicarious replacement for what their disturbed minds conceive as a guide for their misguided purpose left in life. Harsh. Ok. I'll concede, but don't let any thought that mercy will establish hope. That would be indefensible reasoning. The "Blood In, Blood Out"[132] is very real. Each prisoner knows that death may come at any time, during the darkness of the night to the extreme of a full-fledged riot in a cell block or in the prison yard. In a desperate need for what is left the sanctuary of the prison gang is that place.

I remember one of the most talkative, friendly prisoners of all. Every single day he would make it his business to talk to me for at least ten minutes. That may not seem like a long time, but in prison anything longer draws guard attention. I'll say I was well known and I could judge any length of time I wanted, but this was a unique situation. He would touch on so many subjects that I was fascinated with the depth of his awareness and reading. Long story short, he was a monster in his youth. He willfully and viciously raped a six year old girl and then unhesitatingly murdered her. And, at the time I knew him, he was in his late fifties.

What can be said about him when the subject of prison reform arises? I believe I do not possess the gumption to reason a "God issue!" All I can think, reading his computer biography is the degree of spiritual morbidity! And yet, if his current deportment and frame of mind were not corrupted by his criminal record, his core mental and spiritual being have resolutely changed. I can resolutely say he is a changed man, but I am fortunate that I would never have to be on a parole board to pass on his freedom because I simply could not, and would not want to. And, by the way, the parole boards are replete with highly corrupt cronies of politicians who put them there.

The above example is one of many that came to my attention. If nothing else, it caterwauls for "inner city reform". This is really the ticket to prison reform, but nobody takes a regimented leadership role in this regard. All I ever hear is noise and empty promises.

For some reason Simon Baron-Cohen[133] felt compelled in his book to divulge his political position as a "Liberal" in defending his position for prisoner rehabilitation as opposed to punishment without hope for release. As much as I respect everything he says, political affiliation has no role in really excellent work. His book does not have a political inclination; but for some reason, he wants to make it known that his "Liberal" spirit should be public knowledge. That being said, he does not differentiate between the violent versus the non- violent offenders. He purely concentrates his writing on explaining positive and negative behaviors. In this regard, I find his book a must read. It also got me thinking how I view myself. I am a common sense thinker. All life's interactions are political, but I feel that in today's world politicians are warped. They are an ugly social construct and I can take any of my time to support any. Politicians are a fact of life, they are not going away anytime soon, but I have never felt compelled to be any kind of political activist. I will vote at any cycle with reference to the issues of the times and how I reason them at the time. I am not a conditioned follower.

Injecting political persuasions only muddies the thought process because what is right for prisoners and prison life with a societal backdrop requires non-political, common sense thinking. This is somewhat naïve and overly virtuous, but I believe that politicians' bias is an impedance, usually obstructive.

Rather than theorize what is an appropriate opinion about "rights and wrongs" Simon Baron-Cohen compels me to suggest the following (because crime has so many levels which automatically disallows sweeping generalizations).

A great number of people prefer to use the word "EMPATHY" (the ability to understand another person's point of view). So while thinking about the word "EVIL," I reversed the word as a "semordnilap" (A "semordnilap" refers to a word spelled backward, and thus taking on a new and reverse meaning). When the letters are reversed, "EVIL" becomes "LIVE". Or, simplistically treat "EVIL" as an acronym: "Empathy Venerates Inspirational Living." Somewhat off-centered thinking, it is food for thought with a different way of framing an interesting viewpoint. In any case, this acronym is the very polar opposite of core gang thinking and lifestyle. Norman Vincent Peale[134] might reference this as the type imagery he projects in his book: *The Power of Positive Thinking*. As he says so simply: "…our happiness or unhappiness depends to an important degree upon the habit of mind we cultivate".[135] I personally believe in the "cup half full" philosophy of life, but my exposure to the very dark side of extreme criminal behavior taught me very clearly that there is a psychological/emotional edge. It is similar to a cliff with a perilous and steep escarpment: at that point the conditions are visceral, not rational.

I am not committed to the sketchy political status quo, and I would rather determine what is reasonable rather than what a politician or political platform exhorts. Though "the KISS (Keep It Simple Stupid) Rule" has always been popular, I, long time ago, had my own contribution: "RAG's KILL RULE" ("Keep It Livable and Loveable"). Even if a bit treacly and overly sentimental, it's upbeat. It tends to keep people calm and conciliatory in order to present divergent ideas without wrath and disdain. I think historically of "Occam's Razor,"[136] trying to make understandable sense of what may seem very complicated. But simplifying the complex is not always possible and easy.

I remember one prisoner I saw and talked to everyday (and many, many times during the day). He was gentle, kindly and most appreciative of our friendship. An impoverished black man who never asked much of life, was never afforded the opportunity for any education, and was reconciled to a life in prison. He compelled me to recall the rather linear but true Bill Parcells'[137] famous statement: "You are what your record says you are"! Known by the sobriquet "The Big Tuna", he was known for his feisty, arrogant, very direct but knowledgeable and very often accurate analysis of things football as well as life. As an NFL football coach and general manager he saw things with an eagle eye, and, without any diffidence nor fear of consequence, he would customarily blurt out what first came to his rather resolute mind. This prisoner, however, was in for a really egregious murder, so unspeakable that I shall not reveal the details. Bill Parcels, in his very singular manner, would never see this man's plight in shades of gray. A listener may not want to hear as he spoke with splash and an august style, but he always called the facts with crystal clear candor. The parole board had ruled several times against this prisoner so he has sadly resolved to accept his natural life sentence with a very quiet, sullen refrain. The Catch 22 is that he always remorsefully repeated his innocence. He is still there, and lost in the system, the bureaucracy. In meeting and talking to this very quiet and good-natured man, it would be very hard to reconcile the two periods of his life. I always told him I would go before the parole board for him, but the opportunity was never afforded. In a Level III, it was discernibly a "Hang 'Em High"[138] resolve (mainly because the preponderance of prisoners were dissolute and cunning far beyond repair). I believe a parole board's mindset can easily be one- dimensional and clouded by the environment. I tried to convince him that today's DNA testing could be applied, but he had become frail and fearful.

To recall my very long breezeway to the control room and that platitudinous sign the word that remains in my brain will always be "Correctional," a pretext for what should be, but is not! Deep inside (and, in general) I feel this is a continued obsession for public consumption. I wish I could say it is other than a deceptive charade. It is important to be clear. The prisons provide for religious groups, local clergy for support, woodworking schooling, out-sourcing for work details around the city, music groups and gatherings, a library for prisoners, etc. And though a real pretense is made for health benefits, they are ghastly. And, as stated in Chapter One, the atmosphere was one of profound circumspection by all the employees. The feeling was always "what am I doing here, and, I want to quit…for this pay and long hours…oh my God…what am I doing this for? If I heard this once, I heard it a million times. Well, it was for state benefits and health care in retirement for people who came from very meager circumstances. I always thought that such negative feelings never contribute constructive purpose to any organization, let alone a maximum-security prison.

Another prisoner I shall never forget. Either in the cell at the infirmary or out in the yard he was always loud, prodding someone for a fight. The warden would always get upset seeing him alone without a guard in sight. The higher up officers always regurgitated their cautionary alert: be careful because this particular prison had "the murder-a-minute" reputation (not literally, but with so much violence, it was a daily "show"). As I have said it was always dark. Seeing unsupervised prisoners was something I could never comprehend. (Actually, I really did, but it defied my belief system). It was shocking, particularly when prisoners hid in the shadows of the exterior building. Yes, this was "The Big House!" Yes, my heart was "a-flutter" if I got a hello from out of nowhere! There was one particular prisoner I did not know. I knew most, and most knew me. But this particular individual told me he was going to "f-me up!" That was compelling, to say the least! For the sake of my story, I could not write about the American prison system if I had never witnessed some of its untold realities.

Therefore, from my research, reading, experiences and soul searching, I came to a very basic conclusion: that at Level I and Level II there must be a change at some level of government to "reform" more than it resorts to "punish". It is possible if only the powers to be can recognize that non-violent prisoners cannot be in the mix with violent prisoners. And, to repeat what I said: this must be in synch with "inner city reform." Prison reform and inner city reform are Siamese Twin entities! Level III (IV) is a very different entity.

No doubt this is somewhat quixotic, but, in my thinking, the only hope for change. The system cannot mix the prisoners because the range of behaviors is too different. And the next bloodied prisoner should be a quick reminder. Or, just watch the news when prisoners escape and are caught, only to have their mugs on screens nationally. When their crimes are reported, I say to myself: Of course, he wants out, and, he has nothing to lose if he is shot fatally during his apprehension.

As I consider reform the politics reminds me of chocolate pudding as it goes from the heated mix to the congealed refrigerated stage. Unfortunately, there is a bureaucratic freeze on change because of money and a good-ole boy network of professional lifers. They think of change in slow motion, if at all! And unless incompetent or corrupt employees quit or retire nothing moves in a positive direction. State government doesn't fire people to effectuate change. They are shuffled around because most state employees cannot be fired. Only retirement opens up positions which "might" improve leadership.

I am convinced that prison overpopulation is a feeder system for a money grab that masquerades as budget demands. In the hands of crony appointees and politically connected individuals there is an unspoken "partnership in crime." I call this "the invisible hand". Private prisons were supposed to be the white-collar solution to a longer-term issue of state and federal run prisons bleeding money from years of political sludge mucking up any possibility of house cleaning. But even the privatization conjured up another blindsiding bug in the ointment (if that was possibly never foreseen): making money, money and more money to satisfy private investors. How does that translate: more prisoners! And where can state and private prisons lasso the greatest numbers: poor, victimized blacks of inner-city crime mills and backwater white troglodytes with rural hideaway alcohol stills and methamphetamine labs. This is a worldwide problem that reflects badly on corruption in leadership, but human instincts are universal 139[140]. As Michelle Alexander clearly puts her finger on it: "Rich and powerful people, including former Vice President Dick Cheney, have invested millions in private prisons"[141, 142]. I'd like to be a "cockeyed optimist", but as is often said: "follow the money!" Maybe too colloquial, but I think it is as simple as that. Even John Pfaff refers to over- aggressive prosecutorial indulgence[143]. This is just another symptom which accrues to a syndrome that has no antidote. Like the fight against cancer (because the prison system is like an endemic metastatic cancer) there has to be a universal willingness to fight the good fight, a reallocation of money away from wasteful and self-perpetuating funding, and a leadership capable of seeing through bureaucratic muck to right an upside-down ship. Perhaps a Dr. Ben Carson type, knowledgeable, studied, confident and gracious!

At Level III it is not so easy to make the same judgment. This is where Prison Reform is almost impossible. From what I have seen, there must be natural life because of some crime are the most vile, inhuman, mind bending. The criminality is frightfully soulless. I have seen the eyes of such evil many, many times. Life and death is inconsequential to such socio- psychopathy. Most killed multiple times, but were not considered serial killers. One alarming example of the worst serial killer in United States history that "no one ever heard of" was "Pee Wee" Gaskins[144,145]. He was diminutive in stature but one of the most cold and vicious a killers in American history. Why he never attained notoriety status I do not know. But he callously killed 110 plus victims, mostly young women.

There are two other additional people to whom I want to call attention because of their significance. Susan Smith[146] from Union, South Carolina premeditatedly drowned her two boys by leaving them in her car as it submerged in a lake. Then she lied about a person who carjacked her children but had nothing to do with the crime. She coldly attempted to cast blame on that "supposed black runaway carjacker" about whom police eventually cleared. He was the foil for her lies. It was a viciously calculated crime for which she is in prison sorting out her life while still having mental difficulties as she violates all kinds of prison policies (including sexual escapades with guards as well as drug use). She is truly a depraved killer.

The other is Andrea Yates[147, 148] who drowned her five children in a bathtub after breakfast in 2001. She had a very long history of bulimia, psychotic delusions and depression. At the time of the drownings she was on a heavy dose of antidepressants. She was found guilty and given a life prison sentence which was reversed on appeal because of the Psychiatrist's over-dosage of antidepressant medication. He then proceeded to withdraw the dosage amount too quickly resulting in her psychotic rage. The result was a reversal of the life sentence and committing her to a mental institution where she still resides.

I bring up both instances because they clearly differ in terms of the depravity and deviance. I am certain there are people on both sides of the fence regarding forgiveness and rehabilitation for both. However, I do not want to pose an argument because, as the saying goes, this is beyond my pay- grade. I do, however, know from my reading that Susan Smith was a calculated killer whose prison misbehavior over a long period of time during her incarceration has resulted in severe punishment. Ultimately, she was moved to another institution where she is carefully monitored. Conversely, Andrea Yates' passionate and seemingly unforgiveable filicide(s) is hard to forgive for any parent. But even though I cannot bear the thought of what she did, she had a very long history of mental disease and was scapegoated by a Psychiatrist's ill-fated too rapid withdrawal of her antidepressant for which there were warnings provided. Therefore, I put Andre Yates in a classification for monitored rehabilitation despite the repugnant nature of her crime(s). "Pee Wee" Gaskins is without any question the "poster child" who grew into a heartless, cold- blooded killer. Reading about him, I very frankly reflected on some of the cold-blooded killers I came to know quite well. It is for this reason that I have to draw the line and recall Simon Baron Cohen's description of Psychopathy. "Pee Wee" Gaskins is the classic example. And, I know one has to dig deeply into one's soul to envision the abject horror of taking the life of an innocent young child after viciously raping her and not feel the ultimate repugnance. His history is replete with the most vile, sickening murders he committed against young women. He was hollow and as depraved as any human being could be. Redemption was not possible by any stretch of the imagination for the lechery he displayed so mechanically. It would be ludicrous to consider rehabilitation for any serial killer. I am certain a CT scan would display incredible inactivity where natural human emotion should exist and simply does not. Other serial killers simulate the very intrinsic qualities I perceived in so many gang miscreants. Gang members possess this manifest cold bloodedness as they prey on sentient, vulnerable human beings. I shall revisit this later in subsequent chapters.

For many reasons the prison gangs have not only taken over the prison system, but they have grown in numbers. Their crime driven methodology is their creed, and, violence is their calling card. It really is as simple as that. The power structure inures with every passing year. Change the names and faces, but the pattern of behavior stays the same. The sum is greater than its parts. Like government, the entity remains and its occupants reshuffle through time. It's a giant corporation without a "license of incorporation." Wasted words will never dispel their drive to control. And unless there is the desire to finally be proactive, their treacherous conduct of destabilization will persist at a very costly expense.

Jails, Level I and Juvenile facilities are very different. They are not as structurally adapted to handle the violence common to Level II and III (IV in California) prisons because volatility and danger are not nearly as pronounced. But, they do not have to be. The brutal fact is that all the maximum-security prisons are unpredictable day-to-day. And flashpoints spark very unexpectedly.

Like a controlled burn in a forest to stimulate the undergrowth, one of the three tenets of the prison gang is "control." The power structure operates like a business with "drug dealing" buffeted by the massive amounts of money held in escrow (street gangs). Planned violence is established at the top level of leadership. The dominant gangs rival each other for power and control. Morales does a great job in breaking this down. Eventually they tangle in unspeakable and savage murders. Mercy is not a debatable emotion, nor in these rivaling gangs' lexicon. A well-established rivalry is the Aryan Brotherhood blatantly at war with The Black Guerilla Family. These two combatants are the oil and water of forever immiscibility. So, within the structure of each gang turf allegiance is so sacred that each member's loyalty must be sacrosanct. The certainty of death is failure to meet this unwritten contract.

David Skarbek's book offers a crystal-clear viewpoint on gang violence. To assuage the extremes of violence between gangs is unfeasible, being that the prisoner's mindset and temperament is mercurial. Fear engenders their devotion, even if their emotions are so fractious. At spirited times "Helter- Skelter" behavior prevails, and independent reaction is set aside. But, firstly, let's look at Skarbek's point(s):

> The governance theory of prison gangs suggests that a better approach for reducing the power of prison gangs is to alter the conditions that give rise to inmates' demand for them and to identify what substitute mechanisms are available. If removing gangs means that inmates have to rely on norms, then prisons will become less orderly. In this scenario, gangs should not be undermined. Alternatively, if officials can provide formal governance that is more effective or reduce inmate's demand for extralegal governance, then removing gangs can improve prison order. There is a limit to this, however, in that officials will presumably not be willing to adjudicate disputes in illegal markets. Given these concerns, three possible solutions to reduce the influence of prison gangs are to (1) make safer and more liberal, (2) incarcerate fewer people, and (3) hire more police[149].

And:

If we designed a prison intended to meet inmates'demand for governance, it would not resemble the ones we currently have. Radical change, or at least a willingness to question current practices, are in order. Legal scholar Alexander Volokh makes the novel suggestion that we create a "prison voucher" system akin to proposals for school choice, where inmates can choose where to serve their time. As he explains, "vouchers empower the prisoners themselves to reward and punish prisons, creating powerful incentives for prisons to improve in accordance with the prisoners own standards[150].

And:

Prisons would compete against each other for more inmates by offering better and possibly different incarceration experiences. Prisons could specialize in offering a particular set of amenities, including the availability and types of health care, access to therapeutic and rehabilitative programs, high school and university education, vocational training, the quality of gym and recreation resources, a devout religious lifestyle, better visiting facilities, cheaper phone calls, access to the Internet, and location near family. Inmates will avoid prisons known to be disorderly or to lack desirable programming opinions. Prisons would then have an incentive to discover what inmates want and to find ways to provide it efficiently. This might include more training for correctional officers, developing a meaningful internal grievance system, or even establishing an independent system of external monitoring with the aid of a third party, such as the Red Cross. Compared with the bureaucratic incentives that guide prison management today, prison vouchers might be able to generate superior information and incentives to improve prison order. Of course, the system would require restrictions on what type of amenities and freedom inmates could receive. Nevertheless, few people would disapprove of prisons that were more safe, predictable, calm, and rehabilitative, and it seems reasonable that inmates would reward prisons that could provide these[151].

When I read the above. I really did not take it seriously. I thought maybe he was drinking too much wine. Anyone who has spent any more than a week working in a prison at any level might understand that the struggle to keep order supersedes any major change that might upset the normal structure. Prisons are not like schools, colleges, universities, small businesses, etc. whereby change is adaptable for employees. Prison personnel are not amenable at all to a "voucher system." Any break or rearrangement in what is already a challenged bureaucracy would send everyone in a state of confusion and turmoil. There would be tremendous pushback by the employees. As I have tried to reason, there are so many more pressing priorities.

I suppose in an idyllic dream planning could blossom into a reality bearing the fruits of creative programs that are properly budgeted. Then maybe it could make Vololch's thought feasible. I do not see it possible as bureaucracies will never consider prison vouchers. Hey, look at the never-ending argument today within the Department of Education. This political entity is always warring with the enduring American battle in American Education: The public schools versus vouchers for school choice (run privately). And, I say: Vouchers in prisons. Good thought, but never! In theory it would only be applicable at Levels I and II, but "never" at Level III (IV) where the vouchers would be the vulchers laughing cynically and disdainfully.

The voucher argument aside, Skarbek concludes appropriately. But, if he could observe daily the level of venality and ever-present criminality, he would see the impossibility of Prison Reform at the Level III (Level IV in California) prison. There is way too much to overcome. Overriding bureaucratic corruption could make Level III (Level IV in California) run more efficiently. But, unless and until there is better pay and opportunity along with the complete ineptitude responsible for the courses and other periodic instructional compliance methods, there will never be a sense of order and employee satisfaction. Currently, the reality dictates against any possible improvement.

Also, such a consideration goes too far afield. A prison is like such an over-packed suitcase that bulges beyond what a reasonable lock will sustain. As I pointed out in my chapter on "The Misery Index", the level of punishment meted out relates to important variables which ultimately determine a prisoner's classification. Each variable presents so much of a challenge that implementing anything new would rupture the system. An entire house cleaning is needed, but bureaucracy makes it impossible because the people running the system have no incentive (and, believe no knowledge). It's like dieting, it's not physical, it's mental. (Yes, it is physical, but the mindset has to change before the physical will change).

The reality which has to be addressed involves how to manage heinous murderers, rapists and kidnappers when they are classified upon entry. The most important consideration is mental and social status based on prior history. The violent prisoner is vastly different from the unfortunate recidivist whose survival leads to robbing grocery stores. Or, a young ne'er-do-well trying to outrun a state trooper for speeding while smoking marijuana. It is crystal clear that any chance for prison reform lies in a complete reordering of the way prisons are arranged. It seems so simple, but it is not. It will take enlightened thinking, unlike thinking that a voucher program will have any true impact. Fundamentally, Level III (IV in California) numbers must be isolated to be better controlled. Street gangs impact "rehabilitative-programs" because they are so intimately involved with the prison gangs. This is not clearly understood. This requires a more monitored budgetary audit periodically. That would immediately put a restrictor in the wheels of the bureaucracy. As long as Levels I and II expand there will never be resources available for prison reform. Intercept crime at the grassroots (like precognitive, anticipatory planning by well-trained specialists, social programs, attention to the educational needs of the inner-city poor, etc.), and, addressing the bureaucracy issues. This is where the rubber meets the road. Inattention to this reality will just result in business as usual with a continuum of others writing critiques which will just add to the intellectual clutter. It is also very apparent that the writing I have seen does not sufficiently make the difference between prisoner "types" when they discuss issues relating to the prison system (as it relates to overpopulation in the United States versus other countries). There is a reason why this country incarcerates so overwhelmingly greater numbers than elsewhere. Our bureaucracy is drunk with avoidance and reality averse! And Volokh's ideas for vouchers is pure scattershot, not centered thinking based on real life visuals day-to-day. Misery is a potent stimulus, and the "potential" for intra-prison gang violence presents far greater emergency considerations amidst confining spaces where hormones abound and reflexive hostility gushes out of control. As I write this chapter no more poignant example illustrating the height of misery was the riot at Lee Correctional Institution in Bishopville, South Carolina, gaining national news for over a week[152, 153, 154, 155, 156, 157]. During the early hours of Monday, April 15, 2018 a riot broke out due to gang infighting. The ensuing brawling resulted in seven dead and twenty-two severely injured. As a result of rising tensions between internal prison and street gangs, and abetted by corrupt guards (providing contraband for money), a brutal donnybrook led to widespread bloodshed.

In an "n1" facility (a maximum-security prison like Lee Correctional Institution noted above) where violent prisoners abound, the "E" factor (both the expected/unexpected dangers) rises due to a sudden gang clash (for whatever reason). Therefore, the misery index I have delineated dictates that in a facility where violence is already a classification nightmare (because placement in various cell blocks is fragile at best in spite of careful evaluation), any spark can erupt spontaneously from a predetermined expectation of a planned strike. And the strike can be anything from retribution for something that occurred on the street way away from the prison. This scenario is the ultimate misery index price that is paid where gangs contend, prison guards go rogue, and heated exchanges over time result in spontaneous uprising. The "E" factor dangers per numbers of violent prisoners determine the degree of the "misery factor."

At Lee Correctional they peaked to the boiling point. As the numbers of violent, aggressive gang members increase, the expected/unexpected dangers range from a planned one-on- one death to an outright prison riot. The unfortunate fact that makes every violent uprising unique is the absence of a gunas part of the protective gear for guards. This is very controversial to say, but I conclude staunchly that with properly trained guards the proper deterrent is not just power, but the concomitant show of force. This of course is part of the "great divide" (the political correctness) which hampers the resolve and response time guards need to react and bring control to any emergency. The big question: if guards spend so much time at the gun range refining their "gun skills," one should ask "why and for what?" Practice in any endeavor is for the careful display of learned skills! Under current circumstances, understaffing and "no gun use" guards spell uncontained violence. Nothing good can happen, about which reasonable minds would concur. I have personally witnessed young guards in shock after being brutalized by a prisoner. Pepper spray and a stick only goes so far. Every time I saw this, I would think that people on the outside have no idea this goes on. It defies all rational planning. To place a guard (or guards) in any untenable environment where anything goes from day to day is irrational. Make any defense for this and it simply reveals ignorance for what goes on. Elite and more advanced trained guards (special units) are immediately called up from a distant or nearby institution, but so much damage has occurred by the time they get there. When an outright riot occurs, people are already dead and hostages are taken.

Misery, as I tried to capture in Chapter One, already exists as a part of the sheer despondency so rampant throughout a facility. Nowhere in all my life have I experienced so many employed individuals collectively do not want to be where they are. As I stated, most are poor, work two or three jobs, have kids they almost never see, and complain continuously (and rightfully so) about their distress. The very friendly, black female, (overnight) middle-aged, small in stature

Corporal, close to retirement (I discussed earlier) who gave me an earful every night how she was going back to "real" living (never to look back) upon her retirement. She hated every day for twenty-five years. She was filled with an indwelling hatred for the job. Before she let me into the yard from the gate we talked about every social and political issue known to man. I never have met such a friendly, outgoing and graced personality in my life. I always thought to myself that it was her outlook on life, her positive feelings for others that got her through so many years, so many nights in the face of danger. Like so many, many others, being there drained her. But, without being the person she was, survival long-term in that job would not have been possible. I saw so many aspiring young guards (female and male) go through basic training, take all the gun training, all the repetitive computer course updates, etc., all the add-ons that increased the anxiety quotient, only to quit in a fit of rage and disgust for the job. The administrative bureaucrats shrug off common sense, and then wonder how desperation (for just compensation) can lead to the trouble they run into. It's certainly not stupidity. Let's just call it for what it is: corruption twisted around not caring! The tiresome complaint was always the same: little pay, too many hours, and too much danger. Eventually it falls on deaf ears.

I also had a dear friend who was also a young guard, but he was going places. A product of two tours in Afghanistan, he had seen misery in every "crook and cranny" of life. He understood the prison life, but he had been trained to withstand the entire deal. He was either going to be promoted with assured ease or he too would quit. For him it was different because nothing the prison could throw at him could be as miserable as Afghanistan (with all the daily surprise sparking unimaginable terror and fear for his life). But what got to him was the computer compliance courses which he construed as hokey and bureaucratic hocus-pocus! And it was. I could attest to that personally. "Whoopty-doo" he would throw at me when I saw him, casting his right index finger in circles as he pointed it to the sky. When I left, he was still there, but not always positive about whether he would make it. And he was starting to consider another line of work. He was truly a person of strong character, and clever like a fox. He had an insatiable smile and an enduring friendliness every time I ran into him. But, like everybody I knew, the gun issue was always a shake of the head in disgust before blurting out some reflection on the corrupt system. And the strangest irony: prison compliance made them all be at the gun range with sufficient frequency to pass the competency skills test at the end of every calendar year! There is a message in this, I know. But it would be discourteous and just unnecessary rambling. The bureaucracy, the establishment in political control, disabused itself of "the truth and reality" without a wit of concern. Organizations are out of control when their employees are in a world of hurt and disgust.

Tokenism for "reform" is a figment of the imagination for the very pretentious political elite. Nothing advances during lulls between calamities. Once quiet prevails urgency deadens and politicians forget their obligations (hoping, but knowing, people will forget). That is a promise. The misery index is two dimensional. One for the employees, and another for the prisoners. They clash with repeated certainty. Everyone involved constantly feels some level of emotional agony. No doubt, the situation is very different at a Level I and Level II institutions, but the prison atmosphere in general is a repugnant place. Whether there is one gang or 30,000[158], the environment must change at a Level III (IV) institution, but the leadership is woefully lacking and the will invisible. Therecan be no worse context swirling about leaders who think "the working stiff" is not profoundly aware of their do-nothingness.

Consider that to understand what a prison is really like it is necessary to experience it as well as digest the thoughts and opinions of those who have written on the subject. Meticulously researching data to formulate constructive thoughts goes only so far. It is so important to dissect through broad and imprecise reporting. One-dimensional commentary is misleading. It is essential to make very distinctive the contrasts not only in the different prison levels but also the quality of character differences among the prison populations, particularly as personality relates to behavior. The qualitative differences are profound. Level III (IV-California) is otherworldly. Let's conclude this discussion with a review of confinement after a sentence is confirmed and there is a transition from detention to prison.

Before ending this present discussion, I want to get back to prior remarks on danger and vouchers because these ideas engender important points. To repeat, the first statement made by David Skarbek concerns prison gangs. And the second represents a statement by Alexander Volokh, a University of Pennsylvania Professor of Law, reflecting on "prison vouchers" like "school vouchers."

Firstly, in more detail regarding Alexander Volokh's suggestion for "prison vouchers," the idea if ever effectuated would not only allow the fox to guard the hen house, but many foxes. Prisons are not ready for vouchers because the majority of prisoners will reject them as control measures, leaving them under control and not in control of themselves. And this concept begs deeper questions regarding punishments if they do not follow "the prison line". Prisoners do not like to be controlled. They feel their incarceration is control enough. I cannot be dismissive because he has sound ideas, but practically I cannot see them breaking down accepted thinking to create a new program for which they must adopt. And that is why the majority of prisoners just hang around all day doing nothing in particular. I also think bureaucrats (wannabe plutocrats) are one dimensional and defiant against change that does not augment their own position and influence.

Even in a Level I where behavioral issues are, for the most part, easily reconcilable because the personalities are not generally violent. Nevertheless, rigid discipline is necessary because respect is non-existent. The prison system today is what it is, not what theoreticians want it to be. Without strict comportment to measured schedules and oversight, any soft- peddling could lead to deviant behaviors or even an excitation of indiscretions which might make keeping the peace within the yard impossible. Prisoners may not be sufficiently home disciplined growing up nor formally educated but they acutely understand boredom. Lack of some form of discipline spawns trouble. They test the legal limits enough to get them behind bars. Why?

Often forgotten is the fact that once confined the loss of the most precious possession besides good health is the loss of liberty. And, one day each prisoner awakens to this. Maybe not ever aware of this, suddenly a light bulb goes on! Until liberty is taken its appreciation is almost never realized. Allowing them freedom of movement and personal control is necessary if reform ever has any chance to displace the "punish" concept that rules bureaucratic thinking. Politicians talk the talk, but do not walk the walk. Skarbek almost articulates this, but he does not. Fear is always present, but being locked up has a wide range of emotions that lead to no good if prisoners lose purpose and desire. Once laden with the burden of internecine gang warfare, the idea of being productive or reformed is soon a lost idea never to be an opportunity. Finally, the voucher idea may sound nice, and maybe at Level I, but a hopeless thought at Level III (IV in California). It's a lofty ideal better applied to the peaceable world.

What is it about the extreme form of confinement which requires the great amount of attention? Incalculably vacant, often disturbed minds in concert with being nurtured through violence. Think about, for a minute, what happens to people like this when they are warehoused like cattle. Can it be worse? Do people think they are going to behave when confined like sardines in a "can?" Their rejection is inevitable. And where do they turn? To the prison gangs. The prison gangs are thus intrinsically hardened, viscerally one dimensional, and intentionally criminal, yet gangs serve as buffers for protection and a sense of identity to survive. On the one hand it is magnetic-like that the prisoners be drawn to their family-like orientation as their buffer zones for protection and a sense of identity to survive. Morales, however, reminds his readers repeatedly that at Level III (IV) life is "Blood In, Blood Out!" Power, money and control are so bound around their daily lives that they clash and confront each other for "the holy grail" of prison life: drugs. "Reform" as a consideration will never be in the prisoners' lexicon. This would-be fantasyland, a Shangri La of other worldliness. Loose-ended, temporary alliances to maneuver in and around rival gangs for strategic advantages are the true reality and everything by survival arrangements. When they do not work out, someone winds up bludgeoned or curled up face down in a blood spattered, gruesome looking, lifeless final solution. But I always say that at times a blind squirrel finds an acorn. So, perhaps once in a blue moon a Level III thug may have a spiritual awakening and defy the odds. I know this does occur. However, this is not mainstream. The "stock and trade" of a gang member for the most part is the life of violence. And, it will continue until death. This is a fact that all the arguments against mass incarceration statistics cannot overlook. In fact, it supports the importance for classification specificity when making that argument.

One problem is that mixed level populations do support the argument that less violent prisoners should not be in surroundings where violent gangs will draw them in. Until there is more substantive evidence to the contrary this is fact. San Quentin which houses about six thousand prisoners is a good example. It supports a very distinct array of foundational programs with the intention "to reform" and redirect the prisoner's mindset through educational, vocational and religious formats so as to prepare prisoners for a productive life after incarceration. It is a very formal arrangement with highly skilled and dedicated personnel. I see it as more of a show than anything else. It might reveal "do-goodism," but I firmly believe mixed populations will fail in what they want to achieve because of the persistent lockdown threats (which are constant). Maybe someday, but race and gang riots frequently interrupt the schedules causing their lockdowns. Tedious repetition becomes quite unfortunate for those prisoners who are drawn into the explosive rioting (which ultimately will affect their sentencing and paroling). Mixed populations are more common, but reform is almost impossible when gang violence is always present. Gangs are expanding, not decreasing in size and numbers. And the reform prison movement must realize this. The reasons are obvious: inner cities where leadership is in a failed state.

But I have to conclude with a Morales dictum: prison gangs are more violent than street gangs, and to repeat: they fixate on control, drugs and power. But, I'll add this thought: inner city gang violence is on the upswing! And to repeat again: "Blood In and Blood Out" means that each gang member is in for taking life, and will get out when theirs is taken. This is a misfortune that is reality. If some are lucky, they will die from old age and one of the medical diseases which comes with age. Perhaps then the system should concentrate on reforming those that can be reformed, diminish prison overpopulation, and restructure the system to bring it into the 21st century. Is it possible? Yes. Is it probable? No. Or, at least, not at this time.

To bring this full circle, the concept of "the gang" conjures up much more than an antisocial feeling. Otherwise, individuals getting together for a common cause would be defined as a social group, an association, an alliance, a union, an organization, or anything that reflects a union of common positive interests. A gang has the negative ring of a syndicate orientation with a leader drawing from those that follow for pursuit of less than savory and acceptable interests. The gangs of American prisons exist for survival and echo crime driven dividends, be it drug smuggling, murder, child kidnapping for prostitution, gun profiteering, money laundering, or anything that keeps them ahead of the rivals anxious to take them down. There definitely is an emotional commitment as reflected in the body tattoos. Identification with a gang is essential for each gang member to feel a sense of purpose and reason for being needed. For hardworking people this is hard to digest. This thinking is in conflict with the traditional community However, even criminals need to feel a sense of worth even as remote and in cross purpose to the way life's meant to be. In my discussions with hardcore criminals I have always detected a glimmer of natural instincts. If the level of criminality were not so depraved, there would be hope for reform. But gangs dwell and thrive in savage, cold-blooded murderous environments. This is arguable for a lot of people because it is very difficult to accept that there exists such raw evil. Life has lost its meaning, and, within the prison walls their bleak, narrow world continues to darken. Unlike individuals who have committed crimes and are not living in a world of moral perversion (Level I and level II) reparative and compliant techniques of reform are very possible.

If this chapter serves one message, it is to drive home the fact that prison reform for Level I and II individuals is a must. Rather than throwing good money to bad it is incumbent for responsible leaders to make an earnest effort to once and for all establish a legal pathway for prison reform. So many politicians blow empty words into the wind, and that must end. They must be held accountable.

Another very important point: Over-prosecuting, over- sentencing, hardened and recalcitrant parole boards with political constraints, and corruption up-and-down the bureaucratic juggernaut (local, county, regional, state and federal government) are just filling filthy and overcrowded prisons. There they will languish on the taxpayer's dime when so many people would benefit from a reform which would enhance society as well, making lives productive. Think about vocational training, serving industrial job needs, and so many other areas as in agriculture, factory jobs, the fishing industry, etc. When the average person thinks about the prison system, he/she doesn't see the inside of a failing system. The outside world witnesses the heinous crimes on television as they are propagated on the news because "if it bleeds it leads." The far greater number of prisoners in this country are so often victims of a system that has slammed the door shut. Just as there is extreme criminality there are self-serving prosecutors as well as overly punitive judges. As most people read so often, wealthier people seek and receive a different kind of justice just because they can afford more skilled lawyering. Violence is a reflection of mental impairment which employs an out-of- control urge to satisfy a sensibility so profound whereby only an adverse objective is the result. This sensibility according to James Gilligan is "shame". As he clearly describes "group" (as in a nation: Nazism, Hitler's Third Reich) or "individual" shame is elicited because the shamed person or group feels so violated that violence itself becomes defensive. He expresses this thought as such:

"Violence toward others may be thought of as the behavioral equivalent of paranoia, or the behavioral version of it—its hypostasis, the translation into terms of physical reality of the waking dream (or nightmare) which paranoia represents in terms of words and thoughts, fantasies and delusions. But paranoia is the form of psychopathology that results when a person's ability to differentiate between feelings and facts is overwhelmed by feelings of shame…Murder represents (for the murderer) the ultimate act of self-defense, a last resort against being overwhelmed by shame and "losing one's mind", an attempt to ward off psychosis or "going crazy."[159]

The imagery Gilligan captures substantiates my sense that the most violent behavior is the keystone for why prisons exist, namely to protect vulnerable citizenry from such extreme behavior. For whatever psychosis, there is no guarantee that such behavior is controllable enough to protect even the most willing public. Baron-Cohen defines this as Zero negative (Psychopath-Type P[160]). The hyper-empathy he suggests as an approach to what others define as pure evil is too risky. I do not feel it possible for people to grasp the unbelievably dark nature of such violent criminals. Seeing them face-to-face is enough to scare most people working in the correctional institutions. People would not believe such deviant behavior. It's too extreme and spine-chilling. To the lay public, daily stress is burdensome enough. As Baron-Cohen states:

Empathy is a universal solvent[161]. Any problem immersed in empathy becomes soluble. It is effective as a way of anticipating and resolving interpersonal problems, whether this is a marital conflict, an international conflict, a problem at work, difficulties in a friendship, political deadlocks, a family dispute, or a problem with a neighbor[162].

I agree with his thoughts in their totality, but not as applied to violent offenders. The reason: violent prisoners do not understand nor concern themselves with what makes other people tick because they do not have the sensibility to care! As I have stated throughout this writing, there is a viable and truly necessary reason to alter hardcore legal issues dealing with crime, criminality and over-incarceration. It is to a fault that the judicial system is just exploding the prison population. To wit,

Baron-Cohen's statement is a bromide for all people responsible for prison overpopulation. Bureaucrats of all stripes should take "empathy" very seriously. As to the extreme end of the violence spectrum, Gilligan conjures up a certain reasoning for such behavior, and Baron-Cohen wants to extend a fig leaf in the way of hyper-empathy. However, staring into the vacant minds and hollow eyes of the worst kind of killers (as I have many times), so blindly committed to gang retributive justice, I cannot fathom the reasoning that the general public should ever be exposed to such danger. The prisons are overflowing with individuals falsely and overly sentenced, comprising vast numbers, who deserve our attention. Baron-Cohen's statement above exemplifies where empathy should be universally applied. Even then, it may impose too high a standard for many people.

So, to understand that that there is a difference between hardened, savage criminals and people who may commit a crime for any number of reasons is a problem unto itself. As I walked every morning through all the thunderous iron/steel gates in a maximum-security prison, the platitudinous, preachy words like "honesty, respect, responsibility, loyalty…" always rung hollow. Without actionable resolve, what good are the words? I would think to myself that this moralistic preaching and mind control would be far more appropriate in a different setting. Level III institutions are not generally conducive to self- actualization of character values. Theirs are far more fundamental: survival. To gain meaningful action on this very sore subject, a willing leadership has never been more needed. As a previous governor of Massachusetts once said: "A fish rots from the head first."[163] The following line from Len Marrella may be somewhat treacly and pipe-dreaming, but it is meaningful in reinforcing the importance of leadership on behalf of any mission in life: It is often noted that we really learn something when we have to teach someone else. So, if we want to learn, we have to lead. This is not just a matter of winning a leadership position. It is in fact simply taking advantage of daily opportunity. All of us are leaders—those who influence others. Similarly, we are followers—those who are influenced by others. We are both leaders and followers at,the same time. In the process of helping others to develop competence and character, we must give them leadership opportunity and encourage them to take advantage of the opportunity. In the process of continuously developing ourselves, we must exercise leadership, growing and learning from our experiences[164].

There is no doubt that politics and politicians would benefit periodically from reminding themselves of this message from a man who served at NATO, in Vietnam and with the Defense Department after having graduated from the United States Military Academy at West Point. There is sufficient wisdom in this thought without which I only see prison reform being blather from generation to generation.

It should be stated in deference to centralized governance that private prisons were established to take state and federal overflow because private enterprise "can do it better!" Well, private prisons turn a profit, but they also suffer from blatant corruption. The only difference between the entire "group think" bureaucrats is a more subtle form of greed, mismanagement and cover-up. The obvious absence of ethics makes the case for "the irresistible force meeting the immovable object!"[165] Each generation seems to be a blend of givers and takers, and the takers are always in control with the givers like caged hamsters peddling totally exhausted around their wheels, going nowhere fast! Prison reform is needed, but seemingly impossible. It is hard for reformers, but harder for bureaucrats to give up control and money.

CHAPTER 5

Islam and the Radicalization of the American Prison System

"The Sharia is a manual for an Islamic civilization…
All Muslims believe that the Koran contains the precise words of the creator god of the universe-Allah…
There are 91 Koran verses that say that Mohammed is the perfect example for all humanity to imitate in the smallest detail. What Mohammed said and did is called the Sunna…
The Sunna is found in two texts: the Sira (the biography of Mohammed) and the Hadith (his traditions)."[166]
"Islam is not just a religion, but an entire way of life. It is a separate and complete civilization with its own political system. All of Islam is based on the Koran, the Sira and the Hadith."[167] "Sharia is nothing more than a condensation and extrapolation of the Koran and the Sunna. Therefore, it is impossible to understand the Sharia without some understanding about the doctrine found in the Koran."[168]
"We must talk about Islam in the political real, because it is a powerful political system…Islam is called the religion of peace, but its politics are the politics of jihad and war. The peace comes only after you submit. The religion does not affect the non-Muslim, but its politics affect every person."[169]
CULTURE: "the customary beliefs, social forms, and material traits of a racial, religious, or social group also: the characteristic features of everyday existence (such as diversions or a way of life) shared by people in a place or time"[170]

We are always talking about danger and how society deals with it. The discussion almost never frames it by the way I just did, but it is very important that when I analyze the American prison system through the prism of my experiences and my intellectual interpretation "culture" is the cradle in which different peoples grow and mature. Prisons are multi-cultural because they house people from all over the world. Danger within a prison sparks most often as a result of the way prisoners look, think and behave as the result of their country of origin. Gangs, in particular, reflect these differences. This makes their management extremely fragile. Multicultural countries like the United States face the inevitable challenge of ethnic and race assimilation, and it is in the best interest of people to retain their identity in terms of their cultural origin while learning to love among each other with respect and understanding. At best this works harmoniously, but at its worst hostility and an atmosphere of danger and fear are always present. Managing hostility is the greatest challenge of every prison. At its extreme, prisons can be sewers of death and destruction, or, at its best (its ideal) prisons should be rehabilitative. And, this is where differences of cultures impact living in tight quarters in a small community are magnified. The definition of "CULTURE" above reflects the vast array of specific defining characteristics of all people. Thrust together in a relatively small city-like community where cultural differences are magnified is one of the greatest challenges known to man. This observation was the seed for this book. Think about neighborhoods all around the world. The most important ingredient for survival is health. How health is preserved depends on how people interact in order to manage the tools in the hands of educated people to aid in the management of disease. If peoples and countries get along, then health is managed at the highest level. When relations between peoples deteriorate physical and mental disease takes over. For this reason, be it for neighborhoods or very small communities, it is implicit for survival to learn how to respect the people who make up our most proximal individuals and social groups. Survival demands this and failure results in social decline. The best that prison management can do is to recognize this basic tenet of life so that with every level of detention personnel are best equipped with the intellectual insight and training to best supervise multicultural prison communities. They run amok because gangs are perpetually at war with each other. When people discuss "prison reform" it is tantamount for any tangible outcome to understand that not all prisoners can be or will ever be rehabilitated. It is important to fundamentally realize what is possible and exercise common sense to ultimately make it possible for prisoners who will succeed "on the outside." A lot goes on inside a prison, and the greatest threat today is gang growth and the insidious radicalization of prisoners. The following is an in-depth view of the multicultural prison communities. The influences impacting prisons are enduring and highly menacing. Though the dangers of prison gangs are virtually insurmountable given the present construct of prisons, the conversion of prisoners to Islam and their radicalization has escalated them to a completely new level. Radicalization is the eight-hundred- pound gorilla in the room being totally overlooked. It is all about political correctness in addition to a failure to understand the problems that radicalization foments. As if gang violence is not enough to keep in tow, along come newly "radicalized believers" with a hypnotic, literal allegiance to the Koran with an abject fervor and religious zeal. Such radicals account for 9 per cent of the prison population, and yet Muslim prisoners only account for 0.8% of the prison population. The reality is stark because they are increasing in numbers by reason of radicalization of young, wayward American prisoners as well as illegal immigrants who sneak across borders to find their way to Muslim communities where they blend under protective cover. Not taking this seriously is irresponsible and naïve. Key to understanding the grip radical Islam has on this country is understanding what the stringent political side demands of its followers since its inception in the seventh century. I am not here to discuss a person's dedication to any religion, but I want to illuminate the average person who does not understand the convection-like commands delineated in the Koran which Mohammed lays out for his followers. Sharia law is the bedrock of the radical Muslim world. It places the unbelievers (the Kafir, the foreigners) and violators of its dictates to violent submission by death. The law is also a curse suborned through Mohammed to victimize Muslim women who fail to capitulate to prescribed behavior in the Koran through his own words. The soft underbelly for most followers of Western religions does not come across throughout the Koran where the words of Mohammed are literally followed to make all people acquiesce to his commands. "...*Islam is NOT just a religion. It is a complete civilization with a detailed political system and a legal code-the Sharia.*"[171] [emphasis mine] Philip Haney, one of the founding members of the Department of Homeland Security, concludes in his book:

> It's true: sharia cannot be changed, not for democracy, and not even for America. The constitution of the Muslim brotherhood, and Islam, is the Quran (or, Koran, as it is variously spelled). It is not compatible with our political system, which is based on the self-evident truths of life, liberty, and the pursuit of happiness, not the rigid statutes of Islamic law[172] [emphasis mine].

It is important to remember that the United States has undergone a radical transformation since 9/11/2001. American society is no longer a dependably protected society. Many people do not understand the impact of political Islam, and most religious Muslims have not been vocal enough in making the differentiation from the basic tenets of the religion. Many, in fact, do not straddle the line between religious and political Islam, claiming outright that it is purely a radical religion with the Qur'an as their playbook. I personally cannot make this distinction because I am not an expert, but I can vouchsafe those doubters who cannot defend the so-called passive Muslims who do not remonstrate the radical terrorist events in defense of their religious posture. Orthodoxy when it is destructive as it was on 9/11/2001 should not be protected nor excused. The prison system as well, with all its gangs and notorious violence is really not the place for radicalization

Guards and officers right up to the wardens are not educated nor aware of the impending numbers due to conversions. Radical Islam fits right into the gang modus operandi. Sharia law is a deeply rooted way of life in Islamic life. Dr. M. Zuhdi Jasser has been very adamant in his personal mission to defend the average Muslim as a peaceful, devoted and loving person[173]. His message is instructive, but it blurs and obscures the reality. His book is a wonderful text supporting Islam as a peaceable religion. And, for the most part, it is. Since his book was published in 2012 a lot has changed in the United States. First and foremost, President Obama is out of the White House. This has resulted in a change in the language (both in frankness and description) which has restored a sense of honesty which was buried during the Obama administration. In fact, Obama denied the use of the word "radical." Telling the truth has been so cannibalized that its spirit and trust took a nose dive. In fact, the number of mass murder events by radicalized Islamic terrorists became historical events.Obama would not even acknowledge the horror of it all. His language became monotone and disgracefully ho hum! It remains to be seen if the country can rebound to an acceptable sense of good feeling ever again. Listening to the mothers and fathers of mass murder victims of a crazed, radicalized psychiatrist Major Nidal Malik Hasan, July, 2009) of Islamic ethnicity at Fort Hood in Texas was incontrovertibly horrifying and appalling[174]. Yet, Obama slow walked it and couched the words of his post-event statement. His Presidency soft peddled radicalization over so many years that it allowed it to balloon through many pockets of the United States, and particularly in the prison system. His purposefully restricted recognition allowed radicalism to germinate and expand like a subsurface fungus. The country has a proactive President now. He has made very effective changes to the good. Probably his most dynamic and significant leadership has been the elimination of ISIS activity in the Middle East. His message to radical Islam has been loud and certain. It's unfortunate that he can be quite uncouth and loutish. It deters from his message when the country finally elected a real leader. The contrast in the way two Presidents comport themselves could not be more stark. Obama could not tell the truth and his terrible deceit preyed on desperate, uninformed people incapable of seeing through his cynicism[175, 176]. His slanted and tendentious radicalism veiled in an alternating snarky yet eloquence belied his responsibilities to the monolithic nature of the Presidency. The result was an outpouring of a political correctness with all its disdain for truth and justice. History became distorted and fractured, and suddenly our cities became breeding grounds for the worst kind of radicalism ever to hit this country. Obama opened the door for the chaos and confusion taking the country down today. The pity is that his Presidency was effective in two regards: (1) he had a supporting media that covered his lies, deception, and use of the alphabet agencies to go after his opposition (with calumny and complete disregard for honorable, hard-working people); and, (2) his support cabinet who professed bold and lasting lies in his support while they carried out a carefully calculated destructive domestic and foreign policy (which was an unscrupulous transformation of American traditions). The Obama legacy will be positive in his own mind and to those who wanted to believe in change, but, who were handed an ignominious backhand with a luscious smile in his one-man pony act. He did nothing for the needy. The radicalization I experienced is a manifestation of the Obama presidency. The real enemy was not the Republican Party (which historically did more for blacks). It was the ingrained, thorough deceit of the Democratic Party which Obama put under a spell with his 2008 Denver, Colorado acceptance speech for American political "transformation."in the 2008 Denver, Colorado. He dazzled the jejune by vocal romancing! Probably the best speech maker in recent times, he could divert a cat from a fish truck. He was the master of empty slogans and words in a most articulate manner. To this day, his followers still worship his presence and Presidency, guffawed by his image without any tangible sense of his damage. The radicalization his administration allowed in this country, however, will materially affect the country for many years to come. Since Dr. Jasser wrote his book, the witches' brew Obama stirred with an unmatched guile has savaged and divided the country like a cancer eating away at the body politic with ruthless satisfaction. Under his "rule" the Islamic radicalism went from an incubator footing to a starkly disseminated presence. He promised "change" and dealt his full hand. He departed his national crime scene after eight years not like a Kentucky thoroughbred, but like a heavily worked donkey. Now down the street from the White House he is encamped to continue a "deep state" assault on the country. The health of the country is not in his agenda, and it befuddles so many beguiled by his bravado rather than his hollow accomplishments. He was a mesmerizing President who seeded danger through flowery, unproductive speeches while cashing in on a retirement bent on venality while attempting to obstruct and fillet his successor. For Dr. Jasser, as the title of his book states: it is A Battle for the Soul of Islam! With certainty, as the street saying goes: "better the devil you know than the devil you don't know!" Markedly contrasted to President Obama, Dr.Jasser's most benevolent and sincere mission was to explain and disseminate the truth about the gentle believer is an honest appeal. Unfortunately and concomitantly Dr. Jasser's book paralleled the end of the Bush Presidency and the beginning of Obama's. He encouraged in his book that the Muslim family did not reflect the element of radicalism present during those administrations. President Bush established a positive message against the backdrop of two assaults of major proportions (World Trade Center Bombing in 1993, and, the Twin Towers in 2001). As traumatic to the country as these two bombings were, the American mentality was to restore a sense of normalcy while not being naïve to the "new way of life!" Radical Islamic terrorism was in the country to say[177]. President Obama spoke eloquently recalling the horrific nature of the attacks, but time would reveal the shallow nature of his words. For someone like Dr. Jasser, who was forced to his way of life as a Peaceful Muslim, the enormity must have been gnawing at his spirit. Time played out, but President Obama's window of opportunity to recast the spirit of the nation by rallying the country against radical Islamic terrorism was slammed shut by his very passive aggressive approach to the scourge of very brazen sequential attacks around the nation. There is nothing more to say about Obama, but there is enough to say how the pious Muslim should never be in the same conversation with any form of extremism. If one looks at the three major religions (Islam, Judaism, and Christianity), there are extremist groups within all three. The misfortune is that all the senseless killing after 2008 when Obama assumed the Presidency could have been deterred with true (not snide) leadership. The country under President Trump has restored a sense of honesty back into the national discussion so the country no longer fears referring to Islamic radical terrorism. It came with a long overdue spoken truth. It turns out that Trump is also a "truth stretcher" as well[1178], but he is certainly not deceitful. It the nature of politicians to twist words in a very elusive way. What does that mean? Trump is a politician even if he has never held elected office. Life by its very nature demands "truth" to be sold to defend a policy or argument. Everyone has a political side. Let's call it being diplomatic. Trump was labeled as someone who is not a politician, clean of political tendencies. So, let's just call it what it is. He is s genuine politician. He could not have accomplished what he did in the building trade (and, with all the politicians he dealt with along the way) to be "a virgin, untested businessman." So, I do not believe for one minute that anyone who has traveled in the New York circles that he did is not a politician. I would rather say he just never held an official political office. In fact, he appears well-rooted into the land of "politicos." Trump really denies the truth at times, be it out of ignorance or carelessly, but he is not an intentional prevaricator. I cannot say this about Obama. Even Jonathan Gruber, a MIT economist, in a panel at the University of Pennsylvania in October 17, 2013[179, 180], frankly said on video that President Obama lied about the Affordable Care Act (aka Obamacare) to get it passed. Between the two there is a world of difference. Because of my distain for politics and politicians, I will always describe forthrightly what I see and understand. The acts of terror being perpetrated in the name of Islam were being designated as "Islamic Radicalism!" Dr. Jasser carefully justifies his belief system not only to defend his fervent upbringing but to support the plurality of peace bearing Muslims worldwide. Speaking truth to power, Dr. Jasser makes a case with an honor and dignity which contrasts to a Jihadist/Wahhabist-like assault going on in front of the country's eyes (the majority of whom do not understand the religion)[181, 182]. With President Trump the country's divided hatreds have sadly remained intact. He has materially done wonders for the country, but his tone and overly "in your face New York behavior" does not "sell!" It's a shame that he does not get that. With more refinement most of the disharmony might have been averted. His ambitious accomplishments speak for themselves, but he does not seem to care what others think of him. He finds it far too easy to cast people asunder if they disagree with him. He may know the art of the deal, but he does not deal artfully. He would get a lot further if he were genteel and far more politically pleasant. He has an iron will that does not relent, nor does he possess the savvy to understand that sugar advances a cause more than vinegar. His reliance on Twitter has been a gateway to his irreverence and bottled-up frustrations. He is so incapable of a soft, winning touch (maybe with a sprinkle of occasional humor) that he is leaving the other side of the divided country with a venomous foray against his persona. I would say they are exacting their anger in a self-destructive manner, but Trump cannot get out of his way long enough to see he is raining on his own parade. He festers with disdain over the radical left media. Their visceral defiance, on the other hands, does not warrant such scathing defiance. If he could only learn that the office demands a maturity that breeds alliance and cooperation his life would be easier, and he would accomplish even more. He lacks a mature perception of what it takes to restore the honor of the office of the Presidency that Obama decimated. In Level I and Level II prisons there is a greater effort to afford the prisoners productive learning experiences to condition them for their release when job opportunities will (not "might") require familiarity, if not experience, with hiring questions demanding specific answers. The inability to be prepared for life outside is at grassroots of high recidivism rates. As daunting as the challenges of prison are, release into the "real world" again are more so, even cruel because life is not a walk in the park. Level III (IV) prisons are occupied with just keeping a sense of order so that occupational or basic educational programs are offered, but they require the prisoners to be compliant and without behavioral issues. So, right out of the gate this is very chancy and limited due to the environment in which gangs dominate 24/7 with a sad preoccupation for "business operations" which inevitability lead to some violent conclusion. In order for prison reform to become a reality someday there has to be a political will in sync with rehabilitative programs as in Denmark "for all," not "some." There has to be a complete retooling of the thinking by those who run prisons without concentrating on policy paperwork, constant course work for employees which are totally overbearing and unnecessary, a coordinated approach by people who are familiar with occupational and educational course design for specific grade levels, and concentration on bringing the prisoners closer to real world conditioning to schedules and trustworthiness. To return to life as it is, and not as it may be in any prison environment, prisoners must learn responsibility. The only way to reduce recidivism is to restore confidence and provide the prisoners with a defined ability and self-confidence that they can readapt to the challenges of the real world. In this regard, none of this will have an effect if gangs and gang life are not isolated away from prisoners who will eventually qualify for release because gang-bangers are in a different world and are non-rehabilitative. This is an assessment that must be accepted. The reproducibility of violence is a severe hindrance to change as well as a stifled mentality. Of course, there may be "some" diamonds in the rough, but they are limited. If a change to the existing reality is not accepted mixing hardcore killers into any environment is a losing proposition. A willingness to fashion a new way of thinking will ultimately establish positive returns, but it takes revolutionary changes. Reverse thinking is necessary to make a difference because the system is a bureaucratic mess. Languor and laziness in the way prisons are run today reflect a total lack of openness for change and a determination to effect change. The greatest influence on the way prisons are organized and administered redounds in every way to politicians and political influences. This is where all problems start and where they proceed. And, this is the reason why every state has to have the kind of enlightened leadership "to start" on a new course. It would be naïve to think that euphemistic language and frothy promises will be effective. No they will not. However, change requires a brave adjustment in the way state governments do business with regard to prison organization. A great awakening is the only solution because the way the United States population is expanding with a major ethnic expansion which carries language and cultural adjustments. I want to bring into focus a number of thoughts which make gangs both in the inside and outside such a growing and disturbing impediment to both law enforcement and prison containment. They are the bane of those whose lifeblood is the protection of society, and "living" evidence of Simon Baron-Cohen's[110] description of Zero-negative Psychopath (Type P) individuals. Poverty, lack of education, unemployment and drugs lead to behaviors that result in questionable associations, delinquent juvenile actions which grow into criminality and eventual problems with the law. How far each individual distances herself/himself from the mainstream and to what degree of crime evolves will determine a future that goes downhill into a mindset where like-minded individuals accelerate negative outcomes. Prison and street gangs are the results of people who follow a road of crime for lack of no other alternatives. While gangs become their safe harbor, they lead them further and further into darkness and danger. How do such individuals get there? I have to reference a thought which really hits home: ...it is almost a truism that poverty breeds crime, and poor people are certainly more likely than rich people to commit crimes. But poor people do not commit crimes. Thus, there is a serious flaw in the theory that poverty causes crime. Usually, poverty doesn't cause crime...Evil or violent tendencies are usually met with strong restraining forces, most of which can be conveniently categorized as self-control...The immediate proximal cause of violence is the collapse of these inner restraining forces...All that is necessary to stop restraining or preventing it. Once the restraints are removed, there are plenty bearing Muslims worldwide.for people to strike out at each other[111]. Now that is a fascinating viewpoint from a very creditable source. I would agree except when individuals find themselves in prison and refusal to find a group (gang) for protection will lead downhill. At this point self-control loses out to survival. And, this is the difference between scientific analysis and practical considerations that most never see (and therefore do not understand). The most important reason for gang alliance is survival. The more dangerous the prison environment the greater the need for "group" associations; e.g. gangs. Murder and non-violent crimes are in the crosshairs of the demographics noted previously. Prison and street gangs pump and circulate its poisons throughout every major United States city (and today, though not the core area, rural America). The perilous, disruptive, socially upheaving drugs: methamphetamine, cocaine, heroin (and now fentanyl and carfentanil) as well as all the synthetic opioids (oxycodone, OxyContin (the extended release form of oxycodone, etc.). But because it is the most abused among prisoners, marijuana is in the mix, and, to a lot of professional thinking, a gateway drug. Crimes, whether they involve homicide, drugs, gun trafficking, human trafficking for prostitution, etc. are the life force of incarceration. Eliminate them and prisons would essentially disappear. (Maybe not totally because human beings would probably find some other deleterious behavior, but the above point is important). Believing they shall be is unrealistic, and maybe even romantic. Incarceration is a containment process, not an event. For this reason, it is imperative to know and understand it. Before I formulate a few judgments let's examine some pertinent facts. They can be distorted according to different personal viewpoints and what they want to emphasize. That does not concern me as long as they are put in proper perspective. (And, I am using pre-COVID- 19 statistics because I feel they are more realistic. At some point, society will return to a settling normality. The environment today is an aberration and cannot continue). The national homicide rate in the United States has risen 11% in 2015 after falling for twenty-five years. In the cities of Chicago, Philadelphia, Houston, Los Angeles and New York, homicide rates showed the greatest alarming increase, and particularly the percentage of gun murders. (The statistics for the COVID- 19 environment are inflated due to BLM, Anti-Fa, and other radical anarchical right-and-left wing gangs overtaking major cities). The most dramatic change was in the city of Chicago where in 2016 the number of killings rose from 485 to 764[112]. One report (Federal Bureau of Investigation 2012113) reviewed murder, forcible rape, robbery and aggravated assault throughout the United States in 2012. The country witnessed a steady rise in all four categories (murder: an increase of 1.1% in 2012 from 2011; and, 0.2% increase for forcible rape, a decrease of 0.8% for robbery, and an increase of 1.1% for aggravated assault, all for the same time period (2011-2012). In general, though not wanting to diminish the significance of any increase in such a throttling of human-to-human level of crime, these remained fairly constant for the years 2011 to 2012 when contrasted to the horrific increase over the years through the 1980's and 1990's from lows during the 1970's (Bureau of Justice n.d.). However, in an FBI report (FBI National Press Office 2016) comparing the same crimes, the increases were dramatic going from 2014 to 2015. In that period violent crime rose 3.1%, rape 6.3%,robbery 4.6 %, and murder and non-negligent manslaughter was up 10.8 %. Why? The association with the pandemic of drug trafficking. A statistic that is of considerable relevance reveals that from 2002 to 2011 the average homicide rate for blacks was 6.3 times higher than the rate for whites[114]. He is a throwback to Nero who fiddled as Rome burned, and Trump's fiddle is his Twitter feed. There is honor in quiet decency. Disdain inevitably results from crass behavior. A Twitter feed is not a toy for childish outreach. It is a source of meaningful, brief statements to reach out to an anxious country. Yet, despite his puerile behavior he continues to engender a dedicated following. I believe he will retain the Presidency because of his terrific accomplishments which the Democrats besmirch and cavil daily. I am always askance by his reactive nature! It is so myopic and juvenile. When there is a constant barrage of infighting nothing gets settled, and the problems get worse. However, let's be assured that the war Pamela Geller so eloquently lays forth in her books is the same radical minority of Islam that Dr. Jasser describes[183, 184]. Unless and until a consensus emerges to bring back the radically left cities and lands from such entrenched hatreds and violence, justice and calm will not be restored. The number one role a President plays is that of a leader, one who can be building unity and accord. The social pathologies now emerging with such frequency are separating the regressive left states away from the mainstream with remarkable hostility. Displacing people by cynical talk and a constant beat down with rebuke and ridicule is equally childish and subversive. It accomplishes nothing sound, and perpetuates hatreds. Trump is trying to distinguish himself by bringing the country back to pre-eminence. However, his business credentials are overlaid by boyish pettiness and a total lack of refinement. No matter how he speaks out in the hustings (he loves so dearly) somehow it appears that no one ever educated him to the fact that in the long run people will remember you more for your warmth and kindness than the words that speaks for disgust and anger. His pettifogging is churlish and distracting. The pity is that "prison reform" is one of the most urgent domestic needs, yet he does not emote the maturity and sense of steadfast reliance to be a consensus builder. He actually does far better on the international stage. Obama,[185] on the other hand, ran as a left-wing community organizer with a Shia Muslim upbringing. His education along the Saul Alinsky[186] doctrine of communism bamboozled the electorate, mostly unhappy with Republican President George W. Bush. The country wanted a change and Obama was a charmer with the fancy to "turn a word!" George W. Bush was a nice man, but he was incompetent and had leftovers from his father's days who controlled the West Wing. Unfortunately, he was a political marionette with unconvincing leadership skills. 9/11 gave him national exposure, but he could not sustain a pathway to economic profitability. He left the economy with significant trade and tariff issues. Obama took office with flim-flam and inspirited the country with his smile, energy, and imposing mannerisms. Superficially, he would be refreshing after a dullard-like Bush. However, he was, indubitably, insufficiently vetted so his false bravado captured a relatively unsuspecting electorate. From the start of his presidency to its end he ruptured the economy. The "deep state" he now ambitiously sustains through his malevolent minions is deepening an already grand country divide. Most critics complain they have never understood his thinking to reduce the greatness of the United States to the level of a third world country. And he did it with a snide grin as crowds crowed and grinned at his vaudevillian performances out on the political stump. Before more politically sensitive crowds or formal diplomatic presentations the grousing over prior years of American superpower arrogance continued shamefully throughout his presidency. This all continued as he plotted meticulously to destroy the very support system of American life through Dodd-Frank[187] as he over-regulated small business into collapse. If business was not enough, he took advantage of an activist jurist, The Chief Justice of the Supreme Court (John Roberts) to burgled health care from hard-working middle- class families by making ACA (Affordable Care Act, or, Obamacare[188]) unaffordable. Young people were forced to either pay a penalty or over pay for health care way too extensive for their general needs. Unfortunately, Chief Justice was the determinant vote, and, he treated it as a tax to getit passed. In addition, Obama used the IRS as a cudgel to decimate 501c3 Tax Exempt organizations by rejecting their exemptions and forcing unaffordable legal defense. He decimated the United States military by vastly insufficient financial support for significant upgrades from old planes and ships. Many other issues characterized his methodical attack on the pulse of the American way of life. The people whosaid they did not understand were afraid to call out his serpentine behavior. He was simply a cancer to the American individualism which catapulted this country to greatness. All this cloaked his real ambition: to replace American fundamentalism with Islamic fundamentalism All the while he was surreptitiously and meaningfully destroying this country with a coterie of "suits" guarding him like third world lap dogs. At the time, there was no will to expose and curtail this. All anybody could do to face him with public scrutiny was to tread lightly and sheepishly. Obama was a jackanapes with hideous intent. It was sorrowful to see it unfold, but more incredible to view his view following hoodwinked like machined puppets in a toy factory. As John Bolton wrote in the foreword of Pamela Geller's book: Barack Obama is the first post-American president, as his statements and actions since his inauguration have proven beyond dispute. Central to his worldview is rejecting "American exceptionalism," and the consequences that flow from discarding this foundational belief so widely held by U.S. citizens[189] [emphasis mine]. Donald Trump was elected to succeed Obama, and just in time to rescue the country. Without Obama's terrible two terms of killing the economy and selling out American foreign policy, there would never have been a need for Donald Trump. Obama inherited an economy Bush capsized and, with disbelief to those economists in the know, ran it further into the ground. Obama deniers, however, festooned him with extraordinary accomplishments which were empty and overly embellished. There is an old concept that is truthful. When addressing an individual or a crowd for the sake of teaching or just lending a particular expertise psychologists and psychiatrists will warn the following: people want to know that you care before what you know! And this point redounds to the Obama/ Trump difference. Obama is a poseur, narcissist, swaggerer type; aka "Speaker-in-Chief." He is smooth in a very convincing manner. His tones are infectious even as he may promise policies he can never deliver. On the other hand, Trump is raw, lacking style, loud, hurtful, and rough in a most aggressive way. Obama reads his lines well, Trump does not and his delivery is unconvincing and poor. But, Obama provides enough bluster to impress. All in all, Obama is smooth, Trump is very awkward. However, on policy Obama delivers very, very short on most everything. And, without advice knows very little about government. Trump, even in his ungainly approach to people, is a business man, and he accomplished more in three plus years than any President in history. He is a doer par excellence! This essentially the demonstrable character difference between the two. In a willful manner Obama spent his eight years dividing the country. I personally detest politics, but it is hard not to see or deny that Obama is a vicious attack dog underneath his pleasant repose. He carries subliminal anger and revenge. It is hard not to see that he laid the seeds of division in the country: and, as he left office he left his "swamp" politicos in the alphabet agencies to go after Trump. On addition, Trump is hard to watch, but he says what he means, and he does what he says. He is a man of the basic promise, and delivers on it. Democrats will never admit it, but Obama left Trump a nightmare both domestically and internationally, but he applied a "nationalist" best interest for the USA policy and made the country a better place economically, financially, and on the international stage. Trump has not been perfect, but he has made the country a more self-sustaining place for American people. And yes, in his very often vexatious manner, but acted excellently on all policies he promised. This division that Obama sewed his Democrat successors in the House of Representatives and Senators became the mantle on which they have relentlessly skewered Trump. In the end, I am not a seer, but I feel the Democrat bitterness, hate and insatiable grousing will return Trump for a second term. Trump is always with a smile or a straight face, but always with conviction, promise and thrust. Trump continues to follow up on his stump promises with numerous and major accomplishments. Deficient of style and class, void of a tempered demeanor, and clamoring far beyond what anybody expected, he vaulted into the Oval Office like a bull in a china shop. That aside, his resolve was expressed as a compact with the underserved of flyover America. He did not forget, and went at his business with blinders, saying and doing anything despite the heretofore "noblesse oblige" of the American Congress. He treated these Congressional political chumps and their bootlicker constituencies like a snake oil salesman. His blather would make his awkward presence feel like a nail being violently hammered. Trump is grossly inarticulate, repetitive and loathe to refine his temperament equal to his stately office. His comportment is an embarrassment to the expected dignity and refinement associated with global ministerial and regal leaders. The media alludes to his "art of the deal" perceptions as he negotiates, but the overly reverential respect he's paid for what should be an admirable trait is thoroughly swallowed up by his obvious lack of polish. He lacked Obama's urbane comportment. His proverbial "bull in the china shop" approach has been somewhat mitigated slightly after over three years and an embarrassing impeachment while in office. In spite of his continued twitter war with the media and a fraudulent impeachment process, he would have been far more well- served to adopt a more gracious, refined mien. The Washington, D.C. swamp will never accede to his style, and in fact will continue to boil him soundly for the unappealing style he presents daily. His style is incomprehensible because he could accomplish far more with less abusive, childish name calling. His laconically tweeted putdowns treat his Congressional colleagues as if they are dimwitted, frustrated, embittered mafia gangs. Only the true mafia play with more deceit and verbal harpooning. Should he continue with such juvenile behavior on his path to re-election, his material accomplishments may eventually be forgotten in the swing states when people go to vote while recalling his relentless incivility. Most disconcerting is his seemingly carefree concern. It is truly bona fide, basic Trump. Yet, this is what appeals to his base out in the hustings. But, in Washington, D.C., where style and elegance count immeasurably, where communications further legislative support (as a leader of "all the people"), he is refractory to this significant quality. Not caring and carrying on a daily Twitter media carping is puerile and crude. Maybe he is advancing the Presidency into a twenty-first century permanent transformation to accommodate global influence? Who knows his thought process? If so, it will be tolerated at a public level if it supports another crucial foreign policy issue (as the Israel-Palestine West Bank negotiations). Long term it will appear boorish, and his "wheeling-dealing" will be taken as imperious to a fault. Incidentally, this Obama understood in his insidious manner. His smile and cordiality may have been treacly to a fault, but his insincerity and inaction at all times brought obloquy (and devastated both the country's national and international prosperity). The Iran deal in the twilight of his Presidency illuminated a brazen defense of his birthright, the influence of his White House (Shiite) advisers, and his freewheeling with impunity. There is not any doubt Trump is unrefined, but his efforts as a leader appear purposive and true to his declared love in support of the country. Obama may continue his narcissistic plan to take down Trump, but it is wasteful in every regard because Trump is a one-man army and singularly out of Obama's league. If Obama continues with his insidious behavior, Trump will squash him like an annoying bug. With these two very unique characters let's cast a light on how all this pertains to prison gangs and Islamic radicalization. With the backdrop of problematic leadership at the top, the trickle down where prison reform will be affected (if ever) has been demonstrably impactful. As I pointed out before, Michael Dukakis rebuked leadership that cannot perceive its influence and neglect its responsibilities (allowing the fish to rot from the head down). Since the new century, leadership has done more to divide the country, and. in so doing, has handcuffed progress in so many areas of concern (especially where prison reform is more noise than change for "the common good). Rudyard Kipling's manifest dictum wisely summarizes my thoughts on the matter: "Oh, East is East, and West is West, and never the twain shall meet, Till Earth and Sky stand presently at God's great Judgment Seat; But there is neither East nor West, Border, nor Breed, nor Birth, When two strong men stand face to face, though they come from the ends of the earth."190 [emphasis mine.] This is the conundrum both of these presidents are leaving this country. Moderation rules, extremes divide. The volcano that is Trump only forms a blister on top of a very deep sore that deepens in Washington, D.C., the city where thoughts of state prison reform move loose lips instead of sober actions (and federal prison reform seems to gain sway where the state prison populations account for the massive numbers). Violence within political Islam unmercifully asserts its will in the most evil display of savagery to women in particular, and the Judeo-Christian world in general. Its expression is loud and demanding. The havoc and damage fomented are devastating[191]. Depending on where the numbers are displayed the takeaway is a numbers onslaught[192, 193, 194]. No person should be so presumptive as to encourage the dismantling and annihilation of another's belief system. Assuredly, Dr. Jasser believes wholeheartedly in the peaceful nature of the Muslim family, the peaceable way it conducts day-to-day worship, and manages to live in the privacy of its own affairs. Professor Jeffrey F. Addicott, of St. Mary's University School of Law in San Antonio Texas where he is a Professor of Law and Director of the Center for Terrorism Law, has this frank comment: Like the greatest generation in America, this generation has an evil of our time. The many- faced evil wears a single mask called radical Islam. Its ugly head has risen once again and is screaming "Death to America" in word and deed. Whether it is radicalized Shia version (Iran) or the radicalized Sunni version, radicalized Islam is on a global march seeking nothing less than world domination. Denying the reality of jihadi murder might suit modern tastes, but it doesn't stand up to the overwhelming evidence of what is happening[195] [emphasis mine]. Addicott essentially is forthright in his presentation of the degree of radicalization that has overtaken the United States. Its zealous aspersions are aimed at the country's constitutional foundation, and radicalization encompasses a demand for the practice of Sharia law in place of American legal standards. This is foundational to the destruction of American life. I do believe that it is hard for American citizens to swallow the facts because open-minded people truly want others to live free and at will according to the dictates of their own belief system. However, and as I shall show, Islam is failing to assimilate in the United States. If it were not for "political correctness," the self-centered manner in which Muslims demand American cities cow to their commands and stipulations would be denied. But social, educational and religious adjustments to Muslims demands are so overbearing and aggressive that entire American cities and communities are being refaced to the chagrin of long-established families. It is dispositive of a granular failure to demand assimilation which was the marquee of immigration in the late nineteenth and early twentieth centuries. Dr. Stephen M. Kirby condemns Islam as a fantasy and how the allure reflects a false veil of peace overlying its very violent character. Its pretext as a peaceful life force is a lie as it breathes nothing but a demanding, violent takeover of American Society. He intellectually reasons "The Lure of Fantasy Islam" as a sham and corroborates Addicott's position as well in the following: Does it really matter that Americanized Muslim reformers are going around to create personalized, "modern" versions of Islam? Yes, because they are relying on non-Muslims for support. And to get that support, the reformers are presenting "the true" Islam as a religion of peace, similar to Christianity and Judaism, and able to be modified and modernized. And the reformers are presenting the jihadists as outlier who have perverted and hijacked that religion. But the reality is that the Muslim reformers are perverting and hijacking the religion, and it is the jihadists who are following the Islam taught by Muhammad[196] [emphasis mine]. Both in cities and prisons across the United States "political" Islam has become such a disruptive force that it has turned "anywhere and everywhere" upside-down. Politicians have always been shady, elusive and one-minded (intentionally mind bent on re-election at any cost). But now they are complicit in allowing cities and prisons to become swirling and hazardous environments. It would stir the gracious part of my nature to understand and defend Dr. Jasser's argument for a peaceful Islam. But such evidence is drowned out by the noise of radical Islam. The ambition of Islamic militancy is singular: violence for the disruption of the American way of life. If politicians were not so nefarious, this issue would have been nipped in the bud, and Muslims would have been forced to assimilate or suffer the legal consequences of deportation. Washington, D.C., however, suffers from a delinquency of obligation, and operates as its own insulated world, shamelessly ripping off their constituencies. The leader of the pack, and, the man who came with a full-throated speech, a blinding white-tooth smile, and a silver-tongued devil personality was Barack Hussein Obama. His smile is a magic act, his sleight of hand, thoroughly committed to send this country into a political spin from which it may not recover. Should it recover it will mire through years of point-counterpoint distrustful, pugnacious forces of political combat. It will be distasteful and very unceremonious. Obama planted the seed as a candidate, fully warned the country of his intent to "transform" (as I have numerously pointed out), and so he did as a full-blooded Islamic radical clothed in traditional American politician garb. He delivered at the behest of a corrupt Washington, D.C., and, now the writers are writing their books and blogs with festering, boiling-over outrage. It is hard to admit an American president can be so elusive and protected. Looking at the American landscape, it is hard to deny Dr. Jasser's smooth manner as he makes his case for the innocence of religious Islam when the country is burning with disgust. Yet, he deserves not to be put in the same basket of people who want to deceive in pursuit of dishonorable ambitions. He was very vocal on television appearances. He should have made the clear distinction between religious and political Islam. It is the latter that has precipitated such violence across the country. If the very worthy population of quiet, family-oriented Muslims had demanded their Imams speak out against the terror element, they would have gone a long way to rebuff the terror that the radical fundamentalists have propagated. Dr. Jasser had the platform, yet he retreated from the mass of controversy. I cannot say I blame him at all..He spoke eloquently and earnestly, but he simmered quietly without "vim and vigor." Today, Dr. Jasser seems to have quietly retreated from the national scene. But, more than ever the radical groups are most active. Some even hide within cover of some of the notorious Mexican gangs. Barack Hussein Obama was in place to either foster harmony of the religions within the country or to go rogue and precipitate division. There is no doubt that he prevailed upon his inner resentments and could not check them for the sake of his new role as leader of the free world. Elected after 9/11/2001, radical Islam was no longer a secret. The sleeping giant had been awakened and was about to shock the world. Obama had a choice: he could have led with wisdom and honor, or do what he chose to do. He foisted radical fundamental elements of Islam onto the country he promised "to transform." Pamela Geller expresses his true persona this way: …Obama had said that 'one of the great strengths of the United States is…we have a very large Christian population---we do not consider ourselves a Christian nation or a Jewish nation or a Muslim nation. We consider ourselves a nation of citizens who are bound by ideals and a set of values[197] [emphasis mine]. Yet less than eight weeks later, America had become a Muslim nation. Obama was just about to make his major speech in Cairo…he also opened the door to more accommodation of Islam, including---if not especially---its political and supremacist aspects, than had ever before been seen in the United States of America. Some of it was symbolism, like Obama's abrupt cancellation of the National Day of Prayer, hitherto a White House event with pronounced Christian flavor[198]. However, it would have been imprecise to say that it was "mere" symbolism. The symbolism, like Obama's statement about America being one of the world's largest Muslim countries, carried important implications"[199] [emphasis mine]. Barack Obama as the watchword of the United States of America was not a leader. He was a sympathizer of Alinsky communism and Islamic radical fundamentalism wrapped in a determined scheme to turn the country upside down onitself. He was an Islamist to the core, not a Christian. He beguiled a country who, for the most part, never grasped his intentions. He could be likened to a father who comes home from a night out and sees his son drinking, smoking and carousing. Rather than break it up, he carries the party to a different dimension, and, by the end of the wee hours of the morning has the house destroyed and ready to brazenly appeal to his insurance carrier for malevolent destruction by an aggressive group of ne'er-do- wells! As Pamela Geller shows very explicitly, Obama was on a different agenda. It was very clear that the religious Muslim population was going to become the centerpiece of a fractious, unmanageable complex of major political change. His association with Louis Farrakhan, the leader of the Nation of Islam (the radical fundamentalist group supporting antisemitism and the destruction of Israel), the foul-mouthed, radical left winger, Reverend Jeremiah Wright (pastor of Trinity United Church of Christ), and the very left wing, self-proclaimed communists Bill Ayers and Bernardine Dohrn[200] (who led the communist Weather Underground Organization which marauded throughout the United States in the 1960's, and, continued unabashedly to evoke the country's radical takeover. Throughout his presidency, Obama[201] possessed an inexplicable, (almost perverse) manner of lying, smirking and holier-than-thou ignoring suggestions of denying Islamic radicalism as Americans were killed or blown up by Islamist yelling "allahu akbar". As loudly and insufferably as Trump entered the 2016 Presidential election process, now over three years into his term, he saved this country from irreversible harm Obama thrusted upon the citizenry. To this day his believers do not comprehend his animus and his brazen behavior. He now commands the destructive forces of the "deep state." I say this as a pure, apolitical individual who is appalled and disgusted with all politicians, right and left. I view this based on clear evidence and observations of his record. It should be axiomatic that assimilation, not isolation, be common to any immigrant group, particularly to show thanks and pride in one's new country. Resentment is an expected emotional response when a group fails to integrate and prefers to withdraw to create its own enclave to create an island refuge. Bringing Sharia law and barking against American social and religious mores only creates tension. It is beyond pomposity. It is nativist and jingoistic. A case does not have to be made for miscegenation, but social integration amalgamates peoples in a way that has always made this country supreme. It is feasible to perpetuate one's identity. Yet loutish, defiant behavior to secure and preserve old country social-religious tenets is an in-your-face belligerence. This is the unfortunate backdrop for how prison gangs are multiplying like sexually active mice. And, buffeting the winds of violence within the prison system is another algorithm: the silent expansion of radical Islam throughout all American prisons and cloaked in political silence (and supported by a stanchion in a system which relents unconditionally to their every demand). It is financially draining that will make it impossible to make the long-term reforms so urgently required. But the answer is always more government attention because government will always spend taxpayer money. The ease with which government "robs Peter to pay Paul" is going to become the mechanism that ultimately bankrupts state governments.

In the Koran: genital mutilation, stoning for infidelity, taking the infidel's head off, etc. This is just wanton behavior spoken in the Koran that is not written or spoken in any other religion. The politicians want to believe from Judeo-Christian heritage such savagery is not possible, and most Muslim people are peaceful. Au contraire, this is not what is seen throughout major metropolitan areas of the United States where radical Muslim political pockets are summarily trashing the American way of life (Somali in Minnesota for example). They are usurping the American ethos and benevolence in "demanding" their cultural-religious practices be accommodated to their will rather than assimilate to this country's way of life. If a person was invited to spend the weekend at someone's house out of sheer sympathy, and the visitor spent the time rearranging all aspects of the house in a most judgmental, overstepping manner, how long would the visitor last? It is the opposite of what Dr. Jasser suggests in his book where he makes the argument that aggressive, radical fundamentalism is a minority that doesn't speak for peaceable Muslims. Well, so much is written and spoken that contradicts his predicate. As Pamela Geller starts out in the very first lines of her book:

> *To some degree the different versions of the Koran can be confusing. An updated translation (The Qur'an 2015) is softened to some degree, but still commands maltreatment of the kafir (the unbeliever/disbeliever):*

> *Make no mistake. We are at war. Our mortal enemy has made no secret of its goal and stated aim: "eliminating and destroying Western civilization from within and sabotaging its miserable house." And establishing a universal caliphate. Pretending that fourteen- hundred years of Islamic imperialism and expansionism didn't happen doesn't change reality either[202] [emphasis mine].*

> *And:*

> *Your Lord revealed to the angels: "I am with you: give the believers firmness; I shall put fear into the hearts of the disbelievers-strike above their necks and strike all their fingers"[203]* [emphasis mine].

This version of the Koran softens the language, but the Muslim believer is still obedient to commands of violence. As it seems, there seems to be a level of hypocrisy that is quite evident. Dr. Bill Warner, using a different authoritative Koran takes the quote from the same reference page of a different source with a more brutal, savage approach to the unbeliever/disbeliever: Then your Lord spoke to His angels and said: "I will be with you. Give strength to the believers. I will send terror into the Kafirs' hearts, cut off their heads and even the tips of their fingers!"[204] [emphasis mine]. he point is clear: though Dr. Jasser speaks of a religious Islam it co-exists with a very definite radical subset. For people not conversant in the domain of Islamic thought, it is hard to make a case that some Muslim people live by the violent commands of the Qur'an. There is a plethora of evidence that supports the existence around the country of radical Islamists who live by one dimensional belief system. I would like to believe that this is not true, but the past years since 9/11/2001 paints a very aggressive attempt to turn "The Great Satan" (as Osama Bin Laden considered The United States) upside down on "its world!" Within the prison system this kind of radicalization is presently endemic. Not seeing this coming is understandable, but not confronting it is unforgiveable. It just lends another obstructive force restricting prison reform. Between 1095AD and 1291AD there were 9 Crusades in the Holy Land, aside of others known as the Northern Crusades[205]. These were fierce internecine battles in the name of the Judeo-Christian tradition to preserve and protect its civilization against a marauding Islamic Caliphate intent on expanding in the name of Allah. This war is present, alive and well, in the United States, albeit les pervasive but surely purposive. But, once again, the Caliphate (Shiite/ Sunni) is raising its ugly determination to zealously unseat and takeover the American way of life. If it were not for lack of care, blatant ignorance, (and, not for lack of care) blatant ignorance, and an entrenched political correctness, there would be a more attentive defense of the American way of life that is being brazenly bushwhacked. The modern-day caliphate is alive and well, and here, mindfully radicalizing wherever it can. Those citizens who live within themselves in a bubble are not paying attention to the world around them. Just as the country has been transformed since the early 2000's, the state of the prison system is transitioning to an amorphous collective, a cooperative grouping of prisoners from all over the world. The country has allowed this to happen because we have allowed our politicians to freewheel with our safety[206]. Leadership has to be like an effective mountain guide. If it is a feather in a wind storm, then anything but a positive result can be expected. Obama was an effete leader without character. He cared very little about raising up the country. Instead, his malevolence left the country in disarray and divided. Prisons became radicalized under his watch. Under Trump there is a sober concern now for prison reform, and he will listen and be proactive. But his first year has been turbulent because of the Mueller investigation and the hangover from Obama's lackluster leadership (and now his "deep state" contrivances). Only time will tell if Trump may be able to lead; but, assuredly, there will be obstacles at every turn politically. One would think that for the good of the country a consensus would build, but Obama contemptuously sewed so many deep divisions with a smile, sometimes laugh. And a sheer denial. Trump's heart is in the right spot, but his personality was so expressively raw when he was sworn in and now over 3 his churlish nature may be impossible at this point to address this important mission. It seems like he never understood that in life there is only one chance to make a first impression. He has long passed that marker in time. Obama, moreover, was heartless, and continues to be so. Self-annointed soothsayer for where the country should be, he was exposed to be merely the tool of left-wing George Soros[207, 208] to prepare the country for its new path toward pure communism. His was a rejection of capitalism, though he was sure to exploit all the benefits and accoutrements of his office for his personal needs. He handcuffed world of business quietly invoking so many regulations through every governmental agency that the GNP was stifled. His ultimate goal was to grow government so large so as to eliminate private business wherever possible. This was Obama's defined objective. Obama is a study in malevolence. On the one hand his wife's vacations, their Hawaiin vacations and their fanciful Hollywood and wealthy elite associations were so antithetical to his speeches, so publicly disparaging of wealth and Wall Street banks (even while they were overwhelmingly his greatest financial contributors). He admonished with a snicker and a self- flagellating laugh. He materially hurt the "flyover" blue collar Americans while he grifted the rich. It seemed like schadenfreude appealed to him. Trump had his wealthy supporters as well, but the support was not nearly as formidable as how deferential it was for Obama. Trump's rough-edged personality deterred the wealthy so he ploughed headstrong with his own goals. So, where is the United States in terms of leadership? What it clearly shows is wealth can now sow the seeds for transformation. It can bring the candidate the Oval Office where the power and influence can be deliberate, willful and indecent. His promises made to the country were clearly framed in couched language the average person would not understand. Comparatively speaking, Trump spent over three years reversing Obama's attack on private business and unleased the private business sector that restored the "capitalist wealth effect" throughout the economy. His rough-edged personality became a hindrance in ways that allowed his enemies to turn his accomplishments as pure lies. Of course, this is ludicrous, but Trump's success became a double-edged sword, giving his critics fodder to reflect on his gruffy, hostile nature as a danger. It allowed their supporters to believe in his dangerous nature because the media would never report the truth. Trump's perceptions are unfortunately the source of the failings he has experienced. Plain and simple, he would have been immensely successful if he had learned somewhere how to be discreet and low-keyed. It almost seems ridiculous to even write that, but it is certainly the very meaning of awareness. Nevertheless, what he accomplished brought small businesses back to life and would have sustained if not for the corona virus! Unemployment was down to 3.8% before the pandemic and the economy was raising all communities around the country out of the economic doldrums Obama created by his heavy taxation and regulations. That together with the rise in Islamic radical terrorism became the nest into which the prison system found itself with a rising threat: radicalized individuals hell bent on converting young gang bangers. It became an issue that prison personnel could not even sense or understand for lack of understanding. Obama successfully antagonized Republican Leadership in Congress (House of Representatives and the Senate) so prison reform could not be considered. Trump has done Obama one better by turning most everyone in Congress away with his level of highly diminished trust and unappealing personality. Having taken the time to break down the importance of personal conduct and factors which contribute to support, it is understandable why leadership is the most important ingredient to formulate needed programs for the country and, as well, assemble the support to legislate it into the law of the land. Trump really loves the country and has a lot of time to reconcile with congressional opposition. He has the political will and staying power to wear them out.

That being said, a prison reform bill (H.R. 3356) just passed the House of Representative, 360-59, it represents a bill enhanced by Jared Kushner, the President's son-in-law and also one of his chief advisors. The bill reads: To provide for programs to help reduce the risks that prisoners will recidivate upon release from prison, and for other purposes[209]. Senators are already grumbling antagonistically. Senate Majority Leader Mitch McConnell (R-Ky.) has already remarked he will not even bring up the bill until the Senate can resolve differences regarding the bill's details and personal considerations related to its support. Really, this bickering is not surprising. This is why Trump ran for the presidency calling it "the Swamp" and others referring to the United States Congress as a sewer. It has become a place where politicians live insulated with their "friendships," and, make them lose sight of their responsibilities. They become elusive, slippery, and power hungry so that important if legislation fails or gets so watered down or entrapped by add-ons then they quip that the country's needs are not well served. The prison reform bill is a classic example. In my mind, it is just another program to spend taxpayer money on more programs without getting to needs which will truly cut down recidivism and diminish overpopulation, the latter being what prison reform must encompass. This bill does not. And, who knows but that it will take on a completely different substantive reading by the time it is ever considered in the Senate (to resume the process). What the bill reflects is simply a bunch of politicians whose understanding of prisons is unworkable because their "effective knowledge" of the subject matter is so low (if at all). The real beginning of prison reform will enter into a true plan when an eclectic politician realizes that all violent prisoners must be separated out and placed in specific prisons totally away from mixed populations. Radicalization is the prime example. If prison leadership does not appreciate this enough to change then the bureaucratic failures will continue. Just as more government does not solve government failure, more bureaucracy does not solve more bureaucracy. The danger that is MS-13 is not mischaracterized by the media, but it is Islamic radicalism is the rooster in the hen house. The Georgem W. Bush administration awakened a sleeping giant as a result of the second Persian Gulf War[210]. His Hollywoodesque[211] performance on a battleship with the navy appeared so brutally naïve and immature. It is 2020 and the consequences of are still being felt. Radicalization of the prison system, though spreading like a metastatic cancer, is the result of Bush's war and generations of Americans will continue to pay a heavy price in all areas of life[212, 213]. It might have been the singular reason that sprung Barack Hussein Obama from nowhere to somewhere as he engaged the American scene so precipitously with his frothy personality and his deceptive smile. At the time, no one knew the history of this first-term, a very young Senator from Illinois with a spring in his step and such unabating enthusiasm. Who was he? The unleashing of the Islamic flame was to ignite terror upon the United States in every corner of American life. He became a vehicle through which this metamorphosis occurred (after 9-11-2001, and, in defiance of Bush's war). The country was warned[214]; but did not heed the FBI agent, John O'Neil who died on 9/11/2011. His prescience was not appreciated as Murray Weiss depicts in so much detail. More than O'Neill's death in the falling twin towers, he unearthed plans for its forthcoming as well as the unleashing of the fire-breathing mythical dragon in the spirit of Islamic fundamentalism with its radical death program. As Pamela Geller (with Robert Spencer) remarks: "The respect was lacking from the West toward Muslims, not the other way around. Obama listed only ways in which the West has, in his view, mistreated the Islamic world. Not a word about the jihad doctrine, not a word about Islamic supremacism and the imperative to make war against and subjugate non-Muslims as dhimmis. Not a word about the culture of hatred and contempt for non-Muslims that exited long before the spread of American culture ("modernity and globalization") around the world, which Obama suggested was responsible for the hostility Muslims have for the West."[215] The United States has gone even further than Pamela Geller (and Robert Spencer) suggest. Obama may have come out of nowhere, but he suddenly began the transformation of the United States he expressed in his ceremonial "Kingdom" amphitheater post- election speech: a forthcoming tide. It would be a grand transformation of the very social-economic fabric of the country as a substitution of the Judeo-Christian way of life for the Islamic culture. All United States citizens would become "dhimmis."[216] That is, his grand message of "Transformation" in Denver, Colorado was loaded in vague euphemisms. Say what you mean and mean what you say was never an Obama proffer, never frank or lucid. He always spoke suggestively, flowery and confusing. What did he say, what was he suggesting? Well, the country certainly found out: a confiscatory strangling and hold on American prosperity! The naïve American traditionalists sitting in guffaw to his eloquence was actually hearing the words of betrayal of the American way of life. They thought as good Democrats, naively and a savior from Bush's mess. That's not what they heard. They were listening to someone who was going to grow the size and power of the federal government (economic fascism)! It was a primer for "Big Daddy Government" and all the imperial controls. It was, at the time, an outline of the Obama "quasi- monarchical state." And, he carried it out like a masterful Shakespearean play. The dhimmis were in the audience and did not know it because the speech sounded so dreamy. His quiet plan: integrate Islam into the country[217, 218, 219]. It sounds wonderful, and normally it would be. As it turned out, it was an open door for a highly radical area, among others. The economic transformation was a magic act to disguise "his tricks," his grand plan. It did not work, and this is just one of many reasons for Trump's election. The radicalization of American prisons is just a manifestation of all that played out through the first bombing of the World Trade Center[220], to the World Trade Center attack on 9-11-2011, through to the election of Barack Hussein Obama. From that point on the country was suddenly thrust into a social-religious-political maelstrom: to be inclusive while retaining its Judeo-Christian culture. And more important to preserve and defend its constitutional foundation. Rather than choosing to coalesce or to lift people up, Obama in a very snotty, smug manner chose to tear an already frayed, torn public further into a deep divide. At any other time in American history a man like Donald Trump, with a very coarse demeanor, would most likely have never been elected. But the circumstances were calling for a man of his ilk: headstrong, impervious to pillory, defiant, and impassioned. Americans are open-minded and tolerant, but they are not accepting of having their culture twisted and turned the rage and hostility of leadership that wants to totally break with the past and white out American history. On Trump's coattails the country is being defended against complete accession to an aggressive political assault its cultural past. Barack Obama continues to defy the historical transition of government at every conceivable scheme he can brazenly concoct in his Washington, D.C. "fort!" Trump is mellowing on site as time passes! It may not be pretty, but it is what it is (just as sausage is made from "parts"). This is the backdrop for how the prison system continues to be hijacked from underneath everyone's eyes. It is reflective of how government just simply cannot get a lot of things right. However. the people who run prisons are not educated and well-read people so the complex of prison gangs with foreign and domestic radicals is not fully understood. Classification is essential to the minimization of gang violence. It is certain that guards and officers do not always recognize Islamic radicals. The most important point to convey in this writing is the difference between religious Islam and political Islam because the seed of Obama's deceit grew in the latter which he understood perfectly well. People in the United States who may be naïve to the historical context of Islam would not recognize the peaceable nature of a Muslim. However, more certain how a radical terrorist would easily fll through the cracks. And, this accounts for young American born children who become radicalized. And, especially those who are imprisoned and are radicalized during their incarceration. As incidents grew in numbers around the country, it was stark how Obama refused to define them as "Islamic terrorism" all the while innocent Americans were victimized in horrific events of slaughter as the perpetrator(s) yelled "Allahu Akbar" ("Allah is the greatest"). As a reference commonly shouted against the "Kafir" ("the Unbeliever, or, Disbeliever), it is understood as the battle cry in Islamic extreme terrorism. During his public television addresses as president, he avoided any sense of truth to fact by simply casting the events of such wanton bloodshed as if it was aberrant tragic behavior. It was not! It was what it was: Islamic terrorism! It was as disturbing for most Americans as it was overwhelmingly pernicious. Robert Spencer characterizes the political Islamic violence in his book as such: Certainly, this book is not written from the standpoint of Islamic faith. It is, in fact, a guide designed for those who do not believe in Islam, to help them understand why Islamic terrorism and supremacism continue to threaten the United States and so many other countries around the world today. But, while it is not a believer's guide, it is a trustworthy guide. This book is designed to present a 100 percent accurate view of the Koran, so that infidels can know what they should expect from a devout Muslim who reads his Koran and takes it seriously as the word of the one true God[221]. Just as the banter was confusing during the Obama administration the terms Religious Islam and Political Islam were as well. Robert Spencer emphatically delineates the nature of distinct calls to violence in the very Koran that Muslim Imams embrace. The distinction between a peaceable Muslim and a radical, the radical preaches death to the "Kafir." The infidel, the unbeliever, is quite disarming for the United States. Suddenly overtaken with the notion that this country was the victim of a violent takeover of its way of life, and being denied by a dishonest president who was able to mischaracterize and mislead, a new national conversation would emerge to solve this new riddle. Today the American prison system houses a lot of Muslim, but I know for a fact that the guards have no idea which are radicalized until they are thrust into an incident. And, at that point, they still do not understand its long-term effects on gang violence. Whether the average prison Muslim is a "believer" or a "denier" the facts speak for themselves, as 17- 20 percent of prisoners are Muslim who are leading the way to radicalize. To follow the programmed misleading path President Obama took is both startling and dishonorable[222, 223]. I always felt that Obama may be completely uniformed, or, worse, completely venal in his indifference to issues of prison safety. The most important takeaway from my personal experience working in a maximum-security prison is the fact that the criminal justice system is constructed to administer for the greater good, the majority population, and hopefully to err on the side of the common good when mistakes are made allowing the innocent to suffer and the guilty to fall through the cracks. Both the legal system responsible for dealing with prisoner rights centered lawsuits, especially when the laws give Islamic radicals time to overload the courts. In all the research available there is a plethora of documentation where the system breaks down and people suffer[224]. And, as I pointed out in Chapter Three, when innocent people are left "hanging" on death row, time and chance dictate whether the system will rectify and repair, as depicted in the Balko and Carrington book depicting two innocent people, the victims of stodgy, prejudiced Mississippi are caught up and wallowing in the victimization of blacks in the "Old South." It is despicable and sorrowful, more so that platitudinous politicians continue to get elected. Casting a blind eye, and, "a wink and an eye" if it suits their re-election, justice is not served. This book supports my observation that the criminal justice system is warped in its overzealousness in such cases laid out in "The Cadaver King and The Country Dentist." The defiance of the Mississippi legal system operating in an antebellum crucible torching innocent black men is as bad as the reasoning Michelle Alexander makes in her book The New Jim Crow[225]. This is a much more broad view of a very biased criminal justice system against a backdrop of historical victimization of the black man. True? Oh yes, more vividly laid out day-to-day as I paraded through a prison each day, always getting to know so many very personally. The travails of the imprisoned innocents are legendary. It demands a more meticulous and scrupulous approach to prison management. There are varying levels of misdemeanor and felony criminals. The advent of the "new" breed of criminal, the radical Islamist simulates metaphorically a diabetic on a steady diet of Hershey chocolates. The prison culture is drowned in tattoos and violence. On surface it presents a constant level of fear, worry and belligerence, feelings that do not mix well. Re-iterating the statistic that there are 33,000 prison gangs, motorcycle gangs and street gangs, this makes for daily incidents. This will make the prisons become internally explosive, probably not recognizing the difference between a radicalized prisoner versus a "soft" Muslim. This is quite significant because the younger ruffians are integrating into some of the most sinister gangs. This is going to grow as a severe challenge to the criminal justice system. Bill Warner[226] and Stephen Kirby[227] offer a factual basis for why it is important to come to grips with the inarguable reality of political Islam. Tattooing is the ineluctable expression of a prisoner's allegiance to a gang, its belief system and its safety harbor against gang rivals. The Muslim believer is on a mission to convert these vulnerable gang members. To distill what media reports and distorts, there is nothing to deter violence against the "kaffir." This is a real and present danger. I cannot ever forget a young, very violent 22- year-old on a hot summer day rail to me on behalf of Allah. His life mission was clearly altered to erase "the unbeliever" from the earth. And, as I told him, he was too angry and vulnerable to understand what he was saying. He sneered and laughed at me. He yelled out: "Better watch your ass!" He was not any different from the prisoner who always yelled out to me "Hey Goldman, I am going to f--- you up!" One thing I learned early on this was one of a few "attention getter call-outs," but some were "dead" serious! Common sense is not nonsense, and prison reform demands provocative leaders. The rehabilitative underpinnings on which it was constructed in the 19th century have been lost over time because of the numbers and the lack of constructive leadership. Punitive measures are meted out with such frequency that no one thinks beyond the daily routines. This is a grave and serious misfortune that the white collared bureaucrats say they understand but, in my estimation, do not. So much time is frankly wasted on administrative procedures that mentioning it to a bureaucrat doesn't even catch a response. The recent increase in the radical Islamist threat to American cities and rural towns is going to be a lightning rod to further magnify and intensify the whole prison system vulnerabilities. The days, therefore, intensify with so many rendered services that the energy to initiate even discussions seems too overwhelming. I have personally tried to discuss this with influential people, and all they do is roll their eyeballs. This country always prided itself on never experiencing an attack on our shores or earthen territories. Well, guess what, the war is here in spite of media inattention (albeit a different kind of war). Contrary to what Simon Baron-Cohen says about "super-empathy" for the "RadiaclZero,"228 I saw incontrovertible evil when I looked into their eyes and measure the degree of their anger (not anguish) triggering very disturbing body language. It is real and maybe untreatable. But monies should always be spent on progress, not the continuation of open-ended, time wasting projects. I will probe a bit deeper into this later, but for now let's consider

W. David Ball's view that the state prison system is vestigial and afunctional229. Until I read his very concise and lucid arguments for the failure of the state prison system, I thought I was an island missing the obvious. I was not because W. David

Ball ends his long investigation and analysis with a clarion call: There is nothing necessary about a system where state governments pay for prisons, and there are many reasons why we might want to change it. Unless and until we can all agree on what statewide policies should be, we would be better off to agree to disagree and let each locality reap what it sows[230]. Everything I have described throughout my writing thus far support a failing system which could not handle prison reform without a will that overrides the politics which is too unwilling to responsibly "follow the money" and redirect its pathway to effective use. As I said, the current bill for prison reform is just another anodyne for show and not purpose[231]. The first bombing of the World Trade Center towers in 1993 did not even move the needle. Rigid thinking can stifle progress. Overpopulation of prisons was never an issue until the sudden explosion in the 1970's. But, nowhere along the line did anyone significantly realize that a change in the business model may be a benefit for the way prisons do business. Population lowered for a while until inner city violence increased and then it exploded again in the 1990's. Even though prison reform seems to have been an issue during all these years, only recently has it suddenly resounded with the political elite in Washington, D.C. (And, that was at the federal level). However, the political estate had never felt compelled to do something until the Third Estate (newspapers) induced the House of Representatives and Senate to address this issue reverentially. The reading of the House bill itself bespeaks a new sense of urgency. Jared Kushner, the president's son-in-law pressed for personal reasons. His personal imprimatur is all over the bill. There is no consideration for the state system[232]. I do not want to cavil his pleading, but it is obvious he is promoting a reform he must believe is comprehensive. It is not, and his arguments are not vindicated by facts. His motivation redounded to his father who went to federal prison for white collar crime. Inevitably, the radicalization of young Americans (all-encompassing: North Americans, Central Americans, South Americans, and, Mexicans) inevitably will increase because of disaffection. No matter how much bravado the most brutish criminals display the run to gang association begins with a common need for friendship, and mutual understanding and backing. It's as simple as that. It seems strange but most (not all) of the vicious killers who lack any compunction to splay "blood and guts" have a unique awareness for life and death, especially their own. Gabriel Morales, as I have pointed out, defined the gangs of the California Department of Corrections by the "Blood-In, Blood-Out" mantra because gang affiliation required a devotion at any cost. During his years as a guard, he noted that death was inevitable due to such horrendous daily gang violence (outside and inside). The violence when he was documenting was as vicious and mindless as anything that even ISIS can serve up today. And it has not diminished. The blood-letting and mindless deaths are as bad today as ever. MS-13, as noted in Chapter 3, is one of many gangs of young "over-achievers" for gang recognition. Many of the other gangs reveal older individuals whose lust for angry massacre have overtaken the prison system. Age has no restrictions[233]. MS-13 in Los Angeles in the 1980's from their escape from the Salvadoran Civil War) were deported when the politicians sickened from their sickening violence. MS-13 numbers spawned to the thousands back home in El Salvador as a group defense mechanism. It is the illegal immigration of this group now which has caught the media's attention. It is important to absorb this reality to understand that this gang reality (as one of many) makes prison reform at this level of criminality unthinkable (though some radical thinking would argue this point). Key factors which totally go unreported are the vast array of other gangs which, if it can be believed, are significantly as brutal. Is it possible that such violence can be so pervasive? You bet! However, as I also noted in Chapter 3, MS-13 does not even finish in Morales' top 10 list of dangerous gangs. I repeat this (and probably not often enough) because it is germane to an understanding of why the under reporting of radical Islamists is so dangerous. Just as ISIS is an outgrowth of Saddam Hussein's resurgent Baathist Party after the Palestinian defeat of Arab forces in 1948[234], the Shiite sect (aka Shia) has expanded in the Middle East through support of Shia Mullahs of Iran (especially Gaza and Lebanon). The Shia sect follows Mohammed's line (also a few variation spellings: Muhammed,

Mohammad, Muhammad, etc.). The greatest number of Muslim live in Indonesia. Of the approximately 1.6 billion Muslim worldwide, 87% are Sunni and 13% are Shia. The Alawite of Syria are an offshoot of the Shia (split off from the Shia a millennium ago). Some authorities claim 15% of the 1.6 billion Muslim are radicalized. This would account for 240 million individuals. However, some Israeli researchers say the number of militants can be as high as 800,000.235 Whatever, it demonstrates how significant the numbers are. Knowing all these numbers, it is apparent that radicalization of prisoners is a reality the country should never forget. An admixture of radical Islamists and any of the 33,000 prison, street or motorcycle gangs compares to imbibing a drink of 200 proof Vodka (100% alcohol by volume-ABV) chased by the highest alcohol content of Grain alcohol (through fractional distillation). It's a death mixture! This is where American prisons are headed. It's worrisome! The idea of "see no evil, speak no evil" is injudicious thinking. It is important to make a key distinction between a mixed population of prisoners versus a maximum security prison. Plain and simple the difference is comparable to two different burglars who go into a country store intent on the cash in the register. One pulls a gun on the shopkeeper, gets the cash, and then high-tails it out the store. The other puts a bullet between the shopkeeper's eyes after he gets the cash (and runs). The first may understand the value of human life. The second lacks not even a sliver of feeling and is, pure and simple, cold-hearted and thoughtless. All radicalized Islamic terrorists are cold-blooded killers! Another danger that I observed was the presence of many Muslim (and, recent converts) who are religious, not radical. But they were few in number and intentionally quiet. However, since the radicals assume a very secretive demeanor, it was very difficult to discern what is going on. I can only assume arrived that it was practical to assume the worst. Most of the officers assumed the worst and hoped for the best. I knew in my heart that no one discerned the difference, and this is terrifying for the guards. I never bantered pleasantries with the young, virulent, full-body tattooed prisoners. A few times I would be in my office when "a wanderer" would saunter in to "test me!" That's until a guard heard voices, came in, and grabbed the prisoner to haul him back to the "wait cell." Then I would look up the criminal's history only to feel my heart pound as I glanced at the murder and psychiatric history (and the depressants he was taking). It was astounding. Most of the criminal youth could barely speak an English sentence, could not read or write, and were always with their hands in their pants as they "fondled" their genitals. In fact, the beautiful trees, bushes and flowers along the yard breezeway had to be eliminated because they were always secreting behind them to masturbate. They were told to keep their hands in sight, but they did not care. There was a limited aged population admixed, but they were wizened, and many moribund.

Three died while I was present. It was very sad to experience, but after familiarizing myself with their history I recalibrated my emotions to understand that the youthful hellions are too blind to see that this is their future if they should be lucky to survive a yard shiv or shank, or, even a fight during a riot. I always tried to stay on the good side of the most menacing and unpredictable because the prisoners find out your home address so, if they have to, will contract out someone to contract out my assassination. When I was in a Level II mixed population prison (prior to the maximum- security prison where I moved after three months), I experienced far less disorder nor harsh interaction. My risk assessment was easy because the maximum-security prison always made me feel threatened, and, the quality of prisoners was so collectively brazen and willfully headstrong that their hormones regulated their actions senselessly most of the times. The educational, vocational and agricultural teaching was, to my observations, so very hopeless in the Level III setting. If a dog and pony show(s) can reflect positively on the prison for statistical relevance, I thought fine, but who is kidding whom. I knew that at the end of my shift my walk through the yard to the control room was a daily reminder how dangerous exposure to this environment is. It was no joke. The number of incidents which resulted in near fatal and fatal injuries was daily. If anybody thinks that the television shows on cable reveal the true experience of a Level III, it is very misleading. A pre-sentencing or trial lock-up in a jail unveils sad stories, but none reveal what is really going on as the most calculating criminals are being radicalized. I am convinced that even the officers are not educated along this line of thinking to truly perceive the change that is active right under their noses. For the most part, the administration does not want fatal and near fatal incidents to get out to the local news. When it does get out, the result is family going right to the newspapers and television outlets. Public exposure hurts hiring an already skeleton guard contingent. In fact, one of the very common occurrences that always was a head-shaker for me is the number of officers/guards who wind up sneaking contraband in for the prisoners for the exchange of sex or a financial bribe. I could not believe how often it occurred. Whether by desperation for money or out-of-control hormones, the thoughts I had were always: "Why, and do these people realize what the hell they are doing"? Of course, I knew, but my reaction was always the same. (A 10-year sentence, for what? And, this is a guard mentality.) And, it never got old. There is no doubt that a maximum-security prison is a cesspool of perverse activity by criminals with pent up hormonal drives which lead them to abhorrent sexual behavior and uncontrolled impulsive hostility. Unlike the traditional gang-banger, the religiously inspired radical will kill in behalf of Allah against an enemy who simply does not understand. Prison gangs are about control, power, and money. This new enemy is about a religion totally foreign and incompatible with their lifestyle. The tell-all prison books I have read render a false impression to the public about the true dangers of a Level III facility. The viewpoint is narrow. Radicalization is fomenting a level of peril that has yet to be tested. It is incubating, clear and simple. At some point, it will explode as the population of Islamic radicals increase. And, I am certain that leadership does not understand the destructive nature of political Islam to properly deal with the problem. In fact, there is a quantifiable disinterest to learn about the enemy in order to head off the dangerous mess forthcoming as the numbers grow. It will not be a picnic, and, there will be panic as the deaths rise. Radical Islamists are not game players, and they are at war with the Judeo-Christian ethic and lifestyle. The "irresistible force paradox" will be inevitable. It is a mind puzzle asking what will happen when the irresistible force meets an immovable object?[236] The paradox lies in the fact that if the force is unstoppable, the immovable object cannot be immovable (and, vice versa, if the immovable object is truly immovable then the irresistible force cannot be irresistible). There are many very religious, peace- bearing Muslims, but the fact that none speaks up in defiance of political Islam speaks volumes about submission and the force of radical fundamentalism. In time, the paradox will spring forth because the irresistible force (the force of radical Islam) will come nose-to-nose with the immovable object (standard bearers of gang-bang allegiance). Which will capitulate? "The Arabic word 'Islam' means 'submission' and derives from a word meaning 'peace'. In a religious context it means complete submission to the will of God."[237] Taken from the website of the Royal Embassy of Saudi Arabia in Washington, D.C., Stephen Kirby presents an interesting conflict when he asks: "How do you reconcile the peaceful verses with the violent verses in the Koran? Is violent extremism irreconcilable with Islam?"[238] This, as the saying goes, is "above my pay-grade." Like oil and water do not mix, religion and violence are not compatible. And, radical, extreme violence certainly is all over the historical record (Goths, Visigoths, Vandals, Knights Templar, etc.), but it is hard to accept wanton, rapacious brutality (maybe even savagery). Yet, Bill Warner, PHD[239] and Stephen M. Kirby, Ph.D.[240] meticulously trace the call to violence right from the Koran. So, the issue cannot be dismissed, and, it is remorseful for Muslims that there is really a wise, sensible voice speaking and writing so emphatically in behalf of the "peaceable Muslim," Dr. M. Zuhdi Jasser[241]. It is disturbing to come face to face with some of these virulent prisoners who can cite line and verse, some casually and others angrily. This is where the research and written word do not have the sway that the visual leaves. Totally mind bending! Only time will see how this plays out. As I have already commented about prison reform, the present bill which just passed a vote in the House of Representatives and is working its way through the Senate has bite and substance. Suggested by President's Donald J. Trump's son-in-law,

Jared Kushner, it should be the example for state prison reform. Jared Kushner appears committed just by bringing awareness. And, understandably so, because it is so much more complex. Listening to politicians discuss the issue it amazes me that no one offers discussion for the state prisons. I have talked about separation of the violent prisoners to make way for real reform. Then, and only then, can the important issues translate into effective planning. Overzealous prosecutors; over sentencing; "three strikes" policies; reform of parole boards; reform of prison administration; reform of training policies for guards; monies to hire more guards with a livable wage; these are some issues that have to be addressed if and when politicians get serious about prison reform. And, there are other concerns. And, the more time passes, prisons will become even more dangerous as Islamic radicalization increases and interacts with existing gangs. Letting inattention to snowball into an avalanche is a shame. Political Islam only understands the enemy as the "kafir," the unbeliever. There lies "the rub" for western thinking: separation of political Islam from religious Islam. For the well-read, the uniquely educated, or family understanding through marriage, this is conceptually understandable. However, for the majority, this is thoroughly misunderstood. Western thinking is not suspect nor taught to think a religion may, could be, or is the spark for violent thinking or actionable offenses against laws or humanity outright. Americans, for certain, do not think along these lines, except for the well-informed. And, despite being in tune with this fact, it is so foreign to Judeo-Christian thinking. Unfortunately, it is not some myth, a political construct, or even wildly a personal confabulation. To understand the problems besetting the American prison system now, as well as the American city (cities), this had better be accepted if a remedy is to be developed and effected by people in the criminal justice system. Military wars are gruesome and violent, but slow, progressive destructive forces mercilessly trying to degrade and take over the American way of life is a slow, painful death. It pries people apart and creates continuous, nasty inter-personal dissension. As I have mentioned and want to repeat: there is a problem with the fact that there is almost nothing from the Muslim community regarding the very real growth and spread of fundamentalist Islamic radicals into American cities. Middle America is unaware. It is sinful and unforgiveable. (It is the population that Barack Hussein Obama misled, lied to, persecuted by "weaponizing" the IRS, the EPA, Homeland Security, the ATF, the FBI, the Justice Department, etc., and every other government agency at his disposal to make life a nightmare for people trying just to live their lives). This was a back-and-forth every day and everywhere for a divisive, seemingly irresponsible and lazy media to argue[242, 243, 244]. The years Obama was the president were indeed transformative, and preclusive to the uprising the country is now witnessing. It was the very flagrant Islamic Radicalism that came to destroy lives for which he cradled his sanctimonious TV appearances with indifferent "political speech," always failing to lend truth to the surge of coldhearted, unreasonable deaths to everyday Americans. His snootiness was as wanton as it is today. Had he been truly a valiant, honorable leader this spontaneous explosion of Islamic radical violence could have been nipped-in-the-bud. He knew exactly what he was doing and did not care! Unfortunately for this country, he possessed a vulcanized personality that allowed truth, feeling for country, and leadership bounce off his "mission oath." [245, 246, 247, 248, 249] The division this man setupon the United States was actually so obvious that it was disturbing to a fault. A Hollywood actor could not carry out such a bold, convincing display of self-righteous, priggish behavior, and render the feeling that pain was of no concern unless it was his own. In another twist of an expression: the "soft bigotry of low expectations" created an incongruously feeling because here was nothing soft about it! It is impossible to know what a person says in private, but he administered to and blathered to supporters who trusted the squeaky-clean manner he foisted upon them. The Nobel Prize[250] given to him before he attempted to accomplish anything on the worlds' stage was a sham and falsely authenticated accomplishments in platitudinous speeches. He had not even attempted to legislate anything. What an embarrassment to the world! "Change!" What kind of change? Well, he was still a neophyte on the world's stage. Yet, he was embellished with one of the great worldly prizes illustrative of great wisdom and innovation. It was a complete disregard of worthiness and indelible accomplishment[251, 252]. This was simply the result of such a profound mistake of judgment that it fueled so much resentment for a man who had accomplished nothing more than being a community organizer, took advantage of his being half-black, and covered up his long left- wing associations as he began his eight-year betrayal of both those who longed for a leader and those in the left wing of the Democratic Party which was captivated, deceived and both taken and over-taken by "sleight-of-hand"-type hucksterism. While Trump today is known for "The Art of the Deal," Obama became known for "The Art of the Spiel!" He was (and still remains) an unmerciful burden, not a leader. Nowhere was this most evident than at the recent Democratic National Convention where he pilloried and abusively slammed President Trump in a vicious putdown![253] This scathing and concentrated personality droning was as empty of facts as it was rife of jealousy and evident of "littleness" becoming a former President. It should have been an encomium of his former Vice President as well as a charge to his forthcoming campaign season. It was not. It was glaring evidence of the toxic prevalence today of Trump Derangement Syndrome[254] (which he so comfortably propagates). It is difficult to treat him so harshly, but there was so much sophistry and prattle. It was to a fault! He ambushed human expectations he lifted so high and then squashed so ungracefully. His presidency played out in mockery of the country with hate and resentment. It's hard to understand why? Now in the rear view mirror, his lack of accomplishments are becoming more and more apparent. No longer are societal problems isolated because the world has turned global, and, a problem abroad is ultimately going to find its way to this country, and vice versa. It is therefore incumbent that leadership be consensus building to capture the attention of leaders worldwide to the interest of peace rather than war. The forgotten, unmanageable children of this country are finding their way to our prisons because the country does not have a leader who understands the prison system. Politicians are guided by their own political interests too introspectively. Rather than be proactive most are reactive. For this reason, federal prison reform goes more attention so it is more "politically sexy!" To take on prison reform at the state level (where about two thirds of all prisoners are incarcerated nationwide) is not so "sexy" to work at. Why? Because it takes work and persistence where glamorous attention is not paid. The facts are real: about 45% of state prisoners are non- violent. Federal prisons and local jails also have non-violent prisoners as well, but in much lower numbers. Violent state prisoners make up over 50%, and the local jails and Federal prisons house violent prisoners as well (about 34,000). The total for the entirety of American prisons is about 2.2 million. The key, however, there is no push at any political level to make a concerted effort to resolve a state prison reform plan. The United States is supposed to be intellectually advanced and prosperous enough to realize the source of crime and engage the political challenge. We are not the old Soviet Union Gulags[255] nor the present day North Korean Gulags. Nor are we the Chinese Communist Party silencing their citizens for free expression or the imprisoning of Muslim Uighurs in "re- education camps" (translation: "torture camps"). In WWII the Japanese had "LIVE" (no anesthesia) medical experimentation prison camps in occupied China[256]. African countries, Thailand, Myanmar, etc., also torture their prisoners. This masterfully documented. Overall, it is as scary as it is pathetic. The worst example of man's cruelty to man! If we are led to believe we are too civilized to become gulag-like, just study the Civil War prisons, and especially Andersonville (in Andersonville, Georgia) where just under 13,000 Union soldiers died from disease, malnutrition, overcrowding and exposure. It was vile, just as so many of the other northern and southern prisons during the Civil War. The story of these prison is really man's inhumanity to man. It was so horrific at Andersonville that at the war's end Henry Wirz (the commander of this military prison) was hanged for his complete mistreatment of incarcerated soldiers[257]. People are people, and we are just as vulnerable and capable of disintegrating to such a level lacking totally absent of moral rectitude. There are too many to recall here, but the point is made. From my interpersonal relationships with guards and prisoners I could see we are very easily susceptible to loss of our civil sensibilities. State prisons can be very near to city and suburban communities, but once inside the reality is that they might as well be miles isolated because they are worlds of their own being. Maximum security prisons are generally more sterile and cold, which makes the atmosphere brutal. If only young juveniles could be witness to such turpitude, they truly might be "scared straight!" The radicalization of American prisons is a real threat. It has societal spillover and implications increasing exponentially. It is also part of a loose immigration policy as well. This is political fact. Walk around and it is quite evident that In general, I find politicians a very sorrowful lot. Every two, four and six years our national leaders come back to the food chain and begin the false bravado and conventional lies to winvotes to retain housing in the nation's capital where they insulate themselves to get rich on "political-animal-husbandry!" What do they breed: only policies to further their cause for re- election. Other than that, they say what they suspect you want to hear and then leave the camera to relish and savor their benefits in the quiet of their offices. At some point their brazen lies and behavior are exposed and they are voted out. In the meantime, our problems continue. I hate to be so brutish, but after many years it is tiring to listen to their false bravado, their empty words, and their lying testimony. Yes, there are two sets of laws: one for politicians, and one for the citizens. Wouldn't it be nice if this were not true? The most alarming, as I have tried to emphasize, is the increasing radical mix with ongoing gangs. Just think about the monies that could be saved if the system would separate them away and use the saved expense for rehabilitation of non-violent prisoners. Most over-sentenced non-violent prisoners record their anger in many of the books I have recorded in my bibliography. Some of the stories are tiresome to read because they are so vexatious. Radical fundamentalist Muslims, either in the country illegally of American citizens individually radicalized, run amok against the backdrop of our current system are a very real problem.

Eventually there will be a price to pay that will be out of possible control of prison administration. And, they'll be blowing up citizens and the brick-and-mortar foundation of our cities.258 This cited case in Belgium is a typical example of terror borne of the radicalization of a young prisoner radicalized while incarcerated. In Brooklyn, New York we allow an Imam to rail against Jews and pronounce the total destruction of Israel[259]. And, in Malaysia, with the largest Muslim population in the world, the newly elected Prime Minister assails Jews and Israel. To make it worse his radical fundamentalism is approved and lauded by American Islamists[260]. I have personally discussed this with prisoners who unhesitatingly admonish the United States and are shamed by their hate for everything about the United States. It is disarming to hear. The bothersome gnawing in my brain tells me that ignorance is no longer an excuse. It is about time the political elite understand the reality. They spend more time vituperating each other rather than seek cooperate legal measures to keep us all safe. It is sickening how they spent so much time of "Russia collusion" and impeachment when the evidence clearly shows its falsehoods. I do not appreciate any of them, but I know "serpents" of greed and invective when I see it. To put the country throughout what they did with so many more purposive issues to discuss (the deficit and national debt) is debasing! Infecting all aspects of American society by defiling each other by casting unmitigated aspersions and low-level gratuitous criticisms is nothing more than opinionated slander. To demand an ideal is non-sensical because it is never going to happen, but the adults should wake up, smell the roses and get a leg on reality. Politics was once combative, but tolerable. Now it is a blood sport played like a foul-mouthed boor with the mental acuity of a lubber! It is embarrassing that these politicians have no shame. They may viscerally hate Trump for trying to clean up Washington, D.C., but their unprincipled lifestyles and dishonor were exposed like the vile personalities they are. Such exposure would have been more deserving if they have not been so protected by the media for so long. It is amazing how Democrat supporters do not even know what has been going on for almost four years. It is disgraceful. This sounds like the language of a disgruntled

Republican. However, it is not. I do not think the Republicans are any better because they allowed it to happen. Washington is truly a swamp! What is youth to expect if leaders lack enough sensibility to lead with authority and respect. How is it that a politician goes to Washington of average and humble wealth but leaves a multi-millionaire? How is it that Obama goes from being a community organizer to serve as an Illinois senator for under two years, accedes to the Presidency and leaves after eight years to buy a 12-14 million dollar home in Martha's Vineyard and a multimillion dollar home in Washington? Watch the House of Representatives where the politicians harangue, lie and defame each other, or the more gentlemanly Senate where their boring performances are witless and empty of tangible results, what do you primarily see? Fancy empty suits, carefully coiffed hair, large pinky rings, Ben Franklin glasses hanging on the tips of noses to look erudite, and pancake covering their guilt skin lines! The televised hearings are reduced to castigating caterwauling and caviling! Republicans and Democrats differ only by their nomenclature. Making a case for prison reform seems like a hapless, hopeless task! The outrage that is our prison system resonates with a "political correctness" that stultifies its management and magnifies the drudgery of employees. Pamela Geller gives the example of a Muslim prison guard who refused to wear a conventional uniform consistent with prison policy. She continued to wear her khimar (a headscarf), and she was eventually fired for her stubbornness. She refused to understand that it did not comport with correctional officers' policy. However, Obama and his Justice Department sued in her behalf and reversed prison policy to adjust to Sharia Islamic law. This was typical of Obama's allegiance and lack of leadership of a country he took by surprise[261]. He defaultedto Islamic Sharia law in everything he did as President of the United States, assuming a chameleon demeanor for his persistent outreach utilizing all the agencies of the federal government. And yet he always denied the exceptionalism of the country for which he wanted to be President. Obama is elusive and cunning, and his followers in Congress accepted this if it enhanced their own personal gain. During his tenure global transition to radical Islamic terrorism prospered by his soft peddling relations with countries of Islamic Fundamentalism and Terrorism: Syria, Iran, Turkey and Afghanistan. His famous "Red Line" threat to Syria was empty blather[262, 263]! What Obama did, starting with Benghazi[264], and the fall of Egypt and Libya[265 266], played out like the first act of a play that unleashed a reactive dragon (the Islamic State). Obama's failure to act presidential in behalf of this country and not in sway with Sharia law gave rise to a thunderous outpouring of extremism, immigrant migration, and, above all, insecurity and violence on a global stage[267, 268]. The byproduct of Obama's foreign policy failures and history with Shiite Islam uncoiled dramatic turmoil in the Middle East capped by the egregious payment to Iran (1.5 billion dollars in cash and an additional 150 billion dollars flown in on palettes). In addition, he surrounded himself in the White House with Iranian sympathizers, followers and political comforters. The prisons today now reflect the disruption in the Middle East due to a very awkward, soft administration handling of turbulent uprisings provoked by Obama's wishy-washy promises, and then hesitance in dealings with Syria, Iran and the Gulf Arab countries. The Islamic radicalization of American prisons is here to stay, and like young children playing in a mud box our crusty, defiant politicians are throwing mud at each other as Obama snarks from his deep state headquarters in Washington, D.C. This is the zenith of chutzpah. And, he performs like a pretentious thespian with his body language and verbal delivery. It harks of disquieting insincerity that makes one bemoan and question his devotion to the country. The radical Islamic prisoners are now teeming in our cities and prisons, following the Koran literally, and the "good" family oriented religious Muslims say nothing in defiance. Why they recede timorously is hard to understand. The teachings of Islam are far more complex, but, as far as a Level III prison where violence is already a daily matter, the serious religious considerations will bring havoc to a new radicalism which will go face-to-face with established gangs. I am certain the prison leadership has no understanding of radical Islam and the Koran[269]. The question is: How long will political correctness allow prisons remain in this unreality? This pure evil will sustain and infect our cities until someone wakes up to this danger. Even as Dr. Jasser argues the side of tolerance, there is a very radical side that is upending and united in its mission to destroy those that do not live by the words of Mohammad in the name of Allah. This is an unfortunate reality. It certainly does not detract from his earnest efforts to defend all that he, his family, friends and religious associations stand for. He cites from the Qur'an the following: The believers, the Jews, the Sabeaens, and the Christians who believed in God and the Last Day and did good works have nothing to hear and shall not be sad[270]. Dr. Jasser[271] threads a stream of consciousness in writing a noble, humbling attempt to defend the Muslim and the religious Islam as noted in the verse above. He is obviously an incredibly studied, well-meaning, humble and honorable man. On pages 129-131 he lays out a wonderfully idealistic call to reason for a reformist Islam. He valiantly makes his case to "separate the wheat from the chaff" in his distillation of the purity of Islam's religious qualities, a call to spirituality. He recognizes the political/military cauldron that is the Middle East, and his modus vivendi is to deflect the radical political Islam and emphasize the religious Islam accommodation to the Judeo-Christian model. This permeates his call to Imam Rauf on page 177 to recognize the sense of holiness following 9/11 and, in recognition of neighborhood sensitivity, not push for the building of his Mosque in that area where so much public pushback immediately resounded. There is no doubt that Dr. Jasser is both conciliatory and well-meaning. The problem is that in today's world of the three major Western religions, Islam, Judaism and Christianity (purposefully putting the Asian-Pacific rim aside for the sake of this point), Islam is the only one of the three that presents a radical-militant element. Radical Islamist militarism is a fact of life, and, for this, it is so unfortunate for Dr. Jasser to spend his life making the case for the soft-centered mainstream Muslim population. I understand his reticence, but his national platform could influence a tamping down of the radicalization of so many young people. It is outrageous that Islamist militancy is so virulent in its attempt to destroy the western democracies. It is not a sheer mystique; it is violence that has and will continue to transform American society in its nomadic pursuit of American destruction. To people who are not schooled in the religion, and even the schooling of youth in the most extreme form of Islam[272, 273], none of this has meaning. However, what is clear is that the political component of the religion is unlike other religions which do not have a defined political edge. Notice above that the verse starts with "The believers..." However, let's look into the Qur'an's view of the Kafir (the "concealer," one who conceals the truth of Islam; or, the more common translation: "unbeliever," a very prejudicial word), with verse 29 in Chapter 9 from two different Qur'an translations: Make war on those who have received the Scriptures (Jews and Christians) but do not believe in Allah or in the Last Day. They do not forbid what Allah and His Messenger have forbidden. The Christians and Jews do not follow the religion of truth until they submit and pay the poll tax (jizya) and they are humiliated[274]. And, the same verse from a different version of the Koran, aka the Qur'an: Fight those of the People of the Book who do not (truly) believe in God and the Last Day, who do not forbid what God and His Messenger have forbidden, who do not obey the rule of justice, until they pay the tax promptly and agree to submit[275]. The Kafir (the "concealer," the "unbeliever") is contemptible in the eyes of Mohammad in view of the following from The Koran Chapter 33, Verse 60: They (Kafirs) will be cursed, and wherever they are found, they will be seized and murdered. It was Allah's same practice with those who came before them, and you will find no change in Allah's ways[276]. And, the same verse from the same Qur'an cited immediately above: If the hypocrites, the sick at heart, and those who spread lies in the city do not desist, We shall rouse you (Prophet) against them, and then they will only be neighbors in this city for a short while. They will be rejected. Wherever they are found, they will be arrested and put to death. This has been God's practice with those who went before. You will find no change in God's practices[277]. These referenced remarks from the Koran (Qur'an) are highly significant because they dispel what Dr. Jasser would like to disappear: that there is bona fide existence of "radical" remarks which preach outright violence. Clearly, there is a separation of religious and political Islam. This is quite evident. The individual who translated the 2015 edition of the Qur'an tends to mollify and detract, but the message still bleeds through. To someone who knows nothing about Islam there will be very little understanding; but, suffice it to say, that these are remarks to which both non-violent and violent offenders have been (and will continue to be) converted. Sharia is not just a way of life for the Muslim, it is a call to violence for those who are radicalized either in prison or even in cities around the world. It is a global danger. Shamefully the United States experienced eight years of a President who understands all of this and insulted a nation with his hyperbolic verbal camouflage. He reversed the understanding of the United States' exceptionalism, its history rich in accomplishment and a wealth of tradition. He made a mockery of the country that gave him the leader of the free world. He concealed all he did to make life difficult for so many by weaponizing all the departments of government with the vicious intent of bringing an innocent citizenry to its knees. He is arrogant and shameless. His personality is contemptible and his ignominy on the world stage never bothered him. He seemed to embrace a very casual pride in the country and paraded around the world making a mockery of the country's greatness while making excuses for its historical pride. His brash attitude and snarky countenance is intolerable and audacious. He is willfully argumentative and seems to relish opportunities to fault people he cannot overshadow. But, his most destructive action has always been to deny Islamic terrorism and allow it to permeate American cities. He opened up a floodgate that is pouring problems into an innocent population which now has to confront radicalism and criminal behavior.[278, 279] The American prison system has always been weighed down with built-in, bureaucratic policies standing in the way of safety and personnel turnover. First and foremost are all the gangs which daily make life a nightmare. As radical Islamic prisoners increase in numbers, prisons may never identify the radicalization process right in view (because it'll be covert .Political Islam that has the will to subvert and destroy so there is no doubt that every attempt must be made to recognize its presence, diagnose patterns of behavior, and have a strategy to forestall violent riots, which will happen). This is a short-term need, but in the long run there must be prison reform as a reality to checkmate its increasing size (which should allow greater command over the prison environment). It is necessary to drive one more point home, which may be illusory, but it is immensely on point. It is impossible to mix populations of prisoners because "the bad" will infect "the good." That is, it is for some prisoners to be drawn in by poor associations and descend deeper into crime. Prison incidents result in furthering legal entanglements and longer sentences. It becomes a vicious circle. The non-violent/ violent prisoner mix is a nightmare. Think about prison gangs, radical Islam conversions, guard deficiencies, gun carry versus no gun carry arguments for prison guards, prisoners' use of incident reports and lawyering handcuffing the system at a terrible financial cost to the taxpayer, the nightmare of contraband, and daily factional warring. Prison reform is not the simple resolve as purported by uniformed politicians. It is complex problem and will never be realistic until so many other issues are resolved. Politicians are a slow-acting poison to noble intentions. David Skarbek reinforces the most important point that should be understood by anyone who tries to make the case for prison reform:

> Going to prison provides a networking opportunity to offenders. One study finds after controlling for other factors, that being locked up with more serious offenders and with people serving longer sentences, a person engages in more crime in the future.[280] Incarceration increases future illegal earnings. Meanwhile family and community ties strain when parents go to jail. This collateral damage weakens the social network of a community, and breaking the law or going to prison can become destigmatized. Crime is a complex social problem, but if these estimates are roughly accurate, then both the prison population and the crime rate can be reduced at the same time.[281]

I would argue that the "social network of a community" is thoroughly disrupted, understanding that the majority of state prisons are filled with inner city and rural populations who are not fortunate to be the recipients of middle-class education and stable families. In any complex problem solutions do not fall out of thin air. It is a prodigious effort of concerned individuals who possess the wherewithal and specified command to think through the issues and lay out a specific, organized plan. Otherwise, it becomes banter, blather and bloated bunkum for the next book, investigation, or even another political platform. The danger swirling about the country dealing with drugs, guns, open immigration, gang violence (MS-13, for now), school murders, and radical Islamic terror may ultimately reach critical mass to spontaneously demand for consensus thoughtful resolution. Hopefully, cheap political bickering will end. How does the focus on political Islam get attention to compel changes that would make everyday a better day for all involved? It will take a serious appeal to all contributing to the welfare of prisoners and guards alike. For the most part, it is a zero-sum game for now trying to avert intra-prisons riots and fighting. These are issues which will not disappear any time soon. At this point I believe it would be timely to summarize the known and unknown factors which are tantamount to the "silent nightmare" that is prison life. As a realist I do understand that some will be flummoxed because the raison d'etre of this writing is rooted in the outside world being in the dark of the life inside the prison world. Nevertheless, here are relevant considerations for review:

> ***Prison gangs are real, and "a clear and present danger!"**
> ***Radical Islam is now part of American life (of which the American prison is now an unfortunate "bete noire!")**
> ***The soft side of Islam is the religious Islam. There is vast confusion in the media when referring to "Islam" for the spread of radical Islamic terrorism. Islam is a peaceful religion, but there is a radical entity which, for all intents and purposes is a political Islam. This Political Islam has the will to subvert and destroy so there is no doubt political entity is**

an extreme form of which ISIS is a SUNNI entity (the former Baathists of Saddam Hussein). This is just one example of political Islam, just as Al Nusra or Jabhat Fatah al-Sham is al-Qaeda in Syria or the Levant. Essentially, religious or political Islam in the United States is just not one entity. The political extremes are the jihadists reported in the American news groups as radical Islamist terrorists. They are seminally a United States nightmare.

*Wahhabism and Salafism are two different entities as well: the former the reactionary sect of Islam in Saudi Arabia, the latter an offshoot of Wahhabism in the 18th century as a reform-revival movement in Egypt.

*9-10.5% of the cumulative American prison population is Muslim. There is no certainty exactly how many are radicalized, but it is certain that radicalization is an ongoing phenomenon.

*Expanding gang violence and radical Islamic fundamentalist-associated terror are now realities of American life. Political differences are enhancing incidents of depraved crime and terrorist assaults against assembled crowds or congregations.

*This is the era of "Political Correctness" and it is ripping the heart out of people and fueling anger, jealousies, and loathsome behaviors.

*Prison governance from the wardens down to primary entry guards, and all other associated personnel are hardworking and devoted, but they are continuously challenged and rebuffed by prison bureaucracy.

*Three strikes policy is lazy legislation and should be eliminated. *Violence involving murder should involve different sentencing than other violent offenses for which rehabilitation and length of sentencing should be linked.

*Non-violent offenses must have rehabilitation built into the sentencing; punitive sentencing alone is costly and unproductive.

*Classification is a primary means of placement during incarceration for the good and welfare of guards and prisoners. Therefore, it should be in the hands of psychologists or psychiatrists, not just trained guards or ancillary operational personnel. And, classification should be directly tied into rehabilitation planning.

*Prison Budget Reform: money redistributed to rehabilitation as it is saved by decreasing length of sentencing. *Legislation to change sentencing to shorter terms for non-violent felonies. *New restrictive sentencing guidelines in concert with rehabilitation to intercept overzealous prosecutors and overextended sentencing that averts rehabilitation as a pro forma standard. *Eliminate mixed population incarceration. Costs would be absorbed by money saved through length of sentencing remediation and rehabilitation. *Increased pay for guards along with eight-hour shifts (for all).

*All guards should carry guns, and gun range practice should be weekly. Range proficiency evaluation should be monthly.

*Self-defense proficiency should be monthly after initial training. *Eliminate all computer directed courses except for those related to PREA, suicide awareness and training, and CPR. Other courses are time wasting and can be learned onsite within the framework of job function.

*Directors of Prisons should be elected and not political appointments of Governors. It would reduce corruption and give a toe-hold on Directors to have a constructive input for "prison reform."

*All state prison employees should be immediately fire worthy under new legislative guidelines. Featherbedding restricts proper redress for serious violations of professional conduct.

*A panel for each state to optimize prison policy format. The format should be a living document and be reviewed annually.

*Wardens and Associate Wardens should be appointed by review panels of six appointed citizens by an elected Director of Prisons. This will enhance effective Director leadership.

SECTION 4

The Inside

Chapter 6: The DNA of Reality The realities which are so endemic that without change in this core Achilles heel prison numbers will ineluctably increase.

Chapter 7: Simmering Irreverence The bureaucratic corruption acts like old, congealing oil gumming up an engine with low level stubbornness. This is really the bastion of the self- sustaining "power-greed" complacency which propagates "mass incarceration."

Chapter 8: Collective Plausible Deniability Please, how dare you blame me! I hear no evil, see no evil, and do no evil! It can't be that bad! Oh, yes, it is!

CHAPTER **6**

The DNA of Reality

"If the prison does not underbid the slum in human misery, the slum will empty and the prison will fill."[282]
"He who opens a school door, closes a prison"[283]

"Giving money and power to government is like giving whiskey and car keys to teenage boys."[284]
"…we cannot take the development of character for granted…The process of character development is life-long, and people can learn to be good, and they can get better at it---but, not by accident."[285]

Misery, whether hidden deep inside or displayed in the open through physical displays of anger, is the way the DNA template in each human being is coded to express itself through its many "unit components." Safety within the prison system is specifically rooted to serve as a buffer to the outside world: the American public. My research did not unveil any other complicated or secretive documentation separate from what is already known in recognized public documentation. The presence of radicalized individuals or part of Islamist radical groups is widespread, and a known threat to the United States[286, 287]. The presence of Muslim prisoners is very well established (some of whom have been tried in American courts for terrorism as I have noted in Chapter 5). What is not known precisely is how pervasive the numbers are. Nevertheless, there is far more to the serious nature of Islamic terrorism, particularly behind bars[288 289 290]. I have tried to display in the Misery Index in an easily explained formula that the "expected/unexpected dangers" per prisoner increases as they increase.

It is the difference between having a cap gun versus an AR-15 to kill. The Misery Index ultimately reflects danger zones and flashpoints as a product of elements within the prison which are explosive. Before now, gangs and the trafficking in guns, drugs, prostitution, money laundering, etc. was the elephant in the room. However, what is known now is paradoxically what is not known. The degree of corruption involving state prisons complicates prison function at every level, but especially at the highest administrative level[291] [292]. In 2000, Jeffrey Goldberg[293] writing in the New York Times Magazine reported on the Wahhabist Madrassas in the North- West Frontier Province of Pakistan. He investigated the Haqqania Madrassa (a Muslim religious seminary) in particular. Composing 2,800 of the poorest students ranging in age from 8-9 to 30 (as old as 35 sometimes), they are taught (indoctrinated) by mufti (a cleric who is allowed to issue "fatwas," "rulings on a point of Islamic law (which to the western mind has come to reference "death sentences"). They are programmed in one educational format only: Islamic jurisprudence and history. They are repeatedly schooled in religious rulings on matters ranging from family law to waging jihad ("holy war"). It is essentially a training camp for "terrorists" and financially supported by very wealthy Pakistani and Saudis. As Mr. Goldberg points out, they become "perfect jihad machines." And, over the years hundreds of thousands have spanned out worldwide. I know this is not a comforting thought! As I pointed out in Chapter 5, Murray Weiss[294] wrote an entire book on John O'Neill, the counter-terrorism FBI agent who warned agency leadership about 9/11 long before it happened. And Dr. Yousaf Butt wrote a blog about Saudi Wahhibism[295] while Obama was president. On PBS, Frontline did a story on Madrassas[296] rendering the terrorism side of their Wahhabist (Salafist) education. John O'Neill was a man of profound integrity whose love of country was passionate while his devotion to the FBI was profound and borne of idealism and purity. But his career was twisted in a ball like yarn and it inevitably hurt him. In May, 2000 he was passed over to head the FBI's New York office and he clashed with United States Yemen Ambassador Barbara Bodine. She blocked him from flying to Yemen to investigate the USS

Cole bombing[297] in Yemen by two Al Qaeda suicide bombers on October 12, 2000. He was politically conflicted but remained vigilant to the demands of his position because of his unwavering dedication to his country. He lost a briefcase holding a classified report on terrorism (which was found), and, had he lived, the FBI was dogging him for a formal investigation. On August 16, 2001 he became director of the World Trade Center only to die in its collapse on 9/11 with about 3,000 other victims. Murray Weiss whose book on John O'Neill captures the essence of an incredibly loyal FBI agent. He also points out how his forecast of Osama bin Laden was shunned by Ambassador Barbara Bodine in a very inexcusable and unrelenting continuum of abuse. It is a wonder how this woman succeeded. Murray Weiss points to it like this:

> Throughout his life, O'Neill believed in the best in all of us, and brought that belief alive day after day, and hour after hour, with a passion and intensity and joie de vivre that rubbed off on others. He spent six years at the tip of the spear in the fight against international terrorism, and he tried hard to convince the Clinton administration that bin Laden would mount a massive strike on U.S. soil. Right up to the end of his life, in the collapse of Twin Towers, he insisted: "We are due…for something big."[298]

If one were living in a cocoon or on an island, this would be new. But it was evident to so many. However, denial was first and foremost in the minds of our politicians, and "political correctness" to the extreme was still in its infancy (only to be exacted as a government instrument of mind control and "transformation" when Obama became president). Now, President Trump gets his thoughts with Twitter because the media blocks the truth. If not through Twitter President Trump would be filled by his enemies. The criticism of his daily running commentary is mocked by everyone, even the never-Trumpers. The question is: being the President of the United

States, what is he to do if newspapers are not delivering the truth?

Though this may appear unimportant, it is. The country is so divided politically that people cannot see through their hatred. This is a grave mistake. As Mahatma Gandhi said: "Resentment is taking poison and waiting for the other person to die."[299] This divisiveness is a two-way street, and it endangers the safety and health of the country. If people do not tolerate Trump, vote him out. But, skewering his very image is childish and dangerous. Obama was hardly a saint, and continues his subterfuge. Yet, he passes with unbridled acceptance despite his deceit, flagrant lying and being a man who sewed the very divisions in the country today (not Trump)! Today, Islamic radical terrorism is incubating within the razor wires of our prisons (as referenced at the beginning of this chapter). How much does the country have to be battered around before someone wakes up to a growing sense of urgency (over which John O'Neill spent his professional energy)? If prison life were not so diabolical, captive of "political correctness" and the bastion of bureaucratic waste, then its relevance would not be so important. But it is so intimately connected with the outside world that more than ever its serious concerns should garner the attention for which O'Neill paid the ultimate price.

All the warning signs are around us, in newspapers worldwide, on news channels (especially the BBC), and periodicals like "Foreign Affairs," and "The Economist." Sadanand Dhume writing in the Wall Street Journal unveils for western edification the dangers boiling over from eastern portions of Afghanistan into Pakistan[300]. The mixed populations are as mutable as the winds in the dangerous mountains they inhabit. The Mujahideen (who have ranged into the Middle East as well as Indonesia)[301] fought alongside the United States against the Russians in Afghanistan before morphing into the Taliban against the United States (after Russia pulled out in defeat of their ambitions). A Muslim Rohingya population fled Myanmar (formerly Burma) to India (a Hindu population in direct war with Islam). 40,000 fled and wound up in Bangladesh. In Bangladesh they are living in ,hovels, groveling for food and opened to numerous communicable diseases. The pity is a youth involvement with methamphetamine concoction trading to make money. And youths are being converted to gangs involved in Islamic jihad. And, a Pakistani population, comprising about 15 %, known as Pashtuns claim persecution. The problem with all these groups are twofold. Firstly, as they do have militaristic segments, they weave in and out of country populations and breed radical groups where they contest for their own survival. Like the Haqquina (a cold-blooded radical Islamic terror group) a great deal of these populations seeking manifest destiny survival breed their own radical terror groups. They are connected to the Islamic State much like Boko Haram in West Africa. They weave in and out of the normal populations in the name of Jihad, and are not only living rent free courtesy of leaders of the western monarchies and democracies, but they are freewheeling (independently) as well. Secondly, the time has now passed that the so-called free world acknowledges that the eastern waring places the world at great risk despite that "they are there and we are here." Those days of distance separation isolates western countries from terrorism are long gone. Al Qaeda was all this country understood during the onerous wars fought in Iraq. In just the last 25-30 years the understanding of radicalism has grabbed global attention. Terrorist groups, however they are dignified with foreign sounding names most Americans cannot even pronounce, are not only present in numbers in the United States, but their presence in state and federal prisons are well known.[302,303] This is a new fact of life that most Americans do not fundamentally understand, and particularly those that run our prisons. They understand gangs to a certain extent, but they certainly do not comprehend the subtleties of eastern terror groups (especially the vagaries of Islamic fundamentalism). Political correctness subverts this perception because some "ethno-ism" condemns the reality of what is happening in this country. While a good number of politicians refuse to admit to this reality, people are dying in acts of terror which may color their understanding. That is hard to understand. Radicalization with malicious intent could be suppressed if its existence was not politicized, or, if it affected a loved one or family member. In the meantime, politicians getting re-elected overrides dealing with the problems associated with third world terrorism.

Unfortunately, the prisons are housing the unfortunate with this growing population of radical ideologues. Radicals have been nurtured from a very young age to commit jihad and convert where possible. It is a form of imperious "theory reductionism" whereby "good reasoning-bad reasoning" is a media tool to simplify the terrorist acts growing in the country. In reality, the impoverished and dangerous cities versus the reality of growing radical pockets in cities are separate issues, though they may converge. Attached to arguments of racism, xenophobia, religious bigotry, and wholesale character assaults with foul-mouthed language is tragic. It is nothing but abusive invective which does nothing more than stir up resentment.

The reality of prison life is to heal those non-violent prisoners who can be taught that breaking the law is not self- fulfilling, and advancing them a measure of independence by teaching them that a trade is their way out. When the prison becomes infected with a radical element, the possibilities for reform are affected. Calling out radicalization is essential to expose and deter it within the prison system. Otherwise, the problem of reform will never be advanced. Using peaceful Muslims as a political cudgel does not add to the discussion. As much as that is wrong, it is also unforgivable to deny the radicalization of elements within the national prism system is a problem. As the Irish playwright Oscar Wilde adequately pointed out: "There is no sin except stupidity."[304]

Part of the reason (as numerously stated) for overpopulation of American prisons is tied to corruption, be it in sentencing, parole boards, prosecution, and prejudices associated with political beliefs and associations. An entire book could be written on these points, but suffice it to say that there are reasons why the prisons are littered with individuals who are victims of political chicanery. It may be a bureaucrat with some basic animism or some administrator gaming the system. It is imperative to eradicate violence but also to discontinue the nonsensical flooding of jails and prisons at the taxpayer's expense.

There are many imperfections in all bureaucracies, and even the court system. Centered amidst all of them is the prison system. It includes the state, federal and private prisons, but particularly the state system which houses by far the greatest number of prisoners. The prison system should never be underestimated simply because our prisons are protective barriers for all citizens. They are foreign to most people who essentially never have any reason to think about them in their daily lives. However, families with members incarcerated are always active to support a family member. I have seen many examples of a mother or father (or both) in serious pain from the expectation of a son or daughter in prison for a non-violent crime that appears excessive. It is a fairly discouraging and helpless position for a mother/father. And, as well, a great number of very young marauders or killers who will never see the light of day again. This ratchets up the pain for a family. For those who have never experienced the day-to-day burden there is nothing comparable. Prisons are a shock to the newly minted "lifer," even a youth given a 10 year sentence.

Many have written that they have devoted time to meet with prisoners to encourage and support some educational remediation. I refer to these people, the do-gooders, to promote some personal cause (be it institutional or political). They never see at any lengthy period of time the core of the prison yard. And, it is not being in the actual institution because the meeting places are situated away from the yard and cell blocks in rooms just off the central call center. These are buffers to the internal prison. Then they claim they understand the misery of incarceration. This hardly accounts for seeing the minute-to-minute life within the internal housing. Seeing where prisoners live their days in a maximum-security institution is an eyeful!

The more dangerous, the greater the vulnerability for psychology case workers, medical-dental professionals, and guards who are alert to any eventuality. There are many different personality types, and the most aggressive are, capable of any move on someone at any time for any reason. This is jaw dropping the first time a prison guard neophyte sees physical violence or becomes the object of some prisoner's beatdown. For this reason, lay people, educators, or visitors are not permitted into the yard because prisoners are capable of physical reactions within a split second. As I said in the first chapter, it took me a very long time to accept that I could actually be assaulted at the blink of an eye. And, this is why visitors and professional tutors, legal aides, as well as family, are kept away from the guts of the prison yard. Therefore, even though some professionals give of their time to certain programs for incarcerated small groups, this does not provide precise exposure or gain insight to the way prisoners deal with the demands of prison life. Prisons are tense places, and it runs a sense of terror right up the spine of a prisoner at the outset of a lengthy sentence.

There are valid points as to why such a surface view of the in-house lifestyle is so deceiving. The sudden change in the everyday culture is challenging and intolerable to the majority. Idleness and frustration are a precarious mix. Working in a prison is impactful because at every level it becomes clearly evident that something is very wrong in how the system is managed and why basic thinking about how to manage the institutions is missing. The DNA of the prison genome reveals fundamental errors of expression. Three very sensitive cases gained notoriety and saturated the newspapers and media for the last few years. Two involved sexual predation. One additional one involves the university admissions through a cheating scandal[305, 306, 307]. There are many legal cases (probably hundreds) which can be cited, but I point these out how the prison system can be unnecessarily misguided. The first involves Harvey Weinstein, the Hollywood producer who serially raped women (in a sex-promotion scandal for burgeoning actresses: kind of a pay for play!), but was tried on one outlandish one and was given a multiyear prison sentence in New York. He has yet to be tried for cases in California, but he is old enough that his New York sentence is a death sentence. In order, the second is the cheating scandal involving Lori Loughlin and her husband, Mossimo Giannulli, who paid a huckster agent hundreds of thousands of dollars to lie about athletic skills and athletic prowess in rowing to get into the University of California. Lori is getting two years in prison, and Mossimo five months. And, then they'll do community service and payment of hundreds of thousands of dollars in addition to the heavy legal fees. The final one involves Senator Robert Menendez who, for many years, lived a seemingly scurrilous, cheating life. In this case, he had a prolonged relationship with a Palm Beach County, Florida Dermatologist for whom he did the favor of trying to extricate him from Medicaid fraud for sexual favors. He was tried in New York City in a jury trial but skated with good lawyering.

Why should these cases be cited? Because they crystalize the crux of "Prison Reform!" All three cases, to me, are horrendous because it cuts to the core of the "Rich and Famous" exploiting their wealth, position, and connections to advance personal schemes. For me, these kinds of people should not escape, but they should not serve for this reason: who will pay for their care during incarceration? The taxpayer. Their sentencing should perhaps involve house confinement for the length of their sentences followed by paying their fines and doing community service afterwards. Menendez is the typical example of a corrupt Washington, DC senator who can skate because he can afford expensive lawyering. His behavior over the years has always been edgy, borderline illegal, but always meretricious. His sentence will ultimately be served in his own mind and confronting his maker.

Nevertheless, the point to be made, is that is where prison reform begins: the sentencing of people who can be kept at home with anklets with homing device attachment. I am sure many people will disagree, but I then say, spend some time in prisons and then try to understand that the reason for the out- of-control American prison system is grossly overpopulation. All through the judicial system there has to be creative thinking and processing. Violence, on the other hand, requires the full measure of the legal system.

Let's now contrast the above conversation with the following. The black population in the United States is approximately 13%, and yet make up about 40% of the prison population (state and federal). From a visual assessment, I construed from my time working in a maximum-security prison that blacks seemed to account for about three-quarters of the population. And, then whites (about 39%) and Hispanics (about 16%-19%) made up the difference. And yet, when I started in a Level II mixed population security prison there was a noticeable breakdown, much closer to the national statistics. There seemed to be more Hispanics in the Level III prison as well. Prisons in general located in rural areas have very few people of color in their prisons so that the District of Columbia, Mississippi, Louisiana and Georgia have the highest numbers of people of color (where their prisoners are reflective of the national statistics)[308].

When looking at statistics from the Bureau of Justice Statistics from the year 2007, the National Prisoner Statistics were divided from all prisoners into the following categories: violent offenses, property offenses, drug offenses, public-order offenses and other/unspecified. They were subdivided into all prisoners, male, female, white, black and Hispanic. In breaking down all categories into very specific offences, blacks had the highest "estimated percent of sentenced prisoners under state jurisdiction." Hispanics were close behind followed by whites very close behind. The differentials were noticeable but not egregious; and, females less than males in the "violent categories," but females considerably more in the "property offenses" categories. In general, 7 of 10 convicted felons were sentenced to either jail or prison, the average sentence lasted 5 years. Violent felons and non-violent felons were sentenced to prison for an average 8 and 3 years respectively. The Federal prison rates compared with approximate rates, but the statistics were upgraded to 2018. The 5-year sentencing for all categories were quite similar. The key, however, is when population differences are examined: Blacks and Hispanics seemed to have higher sentencing rates, and the former more than the latter. And, looking over several sites, the numbers match up to the extent that sentencing is similar over the past twenty years[309].

The website "Prison Policy Initiative Updates" records the following from a very recent review: Mass Incarceration: The Whole Pie 2018:[310]

> Beyond identifying the parts of the criminal justice system that impact the most people, we should also focus on who is most impacted and who is left behind by policy change. For example, people of color are dramatically overrepresented in the nation's prisons and jails. These racial disparities are particularly stark for Blacks, who make up 40% of the incarcerated population despite representing 13% of U.S. residents. Gender disparities matter too: rates of incarceration have grown even faster for women than for men. As policymakers continue to push for reforms that reduce incarceration, they should avoid changes that will widen disparities, as has happened with juvenile confinement and with women in state prisons[311] [emphasis mine].

Michelle Alexander makes the following points:

> State legislatures were eager to jump on the "get tough" bandwagon, passing harsh drug laws, as well as "three strikes" laws mandating a life sentence for those convicted of any third offense. These mandatory minimum statutory schemes have transformed an enormous amount of power from judges to prosecutors. Now simply by charging someone with an offense carrying a mandatory sentence of ten to fifteen years or life, prosecutors are able to force people to plead guilty rather than risk a decade or more in prison. Prosecutors admit that they routinely charge people with crimes for which they technically have probable cause

but which they seriously doubt they could ever win[312].

And this point which confirms my research observations:

> No. Studies consistently indicate that drug markets, like American society generally, reflect our nation's racial and socioeconomic boundaries. Whites tend to sell to whites, blacks to blacks...The notion that most illegal drug use and sales happens in the ghetto is pure fiction. Drug trafficking occurs there, but it occurs everywhere else in America as well. Nevertheless, black men have been admitted to state prison on drug charges at a rate that is more than thirteen times higher than white men. The racial bias inherent in the drug war is a major reason that 1 in every 14 black men was behind bars in 2006, compared with 1 in 106 white men. For young black men, the statistics are even worse. One in 9 black men between the ages of twenty and thirty-five was behind bars in 2006, and far more were under some form of penal control--- such as probation or parole. These gross racial disparities simply cannot be explained by rates of illegal drug activity among African Americans[313].

Within very small differences, depending on the research site, these facts capsulize the uphill battle blacks face every day against racial bias every step of the way through the court system. There is no doubt that it is onerous and prejudicial. It is one thing to research and write about findings as Michelle Alexander so aptly does, but it is far more striking to be a witness day in, day out.

I have never seen anyone proffer any reasonable and realistic solution except for more bureaucratic interference. As I stand hopefully as insulated from bias as a human being can possibly be, "prison reform" for me is code for the government kicking the "bent out of shape can from so much knocking around" further down the road. And, as the politicians change, the music spanks out a new sound but with a different riff to update the times, but with a similar message as if the public hasn't heard it before. They do it because they have the stage to do so and because, I do believe, they hold very tight-lipped the feeling that "Joy and John Q. Public" are not very razor- sharp observers of the news scene. So, day by day, week by week, month by month, and year by year they pump out the same political drivel. A politician, in fact, just wants to appeal to her/his constituency, nothing more. As H.L Mencken, deceased years ago, but an erstwhile columnist (Chicago Daily News) and editor (The Baltimore Sun), once commented for the ages: "No one ever went broke underestimating the intelligence of the American public."[314,315]

Whether you laugh sarcastically or knowingly does not matter. What matters to me is that I believe that politicians will say and do anything to get elected and then re-elected for as long as they can (and want) to play out the string. It is amazing how so sincere and convincing they all sound. In the long run they all sound out the same twaddle and then return home in retirement as millionaires. Unfortunately, "the peoples' twaddle" is critically important and often timely significant. Their verisimilitude can sound so convincing. At times, the repetitive daily outpourings can make a person momentarily forgetful because most people do not spend their lives tracing the whereabouts of their Congress Representatives and Senators. Cynical? Yes. Truthful? Yes, unfortunately! I think they learned from passed on "political genetics" that to play the game always remember the rules as to how the game is played. Most of them play like impressarios par excellence, others not so!

In this vein, as I read Michelle Alexander's book, my memories of my daily toil at the prison came alive. I would estimate that the maximum-security prison where I worked was about 75-80 % black. They were primarily in for violent felonies: straight murder, gang related murder, kidnapping and murder, pederasty and rape (and often murder), robbery and murder, etc. An entire cell block was filled with those who, in addition to their violent felonies, were psychologically disturbed or deranged. I talked to most, quite repeatedly, during my time. And, I got to know many very, very well as I interacted with them daily for over a year. That is why I so identified with Michelle Alexander's book. And, gradually, being the cynic (but, always with a smile and a gratuitous joke), I realized I could return to the world many generations from now and nothing regarding prison policy will have changed. That's if the world is still here and we haven't "nuked" each other.

I have read a lot getting ready to write this book because I thought some of the thoughts should be relayed on paper. I had an epiphany one day as I was walking across a very large "yard" as many, many prisoners were yelling their hellos and high fives to me. Oh, there were some who wanted me dead, and I was many times warned. But I was told they were just sickos and not to pay attention. I ultimately knew my time was up one early spring day when the air was clear and wholesome, the breeze was satisfying, and the planes were passing above framed so eerily stark against a baby blue sky. My brain in a fog, I was so suddenly accosted by a group from the "the psycho cell block" all talking smack to me. There was not a guard in sight. The pounding of my heart and subtle evidence of sweat around my brow conveyed a message. I was done, simple as that. I no longer wanted to "push the envelope" any further!

This was common because the prison could not hire enough personnel to fill a markedly deficient staff. As I previously stated, never had I been witness to so many overworked and underpaid guards in my life. Many would work as long as they could take the intense pressure, and then quit. I knew a great many of them very, very well. They were treated so poorly for the risks to which they confronted, often many times in a day. Working 2-3 other jobs, they were exhausted most of the time. Everyone knew it, right up to the warden, but they were always confronted with an ironclad bureaucracy.

As I saw myself in clear danger, I did something I have never done in my life. One of the real young prisoners grabbed the papers I was carrying underneath my right arm because I had my hands in my pockets. I was walking very slowly to take in the beauty of the day. I looked up to the cloudless azure- laden sky when I was blinded by an overhead plane's silver skin reflecting right in my eyes. The plane's silhouette was passing its shadow on the ground when suddenly I was jarred and I could now feel my blood pressure rise with the thought of imminent danger. My eyes were blurred by the momentary glare of the sun, but I was alert enough to see several shadows next to mine, blocking my passage. That's how it begins in a prison, with the unanticipated. I have been a runner my whole life as I ran in college and continued marathoning afterwards. So, I am in fairly good shape, even now.

The "looney tunes" who grabbed my papers started looking at them as he laughed and gestured to his buddies. Without any consideration of the danger, I did something that in another circumstance with a more rational composure I would never have contemplated. I responsively grabbed it right back as I yelled at him to cool his heels and get back to his cell block. I reacted so instinctively that I realized later that my friends and colleagues were justified in calling me "certifiable!" Let's just say this was a group from the "psycho ward/cellblock." What was I doing? I felt my heart ready to burst from my chest. Believe it or not serendipitously a new gate had just been installed in the fence just a couple of weeks before. My adrenalin rush lifted me in a sprint to the gate, actually leaving them long behind me. The guard who normally attends several gates in the area had seen me and opened it enough so I could fly through before slamming it shut. I never made a big deal, but I "made hay" to quit that day. I knew the Warden and his two associates would not like it, but I went right to the administrative office and handed in my credentials. I never looked back, and weeks later after the ugly internal payback was relatively gone, I felt that I had probably avoided a substantial threat to my life. After a bit over a year at a maximum-security prison, I had learned more than enough. It took me months before I had an uninterrupted night's sleep!

I got very friendly with a guard (with whom I shared a "love" for The Boston Red Sox baseball team), and I did not even tell him what happened. I did not want the controversy, and I knew he would probably try to convince me to stay. He was a lot younger, and I felt he would not understand.

He was a 6'5" brawny, immensely athletic black man who played linebacker in his home state of California. He was the only guy I ever hugged every day when I left. Much younger, he was intuitively insightful and with an indwelling spirituality far beyond his years. He was the only person I knew I would miss. His intellect and skills are going to carry him right up the ladder of success. One day he will be a warden.

That episode emotionally superimposed on a prisoner who told me he was going to "f" me up gave me enough reason to quit. I knew it had nothing to do with me. Prison is a nasty place where anything can spontaneously take place. Prisoners are cloistered like sardines. The prisoners I knew never practiced any kind of reasonable hygiene so they always smelled. That in itself was quite disturbing. It was the epitome of their *weltschmerz*, a world pain that breeds disengagement and withdrawal. Most of the prisoners typified this mindset until they let loose and rose up to physical violence. So, when I read or listen to discussions or read books dealing with prison reform, I know that this violent subset of prisoner will never be rehabilitated. No book in the world can replace looking into eyes of pure evil in order to witness the extreme limit of wanton and bestial behavior. It moves me to this day.

I thought I would be undergirded by my sensibilities, but, frankly, I was wrong. What one sees the germination of gruesome behavior at an early age, this is the end result when such young people are abandoned and neglected. As I would always say to my colleagues: do I believe what I know through my own life experience or my "lyin' eyes"? There is no doubt that your eyes do not lie in a maximum security prison.

I had witnessed the dangerous and general bad language every day I was at work. Lockdowns were common because they were "time outs" to slow things down and regain control for the staff. So, my decision to quit when I did was convincing, not impulsive. It was predicated on many months of being witness to the unpredictable and the explosive! Maximum security prisons are quirky and offbeat. A place with a lot of disgruntled and mistreated employees entrusted with awesome responsibilities without, in my opinion, a proper defense armamentarium is a combustible environment. Everyone, to a tee, right up to the warden and associate wardens, were the nicest people I have ever had the good fortune to know. But I wanted to live, and I was no longer in the mood for any further incidents. I was employed as a professional so I got to know the prisoners quite well, and from a different perspective. I knew that, for myself, my experiences compelled me to feel that if I had stayed long enough, it was not going to be a happily-ever-after ending. From what I observed and researched there was no doubt that upbringing is everything. The nucleus of childhood is the family unit. And, a complete family provides an atmosphere from which children have a greater chance for education and the benefits which evolve. Black families are fragmented, and the children have less of a chance (statistically, as I have shown) to develop their potential. On this basis, and from what I experienced, there is no doubt that American prisons (not all, but particularly in the southern states) reflect "the new Jim Crow." Prison reform must take this into consideration. But, more significant, is the need "to reform" the inner cities where black-on-black murder is beyond sad.

Michelle Alexander's[316] personal comments with regard to blacks against the backdrop of overzealous prosecution, sentencing, and mass incarceration are incisive and dispositive of an endless loop of "same ole, same ole!" She happens to be far better than I in laying out the framework. It is sinful from my point of view. Two men amidst many, many prisoners I got to know so very well exemplify everything she statistically vouchsafed in her book.

Both men are "lifers," natural life. They both committed murder at very young ages, but were not minors. They are presently in their mid-fifties. One claims he did not commit the murder and has been denied parole. The other admits to the murder he committed, and he has also been denied parole. They are both reconciled to the expectation of dying in prison. Both are already rehabilitated, that's if I can judge them correctly. And, I believe I am not wrong. One talked my ear off forever with a machine gun lilt that took me a long time to truly understand. We are both sports fanatics so we usually reviewed the past night scores every day, with unending commentary as well. The other was extremely polite and serious. We discussed conditions in the world and how angry everyone is. They are interesting cell mates, and their friendship has inured over many years. I can never forget them. This is where the rubber hits the road. As I passed each day and researched as much as I could, I came to the realization that prison reform is very possible with the one caveat that will reframe the entire picture. I have noted this throughout. It would require people with determination and real political clout. As much as I hold almost no trust in politicians, they are all we have. My criticism is that they are not only one dimensional, but they have not one clue what goes on in a prison. Prisons as well are one dimensional, and they are controlled by deliberately pseudo-sensitive bureaucrats. If it were not for the guts and commitment of wardens, they would fall apart.

Prisons are filled with honest, hardworking and level-headed administrators, but they are at the mercy of directors and their political ambitions. Bureaucrats have a very false front and they last as long as they can manipulate their political contacts for another higher government job.

As I said before, but it is worth repeating: the bureaucrat's idea of projecting how well their prisons are doing are the "dog- and-pony" shows they plan to ensure publicity and "faux contentment!" A little lunch gathering, a band presentation for the television nightly news, a convivial spiritual gathering of the religious prisoners, a guest speaker to discuss what life will be upon parole or release, etc. I am not trying to disparage what it represents to the people who rely heavily on this connection. It keeps them grounded with purpose. Through this approach the hope is to one day being reunited with a loved one or a family. Believe me, this is important, but it is hardly prison reform.

What will it take? As I walked in every day in the still of the night, and it was a long, sometimes dangerous walk, I thought it was right in front of their eyes. If they took all the money they spent for punitive imprisonment of the non-violent offenders, rehabilitation would have practical meaning and commitment. Violent offenders would have to be sectioned off because they are so hardcore that most are too dangerous to ever recirculate into society.

Fortunes are wasted on a pure punitive environment. The time should be spent in a far more meaningful manner. The DNA of a harsh reality is wasteful. It contributes nothing more than isolation and boredom. It is like a spreading cancer that kills the spirit and leaves prisoners despondent and requisitioned off to a useless existence like throwaway, marginalized commodities. We do not properly think through why the prison system is a failed one. It is more convenient and easier for everyone connected to the government to draw a salary as well as retirement and health benefits, and not shake up the system. Long term this lazy philosophy is untenable. The prisons can only populate so far. Insanity truly is doing the same thing over and over expecting a different result. Parole is a great example because parole boards are corrupt and generally lacking creativity and beneficence.

There's a timeworn suggestion that all comes to the one who waits. This is so hackneyed, but there is an addendum which offers a far greater chance: that is, work like hell while waiting! That saying is nowhere more true than in prisons. Ultimately, there is no prisoner who wants to be shut away. For this to happen a prisoner must be under probation, paroled or released outright. She/he can be released after time served or early based on good behavior. There's a lot of lawyering involved. Examining the statistics from the year 2016, 4,537,100 were under community supervision (probation or parole). This was down 49,800 prisoners (1.1%) for the year 2016. 1 in 55 adults in the USA were under community supervision by the end of 2016. This accounted approximately for 1 in 55 adults. From 2015 to 2016 the adult probation populations declined by 1.4%, falling 52,500 prisoners. Also in 2016, probation exits increased from 2,043,200 in 2015 to 2,071,400 in 2016. Exits from parole increased from 2,040/, 200 to 2071,400. Release from parole decreased from about 463,700 in 2015 to 456,000 in 2016. Looking at the recidivism highlights is quite significant because the aim is to stay out of prison. The last statistics for this is 1994. Within 3 years of their release in 1994, 61.2% were re-arrested for a new offense. Property and drug offenders had the highest re-arrest rates: 73.8%, (property offenders), 66.7% (drug offenders) respectively, and 64.6% (public-order offenders) respectively. The big one in this survey: 22.5% for violent offenses(murder, sexual assault and robbery). They were all retained in prison. In this survey, 93.1 % had prior arrests, 81.4% had prior convictions, and 43.6% had served prison sentences. At the end of the 2016 year 4,537,100 adults were under community supervision. This was the lowest since 1999. The rates of probation and parole were down, but very marginal. The significant figure of all of these is the re-arrest numbers within 3 years. A significant general figure: 7.6% of all released prisoners were re-arrested for a new crime in another state other than the one that released them. Finally, all the studies are not comprehensive. This means that segments of states are cited, and they are all over the place. The percentage differences are so minor that the figures above are true as reported by the Bureau of Justice Statistics. The interesting observation is that African-Americans account for about 13% of the population, but their incarceration rates are significantly higher for violent offenses (by 6.4 times), for property offenses (by 4.4 times) and for drug offenses (by 9.4 times)[317, 318]. Yet, there are no clear-cut recidivism studies for blacks. One study shows significantly higher rates for African Americans over whites[319].

Finally, current employment statistics show the following: the current overall unemployment record: 4.1%; the African- American unemployment rate: 6.8%; and, the Hispanic unemployment rate: 4.9%. The unemployment rate for African- Americans is the lowest since the government started recording rates in 1972. The Hispanic rate is down from 5.9 which was recorded in December, 2016.320, 321Ultimately the unemployment rate lowered to 3.8% (before COVID-19 set in).

My personal philosophy about statistics is of their representational importance. They can be adjusted to make any point one wants to make unless they are identifiably so distorted that no sane person would believe them. In this case, however, crime, poverty, inability to make a living, and recidivism are linked irrevocably. Desperate people are vulnerable to adopt associations which will enhance. Just like gangs, people who do not have the good fortune to have advantages to prosper will find what they need individually, and most often through their peers.

No greater example are African-Americans. The saying "to go along to get along" defines what they have had to do to enhance their status quo. The misfortune for minority groups like African-Americans since the 1600's during colonial days has been a state of repression, be it through slavery, or reconstruction in the south after the Civil War. During the climb through the Industrial Revolution city growth would change American society. Right through the ensuing years until today all the effects of major socio-economic disadvantages were poised to rear their ugly head.

Crime became a critical survival tool. Crime and the prison system became inextricably mixed. Pain and suffering grew in tandem as prisons began to become substantially crowded. The prisons modernized over the years, but they are still unsterile and filthy as if bureaucrats incredulously boast as new facilities in pockets around the country without any regard to sufficient health standards. The number increases over time were tantamount to "rotting" amidst behaviors which left cellblocks unlivable.

The fact is that the prisons are awfully overpopulated. The statistics delineated above demonstrate, among many suggested facts, a most obvious point: they accomplish very little except to depress the spirit of people, they rehabilitate comparatively few (by the numbers), and nothing of substance is ever planned to make a difference. It is like an autoimmune disease where the system is attacking itself. As long as polemics rule the political world, rest assured nothing will change. A new tapestry of social programs are foisted up as magic bullets to heal wounds, but the scab keeps getting ripped off. The wounds of prison spirit are patched periodically until another corrupt political solution is initiated that fails.

The solution relies on each state to manage its own sets of dilemmas. To get the federal government in charge is like a giant octopus trying to manage too many distant tentacles. Disparate locations cannot be managed in the way resources are needed to allocate them for an entire system change. As Thomas "Tip" P. O'Neill II, Democratic Congressman from the 8th Congressional District in Massachusetts and former Speaker of the U.S. House of Representatives, uttered words of wisdom which has held up brilliantly for terse truth-telling: "All politics is local."[322, 323] It is crisp with logic. He was a master of collegiality. His reasoning was based on his representation of both the 11th (John F. Kennedy's before he ran for the Senate and ultimately the Presidency) and the 8th Congressional districts. He was the first modern politician to understand that Washington, D.C. could never understand the needs of local citizens in his Massachusettsdistrict?

That reasoning was brilliant in easier times. In those days political differences were respected, and everything was reasonably negotiable. The degree of divisiveness of today did not exist. Democrats and Republicans understood their differences and their constituencies. But they never spewed the raunchy and venomous vilifications at one another. They yelled and screamed themselves blue out in the hustings as well as in hallowed domains of the House and Senate, but the visceral hatreds were absent. The last true gentleman was George W. Bush, who was equally as platitudinous as a veiled spokesman for the moneyed elite, but if anything positive can be said of him, he was reasonable. However, he got the country into a lot of trouble: The Middle East War which revived the Islamic fundamentalist nightmare after the 10-year Iraqi- Iranian war settled. He woke up a sleeping giant that is now a worldwide jihad. Bush had a chance at prison reform because of the imprisonment of violent jihadists at the American prison at Guantanamo Bay, Cuba. He was under a world of criticism, and deserved it because of inaction.

He was followed by the "snake oil salesman" in Barack Hussein Obama who lied from his beginning to end creating a gulf between people in this country as never witnessed before. I am apolitical and tend to judge people on their merits. He was a mystery. A youthful, smiling, collegial personality he stormed on the national scene with the plan for "hope and change." He was all words and "nothing!" He never represented the true Black experience, and that was a mystery. Nothing tangible. He never even got involved with the Chicago black infamy, and it just mires still today in horrific murder rates. Today, Baltimore and Philadelphia are suffering from the same abomination. Poverty, crime and murder rates that have swell detention centers and prisons evolved slowly. Obama could have used his sway and the power of the Presidency to improve the black hopes and prayers. All he did was to hang around Louis Farrakhan while Jews and Blacks suffered from his neglect. He was singularly responsible for Trump's election. He left the Presidency with more turmoil and divisiveness in the country than when he entered. And Trump fell back on his heels wheeling-dealing with disreputable oratory and fractious, indiscrete behavior. From Bush to Trump, the mass incarceration rates which had been decreasing in the 1990's are presently expanding again.

Lord knows how Obama won a Nobel Prize for Peace October 9, 2009 when he had not done anything early in his Presidency. He was not even in the office a year. Division can only lead to disharmony and fighting, which it has since the days of George W. Bush. Not one of the three possessed the rare quality of wisdom. No one can predict if Trump's fractious tweets will leave the country irreconcilable for many years to come. This does not bode well for anyone. What this shows is that extremes breed misfortune, consensus builds and enhances good fortune. "Tip" O'Neill taught President Ronald Reagan the meaning of good-measured, civilized communication and consensus building. Today, this is dead in the water of the body politic. The prison is like the closet in a house where unused clothes are stored. In time it's hard to remember what's there. And, if clothes eventually prevent knowing what's inside, then eventually they are thrown away. In modern times, the state prison system has become storage facilities where humans are managed, not cultivated meaningfully for raising their quality of life. There is no doubt that prisoners today are throwaways, in many regards through no fault of their own. At least Trump got the First Step Act[324] passed for implementing release of nonviolent prisoners and revisiting sentencing reform (it is said that prison reform is sentencing reform). The problem as I see it is the fact that the state prison is far bigger in size (and therefore problems), yet there is no leadership to deal with it. Non-violent prisoners are not throwaway clothes, stored and forgotten.

The prison system is a microcosm of life, an assemblage of humanity gone awry. Any chance for prison reform depends on a consensus building of state and federal governments. The factual basis right now in the Washington D.C. mindset is non- existent. Reviewing some facts again, but in capsule form casts a shadow on mass incarceration. More important, it shows that without politicians being true to their appointed tasks it is impossible to "slenderize" our prisons. Legislation is the only way to control prosecutors and give judges a different kind of playbook with which to make sentencing more matter-of-fact (compassionate). Realistically, money has to come from somewhere to become rehabilitative.

The costs are extreme: Inclusive studies of 50 states do not exist, but a 40-state study by The Vera Institute concludes: 39 billion a year (probably higher; it is now 2020). This accounts for approximately $31,286.00 per inmate for each taxpayer. This 2010 study also showed that taxpayers paid 14% more than prison budgets anticipated. The private prisons exist strictly to make money and answer to their investors. The federal prisons are run by a behemoth bureaucracy, the federal government. So, everything about them is usually stodgy and congealed from years of over-regulations. State prisons house the preponderance of prisoners housed in the United States. So, just to repeat what I have delineated: the approximate 2.3 million prisoners are housed in 1,720 state prisons, 102 federal prisons, 2,250 detention centers and 3,300 local jails, 80 Indian Country, 3 military prisons (not including jails which are called stockades in the military), and the Guantanamo Bay detention center (aka Gitmo, the name also for the naval base, but used to house Islamic terrorists). All these numbers are meant to emphasize the meaning of these numbers: White prisoners: 39% of 64% of the U.S. population: Hispanic: 19% of 16% of the U.S. population; and, Black: 40% of 13% of the U.S. population. These Vera Institute statistics were taken from the Bureau of Justice Statistics[325]. The American taxpayer is really held up for a lot of money. Looking at the disproportionate numbers, there is an incredible overboard of black people considering their low population. The numbers just cannot be argued.

The bleak reality is perplexing because on the one hand there is no question that "mass incarceration" is never going to be reconciled if one is cynical and if its reversal of (mis-)fortune (reaching critical mass) resolves only by being "a Cockeyed Optimist!"[326] Hopefully, the reality is more pressing.

There are a multiplicity of factors which make resolution to this enigma almost impossible, real issues: the kind of poverty that is almost impossible to eradicate because elected officials are too corrupt to be proactive, the inadequacy of inner city education, gun violence of the inner cities, drug use and trafficking smothering futures at an early age, the fractured family unit of the inner city blacks, opportunity skewed against minorities, the general cost of college education, the costs of medical care, and many other social programs that never get going because of divisive government. Major issues are too political, which means a political representative reserves his/her obligation to lie if it translates to a fabrication of lies. Why? Because it is not illegal for politicians to lie, but it is for people who lie in front of a congressional committee. Some of the formidable circular firing squads involve the following: cost of immigration and gang violence, merciless treatment of ICE and police departments, denial and mismanagement of political Islamic terrorism, gun violence in American schools, denial of American history, the slugfest over the NRA, politicians using sanctuary cities and sanctuary states mischaracterizing facts to destroy swaths of large communities for the sake of political advantage (and, the costs driving their inevitable bankruptcy), the malice of forethought to destroy American sovereignty knowing perfectly well every non-violent country in the world safeguards their own, and (most of all) the terrible burden placed over the federal government with unremitting diversions of a malicious shadow leadership (best characterized as the 'deep state") tangibly undercutting the peoples' business. This is "the DNA of Reality" which is loathsome. It is reflective of a fascist country like Venezuela or Cuba. Accept it or not, it is the reason why the approval rating of Congress hovers at 18% or less. In any other consideration a normal thinking person would be horrified.

When there is a street brawl, reconciliation occurs only when sensible thinking intervenes and brings the vying parties to the negotiating table. Talk is cheap, and solutions to hatreds default to labored presentations. The laws of the United States are based on the Constitution, originalist (not activist) interpretation. If settled law cannot be respected for its consistency, then anyone or any one body can make up its laws as it proceeds. That is where this country is right now. All the issues that are now coming before the Supreme Court at the present time are a reflection of the degree of fracture impeding consensus in thecountry.

Common sense demands that prison reform necessitates leadership to act, not another government or academic colloquium to discuss tired suggestions. Most anyone who has written intelligently on the subject is familiar with the statistics. Repetitive rhetoric, as Congress seems to engorge like an alligator, is tiresome. Isn't the storyline of "Mr. Smith Goes to Washington," as acted famously by Jimmy Stewart, to present "righteous indignation" for the sorry lot of polluted politicians so over by now? This was 1939[327]. How many generations more does this have to be repeated before Congressional leadership comes to its senses? George Santayana had it right when he acknowledged that "Those who cannot remember the past are condemned to repeat it."[328] This is a self-fulfilling prophecy, to wit an intelligent observer finds nothing but madness and inexorable shame.

No one should revel in the plight of a prisoner no matter what may have been the crime. Only going into a prison on a daily basis can a person begin to realize that losing one's identity is a human tragedy. A human life blends into a blur of insignificance. Only in time does the first-time prisoner learn how much freedom is to be treasured. Liberty is the greatest gift to man, mostly undervalued because people accept it too casually, and especially by prisoners. Life is not a rehearsal. It is robust and term-limited, elements that should not be casually appreciated.

My impression as I got to know many prisoners, they all seem to exhibit either anger, deep regret or a jittery frustration. I could see very early on that languishing unproductively is a slow death, and seemingly worse than the death penalty itself. It sucks the life out of a human being and makes them crazy. I could see some who lost their composure out of shear exasperation. Wallowing in boredom day -in -day out was worse for the uncreative, uneducated and uninspired. Just paying witness to the specter of people living in a vacuum makes a case for much more of an active determination for prison reform. One of my colleagues always commented with a laugh that we were all just one "heartbeat" from a mistake which would put us away like any of the prisoners. Remembering the first time I heard this left me quite lost in such a thought. Opportunity is a gift that most do not begin to fully understand until observing the prisoner's state of depleted meaning. If nothing else, it is the total argument for reform (inner city reform).

The one reference that always stopped me short is always hearing politicians talk about "prisoners" per se when discussing prison reform. It showed me how their brains were oriented. I said in my early chapters that very cruel and abject killers possessed a vacant stare which reflected a total absence of soul. I knew quite a number of these individuals. Common sense convinced me that they are totally irredeemable. I still think about Andrea Yates and Susan Smith who both, in taking the lives of their children, should never see individual freedom again. I never have met them, but I met many who murdered children and they were like empty vessels possessing a remoteness, glazed and hollow look that jarred my sensibilities.

When you examine the financial commitment of taxpayers' money to imprison these types of violent people, it makes sense to isolate them to make a commitment for the preponderance of prisoners who can and ought to be rehabilitated. I know that the maximum-security prison today is a lot more complex and demanding than ever because of globalization.

Prison policies have to be updated because they are filled with meaningless demands and commands. They lack purpose to deal with today's blend of changes as a result of the population changes. They trivialize the importance of making these changes because of self-satisfaction with out-of- date, almost pointless demands on the unimportant. It is incumbent upon leadership to be serious enough to change with the times and not be lost in trivial rules and regulations. Treat employees like children and they'll react with childish, disgruntled behavior. Body searching for household items brought into the prison and treating them as contraband is childish and over-the-top for adult employees (oh, yes, I understand "the chemicals argument"; ridiculous!). If prisons concentrated on what's important, they would not be suffering from constant employee turnover. I do not want to get into it here because it is more important to concentrate where emphasis should be placed: on organization and leadership qualities needed to appropriate a methodology which would broaden a necessary thought process and plan for prison reform. It is not going to come from Washington, D.C. elites who coddle their power and featherbed the system. Prison reform demands initiative, planning and aggressive guidance.

Having spent enough time dealing with people in leadership positions, I see no will to understand a change in direction. I cannot speak to every prison, but it is certain that the people I knew were stuck in dated policies. It always made me feel that the bureaucratic elite were stuck on stupid! They did not seem to understand how ambitious redirection must be compelling, and then regroup to think and plan it through. I am certain the thought is floating above anyone's concern. If people who have written so prolifically on this subject should be concerned, it is this inattention that should be bothersome. For change to take place there must be a change in mindset and a collective decisiveness. I never ever saw this. All I ever witnessed was a level of incivility to employees which burdened them endlessly and saddled their spirits. As Len Marrella pointedly captured in writing:

WATCH YOUR THOUGHTS

WATCH YOUR THOUGHTS
THEY BECOME YOUR WORDS

WATCH YOUR WORDS
THEY BECOME YOUR ACTIONS

WATCH YOUR ACTIONS
THEY BECOME YOUR HABITS

WATCH YOUR HABITS
BECAUSE THEY BECOME YOUR CHARACTER

WATCH YOUR CHARACTER
BECAUSE IT BECOMES YOUR DESTINY[329]

To be a leader "character" is vital to establish a following of people who are on board and feel genuinely what prison reform means. Then, with serious intent, a leader is able to develop a consensus of thinkers who are able to move the "herd" in a new direction. Examine all the old books when prisons were first established[330], and the mindset has regressed, not progressed. This book clearly points out that in the 1800's American prisons were established as "Reformatory" institutions. S.J. Barrows prepared this book in 1900 for The International Prison Commission. The commentary of various prison wardens who wrote about their specific prisons commented emphatically concerning the importance of reform and education, and incidentally, building character. My only comment: what happened? And how far prisons have digressed.

Of course, times are very different, but the bearings are different. Today, the only teaching modality I witnessed of any substance was the very detailed teaching of woodworking with which the prisoners identified and took very seriously. The other areas of educational facilities (library and classroom instruction in various courses) were minimally attended nor taken very seriously. And, as stated before, there were occasional participation in holiday music performances, visitations by locally known musicians, and religious group participation and lectures. These were minimally attended at best.

I did not view this at a serious attempt at education with serious intent. And, there were a lot of group gatherings which I perceived as self-righteous and unproductive (mostly organized fluff).

The intent is not to belittle or besmirch, but rather to emphasize how "reform" will demand a much more provocative commitment. I delineated in detail thoughts on the Presidency because I discern a very distinct lack of understanding of the prison system. I perceive that so many people perceive the distinct need for prison reform, but I see no real "character" in our leaders to direct the country in that direction. Marie Gottschalk renders a very accurate recitation of the observations of the prison system. I may be a bit more doubting than she is, however. She poses a question to which I have a substantive thought because it cuts right to my thoughts. Here is what she queries:

> "The really interesting and pressing question today is not whether the experts, the politicians, or members of the public aregoing to lead the United States out of the crisis of the carceral state. But rather, how do you fashion an effective coalition from elements of all three groups to empty the country's prison and to abolish capital punishment?"[331]

I agree with her motivations for saying what she said because prisons are so hopelessly overloaded, and with many underlying consequences. Her statement cuts right to the core. It is shameful and anathema to honest feelings and sober thinking that the concept just floats around without any serious intent for action. It can be properly blamed on part corruption and part sheer laziness. The way she phrases her statement is very directed to the listless I have exposed. Whether she realizes how repetitive that thought is I do not know. The significant usage of three key words, however, addresses deaf ears: "experts," politicians" and "members of the public."

Experts do not exist, but it took me years to reconcile this fact in my own mind. Instead, I believe there are the "experienced" with deeply vested thoughts based on years trudging through an area(s) of devoted study. In that sense, there is an element of expertise developed, but never so pure as to be the ultimate answer ("the expert"). I have learned that "politicians," though the people who should walk legislation through, never ever get it right. Legislation is always corrupted by add-ons, and politicians use the public forum to administer only what provides "their" best chance to get re-elected. Some of them learn this from the get-go, but others do not. The system is antithetical because a politician who can move legislation in the right direction is just what "prison reform" needs, and requires. And, finally, the public, no matter how stubborn, aggressive, defiant, etc. will always stand for something only if it gets them something they want. Is this cynical? Yes, unfortunately. Selfishness is a strong motivating factor. It drives people to open doors, but there has to be a strong sustaining element to see something through, even it means readjusting for the common good. And, I believe that is the role of "character" to perceive the good that comes from the fruit of labor. I get her query and why she poses it, but such a "coalition" only magnifies the enormity of such a hurdle. It is more than likely why so many over the years have discussed and written about prison reform, and especially mass incarceration. I also think it is extreme to think that prisons will ever be emptied. Prisons should exist to house the innocent of society from the most heinous criminals in society. These are the notoriously vicious killers like Donald Henry "Pee Wee" Gaskins: The Hitchhikers' Killer, Aileen Wuornos: the Monster, Ahmad Suradji: The Sorcerer, Alexander Chikatilo: The Butcher, etc[332]. In addition, there are "the common criminals": the ones that kill a boyfriend or girlfriend, a wife, husband, an intruder, a store clerk, etc. As I have suggested, there is a place for the violent people of society: Level III (IV) prisons. The disproportionate greater numbers are the non-violent prisoners and the violent drug prisoners. These are the people who should be the subjects of rehabilitation. The money to serve this purpose is tied up in government waste, and it will take a profound effort to enable the government to send resources in this direction. Gottschalk wrote her book twelve years ago. The only change since then is that the system is more inured to ongoing procedure and customary thinking.

The kind of violence confronting law enforcement is murder, kidnapping, rape, prostitution, human trafficking, drug trafficking, drug use, mass killing by Islamist terrorists (with different following subgroups), school shootings (involving young people with some psychiatric disorder), etc. Reconfiguration and adjustment must involve considerable management attention (to action, not just talk). Admittedly, it will take political action to invest resources with the courage to reconfigure prisons. Legislation must deal with prosecutors and judges. This is a major task that might take many years during a period of adjustment.

Prison personnel are very hardworking and devoted. The wardens I knew were so well respected and great communicators. They may not possess book knowledge, but they have a high degree of common sense. They manage to keep focus on "order" within the razor wires in spite of the daily grind to prevent lockdowns and mass riots. The greatest issue, contraband, is the rock in the shoe, it's there and must be extricated. With so many gangs in command of their street brethren idleness around a yard is a danger of overwhelming significance. The prisoners whose time is occupied with woodshops, gardening (horticulture), working in the infirmary/cafeteria/laundry areas, etc. are for the most part the minority. Ones that use the library, the chapels, and reading rooms make up the smallest percentage. Walking the yard most are observable working out, sitting around in small groups, or in their cell blocks. The SHU (Special Housing Unit/solitary confinement) and transferring prisoners to other prisons, to hospitals for care, to court, etc. ties up time in arrangements, but it does not involve a lot of personnel. These are major issues today because prisons are guard-deficient. Without getting too deep in the weeds, these factors are important for several reasons: a) prisons do not provide enough structure (only for minimal numbers), b) prisoners are very uneducated and this should be enforceable during incarceration,

c) "grouping" is a distinct potential flashpoint, and d) gangs tend to separate and hang within their own element; this should be monitored with greater care. I witnessed this almost every day where I worked. The danger was palpable. These are important issues which, to my observations, were pressing but did not seem to catch the attention of the officers. Everyday someone, whether a guard or prisoner, was beaten or shivved or shanked.

I understand the academic commitment to writing, and particularly on historical matters related to the prison system. But nothing can replace the day-to-day experience being witness to the inside with all its sudden twists and turns. It never ceased to amaze me how almost surreal it felt at times, just communicating with so many and thinking during my conversations how so many could viciously kill with incomprehensible sanguinity. To smile and laugh while talking about assault, murder, or kidnapping is a fundamental psychological distortion of normalcy that was mind-blowing. This was foundational to the DNA of prison reality that the majority of the outside world cannot fathom as an inside prison hallmark.

Society has to come to grips with pervasive crime on the streets. Police serve to keep the peace. The respect they deserve should never be mistreated by activist political groups nor the savagery condoned by mayors and governors for political support. It's insanity and disgraceful. They do not understand prison life. Mayors and Governors who throw safety of their residents to the wind are cold-blooded and purveyors of crime. Prison reform action will never happen with such counterintuitive politicians. Their voters would never support them if they could see and understand the reality of prison. To be as contumacious as they appear is frankly inexcusable and worthy of their own prison time. When leaders on the outside are as a danger to society as people locked up, how can society's problems be righted? The real danger is in taking advantage of very innocent people who do not perceive their venal and disgraceful motives in defiance of the number one obligation of a politician: the safety of people. If politicians refuse to understand right from wrong, then how can they be entrusted with the influence they peddle and misuse?

Prisons serve a constructive purpose, at least in theory. They serve a very viable purpose. There are also very important reasons why "prison reform" must play into this thought process. However, the "throwing the baby out with the bath water" thinking is naïve. It is impossible to empty them all. There is so much room for improvement of the prison system, but action in this regard cannot be reflexive. It will take a lot of measured thinking and planning that politicians cannot conceive. Maybe they frankly do not care? Perhaps in time someone in the criminal justice system with experience and agency will be able to pick up the mantle and project these considerations.

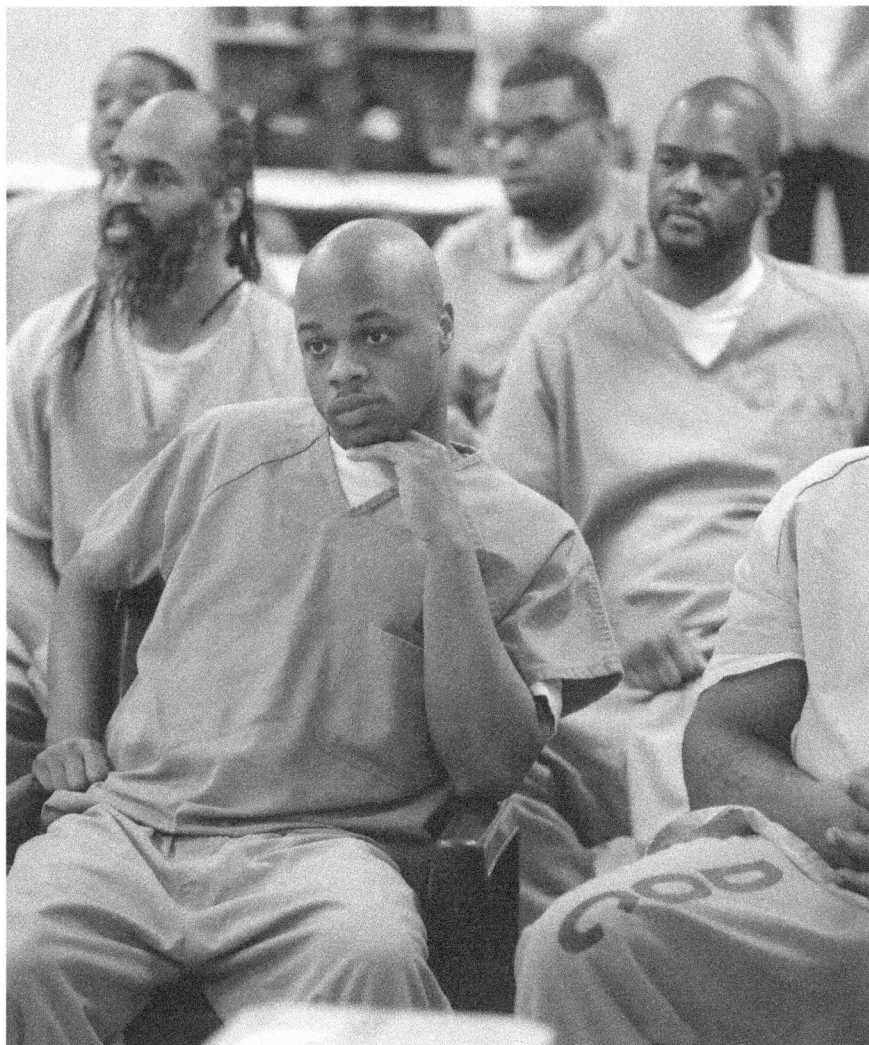

Cook County Detention Center, Chicago, Illinois; Courtesy of
Getty Images

Maine State Prison, Thomaston, Maine, Circa 1950's,
Thomaston, Maine,
Courtesy of Thomaston Historical Society, Thomaston, Maine

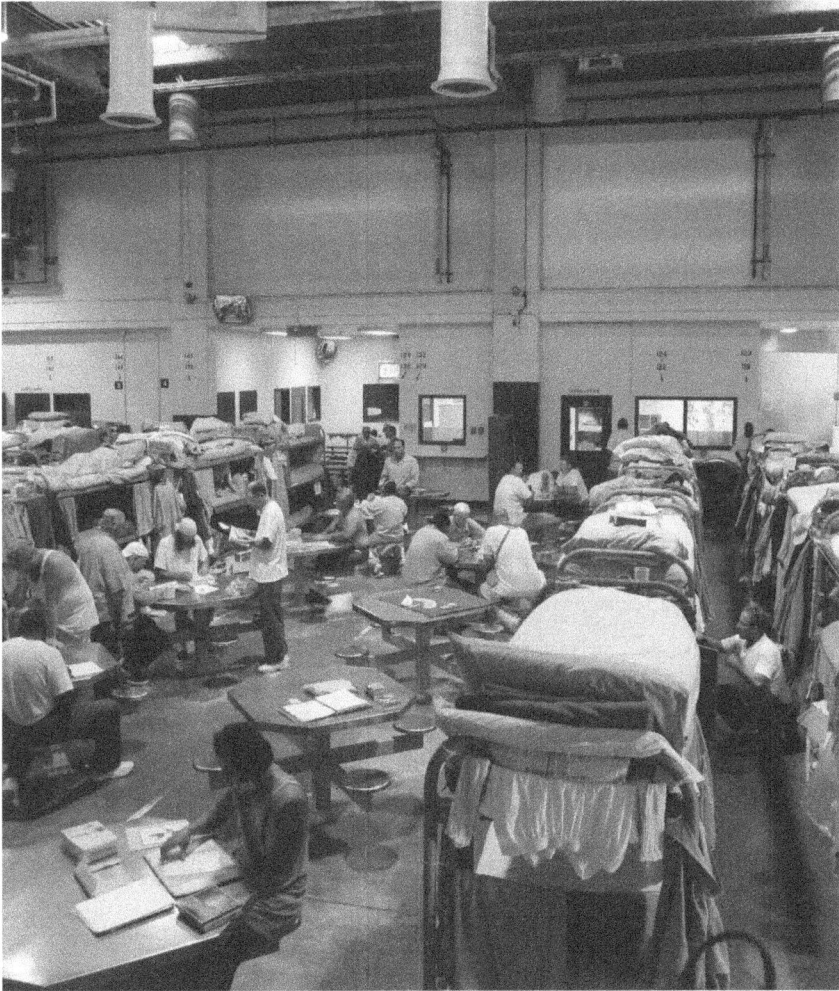

California State Prison System.

"Warehousing of Prisons"

due to overcrowding

Courtesy of Getty Images

CHAPTER 7

Simmering Irreverence

"Being incarcerated does not mean being devoid of the capacity to learn, grow, and think, and it's critical that prisons provide spaces where learning can be both cultivated and encouraged."[333] "Prisons are built with stones of Law. Brothels with the bricks of religion."[334] "When they call the roll in the Senate, the Senators do not know whether to answer 'Present' or 'Not Guilty'."[335]

In Roman times Janus was the "God" celebrated by his two faces looking in two different directions, from behind to the past, and to the front into the future. One would hope that the past would serve as a reminder to improve upon errors of the past in projecting corrective measures. Somehow Shakespeare's play "The Tragedy of Othello, The Moor of Venice"[336] projected a different connotation with the character Iago whose evil was manifested by his two-faced embodiment of deceit. I often wondered why the mythological objectivity made the famous (perhaps "infamous") bard adulterate the viewpoint. Perhaps he properly described what we see in our legislators: one face, but two sides of evil?

To sully politicians with Iago's guile, however, is quite accurate. Conditioned to accept what Washington, D.C. deals the American public may be one of the most helpless, overwhelming positions possible (other than a fatal diagnosis of malignancy). The street expression: "there is no justice, just us" paints a broad stripe across all of Congress, and deservedly so. Yet, this is the body of individuals governing us with a mosaic of laws, a great number of which never pertain to them. They have their own structured retirement programs, health insurance programs, lobbying connections to "K Street" (which makes one wonder who really controls the legislation they deal with the public), abhorrent salaries and Wall Street investments increasing over time, etc. The point is that these are the people we need in spite of the reality that their only motivation is to get re-elected while assuming a righteous posture in the public domain. They are hard to swallow in their well-groomed likenesses with limitless bloviating. Yet, this is all we have. Through telecommunications we have instantaneous impressions to digest. Perhaps their predecessors (all the way back to colonial America) projected equally quirky and loathsome, but over time we have just glorified them for our own benefit. In their day the imagery may have been just as disdainful, but hardly seen. Today we see everything. Knowing and seeing political activity play out so rapidly is a bit more trying on individual patience, and often painful. There was no love lost between Aaron Bur and Alexander Hamilton[337]. Political types who abuse our patience every day with their abusive admonitions are widespread today. And, the record is there to be viewed forever by the public. And then it is sold every day on television, on the web, and in newspapers until it runs out of interest! Rage and demonstrations, political venom and "demagoguing,"financial and social exploitation, money grabbing, the virtue of war and defended with deceit, etc. are sold to the public gift wrapped for consumption. We see and hear everything today. But maybe the historical political elite we so elevate in our minds were just as much the purveyors of "trash talk" and lies? Mass communications have made hiding impossible to hide anything. Therefore, if prison reform is to ever gain a footing, language and behavior will make a difference.

A most difficult subject to capture in its vast extent is that of "good and evil." Adjectives are never ending in the English lexicon to effect context from all the vast ideas used to project a meaning to people and places as objects of those four-letter words. In their bare essence, prisons and the people they hold are the fodder of extensive research and writing to better understand what gave rise to such a vast explosion of prisons and prisoners. There are no definitive answers, just as the subject of "good and evil" will never intuit a final answer for what makes some people transgress, some to display counterbalancing good, and others to be a blend as they live to be the best that they can be. It is unfortunate that life abounds with such a plethora of evil. And, as a prisoner once whispered to me, "there are more evil creatures outside than inside!" And, I smiled and answered" "Yeh, they learned how to fly faster than the long arm of the law!" The research shows how much more is needed to know about "evil." It is pervasive, but often disguised neatly. How does this control our lives?

While good people write their books, blogs, columns in newspapers, and comment on radio and television talk shows, the language contains selective intent.

Noteworthy is the fact that this is the hand American citizens are dealt, and how many times has it been sold that "democracy" is far better than any other form of government? Understood, but listening to the political prattle and yap for many years with the same issues folding in and out like hands molding dough is very old. This is why there will never be consequential prison reform. Generations of politicians will lighten up the hustings with new ears of young cherubs and embalmed older generations who never learned anyway. Our politicians will be as convincing as the redolent smells of an awakening spring morning, and we'll accept the commentary like the brilliance never so reverentially displayed. And, this is the milieu for "simmering irreverence" where the ambitious can reel off the historical context of where prisons fail society, how to make a difference, and then retreat to a cloistered refuge to "pound sand!"

John Pfaff in his book, Locked In: The True Causes of Mass Incarceration and How to Achieve Real Reform[338], makes many indelibly incontrovertible observations one of the most for certain are overzealous prosecutors as a source of mass incarceration. They are the kings of the mountain, and they are able to game the system. And, the system, by the way, is as political as any government system is. However, it is twisted and insincere. Politicians provide the legislation, legislation that looks like a manual for "airplane construction for dummies." If constituencies are not emboldened to matters of crime as a societal need to address, lawmakers will not care.

It's hard to get people to turn out at national elections let alone local elections. Politicians are hard to believe. Words have little meaning to them, they can lie (and do with aplomb), and will drive home their biases like a bull chasing the matador's muleta in a bullfight. They chase a different kind of bull. Michelle Alexander[339] is spot on with the following declaration in her book, *The New Jim Crow: Mass Incarceration in the Age of Colorblindness:*

> "Dealing with this system on its own terms is complicated by the problem of denial." Few Americans today recognize mass incarceration for what it is: a new caste system thinly veiled by the cloak of colorblindness. Hundreds of thousands of people of color are swept into this caste system and released every year, yet we rationalize the systematic discrimination and exclusion and turn a blind eye to the suffering. Our collective denial is not merely an inconvenient fact: it is a major stumbling block to the public understanding of the role of race in our society, and it sharply limits the opportunities for truly transformative collective action."[340]

If Michelle were to reappear in another lifetime, I honestly feeling she would be writing another copy of this statement for a new jejune people who still would not be able to grasp its fundamental accuracy. Memories are short and shortsighted. There are several considerations which I have tried to bring to bear as well. All discussions, pro and con, will ultimately fall to the responsibilities of politicians. And, as I have observed for years, unless and until it is in the interest of a legislator (with clout) nothing but robust, oleaginous promises will emerge.

When I think of her book, I say to myself that it is too bad that we live in a world where important matters are argued by reasons limited to political party affiliation. I agree with her wholeheartedly because of what I have observed over my lifetime, not because I am a "liberal-progressive." I shall not get into it because I detest getting into political discussions from which it is inevitable that diatribes evolve without positive benefits to anyone. Just more bitter expostulations. And, I am categorically averse to politicians and politics. I am baseball friendly so I like to "balls and strikes" as I see them (hopefully better than some I have witnessed). Fortunately, I had a mentor who taught me at an early age to walk the middle road, but not like a wallflower, but as humanly possible with conviction based in common sense.

No greater example of political morphology is the shifting that transpires to support constituencies based on need, be it social, industrial, international diplomacy, etc. The "boll weevil"[341,342]. Southern Democrats aligned with Republicans after WWII because they supported basic conservative republican business-foreign policy principles. But, Democrats (and, Southern Democrats) fostered the "plantation agenda" to obstruct desegregation where the Republicans were obstacles. It is hard to believe, but the Democrat Senator Robert Byrd of West Virginia was an ex-Grand Dragoon of the Ku Klux Klan and aligned with Southern Democrats. It is hard for a lot of people to understand that it was the Republicans who advanced desegregation, civil rights and education. The point: politics makes for strange bedfellows and obsessive disinformation. American history is rattled by "righteous" politicians weaving in-and-out of alliances for high-minded policies. No, nothing is righteous about politicians. They vote their constituencies, "pure and simple." The "boll weevil" democrats were highly conservative and most morphed into Republicans (like Strom Thurmond of South Carolina and John Connally of Texas). The Southern Dixiecrats emerged as a southern voting bloc supporting slavery/segregation against the Free-Soil Movement. The Republicans emerged as the party of Lincoln in 1854 as The Whig Party dissolved. It was the Republicans who sounded off against segregation, not the Democrats. Even the gypsy moth Republicans of the Northeast and Midwest in the 1980's emerged as a voting bloc against Republican President Ronald Reagan who wanted to cut financial support for distressed communities. This became the liberal wing of Rockefeller Republicans who would oppose Ronald Reagan on economics and foreign policy. Even during the post-Civil War Reconstruction "carpetbaggers"[343] from the north who went south for financial considerations, but they were supported by white southern Democrat politicians, aka "scalawags," who supported recently freed black slaves. The "scalawags" (southern democrats) and "carpetbaggers" (northern opportunists who went south after the Civil War for financial opportunity) were not really appreciated by Republican support of Freedmen-Free Slave policies. Not thinkable, but true. The Supreme Court passing *Plessy v. Ferguson*[344] in 1896 upheld racial segregation in public facilities as long as they were equal in quality (aka "separate but equal"), and, it was reversed in 1954 with the Supreme Court decision, *Brown v. Board of Education*[345], that ended legalized racial segregation in public educational facilities (by reversing *Plessy v. Ferguson*). The 1964 Civil Rights Act[346] outlawed discrimination based on race, color, religion, sex or national origin. The *Voting Rights Act*[347] in 1965 reinforced the *Civil Rights Act* of 1964, and gave blacks the right to vote (eliminating poll taxes, literacy tests and other repugnant means to discredit blacks and disallow them from the right to vote). All these issues reflected close votes with support coming fortuitously of political timing, almost serendipitous "chance! The point is that political alliances determined racial harmony that created a "Shangri La" where American people learned to live in mutual understanding and harmony. Right? Absolutely not! Never has divisiveness and sub-rosa political gaming through alliances been more existential and alive. Politicians are all for themselves so their behavior is as unpredictable as the tract of a hurricane (and, they blow air just as hard). If after reading this, one believes in ideal political alliances (eg. politicians), a check-up from the neck up is in order. History shows that politicians are "human slugs," moving earth to pursue self-interests through alliances that comfort their constituencies only (even if it ravages other people in distant parts of the country). Today comity and connected agreements are fanciful.

American history going back to the colonial days demonstrates a roller coaster-like heaving up-and-down in political alliances. The prison system is a microcosm of this country. From what I have seen, both in my education and living experience, I see nothing about what Michelle Alexander has to say deferentially out-of-order. To me, she makes a more living validation of the African-American "pathos" in the court system and prisons. Phaff supports this by his "Standard Story" explanation, but the statistics do not do justice to the sorry state of affairs I have witnessed with my own eyes.

Pfaff is obviously a numbers person. To his defense of numbers, however, (though numbers do not gather my attention except when the curtain is lifted from in front to validate their meaning) I add this assertion: "After all, facts are facts, and although we may quote one to another with a chuckle the words of the Wise Statesman, "Lies— damn lies---and statistics," still there are some easy figures simplest must understand, and the most astute cannot wiggle out of"[348]. Alexander relates the numbers to vigorously substantiate their meaning. She validates descriptively the loathsome experience of black men in prisons in disproportionately shameful numbers. My daily observations corroborate this finding without having made a head count. It was totally unneeded because of the visual reality in concert with census documentation[349].

Therefore, morality and color do make a difference as she justifiably implores. The vestiges of slavery still exist. Prisons are living examples. True, the numbers align with prosecutorial hunger and ambition, but it is obvious from my experience that the stars for African-Americans do not line up with fairness. I cannot downplay what a wonderful contribution John Pfaff's book is despite the fact that I am not a numbers man. Black and white on a page cannot bury the more subliminal messages underneath where I tend to draw the real meaning. Aaron Levenstein, a professor at Baruch College in New York City for twenty years expressed pointedly (and, humorously as well) the difference between "the objective" and "the subjective" (in consideration of truth to meaning): "Statistics are like bikinis. What they reveal is suggestive, but what they conceal is vital."[350]

Michelle Alexander is like abold commentator, interpreting what facts mean and their overall significance. John Pfaff is a computer of facts with explanations and suggestions that I valued as I began my own interpretation.

Overzealous prosecutors are responsible for operating what seems like a well-lubricated, one-way turnstile into prison. The American prison history (from pre-Civil War to now) validates African-Americans are by far are the greatest victims. Maybe subjective, but I witnessed this with my own "lying'" eyes. Of course, looking at the numbers, the variances differ from state to state (especially in whiter states), but, in the deep-south the African-Americans really outnumber whites. Remember, African-Americans are about 13% of the population, but they account for about 40% of the prison population. I want to reinforce this by adding Hispanics (16%/20% ratio approximately) to show that the number results in approximately 60% of the population being minorities[351]. It is an alarming number. Prosecutors will defend their aggressive behavior by standing behind the law. And the politicians who legislate claim to be answerable to their constituencies both at the state and federal levels. In layman's, more plebeian lingo these legal eagles are seemingly in cahoots dancing around the "hit upon" doing the legislator- prosecutor "two-step!"

There are just under 2,700 people on death row. In relation to the disproportion mentioned above, black individuals awaiting execution was slightly higher than the 40% of their prison numbers: about 42%. Homicides, aggravated assault and kidnapping accounted for 3.2% of all offenses. What this demonstrates from the Bureau of Prisons, Prison Policy Initiative and the Bureau of Justice is the fact that violent crime accounts for a lower proportion (by percentage) of crimes, that by population blacks have as mentioned a disproportion on death row, and that drug offenses represent 46.2% of crimes and weapons, explosives and arson 17.6%. Sex offenses account for 9.4%. The remaining 10 crimes are very low percentages[352, 353, 354]. Therefore, if violence is a percentage extraordinarily high by comparison, and particularly high and disproportional for blacks particularly high and disproportional for blacks, but (again) homicides low by comparison, prison reform could politically gain momentum if only an incentive to all others existed. Only legislation could and will change prison occupancy. The facts show that prison sentencing is too long for non-violent crimes. The expense for death row is disproportionally higher than life sentences, and life sentences should be mitigated because the money could be used for rehabilitative programs as opposed to a "throw away the key" mentality.

Juxtaposed to a lackluster approach to changing sentencing guidelines and tracking prosecutorial behavior, there is no push for change. That is a bureaucracy issue because elected legislators understand that most people do not understand the prison system so there is no consensus to care. Even though I present statistics, and rightfully so, the blind spot is the political arena. In spite of what politicians say, they do not comprehend either, and they are not incentivized at the expense of reelection. It is a circular conundrum which cannot straighten to solve the wasteful expenditure of taxpayer money and the one track, ongoing mentality abetting the prosecution-sentencing vaudeville act.

The most disturbing aspect of the political climate is its descent into a sense of vicious disrespect with a violent overlay. This accomplishes nothing. And argumentation that lowers to sewer rattling results in more abuse and mutual disdain. I have always likened Washington, D.C. politicians to "sewer rats." They fattened on the financial opportunity which is the taxpayer dollar. It also loses purpose and constructive give-and-take for the common good. The sententious politicians just make loud noise. And, if anyone believes these politicians will charter a course for reform, it is an unrealistic prospect. I am not quixotic so I view the current state and national politicians far too seamy and irresponsible. Is this overly harsh? Perhaps, but its's hard to see virtue in a sea of greed and self-promotion.

What might be the causation? John Pfaff suggests costs will go down with decreasing populations and that decreasing populations will not cause an increase in crime[355]. I agree with this entirely, and particularly that these cost savings can be diverted to much more significant rehabilitative programs. He also discusses the zeal of aggressive prosecutors because the "legislators… may not have sufficiently precise tools to truly punish overly aggressive prosecutors."[356] Well, the solution would be to put the onus of financial responsibility back on the localities where the force of the ballot box is a powerful implement. Politics is a dirty business, and legislators who do not respond to the local control of overzealous prosecutors can use the power of the purse, particularly in control of salaries. This is pipe-dreaming. The state government will never respond to this. In fact, as normal political course, left to state machinations, prosecutors will most likely see salaries go up whether they are sage in their sense of the large picture or not.

Like all of man's predicaments, follow the money to uncover the facts that are "vital." Take off the bikini as Levenstein would suggest. The man who covered this in relevant detail is Professor W. David Ball, Associate Professor at Santa Clara University, School of Law[357]. He delivers a very lengthy dissertation explaining state prisons from a historical point of view, particularly how the county (localities) versus state financial responsibilities make (or lack thereof) for the predicament they find themselves in.

There was a time when counties ran the prisons and were self-supporting. As W. David Ball[358] points out, this was possible because of the use of chain-gangs for which the remunerations paid the bills. He notes that this held up in Pennsylvania and South Carolina as long as the local prisons retained the control economic benefits. He cites a study that criminality was reduced by penalties for holding too many prisoners. In addition, prison labor was financially productive until the labor movement interfered and politicians passed a bill to restrict this. In essence, prison labor made penitentiaries self-supporting, but eventually private industry and organized labor lowered the hammer to end the financial stream. It was at this point that state prisons lost "local control" and they became dependent on funds from state governments.

This seminal change started in the 1940's with interstate commerce preventing the sale of state prison products over state lines.

This made state prisons dependent. He compares how school systems have learned to exist because "statewide requirements" co-exist with local administration. The contrast to prison management is stark. He concludes by making four points relative to the dependency on state administrations for their existence: local governments should assume the costs as they may be able; local officials would have to be responsible or they would be voted out; force localities to pay for policies; this responsibility would end the whole state paying the costs and excessive spending would be reduced; these would result in the following benefits: 1) greater transparency; 2) the criminal justice system, by making the local system bear the costs locally, justice in every phase would be served more fairly rather impersonal state personnel calling the shots; as Ball writes: "When citizens make policy choices with a willingness to absorb their true costs, those choices are more likely to reflect beliefs that are sincerely held. Decisions that cost less mean less"; 3) "tailor incarceration to local preferences" by decentralization; "society can learn from local experiments…"; "…for the same reasons federalism makes sense"; and 4) lastly, "local criminal justice, rather than statewide criminal justice, is more in line with the values expressed in the Bill of Rights. The Sixth Amendment jury right specifically calls for a local jury, one not only of the state but also "the district wherein the crime shall have been committed." His argument is that local justice for local crime results in more of the local citizenry involved with greater fairness owing to greater person-to-person familiarity with all contingencies. State involvement would still be a sine qua non for limited concerns, but very limited. As he concludes: "We maintain the fiction of a "state" system and a "state" problem when these problems are actually the result of local policies that merely aggregate at the state level…we pretend that the prison population is the state's problem, so we can ignore localities' role."[359] He makes an undeniable summary statement which makes a defining case:

> "There is nothing necessary about a system where state governments pay for prisons, and there are

many reasons why we might want to change it. Unless and until we can all agree on what statewide policies should be, we would be better off to agree to disagree and let each locality reap what it sows."[360]

W. David Ball's (a Professor of Law) 2014 written presentation, "Why State Prisons"?, pretty much lays out why state prisons underperform and consequently fail the states on so many levels. My sense of state government is one of "Johnny-come-lately," if at all, to study and address anything beneficial to the greater picture of mass incarceration. In fact, to the state the issue is "pie-in-the-sky" The point of view: the states' fantasy!

John Pfaff (also a Professor of Law) knows far better than I when he refers to over-prosecution as the great cause of mass incarceration. However, I see the difference in considering non-violent and violent prisoners differentially. The laws governing non-violent crimes are open to both prosecutorial judgment as well as the judge rendering sentences as prescribed by law. In both cases, laggard attention is no excuse. The issue lingers year-to-year as talk like trailing breezes without direction. It is palpable for people who have taken the time to examine this, but corrective legislation hangs in the balance. No one seems to care.

And, as I have stated, Michelle Alexander spells it out crystal clear. She validated my observations. However, I am a bit more concerned viscerally that the state systems in particular do not care. I am not talking about the way wardens run their prisons, for they are subservient to the bureaucratic process that makes their daily management a prodigious effort. In fact, a lot of days it is a nightmare to deal with the incidents that upend the flow and control of prisoners through their very difficult demands and schedules. It is a prodigious effort requiring intra paper work that mounts so voluminously on desks that it's a wonder anything gets done. Just dealing with transfers, incident reports, scurrying prisoners to court and hospitals while managing in-house activity is a pendulous cloud of heavy pressure. But I can only conclude that it is truly a "failed system" at the bureaucratic level. I do concur with Professor Ball that localities would be better served if they served their own needs. Local responsibilities, local input, and local efficiency. Locales identify with their own needs as opposed to depending on state capitals. Indeed, it is certain that "All politics is local"[361] as Tip O'Neill aptly declared.

Political gamesmanship is at the heart of the prison system, and it is a game at any level. Follow the money and the widespread waste would surface right at the intersection of the directors with the legislators and governors. There will never be a change because at the state level the eyes and ears are informationally challenged. Citizenry is ill-informed, and media attention does not capture the truth. The only time people are made aware is the very occasional leak of a prison riot, murder(s) exposed, breakouts, contraband issues or some family member related to a prisoner contacts the local media. Otherwise, what goes on behind the razor-wired fences is a well-kept secret. This is the reality of the way the burdens of a warden are maintained.

If localities were the domain for all financial management, budgetary planning would play a very significant role, and attention to financial waste would be addressed with certain action. The reality is that government is not smooth at any level. But, when local management is "en plein air" with public awareness, the nutmeg stilts bureaucracy. Not entirely, but certainly far less.

To go along to get along is not a realistic approach, but as long as no one attempts to become aware nothing will ever come of the prison issue. Comprehensive reversal of fortune requires lowering the number of recidivates. Finally, change, if ever a reality, would certainly contribute to the more improved reality of parole and probation administrative controls.

The real question which simmers irreverently in a permanent parboiled is what happens to all the money states capture from its citizens. Like a circular firing squad protests for legitimacy in governmental programs recycle from one generation to the next. Oh that legislators did not operate at cross purposes! The obligatory task is to do the people' work. The ballot box is the only mechanism for change when government goes off the rails and gets lost in its own insulated way of life. Prison reform is not a particularly celebrated topic, but it is intimately related to race relations. The numbers reflect this. Yet, prison and race relations are not sexy. And, this is "simmering irreverence!"

The "tabula rasa" of the prison's raison d'etre: rehabilitation is long gone. The "blank slate" is a hieroglyphic morass of empty thoughts lost in time. It will never gain a measure of significance again without enlightened leadership. Pristine purpose would be nice, but it is unrealistic because there is too much disrespect and disharmony in the world today. Everything today is intimately linked to the gap between the "Haves and Have-nots!" Prosperity cannot come from big government, because the government is all the taxpayers' money. Politicians do not have to understand individual sweat and hard work to grow business and offer employment security and growth. The mystery is the economics that half the country does not understand. Government growth is a deterrent to growth. Unions, once a need to protect vile mistreatment of workers in the early to mid-twentieth century, is a major deterrent to individual financial success based on merit. The "right to work" connotes individuality in choice and individual prosperity. Unions are no longer working for the employee. They stultify corporate growth which benefits the worker with increased pay and benefits with prosperity.

It is the same long arms of government which have eclipsed prison reform and inner-city race reform. Educational opportunity is possible with financial prosperity. The cities now that are blowing up, all Democrat cities reflect "Big Daddy Government" where the politicians get wealthy and the poor remain poor. The more the sanctuary mentality continues, the bigger government gets bigger and as long as the poor are taught that they need government to grow, the more adverse their lives become. History has shown that radical left wing socialist or communist countries fail at all levels of life. The more monarchical, the less individualism, the more impoverished, and the more people are imprisoned. Unless and until enlightened leaders produce prison reform will never occur. Big government is anathema to prison reform. Classic overreach are the Democrat politicians today spewing venom because they hate Trump. Admittedly, he is not the softest, cuddly, principled person around, but he has advanced race relations more than any modern leader. Like it or not, this is a fact. And, as long as Democrats lie that they are the answer to race relations, the more this hatred for a man will continue to freeze race relations. The Democrats today are perpetrating a horrible lie: xenophobia, homophobia, misogyny, white supremacy, elitism, defiling of illegal immigrants, etc. These are misery thoughts to turn voters to their party to grow government where individual choice will be eliminated to the will of Big Government. It is unfortunate because the longer this is propagated every four years the more the hope for prison reform will be dispelled, The Democrats do not want prison reform because it contravenes their will to control and prevent individual initiative and prosperity. Individualism is intimately linked with the future of the inner cities. This is fact. The Republicans, not the Democrats, are the authors for legislation which brought desegregation, educational opportunity, civil rights, and opportunity. The politics which brought down The Whig Party in 1856 (and the birth of the Republican Party in 1854, and eventually elected Abraham Lincoln) will bring down the Democrat Party if it continues will its odium, deceit, and false promises at a time when race relations is one-sided. All politics is ruthless and lacking in moral rectitude, but the Democrats presently want to take the country to a position which will ultimately destroy hope and prosperity for all.

I harken to a soap opera called "Days of Our Lives" which opened in 1965 with a gimmicky, but catchy entrée from the tenor tones and rhythmic musical background sounds of a highly energized male actor's voice into the particular day's program: "Like sands through the hourglass, so are the days of our lives."[362] If nothing else this grabbed the viewer's attention because it aimed right at the limbic system of the brain where all emotion-attached reactions begin. Obviously, it has measured up in the Nielson ratings as it still prevails. Thankfully I have never watched a nanosecond, but one would have to be living in a closet at its height never to have heard any of its trailers just once. The actual everyday experience in a maximum-security prison reminded me of this poignant saying, particularly as I entered through the rather austere iron gates in the wee hours of the morning/night and clanked brusquely behind me. As my heart would pick up its pace, sometimes in synch with my feet, I would always hear this soap opera's clarion call in my head. It really objectified the harsh reality of prison. Every day the one thought I always contained was how awful and dangerous such is the experience for which so much is written. Yet our public officials do not care one whit to reform such a nightmare. It makes money, warehouses the most impoverished in a disreputable manner, and leaves the world ignorant about its "truth." I came to the conclusion that the prison system is locked in time, and in the most socially advanced country in the world this is the best it can do. It is irreverent and simmers without change.

The Goths and Visigoths cannibalized its victims; Genghis Khan whipsawed through the modern-day Beijing to the Caspian Sea raping and killing almost a hundred million people across the steppes of Asia to the Caspian Sea; Stalin assassinated thirty millions of his people, and those he did not he threw into his gulags; Hitler killed 6 million Jews, a million Poles, and hundreds of his own soldiers (The SA in "the Night of the Swords"), etc. The Japanese did live autopsies for experimental purposes (especially drugs) in military camps they captured in China; Mao Zedong massacred a hundred million of his own people both militarily and in his concentration camps; and, to this day North Korea and China are filling their concentration camps with enemies of their totalitarian countries. A casual and harsh onlooker might say that American prisoners are doing well with state, federal and private prisons seeming like hotels compared to both erstwhile concentration camps and foreign prisons. It can be said that all through time even early biblical times, societies were always centered about primal military lifestyles. Even today countries like Venezuela, Chile, Cuba, South Africa, Mexico and many others demonstrate an abysmal respect for human life. All of this is part of the historical record[363]. They are all failed, autocratic countries, the mystic and structure the

Democrats want for the United States.

Yet, this is why our level of civil conduct should never lose sight how far this country has progressed. Never should our thinking lapse to a point of inaction so that people in our prisons become lost in that "hourglass of time." It is moral indignation on the part of politicians who recognize the problem and the best they can provide is another search committee, another inquiry, an investigation, or suggest a series of academic colloquia. Unfortunately, greed is too enticing to resist, and, politicians flout the law often enough to the chagrin of hardworking people. It happens so often that the majority of people are numb, and expect it with a fractured smile even though it has lost the romantic glow it used to project.

This characteristic of our legislators convinces me that what should be done will only transpire when a "will to change" makes a presence. The system offers its prisoners stability in all their physical and psychological needs, and all the people who keep prisons afloat are admirably committed to their work. However, the administrators go afoul in paying more attention to so many tedious, unnecessary policies that tire the personnel (guards in particular) grossly inadequate pay, and the real inherent dangers. Ironically, this is what motivated the building of "private prisons." And, in synch with the state prisons corruption is defiantly corrupt.

The incident reports which prisoners file for any and every reason, the ones employees file against each other, and the mischief between female guards and prisoners concerning sex, and contraband-drug exchanges are common occurrences which could be controlled if changes were made. The bureaucracy above the level of the wardens knows perfectly well the prevailing issues, but it accepts the standard operating procedure as it willfully overlooks the big picture concerns. The truth is that prisons (state or federal) do not have to be concerned and just "talk the talk" (but, do not "walk the walk") as long as rioting is kept controlled and prisoners' law suits/ complaints are properly managed. The only way serious prisoner issues (like stabbings, rapes, and serious murders) are held from public scrutiny is to keep families of prisoners away from the media (and that accounts for the media as well as the press). This does work and accounts for a high degree of collective collaboration."

Prisoners are subject to a detailed classification process. Many will reveal that the environment does not lend itself to change because classification means very little unless safety is taken seriously. The question is how serious can the administration be if understaffing is allowed to go on without facing up to vulnerabilities which prevail with impunity. The hardcore prisoners (young or old) know the ropes and can go rogue so suddenly that personnel are left quite vulnerable.

There is a very real difference between Level II and Level III prisons even though there can be some very violent prisoners who wind up in the more passive Level II's. Mixed populations, in my estimation, can be largely mainstream and controllable if all violent prisoners are totally relegated to Level III prisons. In the mixed populations flash points can occur with frequency because rogue prisoners often incite cohorts who would otherwise be more passive. Many of the prisoners who were trades people (electricians, plumbers, carpenters, etc.) before incarceration are exceptionally talented. These are the overwhelming majority whose violations, be they serious or not, can and should be tracked for rehabilitation.

The prison process is either mellowing or inuring depending upon a myriad of circumstances. A judge who has a penchant to over-sentence relative to the statutes can make a prisoner cynical and lose faith. Talking to a great number of them is quite revealing in that they will allude to their freedom with a sense of hope to be a more functional, productive human being. However, to then check their records on the computer, for example, is mind bending. For example, seeing a prisoner who was in his own construction business, convicted for a backyard meth (methamphetamine) laboratory for production, sale and personal usage, and has been in prison for 6 years with 13 more to go is ludicrous, if not a reprehensible over-reach by the judicial system. He was not in any educational programs and lingered around doing nothing unless called upon to repair a sink, an air conditioning/heating problem, a broken lock, etc. I talked to him so often and was one of many with whom conversations were quite revealing as far as how broken a system can be despite the illusions bureaucracy foists upon the public: what grandstanding by hardened bureaucrats. The sludge of pompous, self- flagellating administrations is thick and immovable.

It is also imperative to be up front that there are some very mean, dangerous hombres who should be in for life and never see light of day. Even the most charitable should never be so ill-informed or outspoken to consider these types when seriously considering rehabilitation. It is not being wise to be "super-empathetic"[364] (as Simon-Baron Cohen would suggest) with these types as they would sooner put a bullet in your head, rape your prepubescent daughter, or viciously dismember your girlfriend as say "hello and good morning!" These individuals are very frightening, dark individuals right out of a Hollywood movie set. Explicit discretion is a first requirement in the discussion of prison reform. It is not the world of "the Bird Man of Alcatraz"[365] who has mellowed and demurred to the level of a benevolent ornithologist a la Hollywood. Only the ill-informed or the totally naïve can consider a vicious, blood-curdling criminal for rehabilitation. This is dangerous thinking because visceral evil is not reversible. Even Caryl Chessman[366] went to his death seemingly contrite and stoic, even writing a book before his demise evoking his own human condition as overly burdened. He and Robert Stroud ("the Bird Man of Alcatraz") were aggressive killers. Not everyone can be absolved for the wretchedness of extreme wanton behavior. Stroud murdered with steely degeneracy and Chessman raped lecherously, both with malicious contempt for their victims by virtue of their premeditated vengeance.

A major problem for prison reform is the concern that politicians are too nonchalant. Politicians appear totally ill- informed about the costs which prisons absorb, like swelling sponges. As long as they can raise more and more taxes, they do not deliver a concern for how, with more discretion, the money which goes for punishment could be diverted to more education programs for prisoners. They all talk a good game, but all they do generally is talk. It becomes, after a while, a dog and pony show. I personally became agnostic to politicians who safeguard their biases only for their constituency's agenda just as long they are also in synch with their party's belief system. For this reason, I have been totally convinced that it isn't a political decision (physically or emotionally). Hypocrisy in reasoning life and death should not engage a second hand set of values. It is important to be responsible for legitimate sentencing for cold and calculated violent crime. Tolerance is also a very important noble and defensible consideration of non-violent crimes. Balance of thought is essential to protect society from dissolute criminality while extending redemption for individuals who can be rehabilitated. Referring back to all the statistics I have laid out, the violent crimes for which rehabilitation should not be possible are a minority. By far and away, the preponderance of individuals should not be boldly extended one-way tickets to prison. This is beyond sensitivity for the value of human life. Circumstances can open up vulnerabilities conducive to non-violent crimes.

It would be nice if politicians, our gateway to significant legislative change, could be less vocally divisive and more adherent to their responsibilities. I cannot side with a liberal/progressive, conservative or libertarian viewpoint because I have an open mind and I cannot accept "politics" dictating the deep questions that criminality asks. I think politics is the only vehicle for change so I hope enough common sense legislators exist who do not worship at their political "Tower of Babel."[367] Politicians owe the public commitment to very serious social issues. Like it or not prison reform requires more than blather all the time. They should not use their bully pulpit in Congress to speak the gobbledygook language like it's their Tower of Babel where personal pride is more important than their obligations. There are too many politicians, willfully insulated from society, possess the Lucifer trait and fight crime with conscious neglect. Leadership is necessary for maximum efficiency and to protect against waste and failure. The prison system is a classic example of failure because the people responsible for rigor in maintaining safety are "handcuffed" by the white-collar bureaucracies which are a blend of inefficiency and corruption. Laurence J. Peter and Raymond Hull[368] in their book, *The Peter Principle*, called this "'percussive sublimation": being kicked upstairs: a pseudo-promotion," or, "'the lateral arabesque, a pseudo-promotion consisting of a new title and a new workplace." Government bureaucracy is loaded with lead weighted employees who draw middle grade to very high salaries and just fill space producing poor results. It is the ultimate in their study of "Hierarcheology: a social science, the study of hierarchies, their structure and functioning, the foundation for all social science." And, thus the "Peter Principle: In a hierarchy, every employee tends to rise to his level of incompetence." In this case of a large bureaucracy, incompetence moves up the ladder from one position to the next higher position always carrying inefficiency and waste along the way. Mid-level leadership where efficiency is supposed to churn is nothing but a pit of buck-passing and time consumption with clock watching. Of course, this would not occur in private industry where the resulting lack of productivity would signal the plight of bankruptcy, or, if a public corporation would have to respond to an angry board of directors (which inevitably face an aggressive shareholder moving to take over, fortified by the weight of the most shares in the company). The prison system is stultified by "yes-no" resident employees climbing this ladder, and particularly led by tiered chiefs of "this or that" who listen, conference periodically, telephone a lot, go to questionable meetings every day, and make answers to questions sound reasonable but just float in the ethers without resolution of anything at any time. However, once in a while such "chiefs" conflict with the real worker bees at the prison and feel good that they have inflicted some pain in the process of releasing an urge to display a feckless sense of control and power! It truly is a unique kind of desultory "do-nothingness!"

Constructive and knowledgeable leadership is necessary for prison reform. A mere collection of self- aggrandizing politicians will never be sufficient. People in government who study the requirements will be a good start.

Most of what I have read and observed while researching to corroborate my onsite findings all settle on the same I have thus far delineated. No matter how talented football players are at their individual positions, winning cannot happen without a leader at quarterback who can make the right decisions at the right time. Business decisions likewise emerge from heads of companies who have a vision and a sense of effective communication which filter down to people who take the message and translate it into production with minimum waste. This describes free enterprise as opposed to big government where waste is accepted.

David Skarbeck makes an important statement in his book about which most everyone is in agreement:

> "As the scale of incarceration rises, the resulting decline in crime decreases at a faster and faster rate. The payoff in crime reduction gets smaller at an accelerated rate. At higher levels of incarceration, increasing the incarceration rate actually increases the crime rate. More inmates means more crime[369].

Why do politicians not understand this? The logic is clearly there. This is a consensus finding in staging a cogent rationale for dispelling erroneous arguments and reflecting the supporting numbers. However, it is obvious that politicians have been made aware of this many, many times. It just does not make money, a cynical conclusion. As stated many times, there has to be a will and forceful leadership to move this forward and translate the numbers into bringing change to the system. This is a beginning only. Overpopulation of the prisons does not define how to deal with poverty and education which are synergistically related. Sociological studies are not necessary to understand the stereotypical reasons for so many prison, motorcycle and street gangs. Some people will advance despite adversity, but the collective numbers which make up society's downtrodden need a boost from leadership. Otherwise, no matter how much energy is spent trying to reconcile mass incarceration there will always be a turnstile doorway in-and-out of our prisons with successive generations. What is apparent now will be real tomorrow.

This really should be a "state issue," not a federal one. States manage their tax system so important collective decisions regarding prison reform should alight at the grassroots of each state. Left to the United States Congress the reality will be a mirror image of what exists today: continuous graft, false promises and open-ended blather. Local leadership answers to their constituents so incarceration is a native issue. Politics is a dirty business even at the state level, but the state captures watchdogs who cannot be avoided. Localities within each state should also be directly attentive to their own relative needs. Tip O'Neill was right: "All politics is local!"[370]

Finally, it is incumbent upon all people who want to see "empty" words translate into "meaningful" action to realize that without a national leader who can stir state leaders to challenge inaction, the status quo will linger in perpetuity. Group think is stifling, individual initiative can only prevail through commitment. Informed people must recognize a failing and commit to a coherent, cogent influence over local politicians for change. Indecision is endemic to bureaucracies where time can stand still while mid-level authority figures stand around getting too comfortable with a broken system year in and year out never feeling compelled to act. This is "The Peter Principle" on steroids.

CHAPTER 8

Collective Plausible Deniability

"The world will not be destroyed by those who do evil, but by those who watch them without doing anything."[371] "The nearest approach to immortality on earth is a government bureau."[372] "Government organization."[373]

The last quote cited is the most accurate oxymoron. Government is the antithesis of organization. It is the grand- daddy of waste, fraud, and corruption. It is the epitome of "The Peter Principle!" Government floats in its own polluted reservoir of hangers-on and inefficient employees. Government is thoroughly bogged down under its own weight, and, if nothing else is disorganized in proportion to its size!

The most sacrosanct question to ask is: why the more things change nothing changes? As sure as day follows night and night follows day, all repeated inalterably, government remains an immovable object against all irresistible forces. Even with every empty promise, all politicians continue to optimize the bureaucratic mass of government to their liking. Critical mass is almost never achieved to move key legislation through Congress. Most of the time it is either watered down or adulterated with too many add-ons to preserve the essential elements for long term change and purpose. Government's sense of urgency is reactive only for what serves the "pol's'" individual self-interests. Otherwise, congressional action is as "slow as molasses in January" (when on January 12 and 13, 1919 the city of Boston suffered a molasses tank splitting open releasing 2.3 million gallons of molasses "slowly" moving through the streets: aka: *The Great Boston Molasses Flood of 1919* by Stephen Puleo, a book published in 2003)[374]. Cleaning up congressional messes can be likened as well to clearing away such a viscous brown syrup, lengthy and undignified. This is Congress unfortunately at its "best!"

To simplify what it takes to bring about change it is strikingly similar to the commitment a neighborhood makes to facilitate its safety and cleanliness. Most people countrywide are aware of the slogan "Neighborhood Watch." When individual households make a commitment to be aware enough to alert local police in the face of danger, the cooperative effort facilitates safety. In the same way, each home diligently maintaining the proper management of its own garbage sustains sanitation. And, together, the neighborhood preserves home value for purchase and resale. The converse simply is destructive and conducive to slow decline over time. The ramifications of ramshackle neighborhoods are the slow physical and emotional erosions which result in dilapidation and inevitable dereliction. When federal government is helpless to recognize this picture with a sense of urgency then responsibility should redound to the states, counties and cities. "Slow as molasses in January" is no excuse for the "neglectful supervision" of politicians whose vitriol and defiance against neglect is self-serving and gratuitous. Jaded commentary? Yes. True. Also, yes! Therefore, from a practical point of view, holding the local pol's feet to the fire is more productive than stretching responsibilities all the way to Washington, D.C. The language resounds locally, deafens nationally. When there are multiple cities nationwide, it is 2020, the year when Democrat cities were exposed to willful neglect and degradation of physical property and dissolute murder rates. Watching the floor of a Congressional vote in total feigned disarray and bewilderment is most disturbing. To get away with what politicians get away with would put the average person away in prison for years!

Scott Turow, a lawyer who wrote a book about his first year at Harvard Law School, referenced his first-year experience with

"Contracts" as such: "It was something like stirring concrete with my eyelashes!"[375,376]. Depending on the government to reconcile the plight of "prison reform" is astoundingly comparable. The only difference is that the inertia cannot be excused because of naivete or inexperience. As the trite saying goes: "that ship sailed a long time ago!"

To mount a relevant argument, it is imperative to separate the wheat from chaff. Up and down the prison bureaucracy is a ladder of hapless, misplaced "buck-passers" of incredible "incompetence" as cleverly described in "The Peter Principle."[377] In the prison bureaucracy (not the prison itself) incompetents climb the promotion ladder along with their incompetency as long as they stay until they retire. If the bureaucracy were streamlined (which will never happen), the money saved could be properly used to increase the pay of highly underpaid guards. Unfortunately, I had the misfortune to experience this face-to-face. It was an unwanted reminder of going to an ER with a bleeding body part and the personnel worrying more about paper work than attending the wound. This is the playground for the prison system. It would make anybody's eyelashes stop blinking from all the needless piles of paperwork. It is taxpayer money going to waste, particularly when it could be channeled into so many urgent needs that go to the burial grounds of false promises. Sometimes they wind up in file cabinets under the heading "miscellaneous" which is administrative claptrap for "what should have been addressed, but no one cares right now!"

A sane, healthy and happy family of modest means would not be extravagant nor wasteful in allocating its monetary budget. Likewise, when a public industry is answering to a Board of Directors, which is answerable to its investors, budgetary monitoring is essential. Being improvident will not last very long. It is essential to be punctilious in dealing with any kind of budget or eventually, as myth suggests, the "Grim Reaper" may not be too far behind. Humor aside, the United States debt is hastening toward twenty-one trillion dollars (not inclusive of the Congressional spending spree recently with COVID-19 closedown of businesses nationwide) with a projected budgetary deficit of eight hundred thirty-three billion in 2018 (now in the trillions, but for continuity I want my statistics to remain pre-COVID-19). Somehow, sometime down the road an American generation will pay for this unspeakable sin.

The state prison system is a massive bureaucracy with tiered levels of responsibility. Fluid function is not one of its sterling qualities. From the Federal Bureau of Statistics (last documented in 2001), "Over three-fourths of the States spent 96% or more of prison funds on current operations such as salaries, wages, benefits, supplies, maintenance, and contractual services."[378] This is a very significant amount of overhead expenses. In the private sector, this business would be closed tomorrow. If a car got six gallons a mile and it cost forty dollars to fill up a tank, the maintenance costs alone would make it untenable. In this regard, so much of the overhead costs are so financially draining that the essential guard-to-prisoner(s) demands could not possibly be adequately addressed. The number one cost of any prison is the guard to prisoner ratio. From the 2015 website "vera.org" detailing "The Price of Prisons" (state prisons in this regard): "Thus, Vera's finding reveals that the average cost per inmate is in fact principally driven by the number of corrections officers per incarcerated person, and their average salaries."[379] It is abundantly clear that with the cost of bureaucracy, the number one cause of violent uprisings relates to gross deficiency in the number of guards. Situational difficulties also relate to prisoners suddenly becoming erratic or physically engaging, and they are not explosive enough to promote a lockdown. However, they do relate to bureaucratic failure to properly look at the big picture of business management. Fictitious management in a maximum-security prison can only foment intrinsic dangers which lead to death and destruction within the prison facilities. Management should never be reactive; it should always be proactive and so thought out that flashpoints of physical violence do not evolve into an outright riot. Prisoners can react like a spark and the result can be gruesome. The prison where I worked was so poorly engaged in hiring more guards that it was always a breath away from a blood curdling fight, or even multiple deaths in the cell blocks.

Bureaucracy which violates this one tenet of prison balance and control cannot get out of its own way, and is monitoring an accident waiting to happen. And, when it has to answer to any deficiency within the physical prison itself, the underpinning issues constrain the warden. However, the lack of authoritative planning at the bureaucratic level in any state is central to a systemic failure. I call this "collective plausible deniability," an old military/political reference which allows leadership to escape responsibility for systemic failure by claiming unawareness of causation.

That is state prison to a tee. When a massive enterprise like a multi-institutional entity like a prison system is vulnerable to "life-and-death events" the collective breakdown of internal control does in fact lead to "plausible deniability" of the truth when it leaks to the local/ state press. To an outsider, a citizen who merely reads the local newspaper or sees a television news report, it is often diluted and quickly fades away within one or two days. However, when an outright prison riot occurs, the bureaucracy cannot escape a news conference or interview. The result is a brief statement, but the ensuing days are like a necklace slowly tightening around the neck. The truth is that the cause is bureaucratic failure to properly allocate resources to the one area that counts: guard-to-prisoner ratios. Up and down the administration it is classic for "The Peter Principle." And, where answers are to be found, it is "plausible deniability." It is disparaging when the warden takes the hit for the "cushion set" who gaze into computers looking for answers that do not relate to policies, but in fact relate to basic principles of "common sense." Directors should embrace this fact as the number one "raison d'etre," but they squirrel away from responsibility. It's the Warden's fault! No, it is not as simple as that. It goes right to the top: The Director.

In many ways, the prison system is a reflection of life, very complex and combustible. Personnel who invest a great portion of their lives in this kind of environment do an admirable job. Yes, there is always a small percentage who get entangled in troubling, mischievous behavior. It is unfortunate that some may feel compelled to break the law in behalf of some prisoner. I would always shake my head when the news would filter through the veil of secrecy. The questionable transgressions generally involved trying to sneak in contraband to a prisoner. This was always a head-shaker to me as a check-in involved a full body pat-down whichtouched each body part before a meticulous examination of all carry bags (including food and beverages). Nothing went unchecked, particularly in view of the fact that everyone knew through prison policies certain items were restricted at all times. Perhaps the limitations were overly childish, but the message was certain: no shenanigans! And, yet transgressions occurred all the time. The most incredible misguided behavior involved the number of times female guards would attempt to smuggle in drugs or were caught having sex with a prisoner.

Why? I have thought about this long and hard, but I have no constructive answer. Certainly, the majority of guards and prisoners were young, poor African-American blacks whose hardscrabble upbringing limited their formal education and opportunity. Their narrow vision and sense of life was jarring, but very understandable. I got to know most of them very well. As I opined in the early chapters, they generally worked two or three jobs, were single mothers to two or three children, and always attitudinally challenged due to perpetual fatigue. I personally found everyone personable, fun to work with, and skillful far beyond their training. In fact, given the opportunity they could all handle challenges far beyond the perfunctory nature of a prison guard. They were so underpaid for the overly dangerous challenges during their shift times that it was hard to fathom how all would leave to go to another job, just having enough time to check on their children. This is not to excuse misbehavior, but anyone can identify with low pay, long hours and incredibly high, minute-to-minute stress. I would certainly add to Michelle Alexander's depiction of the plight of the African-American blacks in her book, *The New Jim Crow: Mass Incarceration in the Age of Colorblindness*, the misery of employees within the prison system. Where endemic, particularly in the Deep South, the pernicious circumstances are unforgivable.

I was very much aware how the lack of opportunity forced young black women to train for these jobs. I cannot remember how many conversations I had with them. They were numerous.

The world of possibilities is quite delimited by poverty and lack of formal education. It is a stifling daily pursuit of obligatory drudgery through the prison. To exhibit a smile and sense of alertness when inside there is nothing but an empty pit feeling is difficult in any "misery" borne environment. This is tough, and quite unimaginable for people whose lives do not have an understanding of the life of a prison guard. I know for sure that most sense it dangerous, but glamorous. This is far from the truth. The young single mothers are prisoners of their jobs because they require the medical/dental insurance for their children. It is not the best, but it is necessary.

The male guards with whom I worked every day were also predominantly African-American blacks. Some were married, but most were single. They too were limited in scope for the opportunities available because of their seriously limited education. They came from very poor families and realized that survival could take them in two different directions: crime or employment. The common denominator for the men was extremely high intelligence, but they all freely voiced a quiet disgust for lack of pay, and, the need to be alert in the face of constant demands of childish prison policies while facing the real dangers of hostile violent prone prisoners. My experience with such engaging and very professional colleagues was probably the number one motivation for this book. The hundreds of exchanges I was so privileged to experience gave me insight into the prison system that the research just reinforced. Unfortunately, the research alone is not enough to truly gain insight into the harsh realities of the state prison systems. The prison environment is a measure of the pulse pressure which the writing, charts, graphs and commentary try to capture. The glaring realities would stun and terrify for the cognoscenti if they truly understood the volatile daily exposure.

To see and witness the day-to-day is like a piercing dart into some truthful realities which all the writing cannot even come close to describe. It is enough that anyone can imagine what a dangerous environment it is: gangs composed of combative, angry, vicious individuals for whom the love of life is long past in distant time. A flicker of happiness is not even acknowledged. It does not exist!

These are hardened types whose days are fashioned with deception, lies and schemes. To them, contraband, drugs, money and warring are the very sustenance that give meaning to what would be an otherwise dull day. Pictures of captured contraband would shock the average person. The personality revelations are permanently inscribed on their skin with variegated colorized expressions that only a drug delirium of a tattoo specialist's mind can bring to gaping eyes. Most are revelatory of very sick and twisted minds. These are not your mother's children. Those thoughts are well in the rear-view mirror. Some are moved around in handcuffs; some are additionally shackled. Guided by two or three guards is enough to display the true sense of danger this type individual would pose if not totally under scrutiny and absolute, thorough control. I have interacted with many such individuals. To hear them whisper obscenities, such vulgarity that would make an average citizen blush with covert disdain. It is a unique experience to see such graphic skin art that conjures up the dark underbelly of paranormal depictions of the occult, and from head to toe. Such are the very weird, spine-chilling blend of art with minds that run blank with hollow eye stares which promote shivers. Nothing but evil. The eyes are fixed and penetrating, passing fleetingly around as if photographing the surroundings for future reference. The speech is subdued and mostly incomprehensible. But assuredly this person is exemplary of the most dangerous type of individual who should never ever see the free light of day. Research findings clearly demonstrate that the guard/prisoner ratio governs cost to and safety of the prison system. Thus, an extreme personality as described above necessitates the most direct attention.

Regarding the year 2018, the Prison Policy Initiative[380] breaks down how many people are locked up in the U.S. state prisons: when lockups for drugs, robbery and assault are grouped, they account for 41.82%; for assault, murder and drugs: 24.75%; for assault, murder, drugs grouped with robbery: 63.15%; and for robbery alone: 38.40.

The total number of prisoners on which this is based is: 1,362,028. And, the most key number: those in for murder alone: 12.24%. These numbers do not include those in federal or private prisons, but for documentation their populations are: federal prisons and jails: 225,000; youth detention centers: 48,000; and, adult jails: 615,000. All these numbers are key to understand why the "punitive" versus "rehabilitative" argument is meaningful when the most violent are removed from the overall statistical basis of reform.

As I have stated numerously: It has been my conclusive opinion that without separating the most violent from the prisoner pool, functional rehabilitation is impossible. There will never be prison reform.

The 12.24 % is the key number which reflects the most violent, much like the prisoner I described above. This amounts to 166,712 of the most violent prisoners in state prisons in the United States (from the 2018 statistics). The number has increased since. Each state should extract its share from the other categories and should incarcerate the hardcore. My deductive thinking based upon experience is that this element cannot be rehabilitated. But, for the rest of the prison population, the possibilities are very real.

Leaving these numbers to dawdle through each day without purpose is hard to accept. They languish without any mental stimulation. It is like watching a green plant wither and dry up for lack of water.

When some talk about "reform" the most important ingredient is the ability to see a prisoner through an educational/reform process which will restore them to productivity. To restore human beings to a livable, productive lifestyle is what hardworking, compassionate people expect. Up to now, there has been considered thinking that some form of reform is imminent. Unfortunately, it takes energy to press for that kind of planning. Prisons today can say what they want but they are all, for the most part, massive holding institutions. Some are more capacious than others, but they all function on the old saw: "correctional," which does nothing more than carry out sentences one-dimensionally. The limited numbers who work in laundry rooms, arrange singing or band groups, utilize prison libraries for individual purposes (like researching for their own appeals), work in the prison woodworking facility, take individual classes in English, etc. These are all self- limiting and utilized by limited numbers. It does not represent intentional rehabilitation, and, they are often interrupted by lockdowns and riots. I knew a "lifer" who was interested in horticulture and was amazingly adept at flower arrangements. He taught me a lot that I could personally use, but he really had a "green thumb" and a creative mind. As an AIDS victim he spent a great deal of time in medical rehabilitation.

In a true "correctional institution" a "manifest destiny" would encourage development instead of stifling prisoners. The sine qua non of rehabilitation are guidance and opportunity. From what I could see and learn, prisons today frit money to the air rather than plan to conscientiously plan and transform the thinking of "old guard," parochial standards of incarceration. The lazy, unenthusiastic and almost total ignorance is a big mountain to climb to facilitate this thought process. The instructive message once verbalized (in the late 19th century) has been easily forgotten. The collective leadership at the bureaucratic level today is so entrenched in old-fashioned, backroom political dealing that the "murders" committed inside prisons is no different than the ones associated with the numbing inner city murders throughout the country seen today.

"Plausible Deniability" is the standard to deflect responsibility when, in fact, the whole bureaucracy understands the reality, but lacks the will. Over time, the mountain of money relegated to merely maintaining the status quo could be far better optimized. Unfortunately, underachieving and underperforming are marquis behaviors so very badly endemic. Change in government is as slow as watching an overworked mule churning up a 115-degree sunbaked trail up an Arizona mountain. The animal will get there because its reputation is its DNA and tenacious resolve. However, a prison bureaucracy operates like cold Crisco fat on a cold frying pan. It is just not going to grease the skillet unless heated. It'll just sit pro forma. Year in, year out nothing short of a catastrophic event will bring the right leadership necessary to usher in a turnaround mindset. To reverse old guard thinking is left to people who do not care, and to not want to stir up complacent, lazy attitudes.

I kiddingly said one day to a colleague that prisons remind me of the broken down northern New England outhouses just off the rural roads which lead to forgotten destinations. Forward thinking for its leadership is opaque because it is stuck on stupid. Working in these institutions is convincing in one way: it makes one feel grateful for everything, and particularly to have a productive life, and somewhere safe to rest a weary head at the day's end. Prisoners who should not be where they are cannot indulge themselves with any thought that remotely suggest such a change. And, the ones who should be locked up are where they should be so free citizens may sleep safely.

In 2016, The Hamilton Project produced a report comparing and contrasting the state (public) and federal prison systems. This was the conclusion, remembering that private prisons evolved to handle the spillover of overpopulated state prisons. Mass incarceration of the very late 1970's through the 1990's materialized with the stricter sentencing laws. The following conclusion pretty much is baked into the long-established common sense finding that bigger does not make better, and excess punishment simply adds its own sets of problems, (more "collective plausible deniability" to deny all mistakes regarding oversight:

> "Private prisons do not currently offer a clear advantage over their public-sector counterparts of cost or quality…private prisons do not offer clear cost savings or quality improvements. States that continue to prefer flexibility of private prisons to address surges in their correctional populations might consider policies to better align the incentives faced by those who run private prisons with public need, for example by tying desired outcomes like decreased recidivism directly to payments or the awarding of future contracts…."[381]

The way private prisons survive is to pay personnel less in salary and decrease the benefits which come with public employment (which is the major way state prisons can even hope to retain employees). Twenty states do not use private prisons, and the two largest companies owning private prisons house 55 and 30 percent of all private prison beds respectively. Add a third company and the occupancy jumps to 96 percent. The authors relate a rather "told you so, funny, but not so funny story" about the "Gladiator School" in an Idaho private prison where underpaid guards could not handle the gang violence so the prison negotiated with the prison gang leaders[382]. This is both not funny, and particularly inscrutable.

The argument that another facility will ameliorate conditions is like overindulging anything. More of anything does not necessarily increase quality. If diabetic symptoms incapacitate an overweight person, more medication will not improve her/his health as much as weight loss and nutritional counseling. Prisons, be they public or private, will suffer the same inevitable, mindless consequences of mismanagement/ danger without zeroing in on the most essential issue: quality control. Money is always the issue when the trail is followed to its most logical extent. The Federal Prisons suffer from the same bureaucratic complications. The Federal Bureau of Prisons came into being in 1930, but its three oldest (Leavenworth, Atlanta and McNeil Island) were controlled with partial supervision of the United States Department of Justice with the passage of the "Three Prisons Act" of 1891. Now, even though wardens operate other federal prisons almost autonomously today, there still remains partial DOJ oversight. It is a large bureaucracy with about forty thousand employees with a little over a seven-billion-dollar budget. One might deduce that the feds in charge might institute greater control, but they do not. The federal system suffers the same burdens the state system does: overcrowding, safety and security[383].

It shows that federal government doesn't exhibit any more quality control than the state. And, the private system has been a total failure.The private system makes money because it answers to investors, but quality control is equally absent. At least the federal and state governments can legislate change, but they do not. The private institutions make money without any quality control.

The private sector has a different incentive to streamline the proper management of private prisons. But, it does not. Whether by greed, incompetence, or just poor management, the private prison loses control, money, or even contracts carefully monitored by a board of directors. Government answers to legislators and tiered levels of management, yet they languish with poor management. It's a good example of a private business and government unable to make sense of the same conundrum: the inability to get a handle on "mass incarceration" and definitively deal with it in a rationale way. The private prison system, however, seems to be handcuffed by a "straddling-the-fence" attitude. It seems like half in and half out the door when trying to get their act together. The difference at the very least is that the private prison makes money. Government easily spends other peoples' money, and left-wing legislators never care that they run out of other people's money! e.g., the taxpayer.

The private prison system is profit-incentivized so it cannot avoid scrutiny. The federal system is buoyed by the Washington, D.C. politicians similarly to the Veterans Administration, always suffering from money and management problems. Both cannot get out of the way of their own abysmal, self-serving leadership. All of it speaks volumes for "the Peter Principle!" Being lost in inefficiency, inattentive leadership and, worst of all, corruption. It never excites consequences which would lead any sane person to conclude that hope for change is wishful thinking. This is where prison reform is merely a lot of peoples' useless yearnings and entreaties.

John Pfaff's "The Standard Story"[384] has morphed into the "The Standard Failure." It is certainly not Pfaff's failure to detail all the elements of bureaucratic ineptness, sloppiness and failure. Too many people writing on the subject are loaded for bear with determinative solutions. They wither on the vine without ever moving the needle. Return in fifty to a hundred years and, if life as we know it is still thriving, newcomers to the subject matter will urge a new approach only to wind up having their work taking up space upon some bibliophiles' shelves. To deny that there is something wrong with this picture is to reject failure, and more. It is to accept something quite ignominious. It is to say that American citizens are doomed to accept do-nothing politicians of any stripe: Democrats, Republicans, Independents, Socialists, etc. In today's world, most common sense-based citizens are more likely to consider this indeterminate bloviation without conviction, standing or honor. This is the root cause of failure because rudimentary fixes at the prison, prosecutorial or judicial levels will never have impact. Change must be legislated with bipartisan agreement of men and women with a particle of honor and a grain of responsibility that transcends their alter egos. Reading authoritative texts dealing with prison reform failings just silently scream for bold action. Unfortunately, it is not going to be forthcoming. Why? Because the sense of cooperation necessary to consider and pass meaningful legislation does not exist. Frustration does not begin to define the helpless inability to get this off ground zero. It is American politics in Washington, D.C. par excellence! H.R. 3356, the *Prison Reform and Redemption Act*[385] is unfortunately limited to the federal system.

This bill is the product of Jared Kushner's[386, 387] angst and desire to avenge, in an obvious way, the federal prison experience of his father, Charles. Mr. Charles Kushner, a real estate developer in New Jersey, was convicted of a very devious white-collar crime: illegal campaign contributions, tax evasion and witness tampering (against his brother-in-law). Because his brother-in-law was cooperating with federal investigators, Charles tried to trap him by recording a set-up prostitute liaison. It backfired and he negotiated a two-year federal prison sentence, serving 14 months before being released. Well, good for him to use this as a spring board to effect reform at the federal level. At least someone was thinking intelligently in the right direction. Unfortunately, no politician ever thought: hey, why not the larger state system?

His father-in-law, President Donald Trump (Jared is married to Ivanka Trump, the president's daughter), sprung for a prison reform bill. And, thus H.R. 3356[388]. As I have previously referenced, it is just a beginning. The bill conjures up amendments to the federal criminal code which have already been in the pipeline, but he used them for substantiveaction. Why, when all is said and done, why do Americans tolerate politicians at the state level see this good fortune and draw back on their heels! It is essentially and flagrantly denying their constituencies. In any event, this work of Jared Kushner resulted in a very successful start to federal prison reform with the First Step Act[389]. No other President or state politician in American history ever managed this. So, acknowledge the effort of the Trump administrated and the benefit it brought to the release of 3,000 non-violent prisoners. And, in addition, the Trump Administration acted on The Fair Sentencing Act of 2010[390] and had 2,000 non-violent prisoners' sentences reduced. This is significant to the extent of Trump's concerted efforts to talk about reform, and to actually act on the talk.

As of late, and unbeknown to most people, President Trump[391] paroled a bank robber, Jon Ponder. He had robbed a bank in Las Vegas, but in prison he developed a profound emotional and religious contrition. And, in 2009 he organized a nonprofit group "Hope for Prisoners." His demeanor changed and he is now leading a productive life. Prison reform should be more active in synch with this kind of proactive action by the President. No other President has initiated this kind of policy. Just letting prisoners out of prison through executive clemency (as President Obama[392] did in the last day of his administration) is not prison reform. It is dangerous because they were all drug addicts with criminal histories and no predetermined post-prison arrangement for drug treatment. All politicians showboat, but Trump is making a serious attempt to parole deservedly serious prisoners.

However, what did Congress do? Instead of Congress taking the lead, it besmirched Trump for nepotism and other sins of rash leadership. And, in a typical Trump he goes off on a twitter rant against the "useless" Democrats and "Never-Trumpers". The person who caviled and remonstrated against Trump the most was the Democrat

Joe Biden (candidate for the Presidency in 2020) who has lied so many times it is frankly deplorable. When it comes to prison reform this man was one of the prime movers in the Senate in 1994 when the Crime Bill[393, 394] spiked mass incarceration once again. And, he denied it hoping no one would unearth the bill. Trump is the one who has done more for blacks and prison reform than the Democrats and Joe Biden. It is amazing at this time in black history that blacks do not realize the Democrats have left them behind. If only Trump had a more reserved leadership style, he would engender more support. Trump is agonizingly coarse and without style. That is unsettling and unfortunate at so many levels. However, the old adage prevails: two wrongs do make a right. Trite, yes. Yet, he never learned that a person gathers more flies from honey than with vinegar! And, flattery will always garner support while hostility will always turn people away. And, that is Trumps greatest failing. It is very unfortunate.

Decisions for voting have very anxious bearing if the voter does not know who to vote for. All politicians lie, that is a given. The key for deciding is the following: forget all the smoke being blown by all politicians; the decision reduces to this: do you want a "Nanny State" or "Private Enterprise"? The Democrats, whether they stress Socialist policies (everything for free) or Liberal Policies, it means a "Nanny State": Big Government. The government's money is the taxpayers' money. The Government owns the individual at every corner possible. The Republicans stand for little government and Private Enterprise (freedom of choice for everything). Big Government is just a giant slush fund for corrupt politicians. As much as government is corrupt, there is much more opportunity for success under Republican leadership. Democrats want to make the population servile and needy. The Republicans want to lower taxes and regulations to facilitate private enterprise opportunity. Democrats want to increase taxes (because their Big Government depends on public money-the citizen's money-to survive) and increase regulations to gain control over "everything" related to the country. This keeps people servile. If the Democrats go too far left, the individual will loss his/her identity and the government will own the individual. As Republican Tim Scott of South Carolina described by his "Opportunity Zones" Bill[395, 396]. His bill describes the essence of free enterprise to uplift the impoverished in poor black areas to provide help where business opportunity would allow future growth. As opposed to live a life of poverty and have to resort to crime, his plan was to provide opportunity zones so that people would become self-sufficient and not dependent on government (the Nanny State). Independence, business success and self-worth spring from opportunity, not from free handouts. It is expressed simply like this: "Give a man a fish, and you feed him for a day. Teach a man to fish, and you feed him for a lifetime."[397] The Democrats will give a person a fish, and when they want. The Republicans will teach a person how to fish to enable independence as opposed to reliance on government. Senator Tim Scott's "Opportunity Zones" are modeled on this concept. Finally, it was Trump's Tax Cuts and Jobs Acts[398], which he signed on December 22, 2017, and provided more money in the pocket of working Americans. It further advances the difference between the two parties. It is more convoluted, but the difference between the two parties is singularly stark. In essence, the Democrats who want to increase taxes, and, the Republicans who want to decrease taxes differ in many policies that either favor dependence or independence. And, whether people can step back and look back at the facts, overall history tells the truth: The Republicans have been more supportive of blacks. As I stated before, this is fact and hard to get across because the blacks continue to support Democrats who continue to betray them at every turn. As the great writer Mark Twain said: "Truth is stranger than fiction, but it is because Fiction is obliged to stick to possibilities, Truth isn't."[399] This is not hard to understand. On another note, if someone continues to hit you where it hurts, boy it feels good when it stops!

"The Collective Plausible Deniability," however, is enraging because the so-called leaders who foment trouble never account for the mess that ensues. Up and down in the Washington political world everyone appears to use this as a cudgel to put the blame everywhere except upon the offenders, the agencies who lie and instigate division, and the corrupt politicians who support the lies. All politicians lie, some less (or more) than others. Such was the impeachment of President Trump. For the "Swamp Creatures" the activity was just like another day in a Cajun lagoon in Louisiana. As the truths are starting to filter out, there are going to be criminal indictments of people form the Obama Administration. What good prevailed from such illegal behavior, chicanery, flagrant deceit and such miserable behavior? Just because Democrat politicians and "Never-Trumpers" viscerally hate everything Trump stands for. He was legally elected, and a "soft coup" was executed through the alphabet agencies in the Obama Administration to take him down. The last few years the Democrats obstructed everything Trump tried to accomplish, and yet he did so much for the good of the country. For this reason, he should be re-elected in a landslide. The Democrats lied and created so many offensive political tricks to distract and attack him that eventually it rose to a level of obscenity that many fizzled quickly. People have seen and grew weary of this. These will be the people who will send him back for a new four years. Intractable Democrats have become vile and repulsive, and the majority of people will remember this at the polls. As much as I rebuff "ALL" politicians, the truth is that Democratic Representative Nancy Pelosi and her political twin, Senator Chuck Schumer have become agents of obsessive turpitude. What lost constructive leadership. And, we need prison reform in a country when more crime exists in Washington, D.C. This is "exhibit A" scrofulous!

When Jared Kushner's proposed federal prison reform bill came to Congress, it ran into a derecho-like crush of Democrat blowback.

The politicians in the House of Representatives immediately ushered typically adversarial remonstrations, the Senate (before seeing anything emerge from the House) resounded with an immediate lunatic reaction of its members saying in typical shame that they'll either not consider the bill, vote on it, or pass it. The displeasuring retorts are obnoxious and vile, but living up to their squirrely, self-flagellating behavior. The buffoonery was disquieting and galling.

Well, here is the piece de resistance. With all the collective denial of responsibility to such a "cause celebre" over so many years, this is the best such lame "Wingnuts" could argue? It shows that prison reform has little interest in Congress. If it were nor for Jared's father, Federal prison reform would never have been given selective opportunity. Approximately eighty seven percent of prisoners are in state prisons. Seven to ten percent are in federal prisons. The rest of the state and federal prisoners contribute to the private prisons. Therefore, the magical questions: "Much Ado About Nothing"[400] as Shakespeare wrote. All this political nattering is about the smallest population of prisoners in such a fractious manner with total ignorance of relevance and awareness. The ill-considered significance with such a depth of mutual hostility was borne of inflammatory "cognitive dissonance," so stark and humiliating for those who genuinely made a cogent defense of prison reform.

If legislation is where prison reform must gain footing, then what can be said to explain such a miserable sense of consciousness. This is classic Washington, D.C. Any argument which is rooted in common sense cannot overlook ignorance veiled in partisanship. Carl Sandburg, a very famous American 20th century poet, writer and editor (winner of three Pulitzer Prizes, two for poetry and one for his biography of Abraham Lincoln) possessed a powerful humorous manner to express a serious deficiency: "If the facts are against you, argue the law. If the law is against you, argue the facts. If the law and the facts are against you, pound the table and yell like hell!"[401]

There are many philosophical answers to behavioral differences, and many educators have approached this nuanced subject matter in many ways. Politicians are not all so altruistic to accept their responsibilities with a sense of pride and honor. The character trait which invests in key decision making does not require saintliness, but it should at least be merciful. Locking up prisoners and throwing the key away, and then have the glad-handing arrogance to mislead a constituency with lies and sophistry is sufficient reason to understand why the prison system has remained punitive and never evolved into mostly a committed rehabilitative function. Old guard assumptions that punishments will make a prisoner come around and eventually self-reform, wake up to a spiritual epiphany and become resolute in a new found honor and pride are possible for the very, very few. And, more than likely, such an individual will find an incidental reversal of conduct and appreciation for life's blessings in a narrow flash of awakening. Particularly in today's world where there is so much acrimony it would be almost impossible to have a reset moment. It does happen, but not without education in some formal way to see and understand the possibilities in life beyond crime. The evidence is clear that those who are able to readapt to a productive life are able to understand this wakeup call, and redirect their energies in a positive, productive direction. Unfortunately, there has never been enough political rallying to this mandate. It's unfortunate that platitudinous urging by the political wizards in Congress has never budged the message into an effective movement against mass incarceration. Ellen Chaney Johnson, the first Superintendent of the Massachusetts Reformatory Prison for Women had a lot to suggest, but obviously lost its verve:

"Discipline should aim at change of character rather than at change of behavior, otherwise we rule by repression, by fear, and if a woman does right because she is afraid to do wrong, how long will she continue to do right! Until she has passed beyond the reach of the authority she feared and is subjected again to the temptations under which she fell at first. Discipline is sent to us all that we may learn how to live, soberly, righteously, unselfishly, and society at large is deeply concerned in a prison government which shall teach its prisoners these needed lessons, for only so can society be secured against an endless and hopeless increase of crime[402].

This is not platitudinous at all. Unfortunately, society is victimized by so much group think in so many ways that the benefits of advanced education will get us to the moon (and, perhaps mars soon), but stifle practical decision making here on earth.

The costs of running a prison are horrific, and the idea of a private prison system gathered steam initially to lighten the load in the very late 1970's through the 1990's. It did nothing to ameliorate the sudden expansion. In fact, the private system became as untidy and corrupt as the state system. It has remained a distressful state of affairs ever since. Even after the mass incarceration flood seemed to recede after the millennium, there was no evidence that prison leadership would cogitate over its seemingly ever-expanding conundrum. Ellen Chaney Johnson presaged an evidenced-based plan of ideals which, even if based in common sense, would struggle heartedly to find a practical consensus today for women or men. The hand-wringing bromides spoken on the floor of Congress are stultified by their own impassioned blather that never effectively translates to meaning legislation. And when a Jared Kushner presents an idea for prison reform that quickly runs off the tracks because it truly misrepresents the circumstances, then the politics wavers off on a misguided tangent. The prison system today is run by a bureaucracy which is caught up in a web of effete leadership and very costly management constraints. The misfortune is that the burden of gangs with ever increasing danger, the lack of sufficient security due to low pay and overbearing hours, too many policies which weigh the system down, guards always at risk without self-protection exposure, and administrations bogged down heavily by day-to-day pressure, all combine to oversaturate an already weighted security system. It simply cannot get out of its own way to see the light of day. Itseems that taking on an additional thought might collapse the overblown problems.

A prison, be it state, federal or private is a physical cul- de-sac in many ways. Somehow words flow up and down the rumor mill from the Director's office to as far down as a first level guard. The most often disclosed information deals with two types of corruption: 1) the favorable when danger lurking in the ethers materializes as a forewarning, and 2) the unfavorable which is blind speculation of anything along the chain of command involving any level of the yard-cell block right up to the offices of the Director, the Inspector General or District Attorney. It is a kaleidoscope of endless incidents which may be straightforward or so complex that investigators can grow old during procedural information gathering. Like the whispering circle where a statement proceeds around a circle, the last person is told facts that do not relate in any fashion to the initial ones. Prisoners are going nowhere fast so they fastidiously tie up the administrative law offices with complaints ranging from emotional complaints to protracted complex lawsuits. There are no limits within a system which mimics a closed vessel of opportunity. It subjects all employees with overwhelming stress. Their antagonisms evolve in fighting which often result in major gang violence.

The internal officers who work daily under the Inspector General probing into corruption issues are themselves low paid, overworked individuals who are perpetually very tired, worn out and fed up most of the time. The processing of information is so time consuming that often matters fade or die unresolved. Some are quite serious, but most are mere time consuming and fluffed up through the legal channels. It is a nightmare of persistent daytime challenges.

The significance of this side of the prison system is where the "rubber meets the road," the place where corruption hides until processing unveils the worst side of administration. It may simply reside at the door of a warden, but this is highly unlikely. If such an occurrence sheds light on a rogue warden, it would be rare finding. Generally, the collective plausible deniability hides and protects the white-collar administrative sorts who conjure up contract deals which produce a money trail[403]. The complicated relationships at the highest levels of government are hard to prosecute even if facts reveal quite often that "power playing leaders" assume a denial pose. It takes sharp probing to follow the money where crimes of lust and greed are uncovered. Between the banal prisoner complaints and lawsuits and the nasty, covert white-collar crimes, a pendulous cloud of secrecy overhanging. Even when prisoners are silently murdered sleeping in their beds during the still of the night, the nightmarish facts are hushed most of the time because the media can be like flies around food. Rarely the families get wind of prison violence and stir up a hornet's nest as they lawyer up with opportunistic intent. If administration had an open-door policy with free-flowing information, a great many of issues which tie up the courts and investigation offices could be avoided.

The hidden crime which seems to skate through are the white-collar crimes that are all about money. It is rampant and ignoble. But no one should be alarmed when politicians are involved because they seem to be proficient walking that flimsy line. They know how to negotiate a tightrope averting apprehension be it through connections, power brokering their avarice, or holding other cohorts up to scrutiny for other crimes. They cover to protect themselves. A classic example is when Florida Governor Rick Scott received about a million dollars in campaign contributions from "GEO Group" and "Corrections Corporation of America," both private corporations, in exchange to bid on state prison contracts. Scott was the chairman of the State Board of Administration (which is responsible for the state's retirement trust fund) and was running for Governor (of Florida) at the time. He also had previous ethics complaints which he skirted. In any event, politically bobbing and weaving, he skated and was inaugurated January 4, 2011[404].

All the euphemisms used to descriptively characterize the trappings of politicians are inadequate. To fully capture the misery index necessitates time, not a casual visit. When I was working, I was thoroughly convinced that some of the people in administration should be swap with some of the prisoners. They were real "slugs!" They would "bob and weave" without ever saying anything constructive, only to conceal their true lack of honesty. They talked very little, smiled a lot, and never answered a direct question. The image was one of Kabuki theater[405] (Japanese character acting with Nagauta lyric music: quite traditional, but very representational). The people working in such a dangerous setting reminded me of the very bodacious Kabuki actors.

It is mystical and profound at the same time, similar to the eerie sensation felt within the yard. It is an ingrained feeling never to be forgotten, both in terms of the danger as well as the disbelief.

Research demonstrates that over the last century the quality of life in prison has enhanced the lives of very few. There are some real standouts who leave prison far better off mentally, emotionally and educationally. This is a very certain minority, no doubt. The major issue as I have tried to convey is that change (as I perceive) will never change from within. I have been a witness to a lot of ceremonial speeches which are cosmetic expressions at best. Nothing moves forward because the weighty and meaningful issues have never been accorded fair commitment. From afar it is very obvious that most of the leaders in criminal justice do not perceive where to promote ideas which will instill enthusiasm for prison reform. Unfortunately, it takes a high degree of motivation to want to make a difference, and be creative enough to put the status quo aside long enough to overcome indifferent people who share murky viewpoints and sluggish, lazy thinking. The day-to- day in prison presents a mosaic pattern of people who are thrown together without any sense that life could get any better. Some are accepting of the disillusionment, and some are exhausted from the do-nothing vibes the prison transmits. The feeling is quite linear, always dwarfed by those that can make a difference but never do. Indolence prevails when enthusiastic leaders should inspire conditional change for prisoners who could project desire and purpose. This is almost impossible in a stilted environment.

To most people who have never spent any length of time in a prison setting, it is hard to understand that everyone seems to be simply marking time, be it for work or "doing time" (code for many years). This is a human tragedy. The small numbers who advance on their own ambitions are maximalists among the preponderance of sluggards. It would be ambitious to reverse the majority of minimalists. This, however, is a challenge to political leadership which currently is tepid in its commitment. What a reality!

The reality which is at odds with truth must default to facts. Facts currently show that "reformative" prisons do not exist. Prisons have "reformative" qualities for selected prisoners who suddenly experience "a come to Jesus" spiritual transformation. However, the data suggest that violent prisoners are statistically in the minority. Therefore, the non- violent prisoners wilt like a dying vine without mental stimulation. Non-violence is suggestive of hope, but without a formative challenge in a stale environment like a prison only negative habits prevail. Intellectual development to some degree can only be beneficial. It is true that an idle mind is the devil's workshop. Mercenary behavior guided by a gang dominated environment will only promote transition into violence over time. Violent associations are a danger working against platitudes spoken by prison staff and eventually convert the vulnerable. Learning is productive and is a path to psychological sublimation. If prison leadership continues to produce "punitive victims," their fears will continue to augment, dispel hope, and cast them to a permanent state of primal behavior.

One final point as it concerns "collective plausible deniability": the reality of what is inside the prison razor wires is all about idleness and languishing. There is simply no measure of hope in this kind of environment. It is peaceful to watch paint dry, but it is simply abhorrent to not intercede and ambitiously promote reformative education. Treacly bromides with ubiquitous lingo: honesty, honor, charity, hope, belief, leadership, respect, faith, purpose, love, resilience, etc. This is pap productive of nothing! The meetings, the course for employees, the leadership talks, etc. just ooze with juicy platitudes which is suggestive of a monk's retreat. The use of hokey language is pompous and telltale hypocrisy. Actions always speak louder than words, particularly when words effuse faster than a greased metal slide. Behavior style conveys meaning, and prison leadership has learned to avert "reality" in all its worth through the verbiage of plausible deniability. Never blame bureaucracy, blame the low-level architects of "daily peace!"

At this point, certain conclusions are important enough to reaffirm:

> *The United States incarcerates more prisoners than any other country by an overwhelming margin.
>
> *The number of violent prisoners is proportionally a very small number. The non-violent prisoners represent the lion's share of mass incarceration.
>
> *Overzealous prosecution, lengthy sentences, and imperious parole boards are responsible for mass incarceration.
>
> *Three strikes policies with lengthy sentences account for many life sentences. Three law breaking events is an automatic conviction in 26 states that follow this law. The three strikes must be violent felonies (except in California where a third event does not have to be a felony if the first two are).
>
> *Black African-Americans are disproportionally incarcerated over any other ethnic group: being about 13% of the U.S. population, blacks account for 40% incarcerated.
>
> *Violent prisoners have committed heinous, inhumane crimes and must not be considered for reformative consideration (unless through legal review and DNA testing, they have been erroneously tried and convicted falsely).
>
> *Prisons today, in spite of their naming as "correctional," are purely punitive.
>
> *Prisons do provide many institutional vocational, religious, arts/sciences courses, libraries, horticultural, agronomy, and work opportunities, but they only embrace a small number of the prison(s) population.
>
> *"Prison Reform" is long overdue. It has been on the pipeline of discussion for many years. Some have shown historically that when localities assume the responsibility of prison management as opposed to the state, the costs are reduced. The state(s) is (are) are masters of mismanagement and corruption. The

costs are substantially higher, and management wasteful.
*Localities have greater sway over state prisons because of local oversight being more onsite with more active scrutiny.
*There has never been real prison reform for lack of political will. Federal legislators speak out of both sides of their mouths. They really do not understand the "whys and wherefores" of prison reform. Current legislation which has been written by the House of Representatives at the behest of the President's son- in-law is a wonderful beginning. It is totally insufficient pro forma, and represents only the Federal Prison System (about 6-7% of the total prisoners incarcerated). Based on this beginning, where is state leadershiphiding?
*If "Prison Reform" is to be truly forthcoming, it will have to be the responsibility of the state politicians in their House of Representatives and Senate to take up the mantle! However state and local politicians are ill-informed, elusive and mired in corruption. Look at the numbers of state politicians who have been convicted for white collar crimes. It is obscene. They cannot self-discipline, making prison reform almost unthinkable[406].
*The money saved through "Prison Reform" would be more than enough to manage the diminished population and provide for subsidization of social- educational job programs.
*The goal of "Prison Reform" is to decrease crime and increase self-actualization.
*Poverty and lack of education are at the grassroots of crime.
*Washington, D.C. is the center of bureaucratic logjams that make "Prison Reform" at the Federal level falter. The House of Representatives and Senate are laden with corruption because of self- centered, flip and untrustworthy legislators without any feel for a national consensus on laws that are responsive to "the people", and not just for self-interest.

*States have never exhibited any interest. State prisons will just continue to grow in population.

SECTION 5

The Outside

Chapter 9: The Juggernaut How influential is the "legal-political-bureaucratic" complex that defuses productive change and grows the system for money and power.

Chapter 10: The University of Prison USA I go into a discussion of what it will take to take on the unforgivable level of "mass incarceration." I present a real-life approach which suggests a direct approach to a realistic game plan.

CHAPTER 9

The Juggernaut

"Some have argued from history that major social upheavals have often occurred when social problems were in fact lessening, but not at a pace comparable to rising expectations. If so, it may be more coincidence that the wave of ghetto riots that swept across the United States in the 1960s began just days after passage of the Voting Rights Act of 1965, the capstone of historic civil rights legislation that had preceded."[407] "Education must not simply teach work-it must teach life."[408] "Education means emancipation. It means light and liberty. It means the uplifting of the soul of man into the glorious light of truth, the light by which men can only be made free."[409] "Politics is the art of looking for trouble, finding it everywhere, diagnosing it incorrectly and applying the wrong remedies."[410] "Democracy is the art and science of running the circus from the monkey cage."[411]

Worldwide the prisons are filled with the misbegotten, people set aside from the everyday scenes that life brings on. They may be pale and drab, they may be colorful and exciting, or they may be somewhere between where most people live. However, it is real life, where living is a fight every day. Rich or poor life is not a bed of roses for anyone, though as often heard: "rich or poor, it's nice to have money."[412] People who are earnestly trying to make a living usually do not have the time to get themselves into trouble. Crimes are committed all the time, crossing borders between "the haves and have nots" with unpredictability. Searching for a rhyme or reason is a waste of time because such indiscretions may often set anyone off at any time, though some may deny their own vulnerabilities. It is arrogant to think that being tested is beyond someone's nature. Mistakes are made every day of the week, and it is conceivable to transgress and still be a genuine person. However, when flouting a policy, social norm or even a law because getting caught has never occurred, then it is inevitable that this trend will end. The prisons are filled with people who started this way, soft transgressions evolving into increased chance taking with friends and groups whose associations become very poor choices. In addition, reading a paper daily often appears like a rap sheet for ugly, "high-falutin" white collar crimes. Thus, rich or poor it is easy to wander into such a rabbit hole to find the one-time money grab, or a sudden thirst for a quick return that becomes a psychological, irresistible lure.

Read enough about this behavior and it seems like the longer the article or book the less the author seems to be enthralled to find her/ his own rabbit hole trying to find a conclusive finding, reason, or both. Is crime a manifestation of "evil," indwelling and layered within the subconscious mind? Simon Baron-Cohen[413], in his book, *The Science of Evil: On Empathy and the Origins of Cruelty*, displays a very descriptive "Empathy Circuit" which explains acts of cruelty. This is a very profound rabbit hole! It is a very analytical interpretation of cruelty. For the average reader it is a very well-developed insight into causes of the criminal mind. And, the loss of empathy is depicted as a center-point of three overlapping circles with the center being "Zero-Negative" (loss of empathy)[414]. The non-overlapping portions of the circles are the personality types: Borderline (Type B), Narcissist (Type N), Psychopath (Type P).

There are all levels of crime, and the prosecution- sentencing professionals would do themselves a favor to have this book at arm's length. People who commit crimes have motives which cannot be easily delimited. Upbringing, family, role models, love or its absence, friendship influences, etc. all have their roles. But, causation, being multifactorial, is vital when prisoners fall into what is really a surrendering of their good-fortune or misfortune to a parole board. A non-violent prisoner whose good nature and excellent reputation during time served should instantiate the very respect deservedly earned at a parole board hearing which may turn her/him down simply for fear to speak. This is a blunt reality. The "empathy circle" should be something with which parole boards should make themselves familiar.

As informative as the "empathy circle" is, the issue of prison reform has to be reconciled through proactive means. All the issues which have been very well documented accumulate over time, but, in fact, nothing seems to have struck the right nerve in order to assuage the tension associated with prison overpopulation.

The "disease," mass incarceration, teeter totters up and down depending on the fulcrum point as it changes with all the demographics from year to year. It is problematic that the solutions only deal with the symptoms of the disease. Mass incarceration expanded so quickly through the '80's and '90's that the legal system was in a flutter. Excuses can be made for the corruptive nature of lengthy sentencing and hyperbolic prosecution, but, cynically, greed, money and power are always lurking without being called out. I have always believed that "following the money" has always validated itself, unfortunately--- man's "black hole!" The lust for money is "the juggernaut" that defies man's resistance. The juggernaut is a government that cannot self-regulate, rebuff its passion for power, and fails to advance the truth and perpetuates the endless loop of false promises every four years. Government excites passions which it dismisses very easily when terms are ended or when voting counts. The soft underbelly of people power expands from generation to generation as it swallows the same balderdash without resolutions of matters that count. It's the expanding snowball which strengthens as it gains momentum rolling down the hill swaying right and left from its accumulated largess with only a haphazard endpoint. Politics and politicians have provoked this juggernaut because it has become an aphrodisiac of unimaginable lustful dimension. There is no cure, no possible containment, and it's a drug which leaves the political class in a stupor, deceiving and spewing nonsense. This has led to the divisiveness in the country today fighting over the non-existent leadership from both political sides, the people forced to accept what it is "fed." It is now in this milieu where a solution for mass incarceration must be found. As stated over and over, legislation must evolve at some point when State Government and Congress finds themselves at a weak point where both Republicans and Democrats can see it as a negotiating cudgel to beat each other down. Bills added as supplemental legislation are the negotiating ploys. Without them politicians will not accede where it counts because their constituents are key to the only reason for their consent: re-election. A very adept and keen political (and most likely conniving) mind is necessary to negotiate this game of fortune because this is how it is done.

The two most impactful root causes of massive incarceration which must be addressed are: (1) poverty and (2) education. There will never be a consummate solution which will end crime and bring forth a Shangri La. That is a fairyland, not a world where practicality will always reign. However, this country can do a lot better than how it is currently constituted. As it currently operates, the prison system is a monstrosity bubbling over with unmanageable difficulties. Prison numbers are slightly diminishing, but this trend is not a guarantee. As the social-political troubles are so much in flux right now throughout the country, the increasing patterns of violence will certainly reverse the downward trend if there is no accountability or political resolution.

As assuredly as the sun rises and falls daily, there will never be a uniform sense of social and economic fairness about which every person will feel comfortable. No matter how a loose-lipped politician spiels people should never count on them for their pledges or guarantees. All politicians have a compact with the devil. Only young "bright-eyed and bushy- tailed" young people have not experienced enough of life to understand the motives and modus operandi of politically promotional language and stunts. It is a generational thing. Be it barnstorming around the country or in a small auditorium, the flawed bravado can be most appealing to an ingénue or a jejune, impressionable boy. An august, convincing pol is capable of reassuring already existing beliefs and lighting up crowd excitement into a frenzied excitement. Even a cynic who believes half of what she/he sees and nothing what she/he hears can be drawn in if the tone is right and the effect is appealing. This is the art of the spiel. I confirmed President Obama as the "Spiel-in-Chief!" He learned the art of exciting a crowd, never saying anything! And, this is the misfortune of politics as it beguiles guiltlessly, wildly and unforgivingly. Many of the most provocative social and economic matters hang in the balance on a platform where pundits and politicians alike dance on the head of a needle willfully drawing "group think" into unbridled approval.

This is the venue where the politics of prison reform incubates until it appeared as a formal bill in Congress (as mentioned previously). The same inattention to subject matter and details will resound, only with greater bias about a central theme which may never approximate the really important considerations enunciated for many years at the state level. For this reason alone, the political disinterest shows up as a very softened bill which barely addresses rudimentary changes relating to prison needs (merely cosmetic suggestions which will inevitably be rejected somewhere along the chain of legislative direction). The Federal bill does this because there is much more to prison reform than just springing prisoners. Nothing about education. This is its history, and at it appears right now, nothing will instantiate a turnabout. Congressional politics is an unsavory juggernaut.

If Congress can step up and do what's in the best interest of "Hometown. USA," then certainly the states, municipalities and localities must be responsive and responsible. What seems so obvious even at the local level requires an educated leadership to address a more sensible, balanced approach to draw down antiquated thinking about how the law impacts incarceration and what can be done to rehabilitate prisoners whose fate has long been the consequence of poverty and lack of education. It'll take a courageous sense of fairness and understanding to see where elementary, but dramatic, change is necessary.

Referencing two compelling studies and reports which get right to the heart of this subject, they are very detailed in showing a positive influence: *The Effect of Education on Crime: Evidence from Prison Inmates, Arrests, and Self-Reports* in 2001 and 2003 by Lance Lochner and Enrico Moretti[415,416]. The most important argument for education is the money which could be saved and contribute in a positive way towards rehabilitation. I make this argument because "punitive" institutions as they exist today are for the most part end-stage repositories, a holding terminus, for lost human beings. They conclude the following:

> "…the impact of education on crime implies that there are benefits to education not taken into account by individuals themselves, so that the social return to schooling is larger than the private return. The estimated social externalities from reduced crime are sizeable. A 1% increase in the high school completion rate of all men ages 20-60 would save the United States as much as $1.4 billion per year in reduced costs from crime incurred by victims and society at large. Such externalities from education amount to $1,170- 2,100 per additional high school graduate or 14- 26% of the private return to schooling. It is difficult to imagine a better reason to develop policies that prevent high school dropout."[417]

Education is not a status quo that marginalizes a human mind. It is a dynamic of immeasurable potential for each and every person. A lengthy punitive state is de minimis and, for all intents and purposes, a wasting process. Extrapolated out, the cost savings in 2018 is increased. Whatever the precise savings from a decrease in criminality in concert with an increase in education is highly significant. And, that argument is incontrovertible.

From the Bureau of Justice Statistics[418] in the same year (2003), 68% of State Prison inmates did not receive a high school diploma, but 28% claimed they completed a GED while incarcerated (so that figure is speculative). Prisoners took high school level

Courses. Yet, lacking specificity, this substantially does not contribute to an enhanced employment skill. A very significant statistic from this 2003 report s that 63.3% having less than a high school diploma had less than a thousand dollars in the month before their arrest. And, 22.6% were first time criminal offenders, 40.1% had prior juvenile sentences, and 37.3% had prior sentences as adults. The statistics demonstrate a pattern of behavior which is negative and habitual. Whether they lived alone, with someone else or in a family setting, the lack of education and structure in their formative years favored wayward lifestyles, thus enhancing the potential for repeat incarceration.

It is easy to fall into the trap of aligning populations by reason of pertinent statistics alone. This is not to discredit their relevance (and, poignancy as well), but sheer common sense drives home the significance of educational opportunity (even for middle class people). Education is not everything, it is what an individual does with her/his education. Opportunity is a vague word, yet it is a driving force for employment. It seems sensible to state that a person who is motivated will increase her/his chances of employment, and additionally within the scope of a personal choice area. What has been shown is that people may sit out of the employment process when the unemployment rate is high and salaries are low (notwithstanding the controversial minimal hourly rate argument). And, during periods when the unemployment rate is high (as during the Obama administration), criminal activity increased. Now, during the Trump administration the unemployment rate is at an all-time low (pre-COVID-19 from which the economy is showing signs of rebounding), but employers are finding it difficult to find people to fill skilled positions (a pre-COVID-19 concern; shows how well the economy was doing). And, just as the unemployment rate reverses to a measurable degree, Trump increases tariffs so that corporations (foreign and domestic) are starting to recalibrate their needs relative to the cost of business as well as rethinking the "inversion status" before the corporate tax controversy was settled. So, while all these issues are playing out, there still remains the poverty rate. This significantly plays a role vis a vis crime, criminal activity and incarceration rates. From the United States Census Bureau for 2015, 2016 and 2017[419, 420], some of the statistics are worth examining to underpin how they relate to education and crime. Alone they fill space on a printout, but together the numbers paint a rather bleak picture. The percentage of people living in poverty in the USA: approximately 14.06%. The most impoverished states in 2016 and 2017 were (and continue to be) : Kentucky, Mississippi, Louisiana and New Mexico with Georgia, Alabama, Arizona and West Virginia not lagging too far behind. There seems to be a recurring theme that raises its ugly head every election cycle. Then it fades away 'til the next time. California, Texas, Florida and New York in 2016 and 2017 had the highest rates of people living below the poverty line. For cities, the number and percentage of people with income 50% of the poverty level for the twenty-five most populous metropolitan areas in 2016: the top five in descending order: New York City, Los Angeles, Chicago, Houston and Miami. The most important statistic, however, is the fact that all of the fifty states and twenty-five cities were shown to have decreasedin poverty levels (and rates) from 2015 to 2017. However, examination really is misleading because the decrease in poverty levels and rates were very minimal. Finally, there are nineteen American cities with the number of African- Americans over fifty percent (cities with populations over 100,000)[421, 422, 423]. The significance of this statistic is that cross referencing to the numbers above shows that many of these heavily African-American populated cities closely correspond to the states and cities of high poverty levels and rates.

It would be a herculean effort to create a panacea for the concatenation of poverty and education as they relate to all ethnicities. It would be like creating Voltaire's El Dorado[424], the happiest place on earth. What has been depicted above are dystopian cities where extreme poverty and deficient educational opportunity serve as the precise mix for high crime rates. It would also be a false bravado to suggest Voltaire's romantic dream for such a utopian existence could possibly exist. From a practical point of view all anyone with a modicum of common sense would want is significant improvement over what exists. This would require a good deal of money, purveyors of leadership, and consummate urban planners. What really smacks of a ringing endorsement for the reduction in crime is the 1.4 billion-dollar savings per year. And, this is a statistic from 15 years ago from the Lochner-Moretti study (cited above). The cumulative effect from year to year could provide enough incentive for the perceptive leader. It makes one wonder if there is just one politician who has ever read or heard this statistic. Very Doubtful.

Considerations related to poverty and education are employment data. Job opportunities intimately relate to the direction a young person goes in order to fashion a reasonable degree of prosperity, not just surviving on the edge. Self-worth and self-actualization are the greatest crime deterrents. As seen statistically, the preponderance of individuals were unemployed at the time they were arrested. When Trump saw the African-American unemployment rate go down to 6.8% in January, 2018, he took full credit (and, naturally, he blamed Obama for it being so high previously). The rate of unemployment was also down to 4.9%. The overall rate across the statistical charts was 4.1% (reaching a low of 3.8% in January, 2020 just before COVID-19 hit). These were historic recordings, but Trump should not be so quick to jump ugly with aspersions for Obama's mercurial, selective cherry-picking for statistics-good/bad-because such changes are gradual, not abrupt. But, as I noted previously, neither enjoys a sense of complete honesty. It's the nature of "the political business." An argument can certainly be made for shared good fortune, both being severely challenged by florid egocentrism. The numbers are correct, but Trump's self-flagellation was very much over-the-top[425]. The current figure today as reported by the Bureau of Labor Statistics[426] is an even 4.0%, with the long-term unemployed (those not working 27 weeks or more) 289,000 to
1.5 million. About 5% of working Americans (about 126 million) had multiple jobs. The bottom line is that the cost savings benefit mentioned as 1.4 billion per year (as Lochner and Moretti reported) was at a time when the unemployment rate was 6.3%. This is highly

significant when considering the potential for prison reform. The money can be found by a scrupulous political numbers' cruncher. The rehabilitative concept in sheer numbers is stark. Qualitatively, it surmounts anything suggested by any legislator. Education can provide a pathway to reasonable accomplishment in some remunerative employment opportunity. Success? That is individually determinative. The predicate for success is desire and viewpoint. So much is made of race, ethnicity, religion and family. Certain levels of "predetermined musts" are necessary to open doors and garner windows of opportunity. And, certainly the reality is that people with the right pedigree will open up doors more readily. This is a fact of life, and nothing is ever going to change in that regard. It cannot be a deterrence for the ninety-nine percent who will have to knock doors down to grab opportunity and ride it for all its worth. Somewhere along the achievement ladder mentors can be found who will serve to guide those in need for direction and purposive advice. Even prisoners whose misfortunes are the result of poor associations can be rehabilitated. The mentality of prisons today is very parochial. Let's just say "the bright lights" running "the hole" are ingrained into habitual management and really do not shine that brightly! The people who are immediately in charge of managing prisoners are challenged daily with uncertainty and fear. And, if the minds of prisoners could be openly read, it is certain that they are fearful as well. The greatest challenge to control of danger in a prison setting is "idleness." The atmosphere is its own juggernaut, a perpetual state of anxiety. Some of the guards are nonchalant, but most, being very fearful, are guided by chronic agita. The guards always warned me to be circumspect and always report a wandering, unsupervised prisoner (which was ludicrous because the prison was so understaffed the most violent prisoners were out and about all the time without supervision, especially in the wee hours of the morning dark when I entered the yard). My heart was always racing then. I could feel my temporal arteries pulsating! (What's the saying: Oh but for the grace of God go I... insanely...I survived somehow!) Just gazing around this very stilted, open environment can only lead to inopportune provocations. There was an elevated sense of strangeness that imposed a real pattern that, to a conditioned observer, became hard to relate. One of my co-workers advised me to always watch my back and to condition my ears to voices, near and distant. Looking back, she underplayed the advice as I learned to observe the stealth manner of prisoners calculating their immediate environment. Their eyeballs flitted, their gaits danced in angular motions, their hands very active, and their bodies walking in a speedy, twisted manner as if to skirt any potential threat. It seemed very mysterious, but, no doubt, very self-protective. The more I observed this over time I realized that my surroundings (about which I always very loose with a"hey, what can I do" attitude)) were fickle and potentially a sudden battle zone. Does this sound like unimaginable hyperbole? Well, let's say: spot on, at least at this prison! As an outsider I would never understand this. Like Freud's "conditioned reflex" behavior, I had to develop a new learned behavior to safeguard my natural safety and life. This is a statement of fact, not a Don Quixote fantasy! When I got home every day (the following day) it took a while to settle down and take notice of the peaceful world around me before I could be of any use to myself! This perpetual state of danger is another kind of juggernaut. This existential conditioning is camouflaged by the media, staging for good behavior prisoner bands, occasional religious gatherings, at Christmas celebration, or a small occasion for a retiring officer. Generally, it is no picnic. I have witnessed all extremes of behavior: from a screaming, crying guard who just suffered a beat-down from a few prisoners, a prisoner who came into the infirmary on Christmas ever with left lip, cheek and forehead gushing blood from being knifed. After suturing him up I earned a friend for life. Had I not been there he might have bled out because the EMS was an hour away. After that experience he would always call out to me as I walked the yard. By the way, he was in for pederasty and child murder! Prisoners would bleed out often if abdominal shivv/shank wounds were too deep and the EMS could not get to the prison fast enough to transport the victim to the hospital. In general, the prison was no picnic. It was like a third doctorate in "physical violent behavioral risk management!! Realistically, this is the essence of "the punitive" nature by which prisons live in arrested states of existence from year to year, decade to decade without change. This is the "old reality" in self-perpetuation because there is not a scintilla of courageous discussion how might the system change. It is obvious to the outside observers and authors of critical thought and information. The reality is, I repeat, a juggernaut, a force of an indisputable time lapse where the prisoners are contained like moments in time that are unidimensional, immutable parcels of lost humanity---as if clipper ships nesting for eternity in a glass bottle. This alone is emotionally punitive. My daily ruminations serve as a reminder of Ben Sherwood's poignant, but truly exacting reference to fear he references in his book, *THE SURVIVORS CLUB: The Secrets and Science that Could Save Your Life*[427]. He noted the fear effect as "The Baskerville Effect," from *The Hound of the Baskervilles* by Sir Arthur Conan Doyle (of Sherlock Holmes fame). The effect (aka the Baskerville effect), as he recounts, was discovered and name by Dr. David Phillips, a sociologist at the University of California, San Diego. It is not so much the death that sudden fear brings upon its victim, as in "he was scared to death" or "he was thrilled to death," but the essence of the atmosphere of stress brought to the prison environment no one seems to recognize. Let's digress and explain what a totally "punitive" environment favors as opposed to what a "rehabilitative" one may encourage.

The essence is the suddenness that releases brain hormones which acutely interrupts the rhythm of the heart so shockingly that the individual dies abruptly. Or, the suddenness of overwhelming rejoice of accomplishment can have the same net effect. Moreover, if the individual does not succumb, the scarring effect on the heart leaves a lingering vulnerability. If there is a cumulative effect, people as he described are potentially walking around weakened. The aspect of this Baskerville effect which resonates with me is the high degree of tension, manifesting as acute and chronic (sudden and self- sustaining), which lends itself to a continuous undercurrent that is fraught with "cause and effect" wrapped all in one. Such is the plight of people totally living in a small, self-contained bubble. Ben Sherwood relates the acute shock brought on by startling fear which, if it does not kill, leaves a scar. If deep enough, the Grim Reaper may reappear with a vengeance. This was once labeled as "frightened by the fickle finger of fate!" The prison, at any level of its danger lurking in the dark shadows or the bright light of day, opens all incased within to this vulnerability at any time, in any of its venues. This is fact, not fiction. It possesses a very real and living Baskerville effect.

Of the approximately one million two hundred ninety- one thousand state prisoners 713,000 are designated as violent, and 183, 000 as murderers. This data is for 2020428. Violence entails assault, robbery, rape-sexual assault, manslaughter and murder. The remaining numbers in the state prison system (property convictions: about eighteen percent; drug convictions: about fifteen percent; and, public order convictions: about eleven and a half percent) make up combined about forty eight percent. There are about seven hundred and forty-six thousand people in jails, about forty-eight thousand youths in detention youth centers, and about two hundred twenty-six thousand prisoners in Federal prisons and jails. These figures from 2020 total approximately two million two hundred ninety one thousand prisoners, the largest of any other prison system in the world[429]. These facts are important to understand some basic thinking when trying to understand "mass incarceration."

People living their lives expect one basic payback from their taxes: protection and living in security with the feeling and knowledge that wherever their travels take them throughout the United States and its sixteen territories they will be reasonably kept unharmed. There are no guarantees in life, but the expectation of a fair-minded government standard is understood. The fact that violent people are around unbeknownst to most, the statistics resonate loudly. The result is that standards really have been totally broken down, but the citizenry must endure for the most part by its own awareness and initiative. Government oversight and protection is swiftly breaking down today, leaving enhanced vulnerability and exposure to unexpected crime. Yet, the prison system is hardly serving to maximize community safety because of factors mentioned in previous chapters. The way the prison system exists today it suffers from very poor management at the administrative level (as I have discussed). The breakdown numbers are key to understand why people in their daily lives surrounded by a juggernaut that expands and contracts by a government's giant hand which squeezes and loosens with impunity. The remedial effect of sound legislative reform would be a citizen's dream if she/he really understood the conundrum: the criminal justice system is like trying to remove spilled molasses from a shag rug. Its whole engine and bodywork is a "sticky wicket!" Some defining statements:

*Established facts: money drives life; both state and federal government are corrupt; "The Rubicon," the cutoff line between integrity with responsible governing and its total collapse is long behind; Washington, D.C. is a snake-pit filled with wayward elected officials;

*What the United States has is still better and more advisable than any other country; a quasi-democracy (see the last quote at the top of the first page of this chapter) is what's left of a constitutional democratic republic; its three-headed body: Executive, Congress (the House of Representatives and Senate) and Executive are polluted by political depravity and bias; but, still far better than what other countries can produce;

*Washington, D.C. needs a colonic cleanse; its miasma reeks with its uncontained foul scent passing through into local and state government; Congress's approval rating at the end of July, 2020 was 12 percent, but in some polls (was as low as 6 percent)[430]; Listing the least-trusted jobs in America car salespeople and Congress were at the bottom of the list at 8 and 10 percent respectively[431]; with such low conviction for Washington, D.C. leadership, the real ques-

tion is where do the people go to find an honest legislator?

*Accept these facts as reality: if not, look around and see how divided and diminished this country has become, not because of its citizenry, but because of self-centered, greedy politicians whose "carpe diem" is centered on money grabbing, lying and betraying the country with unforgiveable greed. Republicans, Democrats, Independents, Libertarians, etc. (call them what you want: they wear the same kind of masks as they rob and lie), they are "fool's gold," the people from all over the country worshiping as if they'll return the favor; but, their less than honorable pretexts and pretenses are needed more than ever;

*The life of the American prison system requires a thorough going over; writers of all stripes have dissected its failings, statistically and historically; it now requires a new look, a new analysis, and a new plan; it needs legislation, but the leadership must be educated and informed so that activist legislators abide by their "p's and q's!" What is now filtering through Congress is like "junk science" because the legislation is written with a kindergarten sense of the problem, wrapped with pomposity, and tied with a red ribbon to exhibit a sense of endearment;

*A LEGISLATIVE COMMISSION of bipartisan legislators (three Republicans and three Democrats from the House of Representatives; three Republicans and three Democrats from the Senate; and, one of each party from the House of Representatives and Senate (a total of four people) who will serve to chair the commission; a grand total of sixteen legislators who will study the totality of the prison system: the states, federal and private; a plan must be laid out over a period of six months to initiate action for complete prison reform. Then all the Senators take it back to their respective states for action. Perhaps a federal commission will

challenge state leadership to get on the ball and do something!

*The Commissioners: they must study the facts: the reality is that it is a punishment based system which marginalizes already marginalized people whose spirits are depleted; there is one basic fact: the stone-cold violent murderers are the only ones who should never again see the light of day; the citizenry must be protected from these hollowed-out people; the rest are fully rehabilitative; follow the money to realize the saving from closed institutions as well as expenditures no longer needed (as delineated from prior discussion);

*Requirement: complete honesty and earnestness: leave bias at the door and be measured in study of fact, thought and planning; pass legislation finally which will reconstruct a system that is old, ill-fated for today's work, and blows air into deflated, lost and forgotten souls.

It is unfortunate to be so bold and perhaps discrediting of Washington, D.C. and the country's leadership. Moreover, it is amazing to see so many in Congress making a mockery of the privilege granted to them. Their "noblesse oblige" has long since been scuttled away and permanently replaced by their sense of "Divine Right!" I sneer (in a laughing manner) when I see people arguing liberal versus conservative with a brazen posture that defies all sense of duty. The rule of law has been so macerated by personal-political alignments, so rooted in re- election and retention of the eternal money-grab that obligatory allegiance to the country's health has long been put on the back burner. A great number of legislators go to Washington, D.C. and ossify with their millions never coming to grips that they'll probably die before they see and appreciate the beauty of life. Instead, they worship at the golden altar of money, power and greed never caring about anything besides re-election. They pleasure their constituencies with programmed lies and false promises, and inwardly feel a contained disdain which, once in a while, leaks out with offhanded remarks that betray the intelligent ears of "their people." The disgraceful manners and boldfaced lies are nothing new, but the recent loss of respect and professionalism has diminished to an almost complete loss of moral rectitude.

The juggernaut that is the American prison system is bereft of needed attention. A band aid will not suffice. I am not into paranormal dreaming, transitioning into an afterlife, supernatural spirits and demons, or in ET's from outer space inhabiting terra firma or parallel universes. I am not a spirit or time traveler either, but, if I was, I would encourage a bit of consensus accommodation in order to retrieve what is being quickly lost: human decency and compassion. It is abundantly clear that there is a manifest display (even overplay) of the seven deadly sins in such coarse defiance of rudimentary virtue that it's unspeakably shameful. Not to be sacerdotal, but there has to be a return to moderation in behavior. Where is the drift? Lust for chastity, gluttony for temperance, greed for charity, sloth for diligence, wrath for patience, envy for kindness, and, pride for humility: these are the extreme changes deforming a society based in honor to country and passion for family. Spiritualism need not completely overlay materialism and the capitalist spirit endemic into our nature, but, at some point, the needle must redirect to point the country back into a sensible balance. The country has gone offline, and its politics is reflecting the carnage. Our leaders cannot continue as they do, violating all ethics let alone the law with the expectation the country will not suffer the brunt of such moral decay. Or, maybe Congress can rebuild the prison system for themselves so we the people can start over with sense and sensibility as they observe the world from the inside!

CHAPTER 10

The University of Prison USA

"3. The prison authorities profess three objects: (a) Retribution (a euphemism for vengeance), (b) Deterrence (a euphemism for Terrorism), and (c) Reform of the prisoner. They achieve the first by simple atrocity. They fail in the second through lack of the necessary certainty of detention, prosecution, and conviction; partly because their methods are too cruel and mischievous to secure the co- operation of the public; partly because the prosecutor is put to serious inconvenience and loss of time; partly because most people desire to avoid an unquestionable family disgrace much more than to secure a very questionable justice; and partly because the proportion of avowedly undetected crimes is high enough to hold out reasonable hopes to the criminal that he will never be called to account. The third (Reform) is irreconcilable with the first (Retribution); for the figures of recidivism, and the discovery that the so-called Criminal Type is really a prison type, prove that the retributive process is one of uncompensated deterioration."[432]

"Expecting the best means that you put your whole heart (ie. the central essence of your personality) into what you want to accomplish. People are defeated in life not because of the lack of ability, but for lack of whole heartedness. They do not wholeheartedly expect to succeed. Their heart isn't in it, which is to say they themselves are not fully given. Results do not yield themselves to the person who refuses to give himself to the desired results."[433]

"Training is everything. The peach was once a bitter almond, cauliflower is nothing but cabbage with a college education."[434]

The road to nowhere leads nowhere. Somewhere leads someone somewhere. The purpose of a destination is travel to a place previously thought out with the desire to get there. This is somewhere, not nowhere. Prison is somewhere, but really nowhere. It is a destination leading nowhere. It is generally where most minds wane and die, but not all. There is a whole population of people who, for one reason or another, wind up incarcerated—many with the proverbial keys thrown away. The prison system is not composed of "correctional institutions." Some prisoners get a wake-up call while serving a sentence, and, upon release, go on to lead productive lives. This is not the joy nor benefit for most prisoners. Recidivism bounces up and down statistically, but it is the Achilles heel of the system. When I was working. I used to think of it as institutional madness at its incarnate best.

One of the great laughs I ever had occurred years ago listening to Vice President Dan Quayle emote the biggest blunder while delivering a speech. He served under President H.W. Bush in the early 1990's. Speaking to a group and discussing education he said: "What a waste it is to lose one's mind. Or not to have a mind is being very wasteful. How true that is" when he meant "A mind is a terrible thing to waste…"[435] It was the talk of the nation, and very tragic to his career.

There was a comedian who was on the comedy circuit during the same period as Dan Quayle. He "cut his teeth" as a comedian, aka "The World's Foremost Authority," speaking particularly to very erudite, professional groups. He was the voice of reason, particularly eloquent, linguistically smooth and brilliant, and sounding insightfully brilliant on very arcane subject matter. The deception was so magnificent that the depth of a "belly laugh" his performance engendered was so breathtaking it could be dangerous to anyone with a heart condition. The delivery was sparkling with nothing but moronic run-on sentences that never ended. His intentional malapropisms were so dazzling a person could drop tears of laughter like water streaming from a faucet. He was one of a kind. He never lost his verve even though after time most one- way acts could (and usually did) lose their kick. His never did, and he always brought his "A" game. An interesting nugget at the time was how long would it take for these really intelligent audiences to sense it was all an act, like the gaseous effusions of cattle grazing! He was one of a kind.

Well, hearing Dan Quayle's remark at the time was the opposite of Professor Irwin Cory's[436] thespian genius. It was a tragedy for a man who was certainly not a stooge, he was highly educated. He had a really bad day! It's hard to cavil such blunders, but it leads into a much more serious concern, and that is the number of prisoners whose missed educational opportunities had their minds not vaporized because of a lack of education. In prison they melded, dressed in their bland prison wear, walking the yard looking like corn stalks in a cornfield. And, yes, I can appropriate Dan Quayle's blunder to a very different circumstance and say: "What a waste it is to lose one's mind..." The majority lose tremendous mental acuity and sheer baseline thinking ability. And, this tragedy compelled my mind to wander to a place that their situation could be so much healthier and beneficial. Prisons are nothing more than the dead ends for violent prisoners. I used to remark to a co- worker that a prison is "Nowhere USA!"

George Bernard Shaw certainly had a lot to say on the subject. His very short book relates one very important fact, and that is: nothing has changed, and people are discussing the same reforms (see the last chapter of the book) 100 years later. Who can sit by watching another human being decay? Unfortunately, the guards are so busy that most of them do not view this picture with any profound viewpoint. Their jobs are rather perfunctory amidst a constant state of danger so it would not be incumbent upon them to be subjective. Shaw wrote his treatise on English and American prisons as a preface to the report of Lord Olivier in England. The report was part of an investigation in behalf of the British Labor Research for the long-term benefit of revising "the common system of imprisonment."[437] The treatise was written right after WWI which, in view of the current state of imprisonment, is remarkable how nothing has changed. As well, most of what he wrote is eerily evocative of the very same feelings today. The aged maxim: "the more things change, the more they stay the same!"[438] The American Prison System being a lot younger actually began with an idealistic refrain as I have numerously pointed out. Yet, it has never come close to being a reformative entity in its totality. Its greatest accomplishment was to segregate the non-violent prisoners from the really violent ones.

The major consideration for "Joe/Jill Q. Public" is the prisoner/convict being just a uniform blend. That is, all prisoners are just prisoners, and that is all they care to know. Any more information is too much and unnecessary. The people who do care, and they care a lot, are the immediate families. I was always amazed for the depth of respect and shared concern/love a great number shared. Where did all this violence come from? Well, I know. Yet, the rhetorical question suggests that these are not prisoners who are not reformative. They certainly are!

When I first started my employment, I had to take a one- week initiation course prior to the real undertaking. There were about thirty newbies, seated in a rather austere, very cold teaching room. I was accustomed to this through my background, but these young novices had no idea what this week was going to bring. When it started, I was certainly put off by the outlandish level of low-grade, ignorant "teachers." They were both corporals with a degree of subhuman communication skills found more in a rustic, remote forest common to a troglodyte never having had human contact. They were about as unrefined, crass and crude as it gets. It was a week of torture. I have really never experienced such a profound level of low-life, tactless, power loving individuals in my life. Marine sergeants carried more sophistication and savvy. It was so ugly that three potential guards got up after one hour and walked out in the middle of their presentation. They did not seem to care because they continued on without losing a beat. They "dinged-donged" back-and-forth, looking at each other, talking in high-pitched, piercing voices with sarcastic, imperious facial expressions. They screamed at the three leaving who paid not a second of attention, except that one of the women anointed them with the middle finger quite noticeably as the rest laughed with a sense of righteous approval. About ten more quit during the week. It was really a very uninviting experience. If that was the prison's idea of luring in more employees (I thought at the time), someone is deeply asleep at the switch. And, as I have previously recounted, the prison was horribly understaffed with very over- worked and underpaid employees. The prison advertised all the time on radio and TV, but its reputation preceded these continuous pronouncements such that it was always a pretty bad employment environment (which no one on the outside ever heard).

Certainly, when I first read George Bernard Shaw's account on the prison system, I thought a couple of mindful notions: (1) how spot on his profound criticisms were, as if he were sitting right next to me verbally recanting these thoughts in terms of my own experience; and, 2) that it is deeply concerning that no one is really concerned about "prison reform" in the real context of exercising some old-fashioned, power-driven influence. The key, he noted, was to make change happen for all concerned, not just a few. He added (mind you, a hundred years ago) that prison is run with a 'throw the key away" mentality!

Many have written with a sense of prolix, and as well statistical authority on the issue. Convincing as they may be, nothing will change less and until someone makes a design for a "concrete" metamorphosis. And thus, I suggest "The University of Prison USA" with campuses in every state and territory. So, let's take a look. Nothing else has worked, words are cheap, and either my words will wind up on the junk heap of history or someone with influence will take up the mantle of responsible leadership and usher in a new horizon in prison reform!

It is quite certain that the prisoners of all stripes are provided private services that most family-centered, blue collar lower-middle to middle class people are frequently provided. On a daily cost basis, prisoners far exceed what the disenfranchised (such as the homeless, families living below the poverty line, the drug-addicted unemployed, etc.) receive from any "helping-hand." The services provided are: food (with special dietary and nutritional services for diabetics, cancer victims, etc.), full legal services, medical and dental services, time for religious practice, library services, educational services (vocational, religious, courses, music, etc.), and miscellaneous social, musical and instructional gatherings). Aside of the "protective services," the general costs to create and maintain such an environment is extravagantly costly for the taxpayer. When I would walk through the yard, the breezeways, and the horticultural escape, I was always in awe of its beauty and calming effect. It was costly!

Across the broad landscape of the country each state is invested into the millions to provide these services. Most people unconsciously walk into a maximum-security prison without any sense of the costs that go into its upkeep, let alone the prohibitive ancillary expenses provided. People who have not or are not paying individually for their own accrued expenses tend to be insensitive to what it takes "to live, breathe and eat." The individual who is the primary wage earner in a family understands the formidable commitment.

Considering what is the overall standards that prisons bear, it would take a complete change of thinking and planning to deal with the criminal mind in terms of rehabilitation as opposed to confinement-punishment.

When looking at applicable statistics from the Vera Institute or the Bureau of Justice, it is staggering to realize what is spent for services, provided and expended for capital maintenance. Sitting back to extrapolate the annualized monies (what I consider "monies," a creative word I conjured up years ago) as I would reduce my anxiety from a major bill with a "deep, prolonged moan"), it is realistic to perceive that billions/ trillions/gazillions are disgorged over time to maintain "punishment" as a basis of criminal management! Even if creating a total reverse approach may be unrealistic (but,this has not ever been exacted-yet!), it is not possible to conceive a "happy medium," a so-called "modus vivendi"? This is why an astute thinking commission with legislative authority (and answerable to the taxpayer) is necessary.

The existing system has so spoiled the prisoners that I often wondered who was running the institution (s). What's wrong with the prisoners in a "shakedown" of the prison, what with their demands and insufferable ocean of "incident reports" and legal filings demanding retribution for one thing or another? Like the insane running the asylum, children screaming in high-pitched, splitting headache defiance of parental authority, or a "crazy" going off at the grocery store checkout screaming nonsense at the innocently sounding board cashier, the thought of a discipline change becomes "manifest destiny" for such a rebarbative system way out of control! In a Vera Institute[439] study in 2012, it reported for the year 2010 in 40 states the aggregate cost was $39 billion for these state prisons. In 2014, the Brookings Institute[440] reported a cost of $80 billion for almost the total number of responding prisons. Also reported by the Vera Institute, 5% of state budgets were invested in juvenile justice programs. Even though the Prison Policy Initiative shows a comprehensive prison population of 2.3 million as well as the Bureau of Justice[441], the numbers are not going. The numbers,(for 2020), of course, are large, and they relate to 1,833 state prisons, 110 federal prisons, 1,772 juvenile correction facilities, 3,134 local jails, 218 immigration detention facilities and 80 Indian County jails. Additionally, to understand the panoramic scope, there are military prisons and civil commitment centers. In a comedic sense, the country spends a prodigious amount of time "spanking" our prisoners! However, I am not a "statistic raconteur" because the statistics are only as good as what they convey. Since the above reporting, the cost of living has increased along with the population. That leaves them viable until the next census report in 2020 (which will not be out until the end of this year or early in 2021).

Having repeated some of these statistics intentionally, it is willfully expressed by so many others that the costs of the "punitive state" reflect an overzealous and over-sentencing zealous climate in the country. The government is certainly not going to guillotine its "cash cow." Despite the fact that the statistics do show a slight decrease in the prisons' populations, the increased numbers are not financially significant. The way crime, immigration and political invective are all making such an enormous newsworthy presence, the numbers could gyrate up at any time. Examining the inner-city plight of so many American cities today (Chicago, Detroit, Baltimore, San Francisco,

Minneapolis, etc.), there is a pattern of rampant social disorder which is a disease crying for remedial treatment (worse lately as the country moves toward the national election on November 3, 2020. Politicians, particularly the local ones, are not beyond their own self-interest so they will say and do anything to get re-elected, particularly in such a divisive time. Chicago is the most disturbing example of this neglect. Gangs, with their omnipresent influence so violent and socially disruptive, are so fixed on their street agenda that sooner than later the dislocations to schools, business and living spaces will be irrevocable. And, with the added riots lately, it is hard to imagine the city restoring itself any time soon. It is a political and administrative mess (just as Seattle, Portland, Minneapolis, Philadelphia, Baltimore, Austin, and Los Angeles). And, they are all Democratic run cities.

Aside of the numbers I cited, the anti-social behavior that they would pose is an overwhelming threat if reintegrated back into society. The potential for rehabilitation has to be evaluated with exacting analysis. There are many prisoners whose missed opportunities would be grateful to see open again. It is my observation that there is a vast majority whose social-intellectual decline is enhanced serving out lengthy terms. Their enthusiasm level most likely would be satisfied by watching paint dry or grass grow. They seem to be in a hypnotic lethargy with a definite wilting energy level. The laziness is very regrettably enhanced by a system is centered on maintaining a status quo. Prisons haven't changed the systemic order probably from its inception. The prisoners are of all stripes, but the vast majority have to be schooled into awareness. This is because they are from circumstances that could not or did not offer anything else. And, left as such nothing will ever change.

I have alluded to psychiatrists and psychologists who have presented thought out good-evil, sociopathy and psychopathy studies and opinions: Simon Baron-Cohen, Baumeister, and Beck. A neuroscientist from the University of New Mexico, Kent A. Kiehl, Ph.D.[442], performed brain scans on 4,0000 prisoners noting "impairments in the interconnected brain structures that help process emotions, make decisions, control impulses, and set goals." These prisoners in his study are psychopaths whose significant brain connections are so compromised that "...the psychopath must think about right and wrong while the rest of us feel it" as Kiehl is cited. Psychopaths have impairments of the connection where thought (the orbitofrontal cortex) and emotion (the amygdala) connect. Yudhijit Bhattachjee, writing in *National Geographic* on "The Science of Good and Evil," confirms an empathy deficit at the core of psychopathic behavior. Whether compassion can be sourced within this kind of personality is still questionable through studies he cites, particularly if "reflexive kindness" can be programmed with training. This is the return to a discussion argument long in the historical literature: "nature versus nurture." For the time being, and has been long since established, more studies are necessary, and thus Kiehl's observations stand substantively inarguable as the neuroanatomical pictures are real and not speculative[443].

From the Bureau of Justice Statistics, in a 2014 statement, 67% of federal and state prisoners released yearly (435,000) are rearrested and half (325,000) are re-incarcerated within three years. And, three-quarters (76.6%) were arrested within five years[444]. This sheds light on the practicality of street evidence versus postulates of the vagaries of nature v. nurture analysis. Psychopathy, from a practical point of view, is not open for discussion when setting them upon innocent citizenry where safety is the first priority and responsibility of the prison system.

When analyzing the mind's predisposition for crime of extreme disproportion, exactitude is hardly possible. An example of violent crime[445, 446, 447, 448] where parole boards can leave mysterious judgment in their wake is that of Pamela Smart and Kathy Boudin (who both were incarcerated at the Bedford Hills Correctional Facility for Women in Bedford Hills, New York). Kathy Boudin was involved with a leftwing radical group at age 27 aka "the Weather Underground." At 38, she was part of a group of former "Weather Underground" and "the Black Liberation Army (another left-wing radical group) that robbed a Brink's armored truck at a mall where one driver was badly wounded and the other killed in a shootout. They took $1.6 million dollars in cash. Boudin drove the getaway vehicle, she made a plea bargain by admitting guilt and was sentenced to one-20-years-to life sentence. Pamela Smart was 22 years old, and, with her pupil-lover (15-year-old William "Billy" Flynn) she cajoled him to murder her 24-year-old husband (Gregory Smart). Though she sexually played into "Billy's" vulnerabilities, she was not present in the house when "Billy" murdered her husband with a pistol. "Billy" had three other accomplices. Pamela was sentenced to life imprisonment without parole. "Billy" was sentenced to life for second-degree murder, but not eligible for parole for 40 years (but 12 years minimum if he maintained good behavior). Boudin was paroled at age 60 after serving about 33 years. Pamela smart has served 27 years and is still fighting for release (though she has exhausted her three judicial appeals).

I am using both in this comparison because Boudin is a highly educated individual, having graduated from Bryn Mawr College, a most prestigious college outside of Philadelphia. And, while incarcerated was a prolific writer and educator. She graduated Columbia with a Doctor of Education degree and is now the Co-Director and Co-Founder of the Center for Justice at Columbia's School of Social Work. Pamela Smart was also highly educated and has been a participant in writers' workshops and participated in the writing of a PBS documentary with a known playwright. It is possible to write three pages on each one as these were highly educated individuals prior to the commission of their crimes. And, in both cases people died. Boudin came from a very left-wing, radical family while Smart grew up in a conservative one, but the academic achievement was not as prodigious as in Boudin's family. Smart had some issues when incarcerated, but nothing that would have compromised her rehabilitative standing. Yet, here are the significant issues. Boudin had a very radical life culminating in a horrible murder even though she "merely" drove the getaway vehicle. She was released at her third appeal hearing and was released on permanent lifetime probation, now leading a very productive life. She served 33 years. Smart has been serving 27 years, no longer has a chance for appeal, and, is a seemingly solid citizen, productive and capable of serving again as a teacher. So, where are the thinking individuals? I know the Smart case very well because the murder occurred in New Hampshire, and I was living outside Boston at the time. I follow the trial every day. Her attorney, Albert Johnson, was one of the preeminent trial attorneys of the day. Yes, it was a horrible crime with the similar pattern as Boudin's: no direct involvement with the actual shooting. Pamela Smart was a young mixed-up young teacher. The bottom line is this: if Boudin gets out (both having served in the same prison), I am amazed that Smart is going to languish for the rest of her life. She could now be a productive member of society, teaching and writing. To me, this is a direct example of the prison system failing immensely.

I do understand that murder was involved, but neither were the active participants. "Billy" was released after serving 24 years for his murder of Smart's husband, Gregory Smart. As Pamela was not present at the actual murder, she claims it was his decision though the evidence certainly disputes that conjecture. But, after all these years, this fact is no longer pertinent. The key is whether she is a threat to society now. From what I studied, I say "No!"

Boudin, on the other hand, had a long history of radical behavior with the "Weather Underground." She comes from a family bent on very left-wing, radical behavior so she slipped comfortably into that thoughtless crime.

A significant feature of the Smart case is the fact that Pamela Smart was only 22 years old. *Mental Health Daily*[449] points out that a consensus of neuroscientists acknowledge that human brain development is completed on average in the mid-twenties. However, they also submit that brain development possibly is still active through the entire 20's decade. As well, healthy brain development is affected by such factors as cognitive challenges (such as brain games, etc. all of which increase IQ), nutrition, exercise, sleep, socialization (friendships and social groups which produce positive thinking and judgment) etc. In other words, internal brain development is the result of what is put in one's mouth as well as external stimuli which determine the final adult status (to which I alluded previously). Comparatively, Kathy Boudin was 37 when her judgment went off the rails. A huge difference in age!

Pamela Smart was a graduate of Florida State University and, though not prepubescent by any stretch, was probably as "wide-eyed, bushy-tailed" as the 15-year-old (William "Billy" Flynn) she seduced to "minister" to her misguided plot to murder her husband. Not married long, one might ask is this a person whose maturity (and judgment) was significantly impaired at the time. I say: Of course!

This is where the rubber meets the road. No one should suggest that either Boudin or Smart did not have proper legal defense. At the time of their trials they were properly defended, and their sentencing proper relative to the facts and sentencing guidelines. Kathy Boudin served at the same maximum-security prison where Pamela Smart is still confined (as I previously stated)[450]. Admittedly, Smart has had twenty- two documented incidents, one of which resulted in major plastic surgery on her left cheek bone (where a metal reconstructive stabilizer was screwed in) due to a major physical beating. Having traced such situations when I was working at a similar prison (only for men), I established that this can happen in circumstances where the victim is not the instigator, Thus, it's unwise to surmise and pass judgment.

The significance of these cases is exemplary of the case which should be made in behalf of prison reform, realistic sentencing, and parole boards. Most parole boards are political appointments (by the Governor of the state with approval of the separate state Senates). The number of appointed parole board members varies from state to state. California does not have a parole board and has "determinate sentencing." Consequently, a prisoner may be released early with "good behavior" conduct as determined by the California prison system (guided by individual prison monitoring).

In New York State[451] the parole board has 12 members, and, as stated, Smart used up her three judicial appeals, and, (again) Kathy Boudin was released at her third appeal.

To my thinking, based upon direct observation while working, parole boards can be the seedy domain of the politically connected with "God Complexes." It is just one area where the hope and dreams of prisoners can be dashed at the whims and bias of lazy, insensitive personalities. It is a very disappointing system. As I have said numerously, there is an element of very vicious, empty-minded killers who cannot be rehabilitated and should be at the mercy of a higher power. I am not going to repeat the statistics again, but this is a small number. The rest should serve a term as repentance for their crimes. But at some period, they should be released (probation to be determined). Pamela Smart should be released immediately with the expectation that she can live out her life in a productive manner. The question is, in spite of her behavior violations (which are so common), who can validate her staying inside where the system will assuredly stamp out the creative spirit left in her soul?

These are examples (probably of thousands) whereby incarceration remains a financial burden on the taxpayer, and a heavy emphasis the system exhibiting an inexcusable degree of imperious behavior. Who are exemplary rehabilitated individuals. While Smart lingers in a state of anguish, her background could be utilized far more intelligently at this point in society where she could help so many young people as a teacher. I would suggest that Boudin's actions were far more insidious with her involvement with a highly radical group, whereas Smart was a one-time event with no prior history of crime. Her circumstance appears cynical and foolish. It makes me convinced that "prison reform" will be on someone's mind just as it was for George Bernard Shaw a hundred years ago. His treatise is an emotional castigation of epic proportions for a prison system without humanity and common sense. Anybody reading it can sense his passion flying right off the page, The Boudin-Smart case would make him roll over in his grave! The case is antithetical to reason, and, a sad reflection on the prison system.

Finally, an internet search is riddled with cases who have been victimized by the parole boards whose minds are depleted of compassion, sensitivity and proper judgment[452]. And, I am willing to bet a great number of people who sit on these boards really do not understand the inner workings of the prison system. I knew a few where I worked, and two appeared to suffer from God complexes. Political appointments are a curse, and it implicitly relegates such delicate and thoughtful decision making up to a "hope and a prayer" for so many prisoners. It is a "crap shoot" for a prisoner whose life disposition rests in the hands of people whose judgment skills are rooted in politics and not necessarily "wisdom."

Imagine now, based on everything delineated, I present a realistic suggestion for how to manage prison reform. I determined in my mind from my experiences at the prison, as well as what I have considered from all my research that the missing element is a prison education system. And, I decided to call it: "The University of Prison USA." Fanciful? Hokey? No, I do not think so. Why hold education from those prisoners whose upbringing and family history kept them from such a vital missed opportunity due to poverty or lack of a proper home life. As a long-time educator of close to 50 years, and having spent an immense amount of time in academia getting a degree in History, a dental degree, training in three specialties, and the a doctor of science. Along the way, education played a major role in my life. So, let's take a look at this proposition.

When I started working at a Level II prison, I had the good fortune to meet a man who taught woodworking. He had retired from being the chief assembly manager for one of the largest furniture manufactures in the country. What a talented man, and even more humble than his well-known celebrity would ever suggest. He was cut from the right cloth, very laconic, but engaging with a forceful handshake and wide smile. He showed me around the wide expanse of a huge prison building totally dedicated to the building of all assortments of both house furniture as well as dishware, eating utensils and beds from singles to kings. His teaching skills were obviously formidable because of the final results so many of the prisoners trumpeted. He left his mark on so many of the prisoners who exalted his praise to the hills. He was respected and admired by so many.

One prisoner told me that he wandered into the furniture area one day, stayed, and acquired an unexpected love for the work. He was a 38-year-old prisoner who happened to be a local. Growing up very poor, he was completely uneducated. He was illiterate and extracted any education he could chance through radio and television.

He was a gang member, adorned with body tattoos emblazoned all over his body, his skin citing his gang allegiance by specific identifying lettering and numbers. His face and brow were a patriotic red, white and blue designs. As I got to know him, his humor surfaced and we exchanged wild jokes when I saw him. He was in for life from a vicious assault and murder of a rival gang member "out on the street." I learned quickly that everything for a prisoner was identifiable through "the street." That's where home was. He had already served eight years and was certain he would never see the light of day beyond the razor wires again in his lifetime. A pitiable thought. Oh that life would have exposed him early to a different influence that might have given him proper values and exposed him to education!

The pity is that this was obviously not the same young man who was imprisoned as a violent, merciless killer (his words). In eight years he had mellowed, was affable, and proud of his learned skills. He would tell me that "God blessed him" with the good fortune of meeting such a wonderful teacher. What he did not know is that I was being transferred to a maximum-security prison, and his teacher was quitting and returning to private industry. I did not have the heart to tell him, so I just smiled hoping that the replacement would continue to light up his life. As I became a good friend of this highly devoted teacher, he would complain to me daily about the bureaucratic "mickey mouse" which hounded him about material costs, proper prisoner management and computer minutia (about which he could care less). I would walk all around the area admiring what he had taught the prisoners. It would blow the socks off any teacher who was worth her/his salt. There were about 20-25 prisoners who came and went on a daily basis, producing all kinds of desks, rocking chairs, beds, armoires, etc. in addition to the previously mentioned items. To this day, I still am amazed by this man's teaching ability to transfer such an amazing skillset. We were so friendly that he surprised me with a gorgeous and comfortable rocking chair that I use every day.

They lost a good man, but as I would tell him over and over, the bureaucratic nonsense would override anything in the system because the leadership up and down was filled with "one trick ponies" who could not identify with value nor think beyond their entombed bricks between their ears.

(I said this to him often and he would always laugh with a sense of disgust and disdain.)

However, this where I put on my daydreaming "thinking cap." If I learned anything while working in a state prison is that there is no respect for value at any level. Thought processing does not exist, and the system is frozen in procedure and piles of paper inscribed with meaningless policies about which no one cares nor understands. Let no one be fooled by the foolish pretenses of their false public image gloating self-righteously about their programs and rehabilitative accomplishments. It is very limited benefit to a very small number, and is presented in as accomplished fashion as a WWII fascist protocol for propaganda! It's an insult to the intelligence of anyone who cares. It is a classic mirage to cover for the true colors of what really is a "punitive" only environment. Some people would call this a well-publicized bureaucratic effort, "a dog and pony show" for the public's benefit. The only virtue is attributable to the very limited benefit to the few who swell with pride as they display their worthiness to be released. The occasioned beneficiaries are truly building a cachet to muster in front of a parole board who might, if they are fortunate, take this seriously enough to consider their release. The micromanagement of very limited numbers of concerned prisoners was hard to view. It was the same attitude conveyed to personnel they hired but could not keep.

With all the billions spent on the state prison system could it be that a total reconfiguration would be possible? Imagine each state prison taking responsibility by the local domain municipality. That is, severing the cord of responsibility from the state so that the financial management became the local responsibility of municipal budgets and management. This type of arrangement is how it all started, but the state capitals drew them all into the bureaucratic netting where financial control would allow corrupt legislators to control the purse strings. What's wrong with this picture (as it exists today)? Today there is no local accountability for a prison out in the rural boondocks! But, let's take this gradually, thinking that following the money trail goes a long way.

To achieve a local municipal self-sustaining prison entity it must be clearly presented to the local taxpayers. The tax base is the key to success or failure. At the outset, automatically remove the corrupt bureaucratic state employees who are now in control: prison directors, attorneys who prosecute prisoners' complaints, the legislators who command responsibility to approve parole boards and prison regulations. The attorney general, the district attorney and the inspector general could be extracted from oversight (or rather the huge monies which flows from taxpayer coffers to adjudicate prisoner complaints). Take all of this away from state government and place it back in the hands of localities where the prisons exist. The millions extracted from the state coffers would be immense, though it is very difficult to slow down a gravy train or redirect a Brinks' truck.

Localities which accept "ownership" of the community prison would have total command to represent the voters' fiduciary interests. If the prison's domain remains an authentic public facility, then management redounds to the Warden instead of the current Director in every state. (Directors are appointed by (and answerable to) the state Governors) are responsible for the fiscal and micromanagement of every state prison (within the specific state). Once the Wardens can be freed to be in total control much of the bureaucratic mess is eliminated. For community oversight, a prison board could be elected, and the Mayor would be an automatic member. The local Parole Board would consist of three members (all elected, not appointed). It has been shown in a previous chapter that local control of any kind of prison can lead to a self-sustaining protocol of management. State control of prisons is a cobweb of intertwining responsibilities where every venture is an adventure. Responsibility for corruption is hard to prove because the state is like an interlacing wool fabric. Untangling a bureaucratic mess or mistake, or even a flagrant crime is time consuming and costly. The proprietors of this cumbersome sideshow accept this measure of design because it pays well and allows for side contacts which deliver favored contracts (which enable kickbacks to enroll a private business entity to a specific need, and there are many). Whereas the finances would suddenly be under local municipal control, corruption is answerable to the local taxpaying and voting population. Detection of corruption at the state level is swallowed up in a cloud of "protective political custody" where no one pays a price because there is no public awareness.

It drifts from the Director at the state level to the state Inspector General who has a group of investigators who take so much time that determinative findings almost never resolved. Like in an endless loop the problems hardly ever get resolved. The bureaucracy is a disease. It's impossible to hide corruption from local authorities. I knew the state issues very well as I tried to push a case of battering against a nurse took months of investigation, went to the Inspector General and died of indolence and lack of urgency (in the mind of the IG's office). However, the nurse quit before any resolution. This is typical bureaucracy and indwelling corruption. Given that what's local stays local it is possible to groom management in such a programmed manner that it pays for itself. The taxpayer must not be an unwitting object of deception any longer.

Firstly, the prison structures do not have to be razed. That is, unless the local population wants to assume financial responsibility to do so. In actuality an internal redesign and remodeling would suffice as most of the foundations to state prisons were built when they were fortified as thick cement blocks resembling an immense bunker. Nothing in today's building could offer the same solid fortress-like construction. An internal architectural redesign could finally be updated to a total rehabilitative setting.

Secondly, careful thought has to be considered by the local mayor and councilwomen/councilmen as to whether the prison (now a school-detention center prison) should be contracted out privately or kept under public domain. Without losing interest in this thought process let's look at the virtues and drawbacks of each. It is incontrovertible that local control can be arranged so the taxpayer is not victimized by a wanton, unscrupulous business concern that parades fealty but displays double-dealing in the name of "the almighty dollar." Localities can control this because of the direct power of the vote. Setting the most practical approach could be advantageous for a local municipality. A municipal state charter establishes it as a municipal corporation with its own government so that the proper management of its local prison could bring a management style that increases higher paid jobs with benefit plans (that are no longer in control of corrupt state politicians) So, now let's probe a bit deeper. And, I am not creating a Shangri La, or, dreaming senselessly like Don Quixote with windmills in my mind!

To repeat, but it's worth repeating (at least mentally all the time because of its laconic message), Tip O'Neill's grand message: "All politics is local" The return of local control is a smoother operation. The chances for corruption would be far less in a small community as opposed to a weighty administration laden with deep and numerous administrative offices. Localities would allow the public to retain much more control and input. One thing a politician understands: a vote. It does not matter whether it is a Senator in Washington, D.C., a State Senator, an Assemblywoman/Assemblyman, etc. They all respond to the citizen vote, and hence much more awareness. In a large capital city, administration is amorphous and often careless.

If this plan is followed carefully, the number of state prisons will diminish in vast numbers. Each state will have to determine the numbers required for permanent retention and place them according to the need. California and Texas have the most prisons while states like New Hampshire and Mississippi have the least. The reason for "Classification" when prisoners are processed is for determination of placement according to a long list that makes cell block placement to minimize issues. Many factors go into this process because it is the essence of prison management. This has already been discussed. Assuredly, there are thousands of Kathy Boudins and Pamela Smarts. These are people who should be processed for parole (following guidelines to report to parole officers for monitoring with endpoints to be determined by compliance behavior). Sentencing guidelines should be more tightly followed (and, not overextended). Parole Boards should no longer be appointment centered. Instead, like any official officers they should be voted in for a specified period of time, and with a maximum of two terms. I have found Parole Boards far too highhanded and overbearing.

The number of buildings housing prisoners will diminish in time because the numbers of retained lifers will be about 12%, and the revolving door of new prisoners with those paroled will also reduce in time. This depends on controlling prosecution standards and sentencing guidelines.

The emotional pitch in a murder case is very high so that families suffering from a murdered member will be understandably (and usually, but not always) towards the death penalty or life without parole. For example, in the case I cited, Pamela Smart was adorned with a sobriquet: "The Ice Queen" for her insidious manipulation of her 15-year-old lover, William "Billy" Flynn, and for her seemingly brazen refusal to speak or acknowledge anyone but her lawyer during the trial. She would come and go in a quick-paced, brusque manner with a fixed, vacant, forward stare. Flynn's parents wanted her imprisoned with the keys thrown away during the sentencing phase. Anyone who has suffered through such a loss would be very revengeful. This is understandable, though I have met and talked to profoundly Christian people who are not. I always thought that I hoped I could forgive, but I really do not know how I would react if such a reality reared its ugly head. But, from a philosophical, psychiatric and practical point of view, when is punishment enough? That is the magical question. I shall not even begin to touch on that subject because it is a no- win discussion. It is not the days of King Solomon who wanted to detect the real mother of two who both claimed to be the "real mother." As the biblical story unwinds the real mother was identified when Solomon suggested cutting the baby in half. Knowing perfectly well, the real mother was so set back with fright she said "no!" Thereby, King Solomon identified the real mother through the real mother's nurturing instinct. Well, the bible cannot transfuse the law, but certainly over time emotions simmer and even punishment must enter the broader teleological argument of compassion. This is perhaps why some decisions require pure "objectification!

For the majority of prison facilities, the municipalities should then transform the institutions into formative aggregates of education and socialization. Several changes have to be made. With all the billions previously squandered somewhere down a political rabbit hole, each converted building should be upgraded beyond what is now old, sterile, filthy and rancid cell blocks. Hire guards with real pay scales, worthy benefits and realistic hours. All the "marine boot camp" training should go the way of the last clipper ship. The only training should be in pistol range practice, and each guard should carry a holstered gun and carry a billy club (truncheon or nightstick)) along with a can of mace (pepper spray). And, the number of guards should be upgraded according to what the population demands. The buildings should retain an infirmary for very limited issues, and all dental-medical issues farmed to local hospitals and clinics. All the money wasted for remedial course training should be rechanneled. The only necessary training should be for pistol competency. The idea that guards should only use guns when on the perimeter is injudicious and foolish. Hire people with maturity and ambition to be in well-paid, meaningful positions. I have pointed out that today's guard is disrespected, treated inferiorly, and left very dissatisfied. It should be a highly respected position with all the material benefits afforded any significant responsibility.

Now for the raison d'etre, the piece de resistance: education and redemption. It is incumbent upon a teaching institution to understand and address the fundamental needs of the students. For the most part, this should not be program to turn out end-products of higher learning. The reformatted "correctional institution" should have as its primary goal the exposure of a basic learning environment to address fundamentals: reading and writing. Does this sound pubescent or infantile? Well, it is not. Most of today's prisoners do not read or write (and, if they do perchance, it is usually infantile!). That is a simple fact. If through the process some advanced students are identified, then remedial subjects in history, math and literature can be considered. In addition, each prisoner should be committed to a vocational program so that upon release each has an identifiable skill to retain a meaningful job.

This is vital because an ex-convict must have a means to earn his/her way in the real world. Through this basic structure individuals who have never had this opportunity (probably the majority) will feel empowered with self-confidence and appreciation for the learning process. The local commission chosen to formulate this program should structure it so that upon release each leaves with a certificate of completion for use on a job application.

As to teachers and psychologists, the commission should extract both active teachers and retired ones (who might want to give back for a year or two). Psychologists as well should monitor the progress and needs of each prisoner. And, might I say, it is not recommended to retain an excessive number. Each classroom should have a primary teacher as well as a teaching assistant. A good suggestion is to recruit temporary supplemental help from local families whereby a father or mother may want to volunteer periodically to aid teachers. Or, if financially possible, pay a daily stipend. Prisoners should have plenty of private time for library use and physical exercise.

All salaries, health and retirement benefits should remain state borne. This arrangement extracts the ballooning bureaucratic mess away from the day-to-day management responsibilities of local institutions. Populations of states vary so greatly that individual commissions should plan a cost study evaluation to plan for operational closures as well as those which would be planned for capital reconstruction (the state assuming all costs, but the locality retains "power of the purse!").

It should be mentioned that parole boards should be filled by local (not state) elections. It is my personal feeling that there should be three members at each hearing, and, that two should have an educational background and one should be a religious notable affiliated with a church or temple. One of the educators should be attached to a law school with a criminal justice understanding (training unnecessary). There will be prisoners who might reject the new format, or might exhibit reckless behavior, or even regress violently. In such an instance, a seasoned parole board and a sage warden will be necessary.

This is an experiment that should be intensely studied, planned and brought to fruition. The learning curve will depend on the quality of the commission (which should be 12 in number with education and criminal justice backgrounds).

The prison is what it is: still a prison, but it becomes truly rehabilitative. The majority will sense their enrichment, their increased self-esteem, self-worth and identification with the effort being made in behalf of their future. There is nothing more fruitful in life than "hope" as well as the chance for redemptive second chances! The reality is that nothing is perfect, and the major impediment will be "the gang effect" which must be overcome. Considering that there are 33,000 prison, street and motorcycle gangs (and growing) the dependence is similar to a Koala bear clinging to a eucalyptus tree. (It's not as farfetched as it sounds when every investigator into prison gangs notes the emotional identification with like-minded prisoners as a draw). It's an imposing hurdle to surmount, but this has been a growing cancer for over sixty years. Rest assured that the process has to start somewhere, and it is a venture that must begin before all efforts will be lost. The prison system as it stands is "a regressive institution!"

As I previously remarked, Dr. W. David Ball,[453] an Associate Professor of Law at Santa Clara University School of Law, writing in the Yale Law Review details this evolutionary process. Many comparisons are made to the state/local management of education, and it makes perfect sense. The state should maintain the costs of the prison structures while the localities assume their management. This rids the states of interference at so many levels, but especially the financial connection. He makes four essential benefits for "localization":

(1) transparency; this is the most vital, eliminating overwhelming bureaucracy and corruption; (2) rendering criminal justice decisions more meaningful to allow prisons to be based more on the social sciences, and not retribution (I avoid all of this with formation of an educational/teaching institution); (3) decentralization; this is essential to allow each municipality the ability to coordinate and personalize its own facilities; and, (4) local avoid all of this with formation of an educational/teaching institution); (3) decentralization; this is essential to allow each municipality the ability to coordinate and personalize its own facilities; and, (4) local criminal justice instead of statewide

criminal justice (as he points out, more in line with the Bill of Rights). He concludes by stating: "Reducing or eliminating state governments' role in imprisonment does not mean the end of either criminal punishment of incarceration. Instead, it simply means that these practices should be reoriented to the localities."[454]

My solution is to keep the prison foundation, retool the inside appearance with a capital expenditure from the state, and make it educational minded (but, not losing site of its prison-correctional status). In summary, the state should use taxpayer money to subsidize all aspects of the structure and teaching salaries (health and retirement benefits included), but the municipalities should retain management control.

The most important element in such an arrangement is making all prisoners feel physiologically healthy, comfortable with the environment, and satisfied enough to be challenged so they want to learn. Maslow's "Hierarchy of Needs"[455] is a pyramid with which every teacher identifies and understands. The pyramid identifies basic needs, psychological needs and self-fulfillment needs. The gradient ascends from the bottom of the pyramid where basic physiological needs (food, water, warmth and rest) are identified and discussed. Without these basic needs fulfilled the learning process is impossible. The psychological needs (safety, belonging and love, and esteem) must be instilled in order feel the desire to learn. And, finally, the self-fulfillment needs (self-actualization: achieving one's potential) cannot be realized without good health and safety- belonging-love-esteem elements necessary to feel the desire to learn.

Nothing is more certain to anyone who has spent time in a state prison than the fact that two elements of the prisoner's persona jump out: neglect and deprivation. I have always said to people I know that if you are feeling like the world owes you something or you walk around with self-pity, take a job in a prison. Your feelings about yourself and the world around you will dramatically change. I feel most of the people who suffer from unhappiness (not real depression with physiological reasons) and anger just live with too many material benefits which suffocate a balanced appreciation of being healthy and alive. The poet, William Wordsworth (1770- 1850) expressed this thought beautifully:

> "The world is too much with us; late and soon, Getting and spending, we lay waste our powers; Little we see in Nature that is ours;
>
> . . . .
>
> So, might I, standing on this pleasant lea,
> Have glimpses that would make me feel less forlorn;
> . . . . [456]

The acquisitive urge of material "things" is a grave disease in present day society. It's nice to own, but it's nicer to appreciate what life means! Given good health, liberty is everything.

This is where the responsibilities of the warden changes. She/he no longer answers to a Director (a political construct who answers to state government like an automaton, drawing a huge salary, operates in a perfunctory manner, and gets caught up in corruption). It eliminates the very nature of government operations so thick with "pencil pushers" that a Director has carte-blanche to feel unaccountable and empowered to conduct business for her/his own benefit. A warden has always been the "viceroy" to the "monarch" (the Director). The wardens are really the honorable backbones of the prison system.

Today with so many teachers and others with educational backgrounds it would be a shame not to tap into this captive reservoir of talent. The structure of the prison should operate as a hybrid, not tightfisted, merely a reprogrammed set-up where prisoners will not just be emasculated (physically and emotionally) as was their history. The new refrain should provide, at the very least, a means by which they can grow and feel a new sense of themselves upon release. Vocational opportunities should be provided if local small business want to partake in this educational process. It is the linkage to local connections that would never happen the way state prisons operate today. The most illuminating feature of a state prison is that only the very few treat it as a productive experience. For most prisoners they are empty vessels where days blend and drain whatever motivation is left. These are a very select few who, for one reason or another, are just wired differently and are inspired to enrich themselves. This is not the norm. These are unique and rare individuals who, in spite of all the violence around them, would draw, learn a musical instrument, cultivate a garden, write for the sake of writing, read in the library, and talk for the sake of conversation because it was appealing. The 99% are waiting out the time in their lives without direction or purpose.

It is not enough to visit a prison without going past the control room into the inner sanctum to truly witness and identify with the lifeless environment of a maximum-security prison. Without going past the entry offices on a daily basis the real sense of the prison system is lost. The guts of the prison lies beyond the gates to the yard where all the prisoners walk, linger and plan. Even during the light of day, the prisoners are woefully calculating because they dream to scheme. And boy, do they ever. Loitering with too much time is as dangerous for these types of individuals as it is for the guards and other employees who are constantly left unprotected.

I do believe that as fanciful as this "dreamscape" may appear it is far-reaching in practicality and feasible if not taken as a silly notion. Otherwise, those who settle for the prevailing arrangement must accept that it can only expand as well as deteriorate as the population expands (and, as the inner cities become even more violent). To me the gangs are the most concerning element because they sustain themselves on pure violence.

The most important facet of this discussion is the reality of the political environment that is satisfied with the status quo, quite ignorant and insensitive to the truth, and the lethargy which fosters the type of inattention which is as dangerous as it is neglectful. It is similar to a hoarder who is told to clean up or get out. Cornered the hoarder will throw everything in an attic or closets convinced things are different until one day the accumulation is worse than ever, but the attics and/or closets are now packed to the gills! This is a very dangerous projection that people do not understand, and certainly the prison bureaucracy would thoroughly deny. To the bureaucrats, the maintenance is onerous, but it is a "cash cow" for the state.

The idea of going back in time when state prisons were financially self-sustaining through the use of "prison working groups" cannot be reinstituted because the revenue stream would be lost to the state pols. But the current change I have suggested can generate income as well through needed vocational services which can be farmed out for a fee. As the prison changes local sources for day employment (similar to Kelly services) can be used for per diem fees. In every manner, possible local businesses can benefit by inexpensive assistance so that the income supports the prison. A productive wood working school can sell advertised products for all local families and businesses. The tax base as well can sustain prison salaries and maintenance. The required planning is no simple task, but a prison reform effort has to be made. The reality is that the "same ol'-same ol'" is not going to work, and, will be headed for a complex reality check down the line. It is a freight train out of control.

Education alone is not the complete package. It is a vehicle through which need and opportunity can meet each other to produce a constructive change. Need and opportunity provide self-reliance. Self-reliance instills a sense of "freedom!" Federal and state politicians have too long neglected this fact. George Bernard Shaw ends his treatise by throwing up the proverbial gauntlet for change: "The conclusion is that imprisonment cannot be fully understood by those who do not understand freedom. But it can be understood quite well enough to have it made a much less horrible, wicked and wasteful thing than it is at present."[457] The original "present" was the first copyright in 1946, not the edition later reprinted (from which I quote 72 years later). If you realize he was born in 1856 and died in 1950, it renders sufficient perspective to cynically feel a sense of chagrin that no one has even tried to understand, let alone explore, the proposition. I know the university from which I graduated maintained an entire school devoted to urban planning!

Does "The University of Prison USA" sound unrealistic? Well, nothing ventured, nothing gained. And, I would suggest that refractory elements will look askance with "hell no," "what are you crazy," and others who may just lazily accept the ongoing bureaucratic status quo. Accepting failure is a very large pill hard to swallow without choking on its real time drawbacks. The prison system as it exists today is an immense maze of retrogressive management. When the numbers of incarceration exploded through the late 1970's to the end of the 1990's (along with the huge impact of gangs), the silence of people in the criminal justice system was deafening.

It is no different than looking at the collapsing infrastructure around the country. When President Dwight David Eisenhower (in 1953 after WWII) was elected President, one of his major legacy contributions (besides warning the country of the future impact of the military-industrial complex) was the building of the American Interstate Highway System. Limited upgrades parceled out with a haphazard approach over the years have passed on very dilapidated, marginalized system of roads. A great number of cities are pretty much irreparable because of total neglect, smoothing over roads with casual attention and inferior patchwork repairs. Neglect in government used to be rare, but not anymore. Many states have passed highway and city road repair legislative bills, but, as bureaucracies are known to behave, somehow the money disappears. The newspapers then grapple with the sudden disappearance, later to expose political bad actors. Infrastructure disrepair and prison reform are wedded in the same milieu where neglect lingers.

This is the condition of the prison system. They are old for the most part (except for new ones here and there) with decrepit plumbing and dangerously old wiring electrical systems. They are dirty, smelly and unsavory. As Yogi Berra, the famous New York Yankee baseball catcher, once said: "When you come to a fork in the road, take it."[458] Well, at this point, all aspects of what the American prison system represents are so old, tired and worn that it really does not make a difference which individually or collectively suggested direction it should go or pursue. Just go and do something, or the country will pay at some point for such passive neglect. Avoidance makes problems worse. "Situation Repetition" (my labeling), or, as Yogi Berra said: "It's déjà vu all over again,"[459] inevitably fails. It evolves ultimately in failure. I referenced previously: "The Peter Principle."[460] The hierarchy of incompetence is so steeped in bureaucracy that with its first cousin, corruption, the way is paved with seemingly eternal neglect. This is a way of life in prisons!

My exposure to the prison system was limited, but extremely intense. My hat goes off to so many wonderful people with whom I had the pleasure and the good fortune to engage in wonderful conversation about the prison system. I never asked the warden nor his associates how they liked enduring such an environment because I knew the answer. They were incredibly street smart with a savvy sense of blue- collar psychology knowledge of human personality. The rest of the employees were extremely forthcoming. Not one had a good thing to say that spoke in support of such a broken system. They endured because they needed the money. The country at the time was suffering from an extremely high rate of unemployment, an all-time low Gross Domestic Product (GDP): a total of goods and services the country was producing, and also an all-time high number of people on food stamps. Mistakes were made by some of the guards I knew, but, in most cases, they were very alert and devoted to their work. I mention this because they were all (to a person) aware of the need for prison reform in any way possible. I had some very in-depth conversations with one guard in particular. At 3AM, when unaccompanied stragglers were meandering around the yard, we would strike up a conversation about families, life in the ghetto, crime, personality types, deception, greed, theft, contraband, the cellblock with the "crazies," etc. We touched all the bases: every subject about prison life and prisoners. I learned an incredible amount about gangs, gang psychology, the untold stories of drug trafficking, and gun violence. The prison was so other worldly that every day was a new experience, usually heated incidents interrupting the expected schedules and quiet with sudden change in schedule, or even lockdown. Engaging conversation with the prisoners explained a lot about the desultory and wasted lives they lead with profound resentment, hostility and disgust. I probably never heard it all, but I am thoroughly convinced that The University of Prison USA is a wise suggestion, a good start, and ready to rollout!

SECTION **6**

Turmoil

Chapter 11: The Bermuda Triangle Where have all those prisoners gone, languishing in a torrent of overwhelming currents which hide those sequestered forever from family and "living!" Lost in a "Bermuda Triangle" where nobody cares, and the system (above all) cares less!

Chapter 12: The Stigma Enigma The stigma of a "prison experience" which society (for the most part) cannot forgive, and the enigma of making a difference through "prison reform" (if politicians ever want to do their job and study what is involved).

CHAPTER 11

The Bermuda Triangle

"But the reality of Andersonville lacked nothing in drama, in fiction and nonfiction, even as part of America's greatest war, racial strife, and societal changes…had a population of as many as 33,006 prisoners and became the largest prison up to its time and for generations to come. Statistically, it would have been the fifth- largest city in the confederacy. Of the roughly 800,000 Americans held in prison camps in all the nation's wars, some 40,000 were inmates of this camp. Andersonville also became the first great example of bureaucratic collapse due to an administration that was unable to manage forces that, uncontrolled, create such horrors…mismanagement of transportation and resources proved fatal for thousands of men."[461]

"…If we become serious about dismantling the system of mass incarceration, we must end the War on Drugs. There is no way around it…So long as people of color in ghetto communities are being rounded up the thousands for drug offenses, carted off to prisons, and then released into a permanent under caste, mass incarceration as a system of control will continue to function well."[462]

"THERE IS A SECTION OF THE WESTERN ATLANTIC, OFF THE southeast coast of the United States, forming what has been termed a triangle, extending from Bermuda in the north to southern Florida, and then east to a point through the Bahamas past Puerto Rico to about 40° west longitude and then back again to Bermuda…This is usually referred to as the Bermuda Triangle, where more than 100 planes and ships have literally vanished into thin air, most of them since 1945, and where more than 1,000 lives have been lost…. Disappearances continue to occur with apparently increasing frequency…."[463]

Since the American state prison system made its mark after the Civil War, it has grown to an extent that it is a Bermuda Triangle[464]. It is a giant assortment of thousands of gangs where prisoners are lost: forms wandering like apparitions flitting through the air. Their real personas are gone, no longer the same. They are swallowed up by a massive system where their vitality is adrift like it was sucked out by one huge inhalation. The mass incarceration to which so many address their rightful concerns is "The Bermuda Triangle," the landfill of the country's lost souls.

Many will say that at least they're in American prisons and not somewhere across Europe, the Middle East, Africa, Russia, the Pan-Pacific Countries or the nightmare confinements of Cuba, Central America, South America or Mexico. The shelf life of a human being in those areas of the world can be likened to a bovine slaughterhouse. And that statement is true to an extent. The fact is that this country prides itself on the most advanced way of life. Comparatively speaking, there may be an enhanced sense of "civilized," and, we know better because we are more discerning in the United States (so we are told)!

The truth is that we have been swallowed by large government which is trying to overly secularize religious traditions because, if it were possible, they would galvanize the idea of more government and less religion. The more government and the less conflict of competing interests the greater the population can be manipulated. "Group think" would be an ideal standard, the so-called "dumbing down of America!" Unfortunately, this more than sad state of affairs rudely applies undercurrents of mind streaming so that our "wonderfully honest" politicians can tell us what's good and bad.

That is why, prisons are in the state of affairs they are now in. There was a time when mass incarceration was not the problem it is today. When Michelle Alexander talks about the drug problem, she is spot on, intelligently so, and a self- fulfilling nightmare for the African-American community (to which I had a front row seat working in a prison housing a huge population which was drowned in methamphetamines, heroine, fentanyl and carfentanil, krokodil, and opioids). And, somehow with the drug issues today, HIV and AIDS has lost their splash across the news, but the viral contagion is profoundly higher than ever. The death rate is higher than ever. It's a virus, and there is no vaccine. It is as rampant today as ever. The problem is that there are so many other problematic viruses (Hepatitis B, Hepatitis C, Shingles, Measles (yes, immigration has brought it back, and others).

I used to have a father who said "what you don't know can't hurt you!" However, there was always a sense of sarcasm and a head shake as he said it. The truth is that the picture is that drugs and their associations with sexual-viral bearing diseases are "The Bermuda Triangle" of this country[465, 466]. And, media has lost its impact because its propagation is not impacting the inner cities (nor to the wealthy urbanites and exurbanites). The expansion of the drug addiction into the white community is a fact, and especially into poor southern rural communities, in and around Appalachia. No longer can this country listen to the puffery of the Washington, D.C. clan of preachy stereotypes to seek common sense. It is understandable that people expect something more from their politicians, but today it is totally whimsical thinking. Their persistence on hardly tangible and meaningful social issues plaguing the country is horribly unfortunate.

Today's drug epidemic can be compared to the "Black Death" of the 14th Century in Europe[467, 468] which killed about 25 million people. The causes are not comparable, but certainly mass deaths in any period of history must be identified and considered as an alarming sociological devastation. (COVID-19 has hit the world like a devastating storm amidst all of the other worldly pathoses, but nothing like the Black Death or the Spanish Flu of 1918-1919.) The drug penetration into American society through trafficking from South America in particular is the modern-day version of the "Black Death." The failure to eliminate the pandemic in the United States is part nonchalance, part failure of government, part ignorance, and part breakdown of the family unit. The prison system is a reflection of this societal disease, and Michelle Alexander is correct that mass incarceration will not end unless and until the "War on Drugs" is won. I do believe that the drug problem, in some manner, is here to stay. It may never be eliminated. Education is essential in this regard, and prisons today are merely misery centers where prisoners do not care. At some point the people who write and speak about "prison reform" will get sick and tired about the labored argument that doesn't resonate in the right quarters: Congress. Thus, my plan for a corrective approach with meaningful and fundamental planning.

The American prison system today is a sociological dumping institution that has expanded with claims of unwitting awareness. It is a "Bermuda Triangle" of lost humanity bounded metaphorically by the federal government, state government and the system itself.

A great deal of writing has tried to answer what has lingered as the unanswerable: why so many airplane and all types of large and small seafaring boats and ships have totally disappeared without material recovery. Scientists postulate, without complete scientific assuredness, that it "may" be due to the alignment of the geographic and magnetic poles as they migrate in relation to the earth's axis and its iron core[469]. Ships and planes are lost into eternity in the magnetic Bermuda Triangle, but despaired human beings are lost into eternity in the prison system.

The federal and state governments are so engorged with largesse today that no one really knows why it is a failed system. Every facet is so political that it takes on a life of its own. Fragmented so that Congress, the Supreme Court and the Executive branch cannot serve the peoples' needs, but instead all three branches self-righteously create shock waves that shatter the public need in quest of their own self-serving belief systems. The states are no better, maybe worse in their greed and attitudes. They both claim to be in touch with national harmony, but their political gravitational wills defy their claims as they breed civil discontent gratuitously and holier-than-thou malevolence. Truth and honesty are lost to the political class. It is the overseer of the taxpayers, and accountability is forever lost like ships and planes in the Bermuda Triangle. The mysterious combination of shock and ambivalence prevails in Washington, D.C. and in State Capitals. The average Americans simply asks for mere function, not dysfunction. There is a time and a place for political platitudes, hustings' exaggerations, lies, and preposterous promises. Not 24/7, 365 days a year, and forever. The country is in a new world order where cultural norms have disappeared and oncoming generations have lost moral compass and direction. This is the milieu into which "prison reform" finds itself, dead in a high tide where all ships should rise (for the right occasion) but crash against each other in a tsunami of name calling.

How clairvoyant were the Founding Fathers who wanted separation of powers to leverage each other's indecencies. Perhaps the rude political boldness was not anticipated with growth and territorial expansion, the old numbers game where individuals can lose their identities in large crowds. Whatever, the call to reason has been shelved because politicians have reached to such a high level of self-serving power that an important item such as criminal justice issues are not pressing.

The out-of-control, sinister murder rate in Chicago, Illinois[470, 471] is "the rapture" playing out for any biblical devotee. The mayor avers to political avoidance, lies and posturing as the murder rate soars. The federal government should prevail on the FBI and ICE to support local police and end the insanity, but it is useful to draw the analogy to "prison reform." They are moving parts of the political games played everywhere today. When a local mayor mimics the same venal approach as Washington, D.C. pols, it drives home the ever- present barrier to resolution of the greatest social problem in this country today: the confluence of street crime, poverty, and the social temperatures rising. Political gamesmanship regarding drugs, gun violence, human trafficking, and inner city street gangs in are out of control. This is the Bermuda Triangle housing all of these fast-moving social upheavals at the intersection of criminal justice and total political failure. As David Skarbek rightfully says: "At higher levels of incarceration, increasing the incarceration rate actually increases the crime rate. More inmates means more crime...."[472] This country still runs with recondite laws. Despite what statistics reveal the lawyers still over-prosecute, the judges render lengthy sentences out of proportion to need and cost benefit, and punishment is not a deterrent.

It takes an experienced car mechanic today to understand a car built on computer generated technology. Years ago the engines were relatively compact under the hood, but today internal car failures and breakdowns are burdened by the complexities of internal wiring so heavily computer based. Resolution can be impossible and the repair expenses almost unaffordable for an average person. A similar confrontation with reality comes to bear on the individual who requires a public defense versus a wealthy individual where legal fees are not restrictive. Money can buy what poverty cannot in the pursuit of a legal defense. This has been a forever reality! (It's the old saying: "money talks and bs. walks") As long as street gangs are able to continue the mission of prison gang leadership, the prison system will be weighed down with self- repeating crime forever. This is a reality for which there does not appear to be any sensible resolution in the near future. In truth the Washington, D.C. "pols" on both sides of the spectrum did nothing to control borders, and they have become so porous that drugs, disease, and crime flow into every part of the country with unfettered abandon. The "pols" then beat each other up without any consideration of the people! They do not represent the people, they represent their wallets and nice homes (no acrimony, just fact!).

Every time I hear "prison reform" come from some politician's mouth I know she/he has no idea what is real or unreal. Today's world is composed of people who talk but do not listen, talk over and through each other, and speak in generalities to support what is a fact-based need. Arguments, loud and nasty, eventually substitute for discussion which might further a common objective. This is referred as consensus building. Aaron T. Beck, M.D., a University of Pennsylvania Professor Emeritus in the School of Medicine (Psychiatry) summed it up this way:

> A common source of deepening distress and anger is an exchange of insults. You do something that directly or

indirectly, intentionally or unintentionally, diminishes my self-esteem, and I am driven to release my hurt by punishing you, most commonly by making a comment that will lower your self- esteem. If you are now angered by my insult, you try to restore your social image by retaliating, thus setting up a vicious cycle of mutual recriminations. And so it goeson....[473]

This is very central to the current political climate in this country at the present time. The grave misfortune is that despite the urgency for a recalibration of the entire state prison system, harmonious negotiation is lost in a political Bermuda Triangle. One fact, however, is quite certain: despite all the statistics I have mentioned, they are like the small wave caps in the middle of the ocean; they lose their individual, identifiable differences as they move over each other moving forward. The supporting factual drawbacks of prison dangers will compound over time as numbers increase. And, I do believe that this is inevitable even though jails, prisons and detention centers are busting at the seams. The fighting over border control and a wall to control the flow of "illegal aliens" into the country willy-nilly (along with all the social consequences of drugs, guns, violence, child kidnapping, prostitution, murder, rape, etc.) is a poignant example of blatant, common sense dangers which have engendered crippling, ill-behaved people expending their political capital.

It is hard to tolerate the unresolvable, tendentious points of view, so repetitive and irreconcilable. In the same vein, however, politicians also feel unencumbered to besmirch or castigate anyone in the line of fire. It was once considered childish in better days. Today it is contumacious. It is awful to witness such intemperate insults which, years ago, would kill a career. Not today, that is certain. Roy F. Baumeister, Ph.D.[474], in his book, *Evil: Inside Human Violence and Cruelty*, he advances the concepts of Richard L. Solomon and John D. Corbit[475] from the 1970's labeled "opponent process." This is a very understandable discussion of "body -homeostasis" and how it relates to behavioral conditions. Homeostasis is a balancing effect which maintains the body chemistry and function in a health state. That is, if the body is exerted, the physiological reaction is to counterbalance the drain of exertion to bring the body back to a balanced state. As he states: "Thus, power is a matter of eliciting responses from others." If the assertion of power causes the object to respond in some direct way, it fulfills the "opponent process" to the satisfaction of person asserting the power for one reason or another. Failure to elicit a response means the opponent process fails. Thus, a politician asserting his will with the filing of a bill must see the bill pass in order to be fully encouraged or empowered. His power is governed by a will to enable a positive showing because the power play in Congress is a typical example of the "opponent process." In a like manner, a sadistic act which brings deeply rooted harm may not mean much if it is carried out with empathy (even without sympathy). If a sadist tortures someone to elicit a response during an interrogation, his sense of empathy will understand what it will take to elicit the information being sought. Empathy will be the modality which makes the torturer sense what it takes to get the information. Sympathy or compassion becomes an obstruction because it interrupts the modus operandi which is the assertion of power to elicit the right answer. In today's Congress, empathy is used in a political battle where sympathy is left behind.

After reading through this book on "evil" it is without doubt a window into the very soul of politicians at any level. To a certain degree they manifest their power in many different ways. But, whatever the style, they are perfectionists in getting what they want. They are the ultimate purveyors of "power." I'll stand short of calling them "torturers," but they invest a great deal of insight into how to get what they want done through this window of opportunity (no matter how disdainful), empathy, malevolently leaving compassion (sympathy) out of the negotiations (because sympathy obstructs the "power play"). What devious behavior! It dose not hurt the "pols" because they do not care; it only hurts the constituents (but, most do not see nor understand this gamesmanship!)

The "opponent process" crystallizes the understanding of the politician's mindset in terms of her/his ability to be so cold-blooded in the assertion of power. Saying what they want with no "sympathy" becomes ingrained and so deliberate that it is impossible for the average supporter to understand this simple fact: politicians do not "sympathize," they "cold shoulder." It is cold and clear. They want to ellicit the approval of the constituency; common good has no skin in the game! That is "the power" doctrine to a tee! If people could understand this, the divisiveness today would have a chance for cure! Maybe!

If in fact the politician is so inured, but insightful concerning her/ his constituency, then "compromise" as a legislator, in my thinking, is a Shakespearean enterprise (I am Henry VIII: do as I will, or your head comes off!)

If anyone who has written or spoken on the message of prison reform without getting this message, well she/he is late to the party. I do not think politicians are bright enough to understand this concept of "power to elicit the right response" (at any cost). But re-election is enough psychological reinforcement to embolden their persistent behavior. Without even sensing the intellectual basis, they intuitively zone into a path of approval that may carry them for years and years. Orrin Hatch,[476] the senior Senator from Utah, a Republican, has been cemented in his position since 1976. He retired in 2019 after the final legislative session that year after having served 43 years (he was in Congress so long that some thought he turned to stone). I cannot vouchsafe for what he has accomplished other than his getting very, very wealthy. And he played and wrote music. I personally believe in term limits, but that is a pipedream! And, speaking of lengthy terms, Senator Robert Byrd[477], Democrat of West Virginia, served for 51 years up to his death. Other than his blather and questionable personal history with Ku Klux Klan (serving as a Grand Dragoon), he was anti-minority of any stripe (and, especially Jews and Blacks!). In his day, he ran the Senate with an iron fist. He always kiboshed prison reform.

Charles Dudley Warner[478], an American Journalist proudly declared that "Politics makes strange bedfellows." They will cross party lines to vote for anything that suits their re-election. Legislation historically has notoriously revealed strange voting patterns which contradict their belief systems and their allegiances, it matters not. They will "get in bed with anyone" in Congress, be it the Senate or House of Representatives, to assure their re-election. Once this simple, basic understanding of how Washington, D.C. operates, then it is not too hard to understand why "prison reform" is impossible to accomplish with this mind-bending, frivolous behavior. The "indecency of unreliability" is what incites the voters' wrath. However, today the visceral disdain between parties is inveterate. Warner wrote in more peaceful times.

On August 6, 2018 the Senate passed the Armed Career Criminal Act restoring the intent of the *Armed Career Criminal Act* (ACCA) in 1984. The ACCA was a law protecting the public from extremely violent people and instituted a 15-year minimum sentence for them. In 2015 the Supreme Court's declared a very significant part of the law unconstitutional, but left the definition of "violent felonies" vague and open to further interpretation. The court said failure to identify what aspect of the conduct could be punished violated the 5th Amendment's due-process clause. Several cases involving some very bad prisoners arose which made revisiting the law necessary to protect the public. A gang member, Cornelius Spencer, imprisoned for nine felonies, was released as the result of the Supreme Court ruling. He immediately raped two homeless women in Arkansas: a 62-year-old and a 21-yearold autistic man. In addition, Jerrod Baum, a neo-Nazi in Utah was originally imprisoned for violent crimes including attempted murder. Again, he was released four years ahead of his sentence. He proceeded to kidnap two teenagers, stabbed them, and then threw their bodies down a mineshaft. Interesting enough, politics entered the discussion because the new law provided the following: violent felonies would be punishable for 10 years or more, but the new bill would require at least three felony convictions before the law would apply. The bottom line is that they used a political platform to close a loophole only to establish another. (How many people can be killed in three felonies before the long arm of the laws catches up?) Appearing publicly as if celebrating the determination as a major accomplishment was as misleading as Washington, D.C. gets. It is egregious how politicians behave. This is a classic exposure how the grand capital functions. On the one hand, they are suggesting the importance of the public's safety. But hey, let's see how many they can get before the hammer is lowered. It's like going to the state fair and you get three balls to throw into three holes to get the grand prize! I want to expose the cynical nature of Washington, D.C. because it is this very jaundiced exhibition that reflects "an attitude" of government. People are of little concern. Leadership is agonizingly distrustful. This the attitude at any level of government which makes prison reform illusory. In political leadership attitude speaks volumes.

In another article in the Wall Street Journal Article, Senator Tom Cotton[479] highlights his view on "prisons" by focusing in on those critical of "mass incarceration," opining that prisons may need reform without going soft on crime. Furthermore, he states "when less than half of crimes are even reported to police and more than 80% of property crimes and 50% of violent crimes that are reported go unsolved citing the Pew research Center." Actually, it is slightly less than he reported. The article by Jon Gramlich[480] of the Pew Research Center says that about half of violent crimes and a third of property crimes are reported in the U.S. to police each year. For 2015, the last year for when data was collected, 47% of violent crimes and 35% of property crimes, tracked by the Bureau of Justice Statistics, were reported to police. And, of those numbers, 46% of violent crimes and 19% of property crimes reported to police were "cleared" (those that are "closed after arrest, charged, and referred for prosecution). There is a margin of error for reporting and clearance rates, up or down, which marginally vary from year to year. So those are the real numbers. What is interesting is that it is based on a BJS (Bureau of Justice Statistics) survey of 90,000 households, asking Americans 12 and older whether they were victims of crime in the past 6 months, and, if so, did they report it. Well, without getting too deep into the weeds, there are so many limitations and variables built into the reporting that it makes for vague "granular messaging." And, it does not give a "stand back" overall view message to the report. First of all, and once again, realizing he is a Senator (therefore, he will tend to "slip" message everything from the federal system and fail to message that there are approximately 17% in the federal prison system, but the 83% in state prisons go unreported. Surveying only 90,000 households of approximately 126 million in the country leaves the entire report suspect. Where were the 90,000, what was the mix, etc. The sample is quite small, especially in view of other facts. And, what was the nature of the violence reported, and, what was the nature of the property crimes? This illustrates one thing: why I hate statistics. Statistics are always slanted to underpin a message. And, Senator Cotton is subliminally casting arrows at "mass incarceration" believers who would only suggest that it is not working. The facts, however, should be properly vetted. I do not feel that there is one person who has written on the subject who would not be devastated by a rape, murder, sexual assault, kidnapping, or a combination, especially if it affected a friend or family member, or even oneself. The clamor, and rightfully so, would be for "true" reform: rehabilitation. Senator Cotton always slants his storyline without verifying the accuracy and relation to the facts.

As James Gilligan, M.D., in his book, *Violence: Reflections on a National Epidemic*[481], very clearly rails against those who believe the solution to preventing violence is "greater violence of our own." I would say that in bringing up children, love and more love (in communication and feeling) may go further than greater punishment for their growing pains and misdeeds. Senator Cotton also makes a blank statement: "Mandatory minimums and truth-in-sentencing laws work." Categorical statements like that (without substantiation) are misleading because I would retort for which group of people (gang-bangers, individual desperation, drug crime, robbery, etc.). I would add: whose "truth," under what particular state laws, and what is the nature of the crime. This is the 83% Senator Cotton fails to acknowledge in his article of the 13% in federal prisons. The point is that Senator Cotton tends to report with vague analysis. Also, the belief in "prison reform" does not make anyone "soft on crime" (and, what is the nature of the crime?) There is an ocean of facts and conversation between each suggestion. The nature of a crime (be it non- violent or violent) matters! Statistics are misleading when the nature of the crime is not related.

To make proper sense of the entire problem one must take a rational approach, which is very hard to do. Also, to throw articles out in credible newspapers without proper vetting makes others (who have attempted to be far more faithful to referencing and application of facts) seem more dubious. This is especially true when making a case for prison reform.

I label them the same self-righteous, deceptive pols whose singular role to appeal to the largest cross section of their electorate base is always on their minds. Nothing is more important. Orrin Hatch is retired because of age, but Tom Cotton is a young man and veteran. Facts must relate, it is important to know to what are they relating. Republican/ Democrat/Socialist/Independent: they are all creatures of a world apart from each other. Each subset will have a generic bias so accuracy in facts and how they relate are the only way to convey a message. Can you imagine how these Hollywood- like props would deal with "prison reform"? They are all lost in themselves and swimming in the depths of Washington's "Bermuda Triangle!"

Aaron T. Beck, M.D., is precise, but realistic, in summing up an innately violent person:

> "…the violence-prone individual regards his entire life as
> a battle. As he defends himself against perceived physical
> and psychological threats, he alternates between feeling
> vulnerable and feeling secure. He is continually mobilized
> to fight because of his never-ending pattern of perceiving
> belligerence in other people's behavior."[482]

Spending enough time around violent prisoners reinforces the fact that the truly violent are conspicuously rebellious, calculating and cautiously observant. Almost with eyes on all four sides of their heads, they are always on the lookout for a surprise, a shivv or a shank coming out of nowhere. Most people do not differentiate violence from non-violence, a prisoner is a prisoner is a prisoner. They do not meld with this blind assumption. The overwhelming majority of individuals locked up are rehabilitative, and do not behave with such a characteristic scornful, suspect manner. The "young hellions" as I saw them were so dangerous that walking in their midst set a shivering feeling right up and down my spine with a flush as blood pressure would instantly rise. The hardcore are like mistreated pit bulls, It was so stereotypical that it's hard to digest that politicians are so blasé about their covetous positions, so deceitful and brazen. Such individuals are cultivated with the desire to hurt, maim, or kill. It is certainly instinctive, and to think othwise would be counterintuitive. Nevertheless, it is a helpless feeling to be in the midst of a person who just as soon take you apart as say hello.

Compassion, understanding and education would go a long way to deter violent crime. The system as it stands is so inflexible and set in its old ways that it would take an overwhelming and cohesive effort to reconfigure the manner in which an individual can be reprogramed to be productive rather than destructive. Education is a vehicle to instill confidence and a desire to succeed. Aside of what the textbooks point out or the psychiatrists write, a person who understands that some cares to make them better will respond. Yet, when they are just left alone like wandering sheep around a prison yard, they are intelligent enough to sense their isolation, boredom, and innumerable fears.

I once talked to a 20-year-old who was running his mouth about an appeal. He was not going to be confined for long because his lawyer was the best. He was actually a very pleasant and highly respectful individual. I talked to him for a long time. He had just been transferred from a Level II and was very nervous about his cell block. I had checked him out on my computer to read his profile. He grew up in a backwater town without a father. His sentence was life, but not natural life. He had raped and murdered a pubescent girl. The big question I always had for the guards or others with whom I was close: is this guy ever going to get out? He was so overwhelmingly pleasant that it was hard to imagine such violence. He obviously never had much of a chance from the get-go, but his pleasing way was dramatic. However, I do know this. He is going to be roughed up in a Level III maximum security prison. There is no doubt. He is a good-looking kid so he'll be made someone's sexual "friend." Over time he'll learn to do the things to survive. He is not the kind to take advantage of wood working, the library, gardening or some class work. Only the few who experience a "come to Jesus moment" suddenly attempt to make a role reversal. Also, I do not feel the "Classification Experts" are not what they should be. The ones I came to know were not very insightful, perceptive or sensitive to align his cell block placement appropriately to enable his safety. Classification for him was going to be a rote assessment which would configure a more than likely dangerous placement. That is what I observed most of the time. It is hard to be young and be slammed into such a dangerous environment. This is where prison is today. And really, when contemplating the circumstances, most of the public, the "outsiders" probably would say: "who cares"? And, it was also catching that he believed his lawyer was actually get him "off the hook!" I saw him in the yard a lot, and it was always difficult because I know his domestic situation never gave him a chance in life.

My thoughts are that given a chance in a real "rehabilitative" environment, it seemed like he had a very compliant attitude. His psychological profile was very upbeat and positive. The current environment is going to inure him to further crime, and perhaps resentment and anger. I profiled a lot of prisoners while I worked in this prison, and I can say "rehabilitation" is a sham, a public advertisement, but not a plan at all. This is the nature of state prisons all around the country. It is just the way things are, and the way they will remain. State prisons are not lighthouses to lost ships in the dark night.

When is enough, enough? How much punishment is sufficient? Is wartime urgency a pass to forget conventions regarding ethics, morality and the law? When and where is the "red line" drawn? If someone feels one way, why is the other person a donkey? Who is the epitome of sagacity and balanced thought that she/he can stand above the crowd to make these grand spiritual decisions? Is the answer found in the roaring waves, the swells and the depths of water laden with gyrating gravitational impulses? Absent of water, the "Bermuda Triangle" of Washington, D.C., with its three-headed monster known as The Executive, The Supreme Court and Congress, has numerously bandied these questions around. Their blather has fitfully stirred up polar opposite opinions from 'The Holy See" in Rome, ethicists, academicians, psychiatrists, theologians, the Dalai Lama, and many other self- anointed specialists in the art of predictions (psychics, numerologists, alchemists, magicians, and soothsayers)! And yes, I am sorry, I forgot politicians, the ones with the telltale hold on the domain of "preternatural astrological seeing!" They are the ones who seem to derive their cognitive insights with declarative certainty above all others! Can you imagine? The magicians of the wood paneled walls, soft black leather chairs, and Gothic arch ceilings…yes, they know more than the Dalai Lama…just ask them!

The fact is that if this young man cited above kills so viciously, should he be treated differently than a man in his 50's who goes into an all-night convenience store, like a "7-11," and blasts away killing the attendant because he thought he was reaching for a gun when he was only trying to open the cash register. Who is the omniscient one who can say one, both or neither is rehabilitative? And, where does the death penalty fit into this scenario?

Some would argue that the young man was too young to know what he was doing because his brain has not fully developed whereby his reasoning centers (in the frontal cortex) cannot endow him with a sense of caution and reason to override the more primitive brain centers where emotional behaviors (the amygdala) take over? Maybe there was a rush of serotonin and the connection between his amygdala and orbital-frontal cortex connection was gone so his actions were entirely visceral without cognition. And, some will believe the middle-age man was desperate, should have known better, but he reacted impulsively without any sense of life-or-death consequences for the attendant. Or, maybe he to experience a serotonin rush…or, maybe he was on medication at the time. So many questions? No answers! These are just a touch of thoughts that have to be sorted out over time.

For me, these are teleological-theological questions to be answered way beyond my pay grade. However, I do believe that this is where exposure to education, a decent family upbringing, solid peer friendships, mothers and fathers, and mentors make dramatic differences in peoples' lives. And, I feel that common sense is most important for everyone in trying to make such significant decisions regarding the prison system. This is the common denominator, the balance where all other specialized thinking muddies answers where all that can really be expected is not "the final answer" but a sense of what's good for the greater good, and, what seems to work best over time.

Why do I say this? Let's look at the arguments back and forth concerning the death penalty. This is the subject that has been discussed seemingly forever[483]. In the B.C.E. societies dealt with crime by immediate and certain death in all contrivances, especially to extricate the devil inside. In the epochs A.D. capital punishment prevailed in horrendous ways. In the third century B.C.E. Socrates was forced to drink hemlock for spewing what was thought of as anti-societal, unconventional thoughts (Socratic Dialogue). His judge panel tried at least to allow him to reconsider, but Socrates was unbending so his death was at least comparatively humane (maybe for the times only). After the crucifixion of Christ, nothing, including Jesus, was passive or soft about capital punishment. Be it during the Roman Empire, The Byzantine Empire, the Genghis Khan rule, or through the 100 years' war, all empires solved crime with brutal solutions. Perhaps the worst exhibitions of torture and death were executions in The Tower of London (built by William the Conqueror after the Norman Invasion of England) where "the rack" and Skeffington's Irons[484] were used to slowly stretch or compress the body until death. Boy, imagine the "great minds" who thought these up! The only "man's inhumanity" equal was during the French Revolution in 1789[485] when the victim was mercifully guillotined. Or, if the hatred was so bilious, she/he was "drawn and quartered" enough to still be alive to be attached by ropes to an open wagon, dragged on the muddy ground with evisceration wounds to be guillotined, and then finally quartered so the final body parts could be sent to the four distant locations in France. I have read a lot of history, but the French were really the incomparable beasts of burden! They'll really knew how to rattle a person's mind. Believe it or not the last person guillotined was in 1977, and "The National Razor" (as it came to be known) was dismantled when France eliminated capital punishment in 1989. Well, at least Gillette never had to compete? (I'll be sure to my shaving devices nice and small, and away from my enemies!

Today 31 states have the death penalty, and the U.S. Government and U.S. Military as well. Inclusive of the District of Columbia, 20 do not. The states where the death penalty still remains, the means of execution are: hanging, firing squad, electric chair, or injection of lethal chemicals[486,487,488,489].

The reason I have gone into capital punishment with a cursory overview is due to the internecine "pro's and con's" engenders. I do not worry for my opinion because, like politics, I do not take sides. Capital punishment is what it is. I believe it'll sustain in some states forever. The facts I laid out were just a miniscule description of how really brutal a society can be in delivering the final solution: including Adolf Hitler and "the final solution." I am certain that brutality is an open window to how evil a person or a society can be. Measured by actions alone, people can sink to the bottom in attempting to resolve their own mental disturbances. One final anecdote I always found amusing: Robespierre[490, 491] (after King Louis XVI[492] and his wife, the Queen, Marie Antoinette[493], daughter of Queen Maria Theresa of the Holy Roman Empire, were guillotined in 1793), "grand provocateur" of The French Revolution, who got heads lopped off like a perverse roll of bowling balls, had his own head abruptly separated from his body a year after "he got the ball rolling!" Payback is a "bixxx!" He was a real charmer. The Jacobins and Girondins tried to outdo each other in bloodletting competition as if it were to become the first Olympic sport in the next century (1896) in Greece. The Greeks were more polite, they separated your head from your body with a rather large steel sword. So maybe, we are really more civilized by comparison than our dissolute European avengers! The people who have served the country as notable academic leaders, politicians, legal thinkers, research fellows, professors of business administration, district and Supreme Court judges, etc. have all weighed in on the pros and the cons of capital punishment[494]. 82 percent of   criminologists surveyed believe the death penalty is NOT a crime deterrent. Like all good debaters, the statistics supporting both sides of the argument flow like butter on a hot skillet. For example, Jimmy Carter, former President of the United States, says: "Southern states carry out more than 80 percent of the executions but have a higher murder rate than any other region." And yet, Michael Summers, PhD, MA, from Pepperdine University says: "There seems to be an obvious negative correlation   in   that   when   executions   increase,   murders decrease, and when executions decrease, murders increase...." I say opine on these two because for every plus I can find a minus. I do know that I have witnessed some very heated arguments which have their origins somewhere buried in everyone's belief system.

It is counterintuitive to think there is a final answer, though politicians seem to enjoy the name calling as they discredit the thinking of their opponents. But this is what politicians embarrassingly do.

In the Wall Street Journal, Joseph M. Bessette, a professor of government at Claremont McKenna College and former acting director of the Bureau of Justice Statistics in the Reagan administration, makes a "pro" argument. His column, "The Pope Makes a Fatal Error," opens with: "When Pope Francis last week declared the death penalty "inadmissible," politicians pounced." He concludes by writing: "Apparently, Pope Francis has decided the death penalty doesn't save lives...By falsely claiming that the principles of Catholicism call for rejecting the death penalty in all circumstances, the pope undermines the authority of the Magisterium, pre-empts the proper authority of public officials, and jeopardizes public safety and the common good." The ability of local authorities to perform their responsibilities is undermined by the Pope (and thus the Catholic Church) ushering a worldwide opinion Dr. Bessette feels irresponsible. He goes on to cite three examples supporting his argument that where the death penalty was enacted the crimes rates decreased[495].

Dr. Bessette knows that the Catholic Church has always been the theological refuge of anti-death penalty thinking. This is nothing new. I am NOT railing against him, merely showing how visceral the thinking is for the death penalty. Both sides, pro and con, are deeply cemented with practical and philosophical reasoning, yet assuredly stirring up rancorous views without any final resolution. Headstrong reasoning alone is upsetting rather than stabilizing.

It's impossible to reason prejudicial thinking because it is emotionally based. The supporting arguments are intuitive, only factual in the use of pro forma statistical support. Who's the final say? Well, if someone is looking for a job, trying to do well on a final exam in a criminal justice course, or just win a barroom discussion, then spouting what rings true will be the right approach. That's unless "a goodie-two-shoes" belief must prevail! (However, expect the approach to likely boomerang!)

From my point of view, the one thing missing from most arguments is "the fear factor." It is impossible to reason "fear." Whether the death penalty or imprisonment alone, fear as it relates to crime is noticeably absent from every "pro or con" based argument. The greatest deterrent to misbehavior or crime is the "fear of consequence." If I pull the trigger, will I get the death penalty (or, as the prisoner says: "Will I get the needle"?) is the common argument for the pro side because the thought acts a deterrent. The opposite is true for those who are secure with the thrust of sticking by the statistics argument (that 80 percent in criminal justice say the death penalty does not consider "the fear of survival" in leading them to crime, and killing is just part of the process. Their fear of dying, particularly as retribution by another gang member, is considerable, but not overriding.

On the street or in prison identification with a gang is a psychological support, a crutch on which to lean. Rogue individuals can be found anywhere. They are generally hollow and vacant, never thinking about much, if at all about anything.

Copycat criminal behavior is reproducible to the extent that killing is so common on the streets as well as in prison that there is a greater fear of living up to gang demands than thinking murder is going to act as a deterrent against the other gang member. I feel it may for a certain number who might think before pulling the trigger, but they are the minority.

Gang membership is inviolable, so sacrosanct that killing is a means to survive. Jeff Wise in his book, *Extreme Fear: The Science of Your Mind in Danger*, notes the following: "How does fear spread from one person to another? As social animals, we're designed to catch one another's emotions. Empathy is fundamental to our nature. Neuroscientists have identified a specific anatomical feature of the brain, so-called mirror neurons that fire whether we see someone else perform an action or we perform it ourselves. You could say we live what others are living via our imagination. When we see someone become embarrassed, we feel embarrassed. When we see someone injured, we feel queasy. The face of a terrified person is itself terrifying."[496] Gang members mirror what their brethren do, and the thought of the death penalty does not enter the picture.

On the other hand, in the normal course of the other extreme, say in a toney suburban home, a husband may kill his wife (or vice versa). However, I am willing to bet that if the death penalty enters her/his mind at all, it will be preceded by a mere instantaneous thought (if the random thought even occurs). I think the actual fear of the event overrides everything, long before capital punishment as a deterrent flashes in the mind. Fear is a trait we all harbor somewhere in our psychological profile, whether it surfaces commonly, uncommonly, or never. We are all wired differently. The fact remains that there is going to be a certain number who will certainly see the death penalty as a deterrent, but I think that in the heat of a crime this will not enter the picture until much further down the line when discussion occurs with a defense lawyer. As Jeff Wise points out: "When fear is strong, the amygdala can trigger automatic patterns of behavior without waiting for involvement by the conscious mind."[497] In other words, there is a cortical time lag while the visceral emotions are firing away!

So, is the death penalty a deterrent? I am not a "mamsy- pamsy" type person, but I have to say: sometimes yes, sometimes no. I am sitting on a picket fence catching the wooden point in a delicate spot so to get off before I scream in pain, I'll say less often than one would think. I cannot prove it, and, I know the statistics. I think they are misleading. I always think about a prisoner, a jocular type, who blew away his pestering wife with a double-barreled shot gun right in the face. As I stated, when I asked him if he'd reconsider seeing that he has a life sentence, I was taken back when he said: hell yes! And then I was overtaken by his laughter as he said it so I laughed. Funny? No. But, proof positive, he never considered the death penalty before the murder. Like so many others I talked to, especially in the throes of street crime, house burglary, or drug trafficking. It's a dangerous civil world, a contradiction in terms: because we "usually" do not sever heads in the heat of the crime!

By the same token, I do not speculate whether Robespierre, the grand prosecutor of the monarchy, ever thought his head would roll like a bowling ball. He was simply an over-exuberant, "headstrong" power-driven sort who probably never thought he would exceed the patience of his peers. Certainly, the guillotine never deterred his tunnel vision: the destruction of the monarchy at any cost in behalf of the very "liberte, egalite, fraternite" principles of the French Revolution. For him, power had an overwhelming "heady" attraction[498].

Man's inhumanity to man is a fact pattern for every generation. Certainly, meting out punishment unearths many different opinions as to the proper manner and way. There is no consensus so politicians are there to legislate for the court system. Nothing is perfect, but with all the shenanigans there is a lot that goes amiss. With all that I have pointed out, true prison reform does not seem plausible because it seems that everyone involved is in a daze, or merely beaten down by the enormity of the problem.

Prisons are tangled webs and the system is so embedded with people just running out the string until retirement kicks in. For the majority of lifers, eternity sits over as a greenhouse or a rolling hill in the distance. It is an uncertainty, a timeless bewilderment. Going in and out renders this feeling: a time warp where nothing changes as the minds of so many dissolve like bubbles being blown into the stillness of the air. There is no dimension except the spirit which diminishes a little bit every day. Everything and everyone is lost in the amorphous mass of this "Bermuda Triangle" where search and rescue is possible for the selected few. It is an amazing reality to behold. And, no one seems to care.

Before laying this particular subject to rest, it is important to realize how barren, filthy and foreboding the typical American prison is. It is always with a sense of emptiness that prisoners in the United States carry themselves from day to day. Level I facilities, for the most part, do not carry this dramatic agonizing, but Level III is always fraught with peril and the unpredictable. Nevertheless, when researching the nature of prison structure all over the world, the one finding which jumps out is how a country's prison structure is reflective of its government. Spending time in and around American prisoners is an arduous task for many reasons, but the most startling is the prisoner's sense of how much the system owes them. Why? Because, unlike any other country in the world, the prisoner does not lose her/his civil rights. I was always amused how most of the prisoners used the law daily to advance what they wanted. Or them, it was an obsession! Most were always sending a representative to an Administrative Law Court for one thing or another. It was unending. I read a great many of their letters to their lawyers. Time was open-ended so they spent hours laying out their demands.

The United States, being a democracy (once a true Democratic Republic, but this is for another time, another discussion), has established a sense of not only equality of justice under the law, but, more significantly, equality of treatment under the law. In spite of incarceration, the American prisoner expects access to the rudimentary accoutrements of the prison on a daily basis: computers, television, books in the library, exercise quarters next to the cell blocks, a respectable amount of cafeteria food, employment to some degree, dental/medical care, formal and informal religious worship time for all basic religions, etc. The point is that American prisons reflect the prisoners' expectations. And, this is provided, despite the fact that the prisoners are so rigid in her demands. Their "incident reports" are so numerous that it's humorous. I read a good number and they are intolerably demanding and, to the extreme, legally incomprehensible. They become like too many knots in a tree. I was always amused with them. The threats and angst were spewed with a vengeance and threats ad hominem! Amazing.

As violent as prison gangs are in the United States, the prisoners are strictly under the watchful eye of the guard system. Somewhere buried in Washington, D.C.'s unsavory self-indulgence is an occasional sense that there is a sense of mass incarceration. However, it is a passive aggressive approach because politicians do not want to deal with it so the state over the years has established its oversight. It is a "taxpayer cash cow," and a "hear-no-evil," "speak-no-evil" corruption enclave. The bureaucracy works the system well, achieving full measure of financial manipulation as possible.

In a very recent lengthy article for insightcrime.org, Steven Dudley and James Bargent[499] review the prisons of Latin America. The piece was printed on its website January 19, 2017 and reveals what a catastrophic mess the prison system is. I chose this article to make an important observation and distinction: that the American prison system is broken and requires a complete overhaul as I have described, but prisons of Latin America are thoroughly "hell holes!" In the way the American prototypical prison reflects this country's values, customs, and cultural norms (as horrendous as they are) so do the ones in Latin America and everywhere else in the world. However, let's confine this writing to people just south of us to get a glimpse at how low a society can miserably fall.

The prisons are jungles of mayhem. It is that defining. As "incubators of crime," the prison gangs are left not only to conduct their business, but the wardens and guards leave daily management up to them. Murdering on a daily basis is a lifestyle making the environment too dangerous for the guards to manage. There are no lines to cross because containment is however the gangs manage to conduct their business within the "Institutional Framework" they design for their best interest. The gangs completely run the daily programs. Rioting and fighting is handled on a need-to-know basis by the military police. Compared to the management of American prisons, Latin American ones merely hang in the balance. They are always one day away from complete self-destruction. In a nutshell, prisons around the world, and, in this instance, the Latin American ones are heated cauldrons of death. The imperious gangs, which feed on each other like piranha, are morally adrift like the fascist/socialist/communist governments which reign terror over their citizens. And, that is the bottom line, it is a system of pure management of guerilla- like frenzy and unnerving desperation. The summary doesn't have the space to justify what the article details:

> "Prison guards, and their police and military counterparts, routinely abuse prisoners and take part in corruption schemes that open the door for more crime. The jails have also become incubators of criminal activity; finishing schools for hardened criminals and places where powerful criminal groups organize, train up their members, recruit and plan further crimes...."[500]

The Italians have an expression that capsulizes the status of prisons: "Paese che vai, usanza che trovi" ("When in Rome, do as the Romans do")! This is a very loose translation, but it conveys the substance of how cultures differ. The American prison system can run far better than it does. It is afoul of expectation because this is not a third world country. Militarism is akin to fascist/totalitarian governments found in Latin/South America, and life is commanded by forceful, demanding autocratic, heavy-handed, merciless thugs propagating endemic corruption as it sucks the life-force out of the country. The prisons are so over-crowded that the prisoners run the yard. It's too dangerous even for the guards. The peace is virtually untenable. And, like an old body riddled with cancer, the prisons are decaying from age, filth and neglect.

Baz Dreisinger in her book, *Incarceration Nations: A Journey to Justice in Prisons Around the World*, she vindicates the officious yet depraved nature of some of the most horrendous prisons around the world. Traipsing around the world to the likes of Brazil, Rwanda, Thailand and several other countries, whether women's or men's prisons, her commentary is revelatory how they reflect the mentality and culture of the country. Reading her book confirms my own thinking and previous descriptions from my own personal experiences, but she distinctly emphasizes a point I made previously. As the following reads, prisons take on the culture that developed them:

> "I explain that the trajectory of my prison journey took me from the broad to the specific, from rethinking overall concepts about revenge, forgiveness, and what "corrections" might mean to more particular concerns like women in prison and the horrors of solitary, to the very practical economics of prison, in Australia and Singapore. In all countries, I found that prisons were, to echo the famous Mandela quote that spurred my odyssey, spot-on mirrors of the society that creates them."[501]

Prisons throughout the world are insufferable, mentally jarring. Whatever the physical is left in sucking the final spirit of life remaining, leaving hollowed out bodies as if embalmed with a forever stereotypical stone face. It is as disquieting as some I personally witnessed, vulcanized and depleted. I do believe the prisons, including American ones, are "...spot-on mirrors of the society that creates them." For certain.

It is plainly not good to be a prisoner anywhere around the world, but there are some that are simply a ticket for death at any moment. The gangs are pernicious, and they are filled with dangerous, rogue prisoners. In this country we give the worst human time to develop contrition in hopes of carving out a new found sense of obedience, a desire to reframe an outlook, and maybe learn a vocational skill to find employment upon release. Other countries are bastions of failing government systems so the social effects are pretty gruesome. In the U.S. there is no need to be anything more than a helping hand for prisoners. In many ways the American system is every bit as brutal as the culture allows. Though rehabilitation requires energy to elevate the best in people, American prison culture may be just too overwhelmingly neglected by indifferent bureaucrats. The U.S. has some gruesome prisons comparable to ones in Eastern Europe, like Angola, Parchman, Soledad, Auburn, and many others where the environment can be brutal. Yet, as dishonorable as may be, Directors always speak about rehabilitative programs. They never say rehabilitation as an affirmation. It's more accurately suggestive of ways prisoners can occupy their time when lockdowns do not interfere. It's not disingenuous, but organized purpose is not the objective. This is typical of American prisons. Individual initiatives are not impeded, but programmed training is limited.

The burden of "this beast" we call the government is to resurrect decency somewhere down the line. Sure, our prisons do not ring of despair like in Latin and South America, but in time they might get there. As I detailed previously, the intense manner in the way "ALL GANGS" have taken over the prisons and the streets in the United States is well on the way to highjack the relative safety and freedoms the country so unwittingly enjoy. This country is "still" a democracy, and this contrasts glaringly to the unspeakable and oppressive prisons in totalitarian/fascists countries. My research elicited a clear fact: the prison "hell-holes" of the world parallel the social- political conditions of countries around the world.

It is incumbent for this country to refrain from divisiveness and derision, and endure with mutual respect for differences of opinions without violent retribution as in militaristic centered societies. The American prison system is in trouble and certainly mirrors a hefty population forgotten and left well in the rear-view mirror. The way politicians have deserted their roles to balance the demands of their constituencies with national exigencies is swaying "group think" rather than a sense of individualism. The malevolence and noxious name-calling, illegal behavior(s) steeped in amoral behavior does nothing more than to heat up name calling and violence on the streets. This does not favor consensus, but opens the country up to far more dangerous incidents: school shootings, terrorism and "weaponization" of governmental agencies. Common sense has a great chance of softening anger and savagery thannonsense.

With all the money wasted, all the mercenary sins politicians commit, surely there must be a will to restore a sense of pride in those incarcerated who still retain a glimmer of hope. Our prisons cannot go totally rogue like those in wasted totalitarian countries. Designed rehabilitation is a must. Note thisobservation:

> The clemency of princes is often nothing but policy to gain popular affection[502].

CHAPTER **12**

The Stigma Enigma

"We remember that Diogenes, lantern in hand, roamed ancient Greece looking for an honest man. If Diogenes roamed New York City today, he might be looking for a policeman to report his lantern stolen. A news clipping tells of a bookstore in Boston calling an affiliate in Washington, D.C., in search of the book *Some Honest Men*. Inquiring whether they had "Some Honest Men," in Washington, the clerk, momentarily taken aback, answered, "Perhaps two or three at the most.""[503]

"While I was at Yale University, I worked with Dr. Peter Salovey, who had spent his career developing the MSCEIT (pronounced "mis-keet"), an abilities-based based test for emotional intelligence. With Salovey's help, we implemented the MSCEIT in a large sample of prisoners, many of whom were psychopaths[504].

Psychopaths showed profound deficits in emotional intelligence compared to non-psychopathic criminals. However, psychopaths had normal general intelligence (IQ) scores[505].

In and around a maximum-security prison the non-prison personnel I saw the most were priests and attorneys, coming and going. There were others; but, somehow, I made contact with them most often. One attorney I saw all the time had an offbeat sense of humor so one day I said to him: "If you are a criminal attorney, what kind of crime do you specialize in," a kind of double-entendre! He was a pretty "with-it" person so he picked up on it immediately and retorted: "murder for hire!" As we got to each other better, he asked me one day what I meant by such a joke with a sense of serious intent. And, I explained to him my feelings how the prison system was broken and lost in time. And, immediately, I added that criminal attorneys are often more "criminal" than their clients. I thought he'd "jump crazy" all over me, but he did not. He understood where I was going. There is a broad-based stigma of prison mismanagement at the bureaucratic levels of government, and it is married to a legal system that fortifies the prison rolls by over pursuit and sentencing. The gift that keeps on giving are the political elite who wrap a nice red ribbon around prison reform as if heaven has finally sprinkled angel dust on the problem.

The stigma of non-reform prison reform is rather the self-perpetuating enigma that as government, both state and federal, continues to expand irreverently and carelessly (both without a sense of caring as well as awkwardly). Without revisiting what has already been reviewed on the prior chapters, if for nothing else, the money savings over time to prison reform would be huge. The stigma is an enigma. Considerations which would energize a discussion are: evaluation and financial planning.

Whenever the subject of prison reform makes the news it confuses people. To a Washington, D.C. pol the term is bandied about frivolously and deceptively because in her/his mind the federal system is always the object of Congress's intent. However, it is only 11.7% of the entire prison system: Federal Prisons+ Local Jails+ State Prisons. The majority of prisoners, as has been stated often, is contained within the state supported system (slightly less than 70%). The administration at the state and federal systems are separate. It is easy for politicians to conflate the generic use of the reference "prison system" in a very misleading manner. There are slightly less than 226,000 federal prisoners of the total 2.3 million (between the federal, state and private prisons). And, at the state level, hearing the idea of "prison reform" is barely heard.

There is another issue, seemingly benign, but as a trained scientist, specifics carry meaning. Nomenclature turns on specificity as the identification of the year and model of a car. The media, for example, most generally will say "prison," but reference to whether it is a federal, state or private prison may or may not show up later in the report. A pre-trial detention center or jail, juvenile detentions center or jail, or what level of a state prison are rarely properly identified. And, in the broader discussion, allusion to the womens' institutions are almost never properly identified. That is how little serious thought exists. "Hear no evil, speak no evil" speaks volumes for the prison system as a "living organism" of weighty economic importance being unimportant. Name it, say it, feel it, and discuss it. That should be the mantra.

The stigma of the state prison system reaches into a dark culture where the enigma expands far beyond the harangue for prison reform. The Level II and III prison environment is dangerous, as I pointed out, with gangs running the institutions with the good soldiering and bureaucratic side- stepping of "fact" prevailing to minimize injury. The fact is that sexual need, exploitation and cover-up pervades every institution. The atmosphere is seedy, graphically disturbing, and generally pathetic. To see a prisoner masturbating behind a bush in the plain of day, or, enjoining another inmate in the shower or cell is as rapacious as assault or murder within the same confines. Female guards compromising themselves with prisoners or male guards endangering their jobs by carrying on sexual relationships with female prisoners is nothing new to anyone who has worked in the system. It is a dark stain that cannot be rubbed out until the day "prison reform" realizes a sense of urgency. I was always aghast by hearing about incidents, not because I am naïve (hardly), but because of the "plausible deniability." Between the filthy living standards, the pervasive sexual activity (accompanied by infective sexually related diseases: Hepatitis C, HIV, AIDS, venereal diseases, etc.), and murders (occasioned periodically by numerous fatalities or rioting), it is a well-kept secret from which "the outside" is kept generally unaware. There are peaks and valleys to the incidents as they occur. Word travels at warp speed in a prison. Seeing a prisoner who had been shivved several times in the neck and chest gushing blood because of a sexual encounter gone bad will roil one's thoughts and leave a permanently ugly memory. This is a common event. If nothing else, these events are reminders of the most visceral needs going on daily without any shyness or fear of punishment. It is just the way it is.

James Gilligan, M.D., confirms a few notions and facts in his book, *Violence: Reflections on a National Epidemic*:

> WITHIN THE PENAL SYSTEM---IN ADDITION TO LEGALLY EXECUTED AND morally defended punishments---there is a dark underside to punishment in the prisons. It occurs regularly, knowingly, and more or less universally. It is a predictable consequence of our policies and punishments. The most egregious example of what I am referring to here is the violence that prisoners routinely inflict on one another[506].

> …the very conditions that occur regularly in most prisons may force prisoners to engage in acts of serious violence in order to avoid being mutilated, raped or murdered themselves[507]

> …homosexual rape is another even more horrendous and destructive form of punishment endemic to the prisons[508]

> …all these authorities tacitly and knowingly tolerate this form of sexual violence

> …so that the rapists in this situation are acting as the vicarious enforcers of a form of punishment that the legal system does not itself enforce formally or directly[509].

These are very accurate. Prison life is a danger to everyone and anyone, no matter who they are or what they do. It is a must to be always aware with a keen sense for anticipation.

Anyone who lives a balanced life commits internally to one or two sentiments: either understand the circumstances and bury it deep down, or, quit! Sexual perversion and punishment is every day, and often upsetting. Particularly in a maximum-security prison where prisoners are brought into the system usually hardened by their street conditioning, they are going to live and die by "the sword!" Between the contraband- fixation, sexual focus as a daily need whether by consent or rape, or beatings and murder, there is never a let up. Some days it's like an out-of-control roller coaster, but always understated and an unnerving palpable presence.

The only time it bothered me was to see a hard-working female guard physically hurt or sexually attacked by a prisoner. I knew most of them, and they were quite vulnerable.

It is simply impossible to be overly idealistic or the other extreme, dismissive, about trying to rectify what's wrong. Psychopathy places people at a terrible risk, though there is a very naïve view that conceives all people are potentially normative through accommodative psychiatric counseling. This is far beyond what seems realistic. Even in a world of windmills and fanciful believers, psychopathic violence will remain dangerous and unfit for socialization. There is a world of difference between "do-gooders" and brazen, cold-blooded killers. Gilligan points to "violence" as reactive as well as calculated to be cold and uncaring, destructive without any compassion. Killing without any compassion or moral compass is where more primitive centers of the brain are in a state of disconnect to the thinking areas of the frontal cortex, the area devoid of interpretative judgment. In this state o disconnection reason is lost and behavior is an instinctive reaction to either carnal or destructive desire, or both. To think that this kind of individual can be rehabilitated would be genuinely naïve. Put in basic terms, it would be like diving head first into an empty pool. There are limitations, and perhaps why it is more sensible to concentrate energy on non-violent prisoners who have simply been over-prosecuted and over- sentenced and innately exhibit a desire to make a positive reversal of misfortune.

There is no fine line between speculation and rigid research findings. The MRI imaging brain scans of psychopaths Dr. Kiehl[510] has provided is like kindle for discussion. It is concrete evidence of complete brain nerve pathway interruption to vital centers upon which psychiatric analysis and intellectually based scientific study can only conjecture. The evidence that imaging can render to show a psychopath's significantly emotional deficit while continue to exhibit a normal level of general intelligence (IQ) can shore up observational and conversational discovery. Noting an absence of brain activity in the higher centers (in and about the frontal cortex) and distinctively increased activity in the more primitive center (the Amygdala) from where emotional behaviors arise speaks volumes for accuracy in diagnosis, treatment and classification criteria (based on criminal history) for prisoners.

An interesting question to ask is why not use imaging as part of the Classification process for dangerous violent criminals? So much of Classification is left to verbal communication and speculation. Practical evidenced based technology is far more informational. Prison reform cannot be exclusively based in theory, statistical evaluations and changes, or unique opinion. There is an expense to this science, but it skirts so much of the already wasted money streaming through a bureaucratic morass of worthless speculations.

In the 1990's, Daniel G. Amen, M.D., wrote a book called, *Change Your Brain, Change Your Life: The Breakthrough Program for Conquering Anxiety, Depression, Obsessiveness, Anger, and Impulsiveness*, which principally displays the effective usage of imaging for the proper diagnosis, neurological evaluation and treatment for many impactful brain changes. So many events (trauma, as in stroke and accidents) and behavioral deficits (ADD and ADHD in children for example) and emotional imbalances (oppositional behavior, OCD, road rage, chronic pain, obsessions, and many others) were diagnosed utilizing imaging techniques. He used CT (Computerized Tomography), MRI (Magnetic Resonance Imaging) and SPECT with supplemental cameras making it more effective than CT. SPECT is an acronym for Single Photon Emission Computerized Tomography utilizing a radioactive isotope injected into the patient's vein. A SPECT "gamma" camera moving around the head localizes where the isotope lands as a supercomputer then displays images of brain activity levels. His work in his clinic revolutionized

Brain activity levels. His work in his clinic revolutionized treatment for many disorders, particularly children with ADHD[511].

I wanted to feature both Kiehl and Amen in this discussion because of the technology which can cut right through very opaque decision making. Of all my observations my most startling was the manner in which prisoners were delegated to different cellblocks. When using guess work based on questionnaire evaluations, pertinent information regarding history of criminal activity, home life, marriage/divorce/ children, background, etc. there is no substitute for speculative analysis than the advanced technology applied to hardcore violent offenders. Without such application, the guesswork involved would be like open heart bypass coronary artery surgery without an x-ray view of the obstructed artery. The psychopaths with a very high IQ can be so incredibly deceptive and calculating. Brain hot zones can be specific in a way that will not mask tendencies for violent behavior. If the technology is available, it should be used judiciously, but used! It removes all speculation.

In a humorous, offbeat way this made me recall the oft used statement: there are more questionable "luminaries" (as in "imbalanced") walking around on city streets than inside mental institutions! Of course, this was always meant to be odd humor with sobering undertones.

It is more than important to utilize proper technology in the 21st century. It is critical. The technology has ushered in specificity and understanding. Maybe if the technology served the subject matter accurately, then diagnosis, treatment and prognosis would be far more constructive and contributory. In every way, technology eliminates speculations that might not further delay a patient from care.

Dr. Kiehl speculates the following: "FACT: one in four maximum-security inmates is a psychopath."[512] And, also: "FACT: there are over 29,000,000 psychopaths worldwide."[513] Finally: "FACT: Psychopaths kill more people in North America every year than the number killed in the terrorist attacks on September 11, 2001."[514]

In his book Dr. Kiehl reviews what is referenced as "Psychopathy Checklist" that Dr. Robert D. Hare developed. He understood where I was going. It is a psychopathy checklist of various topics: "The 20 items   of the Hare Psychopathy Checklist Revised (Hare, 1991, 2003) are a clinical rating instrument and the gold standard for the assessment of psychopathy since 1991: 1) Glibness/Superficial Charm; 2) Grandiose Sense of Self-Worth; 3) Need for Stimulation; 4) Pathological Lying; 5) Conning/ Manipulation; 6) Lack of Remorse or Guilt; 7) Shallow Affect; 8) Callous Lack of Empathy; 9) Parasitic Lifestyle; 10) Poor Behavioral Controls: 11)Promiscuous Sexual Behavior; 12) Early Behavioral Problems; 13) Lack of realistic, Long-Term Goals; 14) Impulsivity; 15) Irresponsibility; 16) Failure to Accept responsibility for Own Actions; 17) Many Short-Term Marital Relationships; 18) Juvenile Delinquency; 19) Revocation of Conditional release; 20) Criminal Versatility."[515] Dr. Kiehl makes two other points relative to this discussion. Psychopaths do not manifest psychosis, which "...is a fragmentation of the mind, leading to symptoms that include hallucinations, delusions and disordered thoughts... is manifest in disorders like schizophrenia, bipolar disorder, and major depression. These psychotic symptoms are not typically observed in psychopaths. Indeed, it was the absence of psychotic symptoms that originally differentiated psychopaths from other patients in mental hospitals."[516] And, "...Psychopaths are resistant to psychodynamic treatment, in part because they typically don't feel there is anything wrong with them; they are rarely interested in participating in therapy or changing. Consequently, psychodynamic therapy was not very successful with psychopaths, and that led to the pervasive view that persists today, that psychopaths are untreatable."[517,518]

My personal experience with what was defined euphemistically as the "Psycho House" was every day. Guard detail was noticeably and habitually absent (not good). I often witnessed groups out in the yard in the middle of the day totally unsupervised. When they would engage me as I passed them coming and going, they were very much always unsettled, fidgety, and extremely excitable. A few of them I remember as terribly aggressive so I had to be extremely careful and aware. They fit Hare's 20 criteria to a tee (a test to measure Psychopathy)! All were extraordinarily loud and agitated. They would daily remind anybody around that their "demands" were never answered. It was like a broken record. When they talked, they were so mouthy that the occasional officer going by would have to tone them down. Every other word was "f that," or "f this!" Unfortunately, I remember how dangerous they appeared (which was corroborated by a terrible series of murders the following month after I had resigned from prison employment).

These are stereotypically the criminal types who should not be out of prison, being a real threat to anyone relatively close by. If these individuals were all subjects of MRI imaging, I have no doubt that they would show lack of activity in the frontal cortex area and highly elevated activity in the Amygdala. While the technology has been available for so many years, they never responded to treatment. They were always obstreperous! Their caterwauling was scary was grating. Of all the prisoners with whom I had contact it was this group which was terrifying they encounter anyone alone in the yard (It was inevitably this group which led to my quitting). By checking the revised Hare Test it is eye-opening to understand how extreme the analytic behavior is. Accost any of these individuals alone and it is certain that a physical end would be certain. Death to any of these prisoners would not be regrettable in any way.

The Hare Test grades the following behavioral characteristics: Glibness/superficial charm, Grandiose sense of self-worth, Need for stimulation/proneness to boredom, Pathological lying, Conning/manipulative, Lack of remorse or guilt, Shallow affect, Callous/lack of empathy, Parasitic lifestyle, Poor behavioral control, Promiscuous sexual behavior, Early behavior problems, Lack of realistic, long-term goals, Impulsivity, Irresponsibility, Failure to accept responsibility for own actions, Many short-term marital relationships, Juvenile delinquency, Revocation of conditional release, and Criminal versatility[519]. How many of these personality traits do you the reader possess? Interesting? Well, do not be chagrined, embarrassed or intimidated. Think of it this way, to quote the western American "cowboy" writer from his story: *"The Outcasts of Poker*

Flat," Bret Harte[520] massaged your soul with this explanation: "There is a little bit of bad in the best of us, and a little bit of good in the worst of us!" So now, do you feel better? No one is perfect! Yet, these psychopaths were way out there, at the far end of life where they would just as soon rip you apart as say hello to you!

When led in shackles and handcuffs to SHU (short for Security Housing Unit, or, solitary confinement) in between two armed guards, it could stop one in her/his stance to just observe the facial mannerisms. If looks could kill, such a person looked terrifying. If losing one's perspective for a minute (and, particularly as many times as I witnessed this), it seemed like a Hollywood set: like which picture is the reality? My mind still wanders back to some of those days, particularly with deep appreciation I left unscathed. It is almost impossible to capture the perspective because it was so surreal, a total aberration from the outside world where people come and go never wondering about such an altered reality. It is also bewildering to conceive how many more out in everyday life wander around: the unknowing, the protected, and the ambivalent! If the outside really knew what the inside was really like? They would be horrified, so, perhaps, it is meant to be kept in the dark about certain things.

The stigma, however, is not about the psychopathic wonders. It is the majority who, quite apart from the minority of vicious killers, are dawdling around day-in, day-out with lost interest, just a total state of inertia. Almost all, and there were too many to recount, but enough to etch a permanent reminder in my memory bank forever. Newton's first law of motion states:

> "An object at rest stays at rest and an object in motion stays in motion with the same speed and in the same direction unless acted upon by an unbalanced force." Objects tend to "keep on doing what they are doing." In fact, it is the natural tendency of objects to resist changes in their state of motion. This tendency to resist changes in their state of motion is described as inertia."[521]

Who knew that Isaac Newton was really a psychiatrist?

This is certainly not a story related to the laws of physics, but whenever I watched these prisoners the thought of bodies always at rest made my mind drift to no better example of inertia. It was like both my optic nerves serving up time-lapse photography where everything was slowing down to a final motionless frame. They were loath to be do anything unless urged by a guard. It was a mindless waste of time. For anyone who would spend time searching for meaning in life this was not "exhibit A." To witness this all the time is tragic, and a thunderous wakeup call for change. They would sit for hours staring almost like in a vacuum where all is still. The idiocy of it all is that I was overwhelmed how easily I could talk to them, generally about sports. But through television they would note subjects of interest and seek me out to give me their opinions. As lazy as their environment was, they were truly interested in learning, but they felt ashamed by their lack of education to feel confident enough to pursue a tangible degree directed program while incarcerated. Some did, but they were a minority. Who knew?

The enigma is that the bureaucracy doesn't see a viable solution because it is primarily concerned about the occasional "dog-and-pony" show for public display. In the meantime, there is a generational loss accruing year after year and spawning habituation to the life of crime. Without leadership that directs young children towards education the marginalization of lost youth will expand to a point when there will be a total loss of the virtues of "self." All the social ills that I have previously enumerated will be the hammer that drives the final nails into the coffins being built. The prisons are visuals for what's missing, reflections of what's badly needed, and showcases of failure. I was always baffled by the "social do-gooders" who would show up weekly for instruction for a defined class for a two- or three-month period. Not that these people are caring to at least share their time, but none ever spent time "inside" beyond the meeting rooms to really see the depths of despair and would impart a message in a book or article claiming knowledge for time in service to a prison. Well, they have no idea what it is like, and a more honest vested interest might engender a more helpfully true depiction of the reality of prison life. A benefit to a limited number for a short time is as valuable as dust in the wind. Concentrated efforts to everyone in a system requiring a massive redo is, unfortunately, the only answer…sooner than later!

I can recall a 56-year-old "lifer" who was sentenced as a youth (early twenties) for murder during a robbery. And, to repeat what one of my co-workers always told me: "somewhere there is a mother crying herself to sleep nightly for the loss of a child!" This is an unspeakable loss for any mother or father. No question. Every day that I talked to this 56-year-old man I was very conflicted. On the one hand, I would ruminate over his crime. One day I asked him about it, and he spoke softly to me with tears in his eyes. As I got to know him over a year, speaking at length to him, I was convinced that his life meant far more than the invisible, deleterious shroud slowly consuming the oxygen from this man's life. From politics, social ills, crime, business, and, oh yes: sports; as they say in baseball for a home run, we touched them all. We laughed and entertained each other. Simply put, he could not read or write, but he should be paroled because he has served more than enough time to live his life out as he wishes (under careful supervision). He may be limited to menial occupational work, but the evidence for his rehabilitation over many years was quite certain in my mind. As I checked out his prison profile, there were no infractions, not any advanced incidents reported. I know many would disagree, but this is not the same man. Murder is unforgiveable, I understand. But, people above my pay grade would agree!

I really never counted the numbers whose lives are being slowly extinguished like a burning candle, but they were over a hundred I got to know well. How many more are there?

As I have depicted, the state prisons in the United States are country clubs compared to those elsewhere in third world countries (especially all the socialist/fascist countries). In proper perspective, however, we expect more from this country because of its "capitalistic economic structure" which has enabled a sense of individualism without government dependency.

Once again, reliance on central government has been the bane of socialist democracies and totalitarian countries. Redistribution of wealth, government dependency for financial survival, and regulatory constraints on small business amounts to a regressive slide to socialist/ communist ills over time. Be it in socialist/communist or democratic oriented countries the wealthiest always squirrel away greater income, but in a small business-based economy the low-middle to middle class benefits through the wealth factor. When people try to survive as government dependents, they do not (or, they do with great deprivation). It is the path to central government power and imperious leaders who drain the wealth of the country. The people become pawns and victims of all the social ills which increase poverty, crime and disease from neglected health standards. Such exemplary countries: Venezuela, Columbia, Argentina, Nicaragua, Guatemala, etc. Many comparable countries throughout the world exist where religious bias is used as the cudgel to beat the poor into oblivion creating pogroms and diasporas. Unfortunate examples are: Myanmar (Burma), South Sudan, Zimbabwe (Rhodesia), Sri Lanka (Ceylon), Madagascar, etc. The wealth factor as a byproduct of freedom and a business entrepreneurial spirit is the independent/ individual spirit that enhances the education and productivity of a country. And, a prison is the classic visual for what a country is or is not availing its citizenry.

Historically, in failed states prisoners subsist in extremely harsh living conditions. Some put the prisoners in the yard to fend for themselves (as in Mexico City: the Mexican Gang; the prisoners are like crazed maniacs where life has no value)!

People who fall for lying politicians who promise everything free from a power structure embracing a massive fascist/autocratic government are victims of their own tragic misperceptions. In third world countries (like Cuba), prisons are bottomless pits of agonizing death, filth. rampant disease, and incalculable mental and physical pain. The prisons are large estuaries of putrefaction and death.

The truism that teaching a person to fish for survival as opposed to just giving up a piece of fish to satisfy momentary hunger pains is reality, accepted or fooled into denial? Education at its basic mission should drive this message. If not, the social ills which build with a slow, progressive creep eventually leads to dependence which cannot be sustained without the heartache of the kind of poverty that ushers in all the other social ills. Chicago today is the glaring example, an island of despair in historically one of the country's most ennobling cities, where drugs, prostitution and murder are ravaging what's left of its south side[522]. Maximum-security prisons are filled with the unfortunate survivors of violent interactions which land them in horrendous gang infested environments which Gabriel Morales[523] defined as "Murder In, Murder Out." The Chicago pre-trial detention center should be a wakeup call to the youth of the city where they are packed like sardines before their first court appearance to begin answering for criminal behavior. It's a tragedy. No education, devoid of perception and understanding, and indifference to long term consequences!

As I have described, Gabriel Morales' book on prison gangs is a chilling, jaw dropping delineation (and visuals) of the most blood-curdling slayings of gang members primarily in California prisons. It's a real-life Sylvester Stallone movie gushing "blood and guts," but the real deal! The staggering sights capture the true nature of state maximum security prisons. It is the toilet bowl of American society. The Hare Test on these prisoners would be a waste of time, knowing that they are creatures of bewilderment. Their destinies are hopeless, and their behavior is either servile or stigmatized by a "dead end" fate. Such prisons in California reflect the misery of its major cities!

It is other worldly.

Prison is not meant to be the land of plenty or the three- star hotel for criminals. It should make its case for punishment. Without restitution for crime society is becomes the zoo-like house for lions

Loose to consume the less secure animals. The very thin line is where prison reform evolves where the prison has lost its bearing in transitioning to a rehabilitation institution. There are moral and ethical considerations. How the prison transitions is a "stigma-enigma!"

Laws are supposed to make society free and safe. Prisons serve to protect society, but today they must be more. The cultural-population demographics of today are no longer those of the 1950's. Idle minds must be developed into "open, educated minds" to enable a self-sustaining, productive human being. This picture paints the most obvious contrast to the miserable environments which have vulcanized minds and traumatized the human spirit.

The moral conundrum: when is enough, enough? The ethical conundrum: whose conduct is so pure that she/he may judge others wisely? These are provocative concerns. Fact: the stigma of serving lengthy sentences. Fact: the enigma of resolving the rehabilitation question. Fact: the reality that American prisons are overcrowded and overburdened. Fact: resolution will make a great number of people dissatisfied and emotionally upset. Fact: if politicians at the state and federal level are too corrupt, what will it take to get prisons transformed properly at the local community level?

Marie Gottschalk at the end of her very well- documented book makes very valid conclusions, but leaves this stigma-enigma up in the air! She decidedly concludes: "With so many millions enmeshed in the criminal justice system, the penal policies of the United States have a certain taken-or-granted quality."[524] I would say she is too kind. The penal policies are defiant and strangulating with a very ho-hum, listless caring for the human and material cost to the country.

The answers to the moral and ethical conundrums can be debated ad infinitum without resolve. There is no one way, but a satisfactory, realistic way to look at the problem is to say: when clear thinking people realize the problem of mass incarceration is getting old and boring because it's on minds year in, year out without any glimmer of progress. I ask: how big should the population of all prisons and detentions grow until they are monstrous and untenable?

Rational minds will be at wits end when they realize a "reasonable" solution is far better than no solution.

The framework for relief I proposed in chapter 10. It looks at all the faltering to this point in time when some conceptualization is better than nothing. Self-reliance is the endpoint for prisoner rehabilitation. The possibilities are immense, but at some point there must be a national panel or commission to develop a standard for the future. I was in education long enough to realize that even great minds keep pushing change further and further out until remembering what was important soon drifts away into forgotten memories. I have seen that movie. I had an uncle who talked and talked about a change for graduate education in dental specialization right after WWII. The thoughts languished while he started a formal specialty program in Periodontics at the University of Pennsylvania in 1950. After many years of trying to advance thoughts for formal education in all the dental specialties, he finally built the Boston University School of Graduate Dentistry in 1962 (and became its first Dean). Today it is the Henry M. Goldman School of Dental Medicine at Boston University. The point is that I am uniquely schooled in dead end talking and planning. At some point, if prison reform becomes a reality it will only come planned discussions and concrete innovation. Politics is always a barrier because the pols always like to be part of the planning. The political uncertainties are exasperating because politicians lack complete credibility when prison reform is the subject of legislation.

The politicians at the federal level never resolve anything. I have discussed their indulgence because of the presence of the president. As I reviewed, Jared Kushner's father spent time in a federal prison. Prison reform is being discussed without specificity. However, it engendered planning. The problem is that The First Step Act is not what I consider comprehensive "Prison Reform." The whole nature of the so-called "Prison Reform Bill" now being discussed in the Senate antes up the politics, but makes the need at the state level out of mind's eye. If only the federal politicians felt a need to apply some of their influence with state politicians to come forth with prison reform and meaningful, constructive legislation.

For me, all the talk is just talk, and that is why I offered up a practical solution from my experiences in the system as well as the research I have done. Perhaps it may seem unworkable to some, but starting somewhere with a defined plan is a must. All the research points to local control as a good start, materially and politically. James Gilligan, M.D., offers up an important analysis which I have found to be in line with an exacting analysis. I found it interesting because he shows what I have been contesting in this writing: the "hitting the perpetrator back harder" philosophy is old and bull-headed. The Visigoth will always remain the Visigoth devoid of a more enlightened outlook:

> "Rational self-interest theory assumes that those who engage in violence do so for reasons of rational self-interest and common sense. Like anyone else in possession of rationality and common sense, those who commit violent acts do not want to go to prison, do not want to be subjected to physical violence themselves, and do not want to die. They will do anything to avoid any of these fates, and all we need to do to prevent violence is to threaten to punish those who would commit such acts with greater violence of our own, such as imprisonment and capital punishment.
>
> There are only four things wrong with this theory. It is totally incorrect, hopelessly naïve, dangerously misleading, and based on complete and utter ignorance of what violent people are actually like…it has led us to shift our attention and resources from prevention to punishment…this theory has distracted us from attempting to learn what actually causes violence; and what conditions would be necessary in order to reduce the need for violence, and from applying that knowledge to eliminating or ameliorating those conditions which lead to violence."[525]

Violence breeds violence, and it increases vengeance and a desire for retribution. It does not solve anything except deepens the prisoner's anxiety. I found that prisoners, be they violent or not, appreciate conversation and being treated with respect. To repeat what was pointed out before, psychopathy is not accompanied by psychosis. Psychopathy presents with an emotional deficit, and the general intelligence is not affected to the degree that it does not equate. But violent psychopaths are conniving and contriving (Hare Test-description earlier in this chapter)). They will try anything to get what they want. The violent killer, or even the serial killer, as Kent Kiehl, M.D., pointed out is a psychopath who is untreatable, and do not hallucinate, or, suffer from delusions and disordered thoughts (the symptoms ofpsychosis)[526].

It is incumbent upon people in the criminal justice system to come to grips with proceeding in an entirely different direction because what exists is simply not working. The prison system is broken and needs to be fixed. This country is just throwing fortunes of money after bad, let alone perpetuating the gratuitous myth that more punishment will beat them into submission. And, of course, the other side of the coin that perpetrates "the state of inertia: bureaucratic corruption."

Common sense cannot replace the value of "the formality" of education for the prisoner, and a "formal" education for children in the most squalid, crime ridden cities in the country. The formality of an education through early learning in an established school with ambitious and creative educators is the traditional design. I am not naïve enough to think that "prison reform" will achieve this apotheosis.In prison, there are many individuals who are illiterate and, tragically, are almost indecipherable when they speak. The limitations of a very small vocabulary makes them inhibited, and, consequently, stutter or speak so quickly that nothing makes sense. It is humiliating in ways that educated people cannot fathom. Most of the prisoners with whom I made contact often repeated what they heard on television, but often they got the facts all mixed up because the vocabulary, as simple as it was, challenged and frustrated them. A prison is a labyrinthine backwater of humanity. Prison reform to reduce "mass incarceration" does not have to make an Albert Einstein grandiose achievement to make prisoners self-supporting and self-sustaining.

The issue today is that media, newspaper journalism and talk shows conflate the word "prisoner" with a one- dimensional concept as if they are paleontologists reducing all prehistoric creatures to one species. Because prison life in many states have become so tribal in very poor, remote areas of the country, nothing stands out to make anybody in the major large cities and towns even aware of their existence. To have a firsthand view of this for a city person is shocking. Admittedly, it would make such situations almost impossible to rectify and bring into the twenty first century. Awareness of this reality is the first step in a long journey. It is not surprising to know that statewide politicians in many of the very rural flyover areas of the South and Midwest in particular do know where a great number of their prisons are. The enormity of the problems today include not only location, but size and numbers. Presently, there are 1,719 state prisons, 102 federal prisons 2,259 juvenile correctional facilities, 3,283 local jails, and 79 Indian Country jails, and 59 military prisons under the purview of the U.S. Department of Defense (for every military service). To the unacquainted, all these numbers represent a leviathan-like, octopus-like assembly of structures housing a vast array of criminals from the United States, its territories and foreign countries. To render some comparative measure that would vindicate how large the United States prison systems are, think this through: The Incarceration Rates comparing South Carolina and the founding NATO countries by rates per 100,000 population are: South Carolina: 764; the United States: 698; the United Kingdom: 139; Portugal: 129; Luxembourg: 115; Canada: 114; France: 102; Italy: 96; Belgium: 94; Norway: 59; Denmark: 59; and, Iceland: 38. For the wealthiest, most desirable country in the world, the prison system is unconscionably mammoth. The United States have a turnstile, in-out, entry-exit prison processing "factory" in the millions per year. The point is to emphasize that its enormity explains why it has become primarily punitive. The manner of its business cannot lend itself to rehabilitation because of the built-in complexities. The numbers alone make the business management and safety issues massive. To thrust prisons into the kind of changes they require are certainly far beyond the scope of the present leadership because it is so focused on punishment in its primary capacity. The real enigma, and it most certainly presupposes great thinking and planning, going ahead might be the realization that it may no longer be possible. This is why a gold star-like commission is needed to make the kind of long-range assessments necessary for the good of the country.

Unfortunately, the country at the present time is obsessed with a collective energy concentrated on "language," a mysterious "coinage" of identification terms, and a "fire and brimstone-like" linguistic assault on each other's ideas and thinking. It is important to put viewpoints into perspective. For example, the historic reference to the way parents, teachers, and other individuals in positions of leadership (a clergyman, a football coach, etc.) correct misbehavior or rules violations is the use of the word "punishment." Today everyone is lost in appropriate language so that content and context are losing out to the verbal jousting. Political correctness is the villain, and, over time it has become the lever opening up cobwebs of distorted thinking which has side-bared all reasoning.

To face the consequences of mistakes, violations and outright lawbreaking keeps a leveling between up-and-down, sideways right-and left, a diagonal shift, or combinations. Effecting balance in life keeps society safe as best as humanly possible. This kind of thinking was first and foremost in the warden's mission of the very first prisons after the Civil War. Yes, springing from societal derangement from a vicious war, these original leaders had "punishment" in mind following the legal formalities. But reading their concerns for the way "reformatories" and "prisons" existed during very bitter and inhumane wartime conditions, it was undeniable that they wanted to soften the approach to prison life. Their language was very direct: correct, rehabilitate and educate. The current language" "correctional institution" has its origins from these early pioneers. The skeletal remnants of the original thinking can be witnessed in very limited cultural posturing by prisons across the country. Otherwise, "correctional" would be a complete farce.

However, people want to view the prison world today, the worldview is virtually all punishment. The thinking today is extremely difficult because the poor are poorer, the middle class is really not the 1950's middle class anymore (it is a rural/suburban "lower" blue-collar middle class), and the one- percenters aka the millionaire/billionaire class. Somehow, however, the country no longer has the luxury of foreboding, fantasizing, or quarrelling because we are overwhelmed with two of the most pernicious societal assaults ever known to man: drugs and disease.

The onslaught of drug misuse and addiction is crushing this country in two ways: 1) increasing both non-violent and violent crime, and 2) the tragic commandeering of America's youth. And, because of drugs sexually transmitted diseases are out of control. HIV and AIDS numbers are higher than others. And, yes, SDT's are still the nightmare they once were, but like AIDS, they do not capture the six o'clock news as they did when there were not so many other pernicious social ills as today. These two societal afflictions are the conduits for all the other related maladies because they are like the blood pumping from the heart giving increased life to conditions the country would be able to handle in a less spasmodic, more methodical manner if they were not so overwhelming.

The intellectual currency is being drained over the dialectic drumbeat concerning globalization, immigration, terrorism, nuclear arming, hacking everywhere from government agencies to social platforms, human trafficking, gun control, and a host of other challenges. And, there are many.

Imagine for a minute if we were all living in Shangri La and we eliminated all disease (especially the sexually transmitted ones) and all hallucinogenic and addicting drugs. Well, the United States is not Shangri La, it is not even close. However, if these two most rapacious malefactors were legitimately under control, think how more coherently and efficiently American society could deal with what appears to be so insurmountable.

This brings these thoughts to the following: the influence of drugs and human trafficking are the two most impactful agents responsible for "mass incarceration." If the country could get at this plague hovering over all our cities like a dark cloud, the numbers would demonstrably decrease. Until the country comes to grips with "mass incarceration," the prisons will further increase in size and numbers (there will be need to build additions or additional ones). I would consider that I am completely apolitical, but I try to think things through for logical, meaningful results. Consensus is impossible today, but common sense cannot deny the complete misappropriation of the human potential through drugs and disease which feed their poisons to the most vulnerable in society. Politicians will always be in the dark and remonstrate against the most ticklish concerns, and will never be motivated to really educate themselves enough to go beyond their constituencies to argue for the greater good. Prison numbers affect all people, indirectly or directly.

The criminal's addiction is not just to a drug but to an entire way of life. There is excitement in every aspect of drug use, even before criminal possesses the substance--
-fantasizing about drugs, talking about drugs, making one's way into dangerous areas where drugs are sold, the thrill of the deal."[527]

Drugs are the catalyst for the impending reactions affecting societies' complex problems, and thus America's prisons. And, our leaders by proxy, if they are up to the challenge (beyond political whiplash)?

Robert Allyn Goldman

SECTION 7

Blowback

Chapter 13: Canards, Sophistry and Truth.

The bureaucratic system is like "soldering gold" with the "flux" that contaminates the reclamation of the prisoner's spirit: the contaminants: legal and political tricks with fallacious arguments which would raise anyone's blood pressure! So, what is really the truth which is the ultimate blowback to such ignoble behavior!

Chapter 14: The Insanity of Repetition.

Well, George Santayana had the wisdom to default to the painful conclusion that if one does not understand history, it will certainly be repeated. Well, the "insanity of repetition" is nowhere more shining like a blinding star than within the American prison system.

CHAPTER 13

Canards, Sophistry and Truth

"Thus it will be seen that reformatory influences are educational rather than retributive. This is partly manual. Greater emphasis is laid upon the value of trade schools...Labor has amoral therapeutic value. A large percentage of crimes for which crimes are confined are crimes against property. Nothing tends more to reduce the number of such crimes than the development of a capacity for honest, efficient labor. Training in reading, writing, arithmetic, and all the foundation branches of English education is carried out in night and in day schools. Good prison libraries furnish the books, and competent instructors furnish the guidance for extended instruction in higher ranges of literature and knowledge for those who are capable of taking it."[528]

> The World is too much with us; late and soon, Getting
> and spending, we lay waste our powers; Little we see in
> Nature that is ours;
> We have given our hearts away, a sordid boon! This
> sea that bares her bosom to the moon; The winds
> that will be howling at all hours,
> And are up-gathered now like sleeping flowers; For
> this, for everything, we are out of tune;
> It moves us not. Great God! I'd rather be A Pagan suckled in a
> creed outworn; So might I, standing on this pleasant lea,
> Have glimpses that would make me less forlorn;
> Have sight of Proteus[529] rising from the sea;
> Or hear old Triton[530] blow his wreathed horn[531].

So much of the research points to the unacceptable conclusion: the prison system has failed its original intent, and, continues to buckle under the force of a dissolute political climate. It may be too far flung to reign in what's left of "bureaucratic sobriety" (perhaps a pastoral wish) to revitalize its original intent and engender capable leaders to rally its support for genuine change. It has certainly gone off the rails.

Most of the literature is so linear that it drones on without really getting to a thought of what it would take to rectify a horribly lame duck institution. The books are primarily "tell-alls," and wither from repetitive daily events so much of a personal nature that they really do not paint a real-life picture. There are a few books I have cited which really offer insight where the weaknesses lay. However, there are "canards"[532] (from the French, "vendre un canard a moitie"---"to sell half ducks," hoaxes or fabricated stories) for purposes of embellishing perhaps the glamour/excitement that whirls about Hollywood prison movies. These are romanticized stories to draw pity for a "lifer" (the Birdman of Alcatraz), to bend reality for a great ending (*The Shawshank Redemption*), or retaliate against governmental stridency and brutality (*Papillon*). The hoaxes are not the story because all three are based in fact, but the histrionics which really do not capture the level of misery and danger on a daily basis. The romanticization is similar to a house upfit to sell tickets. This interplay is most noteworthy in the tell-all books where the situations are a bit exaggerated to exploit sales. Additionally, canards are not as commonplace as a "fish story"[533], which is an exaggerated or unlikely story to embellish or mislead. The sophistry[534] (false arguments) made by prosecution of non- violent criminals or outright imperious behavior of parole board members to leave prisoners on the lurch for no good reason is a travesty. It is condoned and goes on all the time. In surfing the web for parole board hearings it display politicized members who seemed to enjoy the power play of their positions; not all certainly, but too many to be resentful. Such cases make Michelle Alexander's book, *The New Jim Crow: Mass Incarceration in the Age of Colorblindness*[535], transcendent and sad. Her accuracy is seen everywhere, but incredibly at the parole board level. This country does not attempt to physically cripple its prisoners as in the middle-east, Asian countries, the Koreas, or Russia, but the emotional beat down is vulgarian-like.

Once an individual gets into the criminal justice system it is supersized with bureaucrats, clerical types of all grades (secretaries and administrators), police, investigators and lawyers. It is a bureaucratic potpourri. I used to comment to a fellow employee that if most criminals knew what they were headed to, they probably might reconsider crime. Of course, it was sardonic banter, but the reality is that the system is so bogged down by procedure that it handcuffs the person right from the beginning to eventual incarceration, and then through all appeals and the eventual nightmare of head-knocking with people on parole boards who may or may not act kindly enough to listen.

The country has completely gone off the rails from the 1900 Barrows[536] report cited above. The International Prison Commission was set up to communicate on a common ground for a better understanding how to invoke standards for a reformative environment based on education standards. This had standing when most people agreed or made the pretense ideologically for what would be the basis of a prison. It certainly reads with comfort and invokes a spiritual sense of do-goodism. Today the pretense is not even-minded, it is polluted with platitudes when reading institution policies. The policies themselves read like canards, really a bunch of pretentious storylines for dealing with behaviors, admonitions for legislation like PREA (The *Prison Rape Elimination Act* passed in 2003[537]), violation policies, courses for annual performance testing of employees, etc. The most significant is PREA, and yet sexual assault and rape is overly common and so situational that it is almost impossible to eliminate. Storylines are common enough to make the bureaucrats appear priestly in their "earnestness" to control prison rape when in fact it is simply like grabbing water with a hand. And then to listen to the sophistry (false arguments) how well they are doing is patently pretentious for anybody who has worked in a maximum-security prison. Gangs determine and control such dastardly behaviors. And, gangs are flourishing with their own canon-like, unstated laws that are inviolable.

The most regressive canards are those borne by politicians for conduct I have torched for good reason. Convincingly, a Wall Street columnist made the same argument I have about Congress. Mary Anastasia O'Grady in her column, "The U.S. Funds Guatemalan Abuse,"[538] she rails against Congress budgeting half of Guatemala's "Commission Against Impunity" which is supposed to fight crime and corruption when in fact it does the opposite. She cites the imprisonment of Max Quiran, a righteous entrepreneur who, as patterned by previous honorable services to noble causes, agreeing to serve on an executive board providing public health care got him branded a white-collar criminal and landed him in "preventive detention." Like the old saying: "No good deed goes unpunished," Mr. Quiran, certainly a man of honor, is indefinitely imprisoned without bail while a former president of Oxfam International, facing corruption charges, is out on bail. The point is that Senator Lindsey Graham, (R-SC) chairman of the subcommittee on state and foreign operations, would not respond to her requests for comment, and, Senator Patrick Leahy, (D-Vermont) is the ranking democrat on the committee and ennobles the work of the committee while Guatemalan corruption goes unaccountable. Meanwhile, she points out that these two self-serving, tendentious senators are doing nothing to honor and advance the principles of the Commission Against Impunity in Guatemala. Instead, they continue the advancement of financial support while corruption prevails unwaveringly. Sound familiar? Senator Leahy's retort is the ultimate canard, with taxpayer money being siphoned off like other types of political bribery and extortion schemes. Congressional leaders spend the taxpayers' money as wantonly as drunks at a Las Vegas craps table, and not wince, care, or feel the slightest bit accountable. Not only is the Commission a hoax, a universal theme repeated too often in Latin American countries (and elsewhere), but Senator Leahy's sophistry is competitive with the example of prison reform served up by Senators Tom Cotton and Orrin Hatch. As she concludes: "But much of the responsibility for the state crimes perpetrated against these innocent people lies with the U.S. Congress." Real familiar territory, crossing party lines imperceptibly! Trusting Congress to protect the American way is like honoring the Black bear before he tears you apart.

The tragic misfortune is that people across the country are not familiar with the shenanigan's endemic to the American Congress. The general lack of respect is well-earned. It is genuinely unfortunate how even the most convincing politicians are ultimately as cunning and double-dealing as the most obvious, vocal individuals. When getting to Washington, D.C. the predisposition to deceit is already baked into the environment so the skillet is already buttered. It is then very easy and comfortable to fasten oneself to the lifestyle and accepted norms. For a politician truth entails spinning bias and balancing promises with party demands. The truth is not how people want to understand what they were taught. Instead, it is a separate, very distinct language which is similar to an exchange process. It is the coinage of bartering for expected behavior and prospective party-line voting. It is nothing less than outright gamesmanship. When a politician is saddled with such expectations, the lies are spoken with the kind of conviction which sickens those who contrarily would be naïve enough to believe in a scintilla of honesty. This is Washington,

D.C. at its verisimilitude. Historically, nothing has ever changed. All the way back to the founding fathers, the rancor and vile mistreatment of each other was perhaps more nasty. It has continued throughout American history. Partiality recognized for some of American history aficionados is no different than the worshipful following for those in other professions. The one significant difference is the country's dependence on key legislation that somehow is always bastardized as it runs through committees and the voting process. Objectives to keep the process moving forward to a consensus is like a maze where unexpected walls are stoppage points to regather and hopefully find the ultimate opening to the light of day. What comes out is distorted to a blend, a mixture that will anger some and please others. This is about as good as it seemingly will ever get (or, at least the country has been conditioned to view Congress as such).

The most concerning hoax is the very little play in the mass media regarding prison gangs. This has to be re- emphasized because the media gives very little "true" information regarding their influence and outright danger. Much has been discussed regarding radical Islam, and, for certain, this is the other concern. There once was a time when, with the right leadership, these two problems could have been almost completely controlled. This is no longer the case because their numbers are way out of control. Not only do they control the prisons, but they have swelled most of every populated city in the country. Their infamy is their belligerence and control. They defile women and traffic in young girls, spread drugs around like a contagious disease, kill to control territory, and opportune any "deal" which will make money. Extreme violence is like a calling card. As I have said, the Washington politicians are making a big deal about MS-13 (Mara Salvatrucha), and to some degree rightfully so. The Salvatruche have a history as guerillas during the Salvadoran Civil War, and, the Mara was a dangerous street gang in San Salvador. So, they are not "Johnny-come-latelies" where propagation of danger and murder are objects of their mission. Their sudden rise in their coverage by national news organizations has brought significant attention to them, but they do not curry nearly the malevolence as some of the more prominent gangs. Their level of toxicity and dreadful crimes are nothing short of a brutal, bloodthirsty gambit. Why? Because it strikes a chord for the danger that will not go away, and, it is a monstrous gang which obscures more uncivil and rapacious gangs which infest the prisons across the country. Make no mistake, prison gangs control the street with one mission wrapped in the combination of money and drugs through power and control. Anyone in any gang not aligning with the established rules will be cut-up or shot-up in a blood thirsty expression of"example-declaration."

Of all the books, blogs, newspapers, and website reporting the Morales book on gangs, which I have noted many times, is a vast array of such toxic and wanton behavior that it is captivating in a most unbelievable picture staging of real-life prison butchery. An example that Morales cites is that of Jack "Happy" Rice who was killed by NF (Nuestra Familia) as a revenge murder. Subsequently, his wife, Gloria, was murdered as she was to testify against the gang on the way to the courthouse. She was stabbed 94 times pin cushion style.

Morales carefully details the interplay between the most significant gangs. It is an incredibly prodigious effort, particularly for a 30-year correctional officer who obviously made it his intent to get to the bottom of what makes them tick. It was no simple task. Most people would assume that a gang is a gang. Not so. Each represents a singular cultural background, layered leadership hierarchy, and specific demands. How they engage and behave is so repugnant that it leaves the reader with a sense of what happens to humanity when it is reduced to such wretched, vile, primal brawling to which animals in the wild do not engage. Race, ethnicity and geographic origin are central to these gangs, and their days are survival based because of their reliance on bloodshed and mayhem. Their business, as stated many times, revolves around guns, drugs, and human trafficking as vehicles for money, power and control. At times seemingly sophisticated, but really a tawdry descent into a soulless place where death will unexpectedly rear its ugly head in an onslaught of blood- shedding anguish. It is hardly romantic, and inevitable. Morales does not create a literary masterpiece, but the overwhelming concentration of events, and the manner in which prisoners wheel and deal, paints a frightening reality. From the Mexican Mafia to the Aryan Brotherhood, the colorful members are one- way "beasts of burden." They live making the case for their gangs, an allegiance that ends badly when failure is exposed. The violence is nothing short of inhuman. The major gangs swell with members who only abide by one tenet: do and live as expected, or life will be snuffed out.

In a Wall Street Journal article on Monday, August 20, 2018, "MS-13 Gang Tries to Organize An Unruly Young Membership," Del Quentin Wilber[539] attempts to make the case for Mara Salvatrucha (MS: Mara being the San Salvadoran city gang, and, Salvatrucha the guerillas of the Salvadoran Civil War) as young, aspiring violent upstarts trying to make a national splash. The national media is trying to make the case for MS-13 as the most threatening gang (with a torrent of shivv-bloodletting).

It is extremely violent and filled with youthful, exuberant hellions, but MS-13 is hardly a national threat compared to older gangs (Mexicana or EME, for example) with their heels long dug into the national crime scene. As I have pointed out, but worth repeating, MS-13 was a 1960's Los Angeles city gang of illegal aliens from El Salvador. They were so vulnerable that they were forced to return. But those in prison aligned themselves with the far more powerful Mexican Mafia for protection. At the present time MS-13 is gaining attention, but the more powerful gangs like EME, Nuestra Raza and the Black Guerilla Family, the Texas Syndicate, the Border Brothers & Paisas, the Netas, G-27, Trinitarios, United Blood Nation, the Aryan Brotherhood, the Nevada Trece, etc., but especially the Mexican Mafia. There are many, but the lengthy Wall Street Journal article is a canard. MS-13 is exploiting its depravity, but the statistics are disingenuous. Morales tried to make a very valid point that many articles and books do not justice to the most controlling prison gangs.

It is also concerning for how unaware the general public is. Having been witness to it during my employment, it leaves an incredibly chilling memory. Animals in the wild carve each other up for survival. Prison murder is so wanton that all the neuroscience imaging would look like hot lightbulbs flashing with blinding energy. All the prison programs on television do not come close to capture this harsh reality. The tattooing lends full body identifying commitment to the gang as a family where support and retributive response is certain. Of all the canards and sophistry regarding the truth about prison life, it is evident that the ones concerning how dangerous it is take a back seat to nothing else. To be specific, this characterization pertains strictly to the maximum-security prison, the Level III (though a Level II, pending the nature of the mix, can witness a very bad element at times).

The level of Islamic radicalization[540], [541], [542] going on is the silent danger because my research tells me that the population is quickly growing (with a high degree of probability). The canard is that the visuals make all the prisoners appear as peace minded Muslims. The pretext is that the radical Islamist is not a concern because most Muslims in prison are peaceable. Not true. Yes, they are not generally gang affiliated because they are generally run solo or in very small, tight groups. They have an identity that does not match the longstanding North and South American gangs. But, Islamic terrorism around the world is very real. Radicalization is a fact, both inside prisons and within their own groups outside. The numbers are on the rise as a certainty, particularly with a recent wave of radicalized very young Muslims. The nature of Sharia Law as the only recognized form by radicals is both a known and silent danger. False arguments disputing this fact come from the so-called "peaceful" Muslims. However, enclaves all around the country are intimately involved with prison radicals. Very little activism exists to fully identify each member because they keep to themselves. It is a clandestine behavior which self-identifies when violence breaks out. One of the founders of DHS (the Department of Homeland Security), Philip Haney, makes no bones about the danger to which this country has been exposed. Activist behavior by cells representing ongoing and future Islamic terrorism is now a fact of life, and Haney is clearly unrestrained in asserting this in his book[543]. Probably, the great combination of canards and sophistry played out in front of the country's eyes and ears were the denials, excuses and lies written and vocalized to abort any admission that Islamic terrorism was the "new game in town" (the country is in a slow, progressive assault). Haney identifies very willingly the enemy: violent Islamist radicals. Sophistry and canards used to front false imagery and deny fact are as sinful as their exploitive agenda driven narratives. Why? There is no answer for throwing caution to the wind and casting a long shadow of danger across the country. As intimately related to living in freedom and not having to worry about constant danger is the very radicalization process affecting inside prisons and in pockets throughout the country.

There is no denial the dangers to which this laboring effort is surreptitiously our way of life, and expanding without restraint. The very kind of sophistry which confounds common sense is obdurate denial of politicians with irreverent self-interest. Make no mistake that the protective standards preserving safety for American citizens are no longer guaranteed. Prisons are incubators for worse to come.

As Morales[544] states about gangs: "America's Jails and Prisons are out of sight, out of mind, for most of the general public. Only when a riot or major incidents happen do correctional facilities get a couple of minutes on the nightly news. Much of the general public gets their distorted views of prison life from shows..." And, in his introduction to his book, he makes a very accurate statement: "I can see why my personal background might upset some Criminal Justice workers. Many of them spent their entire careers on the outside looking in, but the best gang investigators learned directly observing gangs and talking with gang members. I learned from seeing both sides of the fence, from good mentors, and working gangs for three decades."

After closely following many prisoners for over a year every day, and talking to many, sometimes at great length, I can attest to what Morales contests. He may not be a literary scholar or a professional educator, but he identified the "black hole" of prison life where the energy builds from day-to-day. Murder and contraband are the two daily issues which confound every maximum-security prison under state control. Statistics and cultural life cannot measure the true pulse and explosive dangers because they are sudden and unpredictable. Each day is potentially a riot in the making. Between gangs and the ongoing radicalization of prisoners the future outlook does not bode well. Those in Congress are either in denial, totally unaware, or merely filled with imbalanced political motives. Such indifference must be exposed and the politicians voted out. Congress is over-weighted with people who now work at cross purposes to the preservation of American safety. They are self-absorbed and one dimensional. This is abhorrent and scurrilous. It is important to listen and understand what politicians say because they speak their own language, what's best for themselves, their ambitions, and their re-election demands.

Canards, absurd or misleading stories, are so abundant regarding the prison system that they mask reality. In addition, making a false argument to downplay the dangerous prison atmosphere by overemphasizing and excusing behaviors because of psychological distress or poor upbringing is also distorting. The fact is: maximum security prisons house dangerous individuals. Psychoanalytic reasoning, in my estimation, will not excuse the most depraved minds. Help must go to the support of non-violent prisoners whose "mistakes" should not make them the victims of the courts and prosecutors. That is "the truth" and "the truth" is the basis for the most logical argument for "prison reform."

There are two books that should be referenced because they speak to "the truth." They resonate two completely different themes. They are: (1) Christopher Zoukis's book, *Federal Prison Handbook: The Definitive Guide to Surviving the Federal Bureau of Prisons*[545], and, Demico Boothe's book, *Why Are So Many Black Men in Prison?*[546] Both Christopher Zoukis and Demico Boothe are "graduates" of the federal prison system. Each served time in federal prison for non-violent crimes. Christopher Zoukis served time for engaging in under age sex while still in high school, and having child pornography on his computer. Demico Boothe also served time in federal prison for dealing in drugs. However, as he compares his sentence for such a minimal amount like killing a fly with a sledgehammer.

I wanted to identify both individuals because they exemplify everything I have spent so much time discussing. Christopher Zoukis, a white man, spent most of his young adult life in both a state and federal prison. Demico Boothe spent a bit over eight years in federal prison. Christopher was a prolific writer while he was "inside the wall," and additionally wrote an amazingly detailed handbook for those unfortunate individuals who will be serving time in a Federal prison. It explains everything a prisoner will expect and basically advice on how to deal with it. He has performed a wonderful service. Kudos as well for getting a college degree as well as getting an M.B.A.

He has become an accomplished individual. Lending his expertise to such a book is a rarity, but he is obviously endowed with a sensitivity and thoughtful feeling for those he engaged while locked up, enough so to transfer enough energy to deliver such a gift. He is a super example of what is right in a world of turmoil.

Demico Boothe, an African-American, was sentenced to 10 years in federal prison but served eight years and ten months. He had 91 grams of crack cocaine (what is considered a miniscule amount) which he was dealing at eighteen just having graduated from high school. His book is wonderfully written, with occasional harsh language for white supremacy (which I understand perfectly well). The premise of his book is accurate: black people are disproportionally incarcerated. That is an unfortunate distinction. He possesses a very keen insight into human behavior, and no one should fault him for his disgust. He earned it.

Both individuals capture very explicitly what is wrong with the American Prison System. The argument I have made for "prison reform" is supported by their "victimization." It is overkill to rehash the incredible expense involved with incarceration time they both spent in prison (Christopher for over 12 years and Demico for almost 9 years). Let's just say the expense is considerable.

These are two examples of overreach, over-zealous prosecution, and over-sentencing. When authors talk about "mass incarceration," these two individuals should surface as glaring examples of what is dramatically wrong with the criminal justice system. Unfortunately (or, maybe fortunately, depending how the argument is presented), I cannot put as much blame on prosecutors, judges, or sentencing guidelines as I can to those who legislate the laws, write the guidelines, policies and interpret appeals. I have already brandished my disdain for Congress and why it has failed the prison system. There is no justification why these two individuals should have spent so much time locked up at the taxpayers' expense. Both were excessive, and particularly for the nature of their crimes at their ages. Behaviors aside, youthful transgressions like drinking and partying, wasting lives for non-violent misbehaviors requires that the laws be changed or both should have spent perhaps five years on probation and close monitoring. In Christopher's case, he was on probation only to be put in prison with the pornography finding. This lacks insight and understanding of youth development. Somewhere along the line it would have been more rational to substitute education and probation/supervision.

There is a very warped sense about what is right and what is clearly illogical and excessive. People in lofty, but critical, "power" positions should be educated enough to bring some sense to such an incredible lack of insight. Multiply these two examples by hundreds (maybe thousands), the result is a bureaucratic nightmare and a reflection of extremely poor decision making.

I have spent a tremendous amount of time reviewing literature that assails the prison system from so many different psychological/legal viewpoints. The prison system is meant to protect citizens from violence. It was originally a reformative process for the criminal as well. Its direction has been set strictly in the direction of "punishment" with only a superficial consideration for the person after incarceration. Prison bureaucracy will deny this because of the pretense made for optional training as I have discussed. The cautionary fact is that non-violent behavioral transgressions are not separated from violent criminality when punishment is handed out. The result has left so many prisoners punished far beyond what the legal/political system should allow.

As I have stated many times, the most destructive problems manifesting pervasively throughout the American Prison System are drugs and disease. Drugs are so rampant today that their eradication seems very unlikely. With globalization as a present watershed change, disease is really an explosive force. I put this at the very top of likely transmittable disasters. A quote from the most recent *National Geographic* substantiates my opinion, but I wish I was wrong:

"It's a risky world, as we know, but all the more risky because some of the risks keep evolving. Ebola virus and the influenzas can adapt, ISIS can change tactics; Kim Jong Un can do turnarounds. And now experts warn that we have entered the "post- antibiotic era," during which increasing numbers of people---in the hundreds of thousands---will suffer and die each year from infection by forms of bacteria that were once controlled by antibiotics."[547]

This will no doubt affect all humanity, but the prisons today will be noticeably affected because of very old, unkempt and seamy institutions.

Truth conveys much more than "honesty." It also connotes a commitment to doing what is right, being disciplined about performance be it a job, a skill, or a learning process, or even enhancing the world around oneself. Truth is extending one's knowledge, understanding or consideration because it benefits someone in need and has far ranging positive ethical and moral consequence. Seemingly too ideal or unattainable, it is not. Even with all the flaws inherent in political leadership, alliances can form to bolster a cost benefit to "prison reform" in a rational way. John Keats in his poem, "Ode on a Grecian Urn," captured a precise message about "truth":

Beauty is truth, truth beauty---that is all Ye know on earth, and all ye need to know[548].

Finally, I chose to cite William Wordsworth at the beginning because it is a poem that offers a sensible explanation for man's Achilles heel. "The world is too much with us; late and soon, Getting and spending, we lay waste our powers...." It is apparent that our material world is so over-run and maddening that not enough time is devoted to sitting back and taking stock of what is "right and wrong" (in the most apparent and immediate sense). Political leaders squander their authority ("...we lay waste our powers..."), and, in a rational recapitulation, they should take a serious look at the most over-burdened, over-wrought and over-expanded prison system known to man.

CHAPTER **14**

The Insanity of Repetition

"The man who has never made a mistake will never make anything; and the man who has never done any harm will never do any good."[549]

"The virtues lose themselves in self-interest like rivers in the sea."[550]

There is a great deal of documentation to support some very pertinent statistics, but the most significant information resides in the modern milieu: the worldwide web. The interpretive quality of books, however, can never be substituted. The thinking is living and resides permanently etched in time immemorial. They are the most optimal references because of the devotion to historic fact. They are opinions which are supported by indelible records, and these are important for subject matter that is so poorly understood.

The American prison system has very little value to the average citizen, unless and until she/he is drawn in by personal circumstances. At that point the lesson learned is frustrating and irksome. It is a world so near, yet so far. It is a system which has been allowed to grow under the force of an avalanche of crime and ultimately became bottled up with mixed blessings, but is now an over-weighted, swollen organic mess.

George Bernard Shaw, the great Irish/English (born in Dublin, Ireland) playwright-writer, wrote *The Crime of Imprisonment* as an original title: *Imprisonment* as a treatise in the form of a preface for a report for Lord Olivier on English and American prison conditions. Originally published in 1922, it was republished with the new title in 1946 as reported here. It resulted from commentary dealing with the loathsome environment to which the prisons had fallen. The investigation and treatise were prepared in behalf of the British Labor Office "…in an effort to revise the common system of imprisonment."[551]

Shaw wrote this 125-page treatise 96 years ago, over a lifetime for most people. He was an incredible no-nonsense, exacting individual. His literary assault on the prison systems in both countries is complete with rebuke, but without invective. If he were alive today, writing a critique on the present American system, with all its folly, his treatise might turn into a disgusted screed. Whoever would have thought that one of the greatest all-time playwrights would have written one of the greatest literary screeds (as a treatise) on the American and British prison systems. The writer of "Pygmalion"[552], one of his many contributions was a huge stage success, especially in the United States. Whoever would have thought he would deliver the first to take the prison system to task for the bottleneck of bodies amassed like a huge fish catch of Atlantic salmon. I was astonished when I first set my eyes on the treatise. Truly eye-catching!

Looking at the present circumstances, probably the most assailable link in the system are the "sentencing guidelines." It is possible that if all the money passing through the entire criminal justice system could be properly traced, it might fall back on the minimum sentencing standards for some many petty and first-time crimes. When I read the books by Christopher Zoukis and Demico Boothe, the circumstances represented so many about whom I read while I was first working at a Level II prison. They are still very young people, but the quality of their writing and the presentation of their experiences are reflective of highly mature indiviuals.

Boothe's offense was a first-time drug purchase for which he got the 10-year minimum. To the ordinary person who is unfamiliar with the prison system in general, and sentencing guidelines specifically might reflect: ok, he got what he deserved. Christopher Zoukis, on the other hand, was a frisky youth dabbling in alcohol and partying before he was given probation (which means he did not go to prison, but was under prescribed supervision), but during this period, child pornography found on his computer led him to state prison for the minimum. However, once he was released the feds wanted their "piece of flesh" so he was carted off to a federal prison. So, from 18 on, until he was about thirty years old, he was in prison.

Several points have to be made. For the most part, the system deprived both of their most active mental/emotional growth periods of their lives. As I previously pointed out, the male brain does not fully develop until a range about 25 years old. Both Boothe and Zoukis were very unique individuals. Boothe read over 500 books while incarcerated, and served as a tutor for other prisoners. Zoukis, as I noted beforehand, wrote several books in addition to getting a college degree. This is very different for over 99% of others, who, in similar circumstances are content to vegetate vacuously for the duration of the sentences. Thus, for most prisoners, being locked away does nothing for their development nor prepare them for anything when they are released (except to default into the world of crime, and probably to a greater extent and magnitude).

The two young men are exemplary of what George Bernard Shaw rails against in his treatise. Now almost a century later, the sheer runaway freight train that is the American prison system certainly conflates with Shaw's barrage of well-crafted arguments for the system's lazy, thoughtless management. The impact of the ever-increasing volume of crimes have subdued a criminal justice system that cannot handle the magnitude. It has not been able to adjust, and, its expansion has occurred right under the eyes of Big "Sloppy" Government (adorned with forever countless policies and legislation which expand like galaxies with black holes where its convicted find their resting places).

The most common conversation I would always have with prisoners involved the age-old subject: knowing what you know now how would you change your early, young life. Not all, but well into the high ninetieth percentile, most said that if they had someone helping them, they would never want to be locked up like animals. And, then I would proceed to the next point (which always stirred my emotions to no end) dealt with whether the system helped or hurt them. The answer is simple (and, I'll answer it): made them resentful, angry and fearful because the prison environment was poorly patrolled and dangerous. Some conversations were more cheerful because they trusted me enough so we joked around. However, the significance is shameful: these are individuals who were stilted by poverty, lack of education, vulnerable to drug dealers, partiers, poor associations, no authority figure growing up, and driven to gangs for support and direction. The really young prisoners convicted for the first time were always in shock the first few days of incarceration. It is an image I shall carry the rest of my life. "Shock" does not do the facial-body reactions justice. As I talked to the initiates, it was like watching wax improvised caricatures motionless in place! It was something to behold.

One other point has to be made very clearly (even though I have made it several times): based on population census percentages (13% Black African-Americans) there is an overwhelming disproportion of Black African-Americans locked up, particularly in southern prisons. The only other pertinent fact that makes this far, far worse is: NOBODY CARES! No one who should care cares! That is the real tragedy. My observations lead me to believe that history (and I am an avid follower of world history, especially Civil War history) is filled with political leaders who talked the talk, but never walked the walk for the Black African-American population. And, as a reflection of a broken political and prison system, Black African-Americans certainly need leadership with a value system that is sensitive, caring and understanding. The damage is overwhelming, but hope springs eternal. There is a corrective answer, and the Chicago-Detroit cities of the country require an earnestness "to do" and not "just sing political poppycock!"

Some critical observations relate to how the prison system is infecting society. Immigration and education are not only impacting prison life, but both are uncertainties which are ripping into the social fabric. Both are so formulaic driven that they have lost their importance to the country's safety and prosperity. It is very possible to judge a society by its treatment of immigration and education. The significance is that without a sensible structure no society will advance its people, and people will determine their progress if, and only if, there is a reliable sense of order and prosperity. The country is very much divided over this issue today. I blame the Washington,
D.C. political class, mostly the Democrats, because of their visceral hatred of Trump, they cannot connect on this vital issue. I can understand people may be enraged by Trump's personality, but he has always been open to what's best for the country.

The most dangerous impact on American society today which is demonstrably affecting prison life and inner cities is illegal immigration and a quickly failing public school system. Let me reiterate, I am not a political devotee by anyone's imagination so what I see now is based on personal observations and not related to any political allegiance. In fact, the bluster and ceaseless degrading being bandied about is a reflection of socially engineered divisions in American society. At the basis of all of this is political turpitude, on both sides of the aisle. There is nothing pure about Washington politics. Congress is full of warped, self-absorbed narcissists. It is unfortunate to see so much ill-will being excused for positive debate. It is not positive and it is seeding permanent disaffection and gratuitous loss of respect for the laws which made this country so attractive and safe. The prisons are a very sad reflection of so much discursive sanctimony by all the politicians. Tribalism, nativism, fascism, socialism…all the "isms" which seem to be the flavor of our times. If a country does not abide by its sovereignty and laws, it dilutes its strengths and ability to provide support for all its people.

Social ravaging is occurring full thrust by throwing "legal" immigration to the wind and allowing marauding gangs stream blithely through our borders robbing our harmony and killing our youth with drugs, guns, and disease. Our inability to see through this and reject it is actually pathetic. On one side are leftists being taken over by pandering Democrat politicians who, with their millionaire lifestyles, condemn Republican wealth in the name of socialism…and give free this, free that! Who are they kidding? It's patently absurd. If people could only view them through the prism of "truth," they would understand how misguided they are to think these politicians care one wit about them. All they want is to advance their wealth, power and control through "Big Government."

The prisons are loaded with the consequences of neglected and neglectful leadership that is allowing radical Islamists and pillaging, and other murderous illegal aliens to sneak through. It is pathetic to see people fall for this deliberate lying and hypocrisy. It is willfully damaging and hypocritical. Talk to a Black/African-American prisoner who sees right through this!

Congress is Kabuki theater with wind-bags, harridans and clowns masquerading as leaders in search of serious problem solving. The truth is that Congress is a complete embarrassment, a playground for fools without conscience or shame. People who carry on the way they do with the lying, elusive language, lack of conviction, lack of morality and ethical deportment are without values and should be any other place but where they are making a mockery of the taxpayers' trust and needs!

The news programs, newspapers, talk shows, blogs, social media and special media interviews are rapaciously gobbling up wealth to the detriment of average people who are merely trying to get along. The voices are like blow-torches blasting through the air just setting people against each other with alternating vituperative and condescending opinions. Depending to whom people listen, the slant is different, but the opinion bias is still verbal execution of the other side. Meanwhile, the people who listen to such scatological drivel are just being pumped up with increasing visceral hatred and resentment for the other side. It is mind-splitting and tragic to witness.

Why is the above screed so important? Because it distracts from what is really important to keep the country safe, without allowing the Washington political elite to conduct themselves like runaway freight trains in pursuit of their own money, power and control trifecta! The prisons are being loaded with people who should not even be in this country and saddling the taxpayer for their keeping. Meanwhile they are distractions for the rightful Americans in our prisons with excessive and improvident sentences. Why is this so hard to understand? How many more illegals and radical Islamists should the American prison system absorb before the country wakes up to the boondoggle our political panderers are creating through neglect and ignorance? Again, what is so hard to understand? Lack of respect and attention to people who live and die to protect the country around the world is sinful. The sententious political parasites will manage to take the country down if people do not take it back and demand harmony and tolerance.

Illegal immigration is not the key to prosperity and peaceful living. People who are in the country with green cards are being dealt a terrible dishonor. Rather than worry and argue about who defiled the social order in such a despicable manner by furthering tensions with politically offensive discourse, it is more sensible to restore order and move on. Bantering about who killed the children, the guns or the people with guns, is political scamming for "our local and national leaders," gerrymandering common sense thinking for personal attention and benefit. It should be more important to do what has to be done to improve education standards rather than padding the airwaves and newspapers with invective, and to the delight of radio and television prosperity. School choice should be available to all parents who want and need higher quality programs. The public school system is nothing more today than a labor union's delight, providing diminished educational standards. The labor union is a tool of the past, and only serves to collect money to fatten the wallets of seedy union leaders. The prisons are full of kids whose lack of quality education sent them to the streets to get into trouble.

The prisons are filled with young and older adults who wish all the time that they could have benefitted from what the more wealthy communities take for granted. Watching politicians debunk the "NRA,

GUNS & RELIGION" with insults rather than foster a cooperative, productive spirit is misleading and unproductive. For every sin one side condemns in the other, the true sin lies within the one spewing the venomous lies. It is a reminder of the brilliant wordsmith, William Safire[553], who created the expression, "the Nattering Nabobs of Negativism." If only the political establishment could remember these words emoted by then Vice President of the United States under President Richard Nixon. Of course, William Safire whose brilliant essay every Sunday in the New York Times Magazine section wrote these words never imaging that Spiro Agnew would recall them as he resigned his position because of tax evasion. Nothing really changes about the political Washington elite except for the direction they blow their wind! Ultimately it will be the education of non-violent criminals which will act as the fulcrum point in wresting individual potential away from the misery of extended prison sentences. Teaching discipline to imbue pride and self- confidence is the key to advance prison reform. Discipline is what failed the prisoner, and it comes from the home and schools.

Violent crimes are a completely otherwise consideration. With a return to the family unit over time violent crime would diminish. Family, education and good health sound folksy, but the truth lies that domain.

The answer to "prison reform" is actually making the effort. The perpetuation of the punishment standard is not working, and, the corruptive nature of prison bureaucracy is a direct reflection. Although falsely attributed to several people (Albert Einstein, Mark Twain, etc.), an appropriate quote of unknown origin: "Insanity is doing the same thing over and over again and expecting different results."[554] That is why that triad mentioned above is not folksy. The insanity is that the country has enabled the corrupt political class to misrepresent the peoples' needs. The greasy politicians have led the country down the wrong road for far too long and the oversaturation of our prisons are classically a reflection. It is about time the country get back to purity in government to enhance the needs the future generations so richly deserve (a "pie-in-the sky" thought).

The strength of a society should be measured by its weakest link. Communities elect their representatives and senators to be hands-on guardians of the prisons' responsibilities and "health." The American prisons are the country's weakest link, and it is falling apart. Politicians refer to "prison reformers" as ticklish with the persistence of a buzzing mosquito. They are not. They are concerned citizens who simply understand putative deficiencies and bring them to public attention. It is relevant that people are thoroughly in the dark as it is, and without oversight our prisons might grow into Latin American dungeons. This protective buffer zone is demands conscientious leadership. Like in any industry bureaucratic dysfunction corrupts the system. Diligent directors must be carefully sought for their responsible leadership, and not for nepotistic or political connections. This is a noticeable failing along with deficiencies in parole boards and enough properly trained guards.

Education extends in many directions: a GED, a college degree, a graduate degree, vocational training in an occupational oriented field, and non-degree education training for proficiency in horticulture/landscaping, carpentry, general training to become a handyman, forestry, etc.

To advance prisoners into a competitive working environment requires a fallback skill. To a large extent it'll be the first-time young adults might sense a feeling of self- confidence which is the medicine to forestall recidivism. The message is quite simple: a job as a road to self-sufficiency and a productive way of life. The crush of America's inner cities with the influx of drugs, guns and human trafficking for prostitution is a long existing mountain of habitual deviance to overcome.

The long-range plan is to revamp the entire prison system and take it local in an educational format as I have outlined. State and federal politics is demonstrably obstructive and thick with deep bureaucratic corruption. The only place where reform has a chance is where the political class is directly answerable to citizens: localities. This does not mean that local government is as pure as the driven snow. However, community environments allow corruption or irregular behavior to be addressed immediately and soundly. Oversight is essential to address such planning every step of the way. Without such change the existing prison system will become so robust that they'll become Gulag-like.

An outspoken ex-prisoner, Chandra Bozelko[555], wrote an article in the Wall Street Journal addressing the importance of gainful employment upon release. She cites the 1979 Justice System Improvement Act requiring prisoners be paid the same wage as employees in the outside workforce for a similar occupational task. Referring to prison employment as "slavery," she is absolutely correct. Although I concur, political follow-up to advance measurable compliance is very wishful thinking.

The 1979 *Justice System Improvement Act* is a lengthy 59-page document outlining a complete breakdown of the law, centering basically around reforms which would provide money to states and local communities to provide for not only prisoners but as well for prison guards. It reads like a determined final demand to upgrade vast deficiencies in juvenile, state and federal institutions. With even the most common, basic understanding of the American prison system, it reads like a typical political wish list, everything that should be but will not. Without getting too deeply into all the pages, it important to realize that it is "settled law." But like so many facets of "settled law," it is a continuum of many laws that are on record but inadequately or never administered. It is immeasurably more precise and detailed than Ms. Bozelko's article in the WSJ addresses. This is understandable because she, having spent five years incarcerated, knows the misfortune that 86 cents an hour is ridiculous at any level. Thus her point is well-taken. However, the prison where I worked the per diem was even lower. Furthermore, I started this book discussing the misfortune of keeping guards from quitting for many reasons, most of which being very low pay and lengthy twelve-hour shifts. However, it appears that this 1979 law has been a forgotten entity.

However, I worked where systemic complaints abounded concerning every facet of employment. It is now 2020 so examine a brief statement from the law:

> "It is therefore the declared policy of the Congress to aid
> State and local governments in strengthening and
> improving their systems of criminal justice by providing
> financial and technical assistance with maximum
> certainty and minimum delay. It is the purpose of this title
> to (1) authorize funds for the benefit of States and units of
> local government to be used to strengthen their criminal
> justice system…."[556]

The law then proceeds to enumerate how the detailsof the law are to be followed. It is "the insanity of repetition" that allows Congress to be so lackadaisical and divorced from the reality of national constituency. The Congress would never forget their own pay raises, insurance coverage increases, their pension plans, and their other accoutrements. Their "glam" is a broad smile and casual promises to their constituencies for conspicuous attention to re-election, and particularly the year before the run-up to election day. Their second priority is to spend the taxpayer money on "programs" to demonstrate a sense of responsibility and call attention to their "hard work."

Government is serious business, and it is the business of the people. It is unfortunate at so many levels that politicians know no shame. They caress power like children with their precious dolls, and they get uppity if they are exposed. Their egos do not allow for remorse, and contrition is not in their vocabulary. Let's just admit the prison system is in an unfortunate limbo whereby no one will effectuate change sufficient to address such a plethora of needs. In spite of the 1979 legislative act, it is very possible that the money originally laid out and spent never got into the hands of the right people to be apportioned appropriately. Like social security, Congress has raided many of its agency appropriations for many years. It is not a secret that entitlement programs have been dissipated despite Congressional flim-flam. They also pass bills to which they conflate erroneous attachments (most generally for personal political needs). There is nothing historic about this because this is the nature of a political opportunism so boldly repeated without any sense of regret.

The strange irony is that the emoluments clauses of the United States Constitution[557] (Article 1, Section 9, and Article 1, Section 6 prohibiting federal officeholders from taking any gifts, payments or other things of value from a foreign state or its rulers, officers or representatives; or, the president from the federal government or the states beyond his salary respectively) is a pre-emptive strike against corruption. And yet. with all Congress' splashy lifestyles and the President's pampering community, vacations and surrounding attendants, don't they clear the ceiling for excess? And yet, they all want more! Certainly, doing the peoples' work with a bit more care and attention would be nice.

Given the extraordinary amount of literature encompassing websites and books about the prison system, it points out how difficult it is to invoke change. The most underlying obstruction to "prison reform" is Congress itself. If this were a totalitarian or fascist country like Russia, Cuba or Venezuela, well it would be a prima facie case for surrender to their values and unconditional tyranny. There would be wanton destruction of the human spirit, and no redress. This country was founded as a democratic republic and transformed through relentless political squabbling and usurpation of power into a mongrel democracy. Executive privilege over time made the Presidency appear like a fascist dictatorship, the Congressional climate breathing fire and fury with a madness, defiance and incurable disdain that could never settle with any rational composure. As a gradual sinkhole deepening over time, it is as if the well of the Senate is a foul-smelling bat cave with guano so spread throughout that communication for the sake of compromise is virtually fossilized somewhere in the forgotten past. Some people might ask why, and most would realize that leadership failed because principles and ethical behavior self-destructed for the sake of greed and control.

At this time the politics of the nation is in the midst of extremely incendiary, irrational and combustible conflicts over the illegal /alien problem. In order to truly understand the failing prisons, it is incumbent to recognize the number of fiery cauldrons expanding

expanding within so many cities. The Democratic states are out of control, and there is no hope now for political reconciliation. At least until the November 3rd election is over.

A lot of time has been spent trying to explain state prisons swelling with depraved gangs. They are presently a "dumping ground" for the country's bottom of the barrel. Whether people want to understand the dangers of this mix or not, it is comparable to awaiting a dynamite explosion. The following is a menacing fact:

> "Using data collected in the SCAAP..." (State Criminal Alien Assistance Program of the Bureau of Justice)..."system for 2009, an average share of 5.4 percent of the prisoners in state and local prisons were criminal aliens. The share was more than double that average in California (12.7%) and Arizona (11.7%). Another seven states also had criminal alien shares higher than the national average. They were: Oregon, Nevada, Colorado, Utah, New York, New Jersey, and Texas. The shares of the incarcerated population comprised of criminal aliens are generally higher than the shares of the estimated illegal population in the state. For example, the estimated 2,365,000 illegal aliens California represent 7.1% percent of the state's overall population compared to the 12.4 percent criminal alien population. Nationally, the estimated 11,920,000 illegal aliens in 2010 represented 3.9 percent of the overall population compared to the 5.4 percent criminal alien incarceration rate. This difference in shares demonstrates that the share of aliens in prison for various crimes is disproportionately large. The share of aliens in federal prisons is higher than in state and local prisons because federal prisons house aliens convicted of federal immigration offenses such as alien smuggling in addition to other crimes[558].

This is a very disturbing revelation which any American will never hear or read. From a common-sense point of view, and the political insanity aside, anyone who does not see a foreboding metamorphosis has either nerves of steel or a calibrated denial. Taken alone, this is destructive enough to rob safety from people thinking law enforcement will be able to control this expanding nightmare.

There cannot be any human being who does not see the virtues of legal immigration or undeniable compassion of people trying to escape the imponderable, depraved treatment of citizenry by despots in this hemisphere. It is simply a totalitarian beat down of impoverished people in Cuba, Venezuela and Nicaragua. Anyone who does not have compassion for these people either does not read or does not have a soul. And, it is similar to many other countries around the world (Zimbabwe, The Democratic Republic of Congo, Somalia, Libya, China, Russia, North Korea, etc.). This is subject for another day, but suffice it to say, it is glaringly ugly, and enough to emphasize majesty and the hallmark of openness of the United States.

However, the politics is disturbingly conflating the danger of people requiring asylum and the dangerous illegals coming across the border (where other radicals are cloaked silently among them, such as violent Islamists). I have argued the overwhelming dangers in previous chapters so it suffices just to emphasize the irrational and menacing storm of criminal groups amounting very quickly into a perilous political mix. Politics is essentially feeding this insatiably devouring mix. Probably most do not understand the legacy consequences of such vitriol. It is irrational to construe that legal asylum does not have full support, but there is an ocean of difference between criminality and innocent victims of fascist dictatorships. This leads to the assumption that so many are being denied the truthful message from the Fourth Estate.

One final point of the number of criminal aliens being thrust within the prison population along with gangs and violent killers. It is not a "witch's brew." It is a crucible for pernicious elements that will boil over assuredly into the public domain threatening "Joe and Jill

Public: or their next-door neighbor. This as certain as the sun rising or setting every day! The political elite in Washington must account for their willful neglect in this regard.

It is necessary to put the naivete away, and realize change is fomented only by people sensing this fundamental "truth." Political razzmatazz is shape-shifting of the most vexing sort, but it will always be a fact of life. It is all that exists to make change, but an educated person must sense this elite form of guile, and that it is a real fact of life. Remember: lies and ignorance can be sold with a treacly smile carefully veiled as warmhearted feeling.

Some important summary thoughts:

*Violence is sorrowfully part of American life.
*Islamic Jihad is within the American social fabric.
*The country is experiencing a watershed moment: a population shift.
*The prison system is also experiencing a watershed moment: a population shift as well; along with gangs, increasing criminal elements, foreign and domestic: illegal aliens.
*As a disproportion of population size, Black African-Americans by percentage are locked up in the greatest numbers[559, 560].
*Personal observation: drugs and murder, alone or in combination, are the two most common reasons for incarceration. *Sexual involvement of female guards with prisoners increased while I was working; women prisons also experience sexual encounters (male and female);
*Murder or severe knife fighting occurs when least expected, but it is a reality that is more common with the younger prisoners.
*Guards do not carry guns. If they did, there would be an enhanced deterrent against danger and loss of life. Accept this or not, it is reality. Do not bring a knife to a gun fight. Use the firing range for what it is really for: to keep skills up to par.

*Wardens, Associate Wardens and all other employees are under pressure from the administrative bureaucracy.

*The American Prison System is a multi-billion- dollar industry with a very disproportionate amount of money spent on administrative bureaucracy, but to the misfortune of employees, especially the women who are over-worked and under-paid.

*With everything that has been adequately documented, maximum security prisons are exceedingly dangerous, but there is no political will to correct this.

*Suicide is hard to prevent and rape is overly common.

*Sentences are too long for non-violent prisoners.

*First-time youthful prisoners exhibit a nervous shock when first incarcerated.

*There is a general malaise that permeates a prison environment.

*Personal observation: prison psychiatrists are aloof and do not communicate. *Wardens and Associate Wardens are very genuine, communicate very well, and, are extremely congenial.

"Hope may be a lying jade, but she does at any rate lead us to the end of our lives along a pleasant path"[561].

SECTION 8

Afterthoughts

Epilogue: Some very important conclusions in line-by-line presentation.

Robert Allyn Goldman

EPILOGUE

Perfection is unattainable, but improvement is a legitimate cause.

Government is too big, and, it can never fairly mete out justice.

Government is, however, all we have. Our Founding Fathers grappled with each other, and the tradition continues almost ritualistically.

Prisons have attained profound cultural meaning. They reflect the most basic societal need: freedom from danger.

Prisons are important beyond any measure. If they do not want a regression into Mexican, Latin American, South American, Cuban, Russian, Chinese, Middle-Eastern, or to some degree European, hellfire misery, then the fractious construct must be immediately addressed. The United States is a wonderfully blessed country and should never reflect a derision for the human condition.

Politics is steeped into every facet of American life, and particularly into the prison system. Politics is both a need to produce productive legislation to format more reasonable sentencing guidelines and, as a viable source of oversight, to make resources available for upgrades and changes.

Education is the ticket for self-reliance. American culture should never be subservient to its Pop culture, the former being the gold standard for education and the latter its cosmetic overlay.

Parolees and Probationers will always compete for diminished opportunities because people generally are afraid to offer second opportunities where their businesses are potentially compromised. Money should be diverted to compel education for all non-violent prisoners to make their employment competitive.

Non-violent prisoners should be availed vocational choice to engage them more enthusiastically such that over time recidivism rates will diminish.

Punishment must remain a viable instrument for dealing with criminality, but during confinement keeping prisoners occupied is essential to control the continuous onsite gang violence.

Sentencing, parole boards and bureaucracies managing prisons must be reframed to be more respectful of jurisprudence. They are out of control.

Violent criminals and prison gang violence need more drastic attention. If more attention can be focused on the need to decrease non-violent criminality along with the needs to upgrade inner-city public education, a gradual decrease in violence will occur. This is not fantasy. It is fact. The problem with inner city violence stems from splintered families and lack of proper educational standards. Politicians should understand this, if nothing else.

The prison system should be protective, not a monetary exploit for financial opportunity, even and in spite of the attraction of its capitalist potential. Bureaucrats treat it as a financial opportunity, pure and simple. Monetary, bureaucratic and legal neglect feeds the growth of the prison system.

Gangs, human and drug trafficking, money laundering and trafficking, trafficking in child pornography and prostitution, unsightly murder rates, open and uncontrolled borders, gun trafficking and violence, increasing patterns of STD's and AIDS, globalization and disease transmission of previously controlled diseases (measles, German measles, etc.), and vastly increased vulnerability to radical Islamic terrorism are all prison/societal problems. This is a formidable reality.

Prison gangs control street gangs. They seed gun, human, and drug trafficking. This is now a major source of inner-city deaths. In addition, the danger it promotes spills over into the so-called "sleepy" suburban communities.

The country is flush with the impact of these problems affecting school safety and public life in general. An intelligent approach to prison reform as discussed in this book is to restore safety and improve living conditions for all people. Prison reform is a cultural need and imperative.

ENDNOTES

1. "Ode on a Grecian Urn" by John Keats, in www.poetryfoundation.
org/poem/173742.

2. Emerson, Ralph Waldo: THE SELECTED WRITNGS OF RALPH   WALDO EMERSON, 135, The Modern Library, New York, New York, United States of America, 1992.

3. Emerson, Ralph Waldo: Ibid, 133.

4. Shedd, George H. Dr.:
https://www.mainehealth.org/memorial-hospital/doctor-george-h-shedd.

5. Lapsansky-Werner, Emma J.: United States History, 1264; Prentice Hall, Upper Saddle River, New Jersey, United States of America, 2011.

6. Stennes, Elmer:
https://www.delaney/antiqueclocks.com/186.

7. Carr, Howie: The Brothers Bulger: How They Terrorized and Corrupted Boston for a Quarter Century, 342; Warner Books, Time Warner Book Group, New York, New York, United States of America, 2006.

8. Carr, Howie: Hitman: The Untold Story of Johnny Martorano: Whitey Bulger's Enforcer and the Most Feared Gangster in the Underworld, 464; Tom Doherty Associates, LLC, A Forge Book, New York, New York, United States of America, 2011.

9. O'keefe, Specs:
https://www.nytimes.com/1976/03/28/archives/specsokeefe-informant--in-brinks-robbery-dies-biggest-cash-robbery.html.

10. Levenstein, Aaron: https://www.goodreas.com/quotes/130178-statistics-arelike-bikinis-what-they-reveal-is-suggestive-but-what-they-conceal-is-vital.

11. Barrows, S.J.: The Reformatory System in the United States: Reports Prepared for the International Prison Commission, 240; Government Printing Office, Washington, D.C., United States of America, 1900.

12. Ibid., 129.

13. Johnson, Mrs. Ellen C., Late Superintendent of the Massachusetts Reformatory Prison for Women: International Penal and Penitentiary Commission;133, The Reformatory System in The
United States. Reports Prepared for The International Prison Commission, S.J. Barrows, Commissioner for the United States, 1900.

14. The Big House: https://www.imdb.com/title/tt0020686.

15. Pfaff, John F., Locked In: The True Causes of Mass Incarceration and How to Achieve Real Reform, 231; Basic Books, New York, New York, United States of America, 2017.

16. Orwell, George: Animal Farm and 1984: 385; Harcourt, Inc., Orlando, Florida, United States of America, 1945.

17. Springfield, Dusty: www.azlyrics.com/dusty springfield/wishingandhoping.html.

18. Safire, William: New Political Dictionary: The Definitive Guide to the New Language of Politics, 528; Random House, New York, New York, United States of America, 1993.

19. Hobbes, Thomas: Leviathan: Or the Matter, Forme, and Power of a Common-wealth Ecclesiastical and Civil (Rethinking the Western Tradition), edited by Ian Shapiro; Yale University Press, New Haven, Connecticut, 2010 Reprint-edition), 608.

20. Peter, Dr. Laurence I., and, Hull, Raymond: The Peter Principle: Why Things Always Go Wrong, 161; Harper Business, 2011 (Reprint Edition).

21. Hilton, James: Lost Horizon: A Novel, 272; Harper Perennial, 2012 (Reissue Edition).

22. Gottschalk, Marie: The Prison and The Gallows; The Politics of Mass Incarceration, 451; Cambridge University Press, New York, New York, United States of America, 2016.

23. Pfaff, John F.: Ibid.

24. Sherwood, Ben: The Survivors Club: The Secrets and Science that Could Save Your Life, 383; Grand Central Publishing, New York, New York, 2009.

25. Levenstein, Alan: http://www.goodreads/130178-statistics-like-bikinis-what-they-reveal-is-suggestive-but-what-they conceal-is-vital.

26. Twain, Mark: THE AUTOBIOGRAPHY OF MARK TWAIN: 508; HarperCollins, New York, New York, United States of America, 1917.

27. Bureau of Justice Statiistics.

28. United States Census, 2010: https://www.census.gov/population-breakdown.

29. Pfaff, John F.: Locked In: The true Causes of Mass Incarceration and How to Achieve Real Reform; Basic Books, 2017; 311pages, New York, New York.

30. Gottschalk, Marie, Ibid, 21.

31. Gallup Poll: https://www.news-gallup.com/2017/11/09/Congress-and-thePublic.

32. Francois, Duc de La Rochefoucauld, MAXIMS (London, England, 1959), 120.

33. file://C:/Users/Owner/Documents/2020-08(August)/--Samuel Johnson-Thurs-8-20-2020.html#852ton.

34. Hamilton, Edith: Mythology: Timeless Tales of Gods and Heroes, 75th Anniversary Illustrated Edition, 384; Black Dog & Leventhal: Deluxe, Illustrated, Anniversary edition, New York, New York, United States of America, 2017.

35. Rochefoucauld, Duc de La, MAXIMS, 100; Penguin Books, London, England, UK, 1959.

36. Amen, Daniel G., M.D.: Change your Brain, Change Your Life: The Breakthrough Program for Conquering Anxiety, Depression, Obsessiveness, Anger, and Impulsiveness, 337; Times Books, Random House, United States of America, 1998.

37. Bhattacharjee, Yudhijit: The Science of Good and Evil, 116-143, in National Geographic, Washington, D.C., United States of America; January, 2018 edition.

38. Slater, Lauren: Love: The Chemical Reaction, 32-49, in National Geographic, Washington, D.C., United States of America; February, 2006 edition.

39. Kipling, Rudyard: The Ballad of East and West, https://www.bartleby.com/246/1129.html.

40, Johnson, Ibid, 42.

41. Slater, Lauren, Ibid.

42. Slater, Lauren, Ibid.

43. Bunyan, John: Pilgrim's Progress, 384; Aneko Press, 2nd Edition, Abbotsford,
Wisconsin, United States of America, 2015.
44. Allighieri, Dante: The Divine Comedy (The Inferno, The Purgatorio, and The
Paradiso), translated by John Ciardi, 928; Berkley, 1st Edition, London, England,
UK, 2003.
45. Bhattacharjee, Yudhijit, Ibid.
46. Baron-Cohen, Simon: THE SCIENCE OF EVIL: ON EMPATHY AND THE ORIGINS OF CRUELTY, 257; Basic Books, A Member of the Perseus Book Group,
New York, New York, United States of America, 2011.
47. Amen, Daniel G., M.D., Ibid.
48. Wise, Jeff: EXTREME FEAR: THE SCIENCE OF YOUR MIND IN DANGER, 246,
Palgrave-Macmillan, New York, New York, Unite States of America, 2009.
49. Slater, Lauren, Ibid.
50. Bhattacharjee, Yudhijit, Ibid.
51. Bhattacharjee, Yudhijit, Ibid,
52. Levin, Marc "THE PRISONERS OF THE WAR ON DRUGS: Home Box Office Documentary; Release Date: January 8, 1996 in David Skarbek, THE SOCIAL ORDER OF THE UNDERWORLD: HOW PRISON GANGS GOVERN THE AMERICAN PENAL SYSTEM, 17; Oxford University Press, New York, New York, United States of America, 2014.
53. Kaminski, Marek, Games Prisoners Play: The Tragicomic Worlds of Polish Prisons. Princeton, NJ.

Princeton University Press, 2004, and, MSNBC, 2006. "Inside Kern Valley." Lockup. Airdate: July 24; both in David Skarbek, Ibid, 18.

54. Skarbek, David, Ibid 17and 18

55. Baumeister, Roy F, PhD: EVILINSIDE HUMAN VIOLENCE AND CRUELTY, 1; Holt Paperback, Henry Holt and Company, LLC, New York, New York, United States of America, 1997, 1999.

56. Baron-Cohen, Simon: THE SCIENCE OF EVIL: ON EMPATHY AND THE ORIGINS OF CRUELTY, 47; Basic Books, A Member of the Perseus Book Group, New York, New York, United States of America, 2011.

57. NYPD NEWS: https://www.nypdnews.com/ 2018/04/truth-herman-bell.

58. Boston news report: https:// www.boston.com/ sports/new/england/patriots/2018/Robert/kraft.

59. Smith, Sydney: https:// www.izquotes.com/ quote/287383.

60. Baumeister, Roy F., Ph.D., Ibid, 262-263.

61 Merriam-Webster Dictionary: https://www.merriamwebster.com/dictionary/ corruption.

62. United States Department of Justice, Office of Justice Programs, National Institute of Justice: https://www.nij.gov/topics/gunviolence/pages/ Welcome-aspx.

63. Getting MAD: Nuclear Mutual Assured Destruction: https:// www.strategicinstitutestudies. army.mil/pdf-files.

64. Morales, Gabriel C.: LA FAMILIA: THE FAMILY: PRISON GANGS IN AMERICA, 4th Edition; CreateSpace, Parker, Colorado, United States of America, 2015.

65. Merriam-Webster Dictionary: Ibid.

66. Baron-Cohen, Simon: Ibid.

67. Pfaff, John F.: LOCKED IN: THE TRUE CAUSES OF MASS INCARCERATION AND HOW TO ACIEVE REAL REFORM, 311,231; Basic Books, an imprint of Perseus Books, L.L.C.,   subsidiary of Hachette Book Group, Inc., New York, New York, United States of America, 2017.

68. Pfaff, John F.: Ibid 203.

69. Phaff, John F.: Ibid 231.

70. Beck, Aaron T., M.D.: PRISONERS OF HATE: THE COGNITIVE BASIS OF ANGER, HOSTILITY, AND VIOLENCE, 125; HarperCollins, New York, New York, United States of America, 1999.

71. Garrat, Bob: THE FISH ROTS from the HEAD: THE CRISIS in OUR BOARDROOMS: DEVELOPING the CRUCIAL SKILLS of the COPETENT DIRECTOR, 320; Profile Books; Revised, Updated Edition, London, England, United Kingdom, 2011.

72. Peter, Laurence J. and Hull, Raymond: THE PETER PRINCIPLE: WHY THINGS ALWAYS GO WRING, 161; Harper Business, New York, New York, United States of America, 1969.

73. The Blizzard of '78; www.blizzardof78.org.

74. Phaff, John F.: Ibid.

75. Skarbek, David: Ibid.

76. Alexander, Michelle: THE NEW JIM CROW: Mass Incarceration in the Age of Colorblindness, 167; The New Press, New York, New York, United States of America, 2010.

77. The National Registry of Exonerations: https://www.law.umich.edu/special/exoneration/Pages/about.aspx.

78. The National Registry of Exonerations: https://www.law.umich.edu/special/exoneration/Pages/about.aspx.

79. The National Registry of Exonerations: https://www.law.umich.edu/special/exoneration/Pages/about.aspx.

80. The National Registry of Exonerations: Ibid.

81. Morales, Gabriel C.: LA FAMILIA: THE FAMILY: PRISON GANGS IN AMERICA, 4th Edition, CreateSpace, Parker, Colorado, United States of America, 2015.

82. Morales, Gabriel C.: LA FAMILIA: THE FAMILY: PRISON GANGS IN AMERICA, 4th Edition, 2; CreateSpace, Parker, Colorado, United States of America, 2015.

83. The National Gang Center: https://www.nationalgangcenter.gov.

84. The National Gang Threat Assessment, 2011: https://www.fbi.gov/2011/national-gang-threat-assessment.

85. Census Bureau, https:// www.census.gov/2017/facts-poverty-education.

86. Census Bureau, 2017: Ibid.

87. Dillon, Sam: New York Times: https:// www.

nytimes.com/2009/04/22/education.

88. Wright, Whitney:2012: The Disparities between Urban and Suburban American Education Systems: A Comparative Analysis Using Social Closure Theory: Proceedings of the National Conference on Undergraduate Research (NCUR), Mar 29-31:1612-1619: https://www.pdfs.semanticscholar.org.

89. Pew Research Center: Millenials: Confident, Connected, Open to Change; https://www.pewsocialtrends.org/files/2010/10millenials-confident-connected-open-to-change.pdf.

90. Census Bureau, 2017: Ibid.

91. Drug Enforcement Administration: https://www.deadiversion.usdoj.gov.

92. Diversion Control Division: 2018: https://www.deadiversion.usdoj.gov.

93. Centers for disease Control, 2018: https://www.cdc.gov/2018.

94. The Trace: A Nonprofit Newsroom Covering Gun Violence in America: https://www.thetrace.org/features/gun-violence-2017.

95. U.S. Department of Justice, Office of Justice Programs, National Institute of Justice: https://www.nij.gov/topics/gun-violence/pages/welcome.aspx.

96. The Trace: A Nonprofit Newsroom Covering Gun Violence in America: Ibid.

97. The Trace: A Nonprofit Newsroom Covering Gun Violence in America: Ibid.

98. Centers for Disease Control and Prevention: https://www.cdc.gov/gun-violence.

99. Sawyer, Wendy and Wagner, Peter: https://www.prisonpolicy.org/reports/ pie2018/html.

100. U.S. Bureau of Prisons: https://bop.gov/ https://www.about/statistics-race-ethnicity-etc.

101. Voltaire: https://www.brainyquote.com/quotes/voltaire 106180, accessed May 3, 2018.

102. Census Bureau, 2017: Ibid.

103. U. S. Department of Education: https://www.ed.gov/2015/12/15/news/ press-releases/us-high-school-graduation-rate-hits-new-record-highs.

104. Federal Bureau of Investigation: https://www.fbi.gov/homicides.

105. Federal Bureau of Investigation: Ibid.

106. Uniform Crime Reporting Statistics: https://www.ucrdatatool.gov/Search/ Crime/State/Run/Crime/State/by/State/.cfm.

107. Pfaff, John F.: Ibid.

108. Baron-Cohen, Simon: Ibid.

109. Russell, Craig: Incarceration Around the World Mason, 71,72 and 74 Crest Publishers, Philadelphia, United States of America, 2007.

110. Cohen, Simon-Baron: THE SCIENCE OF EVIL: ON EMPATHY AND THE ORIGINS OF CRUELTY, 256; Basic Books, A Member of the Perseus Book Group, New York, New York, United States of America, 2011.

111. Baumeister, Roy F, Ph.D.: EVIL: INSIDE HUMAN VIOLENCE AND CRUELTY.

431, 262-263; Holt Paperbacks, Henry Holt and Company, LLC, New York, New York, United New York, United States of America, 1997 and 1999.

112. The Economist: 2017 Report on dramatic rise in Chicago killings in 2016: https://www.economist.com/2017-dramatic-rise-in-chicago-killings-in-2016.

113. Federal Bureau of Investigation: https://www/fbi.gov/2012-report-murder-forcible-rape-robbery-aggravated-assault.

114. Homicide in the U.S. Known to Law Enforcement, 2011 & 2013: https://www.bjs.gov/index-homicides-2011-2013.

115. Bureau of Justice Statistics: https://www.bjs.gov/probabtion-and-parole-inu.s.-2016-report-summary./p434over/

116. World Drug Report (United Nations), 2015: https://www.unodc.org/documents/wdr-2015/World Drug Report 2015.pdf.

117. Morales, Gabriel C.: La Familia-The Family, (no page numbers); CreateSpace, Parker, Colorado, 4th Edition, 2015.

118. Cohen, Simon-Baron: Ibid.

119. Uniform Crime Reporting Statistics: https://www.ucrdatatool.gov/Search/Crime/State/Run/Crime/State/by/State/.cfm.

120. Morales, Gabriel C.: Ibid.

121. Peter, Laurene J. and Hull, Raymond: Ibid.

122. Davies, Norman: EUROPE: A HISTORY, 1392; Oxford University Press, New York, New York, United States of America, 1996.

123. Bureau of Alcohol, Tobacco, Firearms and Explosives: ATF Homepage, 2018: https://www.atf.gov/guns-purchases.

124. Violence Policy Center: Research, Investigation, Analysis & Advocacy for a Safer America, 2018: https://www.vpc.org/regulating-the-gun-industry/ gun-trafficking.

125. The National Rifle Association, 2018: https://www.nra.gov/gun-regulations.

126. Gottschalk, Marie: THE PRISON AND THE GALLOWS: THE POLITICS OF MASS INCARCERATION, 451, 20; Cambridge University Press, New York, New York, United States of America, 2006.

127. Gottschalk, Marie: Ibid, 20.

128. Whitman, James Q.: Harsh Justice: Criminal Punishment and the Widening Divide Between America and Europe: 19, Oxford University Press, Oxford, England, UK, 2003, (as cited in Gottschalk, 2006).

129. Gottschalk, Marie: Ibid.

130. Santayana, George: https://www.brainyquote.com/quotes/george/

131. Morales, Gabriel, C.: Ibid.

132. Morales, Gabriel, C.: Ibid (page 60: counted as there are no page numbers).

133. Baron, Simon-Baron: Ibid.

134. Peale, Norman Vincent: The Power of Positive Thinking: Prentice Hall, Inc.,

1952, 1956: Touchstone, A Division of Simon & Schuster, Reprint, New York, New York, United States of America, 2015.

135. Peale, Norman Vincent: The Power of Positive Thinking: Prentice Hall, Inc.,
1952, 1956; Touchstone, A Division of Simon & Schuster, Reprint, New York,
New York, United States of America, 2015, 59.

136. Occam's Razor:
https://www.brittanica.com/topic/Occam's-razor.

137. Pro Football Hall of Fame:
https://www.profootballhof.com/players/
bill-parcels.

138. Hang 'Em High (1968):
https://www.imbd.com/title?tt0061747/fullcredits.

139. Dreisinger, Baz: INCARCERATION NATIONS: A Journey to Justice in Prisons
Around the World, 325; Other Press, New York, New York, United States of
America, 2017.

140. Alexander, Michelle: The New Jim Crow: Mass Incarceration in the Age of Colorblindness: 218; The New Press, New York, New York, United States of America, 2010

141. Alexander, Michelle: The New Jim Crow: Mass Incarceration in the Age of Colorblindness: 218; The New Press, New York, New York, United States of America, 2010.

142. Sherman, Christopher: "Cheney, Gonzales, Indicted Over Prisons"; Washington
Times, Nov. 19, 2008 (as cited in Alexander, 2010).

143. Pfaff, John F.: Ibid.

144."Pee Wee" Donald Henry Gaskins: https://en.wikipedia/wiki/Donald Henry Gaskins. Henry Gaskins.

145. Odeku, N.: https://www.wickedhorror.com/2015/06/15/horror.

146. Susan, Smith: https://en.wikipedia/wiki/Susan Smith.

147. Andrea Yates: https://en.wikipedia.org/wiki/Andrea Yates

148. Chan, M.: https://www.people.com/2016/06/20/andrea-yates-15-years-afterdrowning-five-children-in-a-texas-mental-institution.

149. Skarbek, David: THE SOCIAL ORDER OF THE UNDERWORLD: How Prison
Gangs Govern the American Penal System, 224, 161; Oxford University Press,
Oxford, England, UK, 2014.

150. Volokh, Alexander. 2011. "Prison Vouches," University of Pennsylvania, Law
Review 160(3), 790 (cited in Skarbek, David).

151. Skarbek, Ibid, 162-163

152. Lee Correctional: htps://www.greenvilleonline.com/story/story/crime/2018/04/24/lee-correctional-inmates-cause-death-south-carolina-prison-riot/547751002.

153. Lee-Correctional: https://www.greenvilleonline.com/story/news/local/south-carolina/2018/04/21/why-deaths-and-violence-continue-lee-correctional/532430002.

154. Lee-Correctional:
https://www.greenvilleonline.com/story/
news/2018/04/23/deadly-prison-killings-complete-
coverage-violence-lee-correctional/541764002.
155. Lee-Correctional:
https://www.greenvilleonline.com/story/news/
local/south-carolina-lee-correctional-employees-
charged-contraband-ring/549028002.
156. FitsNews.com:
https://www.fitsnews.com2014/01/12/south-carolina-
prison-system-blasted?
157. FitsNews.com:
https://www.fitsnews.com/2017/07/13/henry=mcmaster-
must-fire-corrections-czar.
158. Morales, Gabriel. C: Ibid.
159. Gilligan, James: VIOLENCE: REFLECTIONS ON
A NATIONAL EPIDEMIC: Vintage Books, A Division
of Random House, Inc., 306, 75-76; New York, New
York, United States of American, 1997.
160. Cohen, Simon Baron: Ibid, 47.
161. Dennett, D.: Darwin's dangerous idea. Simon and
Schuster, New York, 1995
(as cited in Baron-Cohen, THE SCIENCE OF EVIL:
ON EMPATHY AND THE
ORIGINS OF CRUELTY, 256, Basic Books, A
Member of the Perseus Book
Group, New York, New York, United States of
America, 2011).
162. Baron-Cohen: THE SCIENCE OF EVIL: ON
EMPATHY AND THE ORIGINS OF

CRUELTY, 256, 194; Basic Books, A Member of the Perseus Book Group,
New York, New York, United States of America, 2011.
163. Dukakis, Michael S.:
https://www.nytimes.com/1988/07/31/dukakis-focuses-on-reagan-ethics.html.
164. Marrella, Len: IN SEARCH OF ETHICS, Conversations with Men and Women of
Character, THIRD EDITION, Revised & Expanded, 368, 282-283; DC Press:
A Division of the Diogenes Consortium, 2009.
165. Columbia Law School: prison corruption:
https://www.law.columbia.edu/
sites/default/files/microsites/public-integrity/files/prison corruption -
cipi community contribution -.
166. Warner, Bill PHD: SHARIA: LAW FOR NON-MUSLIMS; CSPI Publishing;
Brno, Czech Republic, 2010, 5.
167. Ibid, 6.
168. Ibid, 7.
169. Ibid, 4.
170. https://www.merriamwebster.com/dictionary/culture
171. Warner, Bill PHD: SHARIA: LAW FOR NON-MUSLIMS; CSPI Publishing;
Brno, Czech Republic, 2010, 9.
172. Haney, Philip and Moore, Art: SEE SOMETHING SAY NOTHING: A HOMELAND SECURITY OFFICER EXPOSES THE GOVERNMENT'S SUBMISSION TO

JIHAD, 102; WND Books; Washington, D.C., USA; 2016.

173. Jasser, Dr. M. Zuhdi: A BATTLE FOR THE SOUL OF ISLAM; AN AMERICAN MUSLIM PATRIOT'S FIGHT TO SAVE HIS FAITH, 294; Threshold Editions, A Division of Simon & Schuster, Inc., New York, New York, United States of America, 2012.

174. https://www.nbcwashington.com/news/local/a-history-of-shootings-at-military-installations-in-the-us/1953672.

175. Barack Hussein Obama's false statements-lies: https://www.politifact.com/personalities/barack/obama/statements/by/ruling.

176. Obama's 50 Lies / Obama Not Exactly: https://www.snopes.com/fact-check/Obamas-50-lies.

177. https://www.latimes.com/local/lanow/la-me-ln-san-bernardino-shootinglive-updates-htmlstory.html

178. Trump, Donald: King of Whoppers: 100 Days of Whoppers: https://www.factcheck.org/2017/04/29/100-days-whoppers.

179. https://www.forbes.com/sites/theapothecary/2014/11/10/aca-architect-thestupidity-of-the-american-voter-led-us-to-hide-obamacares-tax-hikes-andsubsidies-from-the-public/#268430327c05

180. https://www.washingtonpost.com/opinions/marc-thiessen-thanks-to-jonathan-gruber-for-revealing-obamacare-deception/2014/11/17/story.html.

181. Jasser, Dr. M. Zuhdi, A BATTLE FOR THE SOULD of ISLAM, 294; Threshold
Editions, An Imprint of Simon & Schuster, 2012.
182. Corsi, Jerome R., Ph.D.: KILLING THE DEEP STAT: The Fight to Save President
Trump, 228; Humanix Books. West palm Beach, Florida, United States of America, 2018.
183. Geller, Pamela with Spencer, Robert, THE POST-AMERICAN PRESIDENCY: THE OBAMA ADMINISTRATION'S WAR ON AMERICA, 376; Threshold
Editions, A Division of Simon & Schuster, Inc., New York, New York, United States of America, 2010.
184. Geller, Pamela: STOP the ISLAMIZATION of AMERICA, 198; WND Books,
Washington, D.C., United States of America, 2011.
185. Scott, Janny: A SINGULAR WOMAN: The Untold Story of Barack Obama's Mother,
386; Riverhead Books, An Imprint of the Penguin Group, New York, New York, United States of America, 2011.
186. Alinsky, Saul D.: "RULES FOR RADICALS," 224; Vintage Books, An Imprint
of Knopf Doubleday Publishing Group, New York, New York, United States
of America, 1989.
187. Dodd-Frank Wall Street Reform and Consumer Protection Act: https:/www.
investopedia.com/terms/d/dodd-frank-financial-regulatory-reform-bill.asp.

188. Affordable Care Act:
https://www.healthcare.gov/glossary/affordable-care-act.

189. Bolton, John in Geller, Pamela (with Robert Spencer), THE POST-AMERICAN
PRESIDENCY: THE OBAMA ADMINISTRATION'S WAR ON AMERICA, ix;
Threshold Editions, A Division of Simon & Schuster; New York, New York,
United States of America, 2010.

190. Kipling, Rudyard: The Ballad of East and West:
https://www.Kiplingsociety.
co.uk/poems eastwest.htm.

191. Ali, Ayaan Hirst: INFIDEL, 384; Atria Books, Reprint Edition, An Imprint of
Simon & Schuster, New York, New York, United States of America, 2008.

192. Downing, Michael P.:
https://www.homeland.house.gov/files/Testimony/9620/Downing.pdf.

193. Emerson, Steve:
https://www.investigativeproject.org/1041/radicals-in-our-prisons.

194. Shapiro, Ben:
https://www.politifact.com/punditfact/statements/2014/11/05/ben-shapiro/shapiro-says-majority-muslims-are-radicals.

195. Addicott, Jeffrey F.: RADICAL ISLAM WHY? Confronting Jihad at Home &
Abroad: Lawyers & Judges Publishing Company, Inc., Tucson, AZ; 2016, 184.

196. Kirby, Stephen M., Ph.D.: The Lure of Fantasy Islam: Exposing the Myths and Myth Makers, 83: CreateSpace, Charleston, South Carolina; 2017.

197. "Obama's Address on the War in Afghanistan," New York Times: December

1, 2009;

https://www.nytimes.com/2009/12/02/world/asia/02prex y.text.html; in Geller, Pamela (with Robert Spencer): STOP the ISLAMIZATION of

AMERICA: A PRACTICAL GUIDE TO THE RESISTANCE, 208, WND Books,

Washington, D. C., United States of America, 2011.

198. McCarthy, Andrew C.: "Alinsky Does Afghanistan," National Review, December 4, 2009; Ibid, 208.

199. Geller, Pamela (with Robert Spencer): STOP the ISLAMIZATION of AMERICA:

A PRACTICAL GUIDE TO THE RESISTANCE, 208: WND Books, Wahington,

D.C., United States of America, 2011.

200. Time.com/weather-undergound-ayers-and-dohrn: https://www.time.

com/4549409/the-weather-underground-bad-moon-rising.

201. PewForum.org/barack-obama-reverend-jeremiah-wright-united-church-of

Christ-Chicago:

https://www.pewforum.org/2008/11/04/religion-and-politics-08-barack-obama.

202. Geller, Pamela (with Robert Spencer): STOP the ISLAMIZATION of AMERICA:

A PRACTICAL GUIDE: TO THE RESISTANCE, 151-163: WND Books, Washington, D.C., United States of American, 2011.

203. The Qur'an, 464: Translated by M.A.S. Abdel Haleem: Oxford University

Press, New York, New York, United States of America, 2004, 2005, 2011 & 2015.

204. Warner, Bill PHD: SHARIA LAW FOR NON-MUSLIMSs, 27: Center for The

Study of Political Islam (CSPI), LLC; Nashville, TN, 2010.

205. Davies, Norman: EUROPE: A HISTORY, 1365; Oxford University Press, Oxford, England, Uk, 1996.

206. New York Post: Emerson, Steve:
https://www.nypost.com/2009/5/23/
radicals-in-our-prisons.

207. https://www.drugfree.org.au/images/pdf-files/library/soros/2019/OrganizationsFundedDirectlyby GeorgeSoroshisOpenSocietyInstitute2015.pdf

208. https://www.citizensjournal.us/sign-up-for-twice-weekly-headlines-in-youinbox/

209. Congress.gov: Prison Reform and Redemption Act: 09/06/2017:
https://www.congress.govbill/115thcongress/house-bill/3356.

210. Britannica: 2nd Persian Gulf War:
https://www.britannica.com/print/article/880815.

211. George W. Bush on USS Abraham Lincoln:
https://en.wikipedia.org/wiki/
Mission Accomplished speech.

212. George Bush Lies: https://www.vox.com/2016/7/9/12123022/george-w-bushlies-iraq-war.

213. George Bush Does Not Lie: https://www.townhall.com/columnists/johnhawkins/2016/02/21/show-this-column-to-anyone-who-claims-to-anyonewho-claims-bush-lied about-winds-in-Iraq.

214. Weiss, Murray: THE MAN WHO WARNED AMERICA: THE LIFE AND DEATH OF JOHN O'NEILL, THE FBI'S EMBATTLED COUNTER TERROR WARRIOR, 450; Regan Books, an Imprint of HarperCollins Inc., New York, New York, United States of America, 2003.

215. Geller, Pamela (with Robert Spencer): Ibid, 182.

216. Jewishmag.com/dhimmis-christians-and-jews-living-in-Islamic-conqueredLands-2002: https://www.jewishmag.com/57mag/dhimmi/dhimmi.html.

217.https://www.cnn.com/interactive/2017/02/us/somali-minnesota-photos.

218.https://www.adl.org/sites/default/files/documents/assets/pdf/combating-hate/Post-911-Islamic-Extremism-in-the-US.pdf

219. https://www.pewresearch.org/fact-tank/2017/08/09/muslims-and-islamkey-findings-in-the-u-s-and-around-the-world/

220. World Trade Center Bombing, February 26, 1993: https://www.history.com/this-day-in-history/world-trade-center-bombed.

221. Spencer, Robert: The COMPLETE INFIDEL'S GUIDE to the KORAN: REGNERY

PUBLISHING, INC., an Eagle Publishing Company, Washington, D.C., the
United States of America, 2009, 21.
222. Geller, Pamela (with Robert Spencer): Ibid.
223. Kirby, Stephen M.: Ibid.
224. Balko, Radley and Carrington, Tucker: THE CADAVER KING AND THE COUNTRY DENTIST, 391; Public Affairs of the Hachette Book Group, 2018.
225. Alexander, Michelle: THE NEW JIM CROW: MASS INCARCERATION IN THE
AGE OF COLORBLINDNESS, 290; The New Press, New York, New York,
United States of America, 2010.
226. WARNER, BILL, PHD: SHARIA: LAW FOR NON-MUSLIMS, 47; CENTER
FOR THE STUDY OF POLITICAL ISLAM, LLC, Nashville, Tennessee,
United States of America, 2010.
227. Kirby, Stephen M., Ph.D.: Ibid.
228. Baron-Cohen, Simon: THE SCIENCE OF EVIL: ON EMPATHY AND THE
ORIGINS OF CRUELTY, 256, 158; Basic Books, A Member of the Perseus Books group, New York, New York, United States of America, 2012.
229. Ball, W. David: Why State Prisons: Yale Law & Policy Review, Volume 33,
Issue 1, Article 3, 2014:
https://www.digitalcommonslaw.yale.edu/ylpr.
230. Ball, W. David: Why State Prisons: Yale Law & Policy Review, Volume 33, Issue 1, Article3:2014;
https://www.digitalcommons.law.yale.edu/ylpr.

231. Congress.gov/congress-house-ill:
https://www.congress.gov/bill/115th-congress/house-bill/3356.

232. Kushner, Jared:
https://www.wsj.com/2018/10/25/jared-kushner-trump's-forgotten-men-and-women-include-prisoners.

233. Morales, Gabriel C.: LA FAMILIA-THE FAMILY: PRISOM GANGS IN AMERICA (no page numbers); CreateSpace, Parker, Colorado, 2015.

234. Aljazeera.com archives:
https://www.aljazeera.com/archive/2005/06/23/2008.html.

235. Shapiro, Ben: Ibid.

236. Blog: paradox: irresistible versus immovable:
https://www.sutherlandcareers.com/blog/paradox-puzzle.

237. https://www.saudiembassy.net/about/country-information/Islam/understanding Isalm.aspx in Kirby, Stephen M., Ph.D.: ISLAM AND BARACK HUSSEIN OBAMA: A HANDBOOK ON ISLAM, CreateSpace, Charleston, South Carolina, 2010.

238. Kirby, Stephen M., Ibid, i.

239. WARNER, BILL: Ibid.

240. Kirby, Stephen M., Ph.D.: Ibid.

241. Jasser, Dr. M. Zuhdi: Ibid.

242. Obama: Weaponization of Government:
https://www.forbs.com.thomasbasile/2014/01/31/obamas-weponization-of-government/#69fec92b1b92.

243. Obama: Over-regulation of the EPA:
https://www.america.aljazeera.com/articles/2014/2/23/e

pa-s-carbon-regulation-rules-come-under-supreme-courtscrutiny.html.

244. Obama: IRS Targeting: https://www.washingtonpost.com/business/economy/ire -admits-targeting-conservatives-for-tax-scrutiny-in-2012.

245. Benghazi Timeline: https://www.factcheck.org/2012/10/26/benghazi-timeline.

246. Ft. Hood Shooting: https://en.wikipedia.org/wiki/2009 Fort Hood shooting;

247. https://www.latimes.com/nation/nationnow/la-nn-fort-hood-shooterislamic-state-death-row-2014; story.html.

248. San Bernadino Terror Attack: https://latimes.com/local/california/ la-me-san-bernadino-shooting-terror-investigation-htmlstory.html.

249. Ft. Hood Labeling: https://www.nytimes.com/2014/04/09/us/at-fort-hoodwrestling-with-label-of-terrorism.html.

250.https://www.nobelprize.org/prizes/peace/2009/press -release. Nobel Prize: Obama:

251.https://www.nobelprize.org/nobel prizes peace/ Laureates/2009/press.html.

252. Nobel Prize: Obama: Outgoing Nobel Secretary Has Regrets: https://www. bbc.com/news/world-europe-34277960.

253.https://www.nytimes.com/2020/08/19/us/politics/ob ama-speech.html

254. HANNITY, SEAN: LIVE FREE OR DIE: AMERICA (AND THE WORLD)
ON THE BRINK; VIVAMUS LIBERI NE AMERICA PEREAT; 55; Threshold
Editions, An Imprint of Simon & Schuster, New York, New York, 2020.

255. Solzhenitsyn, Aleksandr I.: THE GULAG ARCHIPELAGO, 1918-1956: AN EXPERIMENT IN LITERARY INVESTIGATION, 660; Harper & Row, Publishers, New York, New York, United States of America, 1973.

256. Harris, Sheldon H.: FACTORIES OF DEATH: JAPANESE BIOLOGICAL WARFARE, 1932-45, AND THE AMERICAN COVER-UP, 297; Routledge, London, England, UK, 1994.

257. Davis, Robert S.: GHOSTS AND SHADOWS OF ANDERSONVILLE: ESSAYS
ON THE SECRET SOCIAL HISTORIES OF AMERICA'S DEADLIEST PRISON,
310, Mercer University Press, Georgia, United States of America, 2006.

258. Investigative Project: Prison radicalization in Belgium:
https://www.investigativeproject.org/7471/Belgium-terror-attacks-mirrors-an-all-too-familiarpattern.

259. Investigative Project: U.S. Imam advocates violence:
https://www.investigativereport.org/2018/04/20/7409/ipt-exclusive-us-based-imam-advocates-violence.

260. Investigative Project: American Islamist celebrate antisemitism:

https://www.investiagtivereport.org/7455/american-islamists-celebrate-an-avowed-anti-Semite.

261. Geller, Pamela (with Robert Spencer): Ibid, 212-213.

262. https://www.wsj.com/articles/obamas-red-line-debacle-from-the-inside-1528497718

263. https://www.nola.com/opinions/article 3635.html

264, Forbes.com:
https://www.forbes.com/sites/peterferrara/2012/10/25/Benghazi-obama-actions-amount-to-a-shameful-dereliction-of-duty.

265. https://thebestofafrica.org/content/libya-the-obama-administration-and-the-muslim-brotherhood-part-2.

266.https://www.cato.org/publications/commentary/obama-administration-wrecked-libya-generation.

267.https://www.cruz.senate.gov/news-2219

268. https://thehill.com/opinion/white-house/477666-obama-should-apologizefor-shameful-cash-payment-to-iran

269. WARNER, BILL, PHD: Ibid.

270. The Qur'an, Chapter 5, Verse 69 cited in Jasser, Dr. M. Zuhdi Jasser: A Battle
For the Soul of Islam: An American Muslim Patriot's Fight to Save His Faith, 262:
Threshold Editions, A Division of Simon & Schuster, Inc., New York, New York, 2012.

271. Jasser, Dr. M. Judhi:Ibid, 129-131, and, 177.

272. Wahhabism: The Extreme of Islam as practiced in Saudi Arabia: https://
www.pbs.org/wgbh/pages/frontline/shows/saudi/analyses/wahhabism.html.

273. Wahhabism: What is it: https://www.telegraph.co.uk/2016/03/29/what-iswahabbism-the-reactionary-branch-of-islam-said-to-be-the/.

274. The Koran 9:29 cited in Warner, Bill PHD: Ibid, 21.

275. The QUR'AN, 118: A new translation by M.A.S. Abdel Haleem: Oxford University Press, Inc., New York, New York; 2015.

276. The Koran33:60 cited in Warner, Bill PHD: Ibid, 20.

277. The QUR'AN 33: 60,61 & 62; Ibid, 271.

278. Corsi, Jerome R., Ph.D.: Ibid.

279. Geller, Pamela (with Robert Spencer): Ibid.

280. Drago and Galbiati (Chapter 7, page 166, 2011) in Skarbek, David: THE SOCIAL ORDER OF THE UNDERWORLD: How Prison Gangs Govern the American Penal System, 224: Oxford University Press; New York, New York, 2014.

281. Skarbek, David: THE SOCIAL ORDER OF THE UNDERWORLD: How Prison Gangs Govern the American Penal System, 166, 224: Oxford University Press: New York New York, 2014.

282. Shaw, George Bernard: https://www.shawquotations.blogspot.com/2017/06/if-prison-does-not-underbid-slum-in.html.

283. Hugo, Victor: https://www.brainyquote.com/quote/Victor Hugo 104893.

284. O'Rourke, P.J.:
https://www.brainyquote.com/quotes/p j O'Rourke
105432.

285. Marrella, Len: IN SEARCH OF ETHICS:
Conversations with Men and Women
of Character, 368, 284-285; DC PRESS, A Division of
Diogenes Consortium, Third Edition.

286.http://www.cnn.com/2009/CRIME/12/25/richard.rei
d.shoe.bomber/index.html.

287.https://www.csmonitor.com/USA/Justice/2009/122
8/Echoes-of-2001-shoebomber-in-Detroit-attack

288. https://foreignpolicy.com/2020/01/15/radical-
islamists-are-still-a-threat-behind-bars.

289. https://ctc.usma.edu/the-danger-of-prison-
radicalization-in-the-west/

290.https://www.ncjrs.gov/pdffiles1/nij/grants/220957.p
df.

291. https://qz.com/1419802/which-state-is-most-prone-
to-corruption-heres-aranking/

292. https://en.wikipedia.org/wiki/List of American
state and local politicians convicted of crimes

293. Jeffrey Goldberg in the New York Times:
https://www.nytimes.com/2000/06/25/magazine/inside-
jihad-u-yhe-education-of-a-holy-warrior.html.

294. Weiss, Murray: THE MAN WHO WARNED
AMERICA; The Life and Death of
(Feb. 6, 1952) of John O'Neill (Sept. 11, 2001), The
FBI's Embattled Counterterror
Warrior, 450: Regan Books, An Imprint of Harper
Collins Publishers; New York, New York, USA, 2003.

295. Butt, Yousaf:

https://www.huffingtonpost.com/dr-yousaf-butt/saudi-Wahhabismislamterrorism6501916.html.

296. Wahhabism:
https://www.pbs.org/wgbh/pages/frontline/shows/saudi/analyses/madrassas.html.

297. https://www.fbi.gov/history/famous-cases/uss-cole-bombing

298. Weiss, Murray: THE MAN WHO WARNED AMERICA; The Life and Death of
(Feb. 6, 1952) of John O'Neill (Sept. 11, 2001), The FBI's Embattled Counterterror Warrior, 398: Regan Books, An Imprint of Harper Collins Publishers; New York, New York, USA, 2003.

299. https://quoteinvestigator.com/2017/08/19/resentment.

300. Dhume, Sadanandi:
https://www.wsj.com/2018/06/01/fear-of-Islam-leadsindia-to-snub-refugees.

301. Dhume, Sadanandi:
https://www.wsj.com/2018/06/15/pakistan's-pashtunstake-on-army---and---terrorists.

302. https://www.lawfareblog.com/americas-terrorism-problem-doesnt-endprison%E2%80%94it-might-just-begin-there

303. https://www.jstor.org/stable/40210232?seq=1

304. Wilde, Oscar:
https://www.brainyquote.com/quotes/Oscar Wilde 130045.

305. https://www.npr.org/2020/02/24/805258433/harvey-weinstein-foundguilty-of-rape-but-acquitted-of-most-sexual-assault-charge.

306.https://www.latimes.com/california/story/2020-08-21/lori-loughlin-mossimo-giannulli-college-admissions-scandal-sentencing

307. https://www.nj.com/opinion/2017/11/the bob Menendez case a double standard for dems.html

308. Bureau of Justice: https://www.bjs.gov/Index.cfm?ty=tp&tid=2214, and, https://www.bjs.gov/index.cfm?ty=pbdetail&iid=1572.

309. Bureau of Prisons: https://www.bop.gov/about/statistics/statistics inmate/sentences.jsp.

310. https://www.prisonpolicy.org/

311. Prison Policy Initiative: https://www.prisonpolicy.org/2018/03/14/mass-incarceration-the-whole-pie-2018/peter-wagner-and-wendy-sawyer.

312. Alexander, Michele: The New Jim Crow: Mass Incarceration in the Age of Colorblindness, 290, 86; The New Press, New York, New York, United States of America; 2010.

313. Alexander, Michelle: Ibid, 98.

314. Mencken, H.L. (Henry Louis): September 19, 1926, Chicago Daily News; quoted in http://www.thisdayinquotes.com/2011/09/no-one-ever-went-broke-underestimating.html.

315. Mencken, H.L.: MENCKEN: THE AMERICAN ICONOCLAST: THE LIFE and
TIMES of the BAD BOY of BALTIMORE, 662;
Oxford University Press, New
York, New York, United States of America, 2005.

316. Alexander, Michelle: Ibid, throughout book.

317. Bureau of Prisons Statistics: https://www.bop.gov/statistics/stistics/inmate/offenses.jsp.

318. Bureau of Justice Statistics: https://www.bjs.gov/content/reentry/releases.cfm. **319.** Reisig, Michael; Bales, William D.; Carter, Hay; and, Wang, Xia: https://www.doi.org/the-effect-of-racial-inequality-on-black-male-recidivism.

320. Employment Statistics: https://www.bls.gov/web/empsit/cesprog/employment-statistics.html.

321. Unemployment Rates for Black African-Americans, Hispanics and Whites: https://www.npr.org/2018/01/08/6552028/fact-check-trump-touts-low-unemployment-rates-for-african-americans-hispanics-whites.

322. Thomas P. O'Neill II: https://www.brainyquote.com/quotes/thomas p oneill-212119.

323. Thomas P. O'Neill II: https://www.nytimes.com/1994/01/06/obituaries/thomas-p-oneill-jr-dies-at-81-a-power-in-the-house-for-decades.html.

324. https://www.brennancenter.org/our-work/analysis-opinion/how-first-stepact-became-law-and-what-happens-next

325. Sentencing rates by states: https://www.bjs.gov/sentencing-states-byrace=1572.

326. Music Match: https://www.com/lyrics/Mitzi-Gaynor/Cockeyed-Optimist-South-Pacific.

327. Jimmy Stewart Goes to Washington:
https://www.imdb.com/titles/jimmy-stewart-goes-to -
wahington-tt0031679.

328. George Santayana:
https://www.brainyquote.com/quotes/george/ santayana
101521.

329. Marrella, Len: IN SEARCH OF ETHICS: THIRD
EDITION, REVISED & EXPANDED: Conversations
with Men and Women of Character; DC Press, A
Division of the Diogenes Consortium; Sanford. Florida,
2009; 368, 271.

330. Barrows, S. J.: THE REFORMATORY SYSTEM
IN THE UNITED STATES: REPORTS, 240, THE
INTERNATIONAL PRISON COMMISION,
Washington,
D.C., United States of America, 1900.

331. Gottschalk, Marie: THE PRISON AND THE
GALLOWS: THE POLITICS OF
MASS INCARCERATION IN AMERICA, 451, 257;
Cambridge University Press,
New York, New York, United States of America, 2006.

332. Serial Killers: https://www.thisisinsider.com/serial-
killers-from-every-statein-america-2015-5.

333. Smith, Clint:
https://www.brainyquote.com/quotes/clint smith 893473

334. Blake, William:
https://www.brainyquote.com/quotes/william/blake
165313

335. Roosevelt, Theodore: https://www
works.goodreads.com/quotes/tag/
senate

336. Shakespeare: The Complete Works; edited by G.B. Harrison, 1948,
1952; 1668; New York, New York, United States of America; The Tragedy of
Othello, The Moor of Venice, 1059.

337. Ellis, Joseph J.: Founding Brothers: The Revolutionary Generation, 2000, 288; New
York, New York, United States of America; Chapter One: The Duel, 20.

338. Pfaff, John F.: Locked In: THE TRUE CAUSES OF MASS INCARCERATION
AND HOW TO ACHIEVE REAL REFORM, Basic Books, an imprint of
Perseus Books, 2017, 311; New York, New York, United States of America.

339. Alexander, Michelle: The New Jim Crow: Mass Incarceration in the Age of Colorblindness, The New Press,2010, 290; New York, New York, United States of
America.

340. Ibid, 211.

341. Boll Weevil: http://en.wikipwedia.org/wiki/boll weevil (politics)

342. Hornblower, Margot; Reid, T.R.; and, the Washington Post Staff Writers:
https://www.washingtonpost.com/archive/politics/1981/04/26/after-twodecades-the-boll-weevils-are back-and-whistling-dixie...

343. The South and Reconstruction:
https:/www.courses.lumenlearning.com/

boundless-us history/chapter/the-south-after
reconstruction

344. Plessy v. Ferguson: 1896:
https://en.wikipedia.org/plessy v. ferguson

345. Brown v. Board of Education:
https://www.ourdocuments.gov/87

346. Civil Rights Act of 1964:
https://en.wikipedia.org/wiki/civil rights act
1964

347. Voting Rights Act of 1965:
https://www.history.com/black-history/votingrights-act-
1965

348. Courtney, Leonard H. (later Lord Courtney):
https://www.phrases.org.uk/
meanings/lies-damned-lies-and-statistics.html

349. Census.gov: https://www.census.gov/2010/black-
population-prison-statistics.

350. Levenstein, Aaron:
https://www.quotes.net/quotes/15160

351. Bureau of Justice Statistics:
https://www.bjs.gov/racial-prison-statistics.

352. https://www.bop.gov/about/statistics/statistics
inmate offenses.jsp

353. https://www.prisonpoicy.org/graphs/cjrace death
executions.html

354. https://www.doj.gov/statistics/statistics/violent-
crime

355. Pfaff, John, Ibid, Chapter 4.

356. Pfaff, John, Ibid, 143.

357. Ball, W. David: Why States Prisons:
https://www.digitalcommons.law.yale.

edu/ylpr/vol33/iss1/3.

358. Ball, W. David: Why States Prisons: https://www.digitalcommons.law.yale. edu/ylpr/vol33/iss1/3.

359. Ball, W. David: Ibid, 109-116

360. Ball, W. David: Ibid, 117

361. O'Neill, Thomas P. II: https://www.brainyquote.com/thomasponeill 212119

362. Days of Our Lives, Soap Opera: https://www.popcultureaddictlifeguide. blogspot.com/2011/09/like-sands-through-hourglass-so-are.html.

363. Davies, Norman: EUROPE: A HISTORY, 1392; Oxford University Press, New
York, New York, United States of America, 1996.

364. Baron-Cohen, Baron: THE SCIENCE OF EVIL: ON EMPATHY AND THE ORIGINS OF CRUELTY, 256, 185-188; Basic Books, A Member of the Perseus Book
Group, New York, New York, United States of America, 2011.

365. Robert Stroud, "the Bird Man of Alcatraz": https://en.wikipedia.org/Robert Stroud.

366. Caryl Whittier Chessman: https://en.wikipedia.org/Caryl Chessman.

367. Tower 0f Babel: https://www.britannica.com/print/article/47421.

368. Peter, Laurence J. and Hull, Raymond: THE PETER PRINCIPLE: Why Things

Always Go Wrong, 161; 25,27, Harper Business, an imprint of HarperCollins Publisher, 1969.

369. Skarbek, David: THE SOCAIL ORDER OF THE UNDERWORLD: How Prison
Gangs Govern the American Penal System, 224; 166; Oxford University Press,
New York, New York, United States of America, 2014.

370. O'Neill, Thomas P. II: Ibid.

371. Einstein, Albert:
https://www.wiseoldsayings.com/corruption-quotes/page-2.

372. Byrnes, James F.: https://www.just-one-lines.com/ppl/james-f-byrnes.

373. Oxymoron: https://www.just-one-liners.com/misc/oxymoron.

374. Adams, Cecil:
https://www.straightdope.com/columns/read/2577/was-boston-once-literally-flooed-with-molasses.

375. Turow, Scott: One L: The Turbulent True Story of a First Year at Harvard Law
School; 2010, 304; Penguin Books, reprint Edition; New York, New York,
United States of America.

376. Turow, Scott:
https://www.goodreads.com/quotes/8282.

377. Peter, Lawrence J. and Hull, Raymond: The Peter Principle: Why Things Always
Go Wrong; 1998, 161; William Morrow, an Imprint of HarperCollins Publishers; New York, New York,
United States of America.

378. Federal Bureau of Justice Statistics: https://www.bjs.gov/content/pub/pdf/ spe01.pdf.

379. Vera.org: https://www.vera.org/publications/price-of-prisons-2015-statespending-trends/price-of-prisons-2015-state-spending-trends/price-of-prisons-2015-state...; page 4.

380. Prison Policy Initiative: https://www.prisonpolicy.org/reports/pie.html.

381. Mumford, Megan; Schanzenbach, Diane Whitmore; and, Nunn, Ryan: The Hamilton Project: THE ECONOMICS OF PRIVATE PRISONS: https://www. brookings.edu/wp-content/uplands/2016/10/es 20161021 private prisons economics.pdf.

382. Ibid, 5.

383. Federal Bureau of Prisons: https://www.bop.gov.

384. Pfaff, John F.: LOCKED IN: THE TRUE CAUSES OF MASS INCARCERATION AND HOW TO ACHIEVE REAL REFORM; 2017, 311; Basic Books, an imprint of Perseus Books, LLC, New York, New York, United States of America, 21-105.

385. H.R. 3356-Prison Reform and Redemption Act: https://www.congress.gov /115th-congress/house-bill/3356.

386. The New York Times: https://www.nytimes.com/2004/08/19/nyregion/major-donor-admits-hiring-prostitute-to-smear-witness. html.

387. Charles Kushner:
https://en.wikipedia.org/wiki/Charles Kushner.

388. H.R. 3356: Ibid.

389. https://www.brennancenter.org/our-work/analysis-opinion/how-first-stepact-became-law-and-what-happens-next

390. https://www.aclu.org/issues/criminal-law-reform/drug-law-reform/
fair-sentencing-act

391.https://www.independent.co.uk/news/world/america
s/us-election/jonponder-hope-for-prisoners-bank-robber-donald-trump-rnc-a9688731.html

392. https://www.vox.com/policy-and-politics/2016/11/23/13731448/obama-pardon-clemency-commutation

393. https://www.ncjrs.gov/txtfiles/billfs.txt

394. https://www.factcheck.org/2019/07/biden-on-the-1994-crime-bill/

395. https://www.scott.senate.gov/media-center/press-releases/tim-scott-leadscolleagues-in-asking-treasury-to-provide-relief-for-opportunity-zones-inthe-wake-of-covid-192.

396. https://www.natlawreview.com/article/senator-tim-scott-considers-bill-to-modify-opportunity-zones-3

397.https://quoteinvestigator.com/2015/08/28/fish/4

398.. https://smartasset.com/taxes/heres-how-the-trump-tax-plan-could-affect-you-5

399. https://www.goodreads.com/quotes/4650-truth-is-stranger-than-fiction-but-it-is-because-fiction

400. Shakespeare, William: Much Ado About Nothing: https://www.shakespeare.org.uk/explore-shakespeare/shakesedia/shakespeares-plays/much-ado-about-nothing.

401. Sandburg, Carl: quote: https://www.goodreads.com/quotes/918291-if -the-facts-are-against-you-argue-the law-if...

402. Johnson, Mrs. Ellen C., Late Superintendent of the Massachusetts Reformatory Prison for Women: INTERNATIONAL PENAL AND PENITENTIARY COMMISSION; 240, 130, THE REFORMATORY SYSTEM IN THE
UNITED STATES. REPORTS PREPARED for THE INTERNATIONAL
PRISON COMMISSION, S.J. Barrows, Commissioner for the United States,
1900.

403. Center for the Advancement of Public Integrity at Columbia School of Law:
Prison Corruption: The Problem and Some Potential Solutions: https://www.law.
columbia.edu/.../prison corruption - capi community contribution.

404. Scott, Rick: Governor of Florida:New Times of Broward and Palm Beach,
Florida Counties;
https://www.browardpalmbeach.com/news/owner-of-greyhound-adoption-agency-details-abuses-of -dogs-at-palm-beachkennel-club-9679146

405. Kabuki Theater:
https://www.britannica.com/art/Kabuki.

406. https://en.wikipedia.org/wiki/List of American state and local
politicians convicted of crimes

407. Sowell, Thomas: WEALTH, POVERTY AND POLITICS: AN INTERNATIONAL PERSPECTIVE, 328,240; Basic Books, A Member of the Perseus Books Group,
New York, New York, United States of America, 2015.

408. DuBois, W.E.B.: https://www.azquotes.com/quote/543635, accessed July 19, 8 409 Douglass, Frederick:

409.https://www.aquotes.com/quote/683 accessed July 19, 2018.

410. Marx, Groucho: https://www.brainyquote.com/quotes/groucho marx 146422, accessed July 19, 2018.

411. Mencken, H.L.: https://www.brainyquote.com/quotes/h.l.mencken 105483, accessed July 19, 2018.

412. Sheinwald, Alan: https://www.goodreads.com/quotes/904896-rich-or-poorit-s-nice-to-have-money.

413. Baron-Cohen, Simon: THE SCIENCE OF EVIL: ON EMPATHY AND THE ORIGINS OF CRUELTY, 257, 170-174; Basic Books, A Member of the Perseus Books
Group, New York, New York, United States of America, 2011.

414. Ibid, 47.

415. Lochner, Lance and Moretti, Enrico: The Effect of Education on Education:

Evidence from Prison Inmates, Arrests, and Self-Reports, 53: https://files.eric. ed.gov/full/text/ED463346.pdf; December, 2001.

416. Lochner, Lance and Moretti, Enrico: The Effect of Education on Crime: Evidence from Prison Inmates, Arrests, and Self Reports, 51: https://eml.berkely.edu/-moretti/lm46.pdf, October, 2003.

417. Ibid: 51.

418. Educational attainment: Caroline Wolf Harrow at Bureau of Justice
Statistics: https://www.bjs.pgov/caroline-wolf-harrow-compares-educational-attainment-of-state-&-federal-prisoners-to-normal-population/index.

419. Poverty: 2015 and 2016: prepared by Bishaw. Alemayehu and Benson, Craig: http://www.census.gov/content/dam/Census/library/publications/2017/acs/acsbr/16-01.pdf.

420. U.S. Poverty Statistics for 2017: https://www.federalsafetynet.com/us-poverty-statistics.html.

421. List of U.S. cities with large African-American populations: https://en.wikipedia.org/List of U.S. cities with large African-American populations.

422. African-American population facts (2010): https://www.census.gov/Quick/facts/fact/table/US/RH1225217.

423. African-American population facts (2010) https://www.census.gov/black-population-2010.pdf.

424. Voltaire: Candide, 122; Digireads.com, a subsidiary of Neeland Media Digireads Media, LLC, Overland Park, Kansas, 2016.

425. Kurtzleben, Danielle: FACT CHECK: Trump Touts Low Unemployment Rates
For African American, Hispanics: https://www.npr.org/2018/01/08/576552028/factcheck-trump-touts-low-unemployment-rates-for-african-americans-hispanics.

426. Bureau of Labor Statistics: http://bls.gov/news.release/pdf/empsit.pdf.

427 Sherwood, Ben: The Survivors Club: The Secrets and Science that Could Save your
Life, 383, 224-227; Grand Central Publishing, a division of Hachette Book
Group, Inc., New York, New York, United States of America, 2009.

428. https://www.prisonpolicy.org/reports/pie.html.

429. Prison Policy Initiative: The Whole Pie 2018: https://www.prisonpolicy.org/reports/pie2018.html.

430. RealClearPolitics://www.realclearpolitics.com/eolls/other/congressional job approval-903.html.

431. The Atlantic: http:/www.theatlantic.com/business/archive/2012/12/the least-trusted-jobs-in-america-congress-members-and-car-salespeople/265943

432. Shaw, George Bernard (1856-1950): THE CRIME OF IMPRISONMENT, Illustrated by William Gropper, 125, 117-118; Greenwood Press, Publishers, Westport, Connecticut, United States of America, 1969.

433. Peale, Norman Vincent: The POWER of POSITIVE THINKING, 219, 87; Touchstone, a Division of Simon & Schuster, Inc., New York, New York, United
States of America, 2015.

434. Twain, Mark: PUDD'NHEAD WILSON in The Family MARK TWAIN: 1462, 909;
Barnes & Noble Books, New York, New York, United States of America, 1992.

435. Kurtzman, Daniel, writing in thoughtco.com: Dan Quayle faux pas; in:
https://www.thoughtco.com/dan-quayle-quotes-2733512.

436. Professor Irwin Corey:
https://en.wikipedia.org/wiki/Irwin Corey.

437. Shaw, George Bernard: Ibid, 6.

438. Karr, Jean-Baptiste Alphonse:
https://en.wikipedia.org/wiki/Jean-Baptiste Alphonse Karr: translated: "plus ca change, plus c'est la meme chose."

439. The Vera Institute:
https://www.vera.org/newsroom/new-vera-reportthe-price-of-prisons-what-Incarceration-cost-taxpayers.

440. The Brookings Institute:
https://www.brookings.edu/.../more-prisoners-versus-More-crime-is-the-wrong-question...19.

441. The Bureau of Justice Statistics:
https://www.bjs.gov/state-prison-expenditures-2001-statistics.

442. Kiehl, Kent A, PhD.: PSYCHOPATH WHISPERER: THE SCIENCE OF

THOSE WITHOUT CONSCIENCE; Broadway Books, 2014.

443. Bhattacharjee, Yudhijit: National Geographic: The Science of Good and Evil:
What makes people especially giving or cruel? Researchers say the way our brains
are wired can affect how much empathy we feel for others; 144; 131-132; Washington,
D.C., January, 2018.

444. Recidivism Special report from U.S. Department of Justice: Recidivism of
Prisoners Released in 30 States in 2005: Patterns from 2005-2010: https://www.bjs.

445. Boudin, Kathy: https://en.wikipedia.org/wiki/Kathy Boudin.

446. Smart, Pamela:
https://en.wikipedia.org/wiki/Pamela Smart

447. Boudin, Kathy and Smart, Pamela served at Bedford Hills Correctional
Facility for Women; Bedford Hills, New York: https://en.wikipedia.org/
wiki/ Bedford Hills Correctional Facility for women.

448. Boudin, Kathy: Co-Director and Co-Founder, Center for Justice; Director of
the Criminal justice Initiative; Adjunct Lecturer, School of Social Work-Columbia University;
http://centerforjustice.columbia.edy/about/staff.

449. Mental Health Daily:
https://www.mentalhealthdaily.com/2015/02/18/ at-what-age-is-the-brain-fully-developed.

450. Boudin, Kathy and Smart, Pamela: Bedford Hills Correctional Facility for
Women: Ibid.

451. New York State Parole Board:
https://www.doccs.ny.gov/ParoleBoard.html.

452. Example of Parole Board Neglect:
fttps://www.washingtonpost.com/national/the-power-and-politics-of-parole-boards/2015/07/1049

453. Ball, W. David: Why State Prisons, 117; Yale Law & Policy Review: Iss.
1, Article 3; 2014; Available at:
https://www.digitalcommons.law.yale.edu/
ylpr/vol 33: Iss. 1, Article 3.

454. Ball, W. David: Ibid, 109-113.

455. Maslow's Hierarchy of Needs:
https://www.simplypsychology.org/maslow.
html.

456. https://poets.org/poem/world-too-much-us

457. Shaw, George Bernard: Ibid, 125.

458. Berra, Yogi: THE YOGI BOOK: I Really Didn't Say Everything I Said: 127,48:
Workman Publishing, L.T.D. Enterprises; New York, New York, United States of America, 1998.

459. Berra, Yogi: Ibid, 48.

460. Peter, Laurence J. and Hull, Raymond: THE PETER PRINCIPLE: Why Yhings
Always Go Wrong, 161; Harper Business; New York, New York, United States of America; 1969.

461. Davis, Robert S.: GHOSTS AND SHADOWS OF ANDERSONVILLE: ESSAYS

ON THE SECRET SOCIAL HISTORIES OF AMERICA'S DEADLIEST PRISON; 310, XV111-X1X; Mercer University Press; Macon, Georgia, United States of America, 1954.

462. Alexander, Michelle: THE NEW JIM CROW: Mass Incarceration in the Age of Colorblindness; 290, 220; The New Press, New York, New York, United States of America, 210.

463. Berlitz, Charles with the collaboration of J. Manson Valentine: The Bermuda Triangle: an incredible saga of unexplained disappearances: 203,1; Doubleday & Company, Inc., Garden City, New York, United States of America, 1974.

464. Berlitz, Charles, Ibid.

465. Race and Addiction: https://www.americanaddictioncenters.org/race-and-addiction/#the.

466. Blacks and Hispanics Are Less Likely Than Whites to Complete Addiction Treatment, Largely Due to Socioeconomic Factors: https://www.ncbi.nlm.nih.gov/pmc/articles/PMC2377408.

467. Black Death: https://www.history.com/topics/black-death/print

468. The Plague: https://www.nationalgeographic.com/science/health-and-human-body/human-disease/the-plague.

469. Live Science: https://www.livescience.com/41599-northpole.html.

470. Chicago Deaths: https://www.abc7chicago.com/10-killed-53-woundedin-chicago-weekend-Shootings/3892234/

471. Chicago-social media effect: https://www.chicago.cuntimes.com/news/social-media-street-chicago-gang-culture-fueling-violence/

472. Skarbek, David: THE SOCIAL ORDER OF THE UNDERWORLD; HOW PRISON GANGS GOVERN THE AMERICAN PENAL SYSTEM; 224,166; Oxford University Press, New York, New York, United States of America, 2014.

473. Beck, Aaron T., M.D.: PRISONERS OF HATE: THE COGNITIVE BASIS OF ANGER, HOSTILITY AND VIOLENCE, 354, 63; HarperCollins Publishers, New York, New York, United States of America, 1999.

474. Baumeister, Roy F.: EVIL: INSIDE HUMAN VIOLENCE AND CRUELTY, 451, 233-234, and, 243-244; Holt Paperbacks, Henry Holt and Company, LLC, New York, New York, United States of America, 1999.

475. Solomon, R. L., & Corbit, J.D. (1974). An opponent process theory of motivation: I. Temporal dynamics of affect. Psychological Review, 81, 119-145. In Baumeister, Roy F: Ibid, 234.

476. Hatch, Orrin: Utah Senator(R): https://www.hatch.senate.gov

477. Byrd, Robert: WV Senator(R-deceased): https://www.snopes.com/factcheck-robert-byrd-kkk-photo.

478. Warner, Charles Dudley: https://www.brainyquote.com/quotes/charles Dudley/warner 379741.

479. Cotton, Tom (R-Senator, Arkansas): https://www.wsj.com/2018/08/16/ reform-the-Prisons-Without-Going-Soft-On-Crime/

480. Gramlich, John: https://www.pewresearch.org/fact-tank/201703/01/ most-violent-and-property-crimes-in-the-u-s-go-unsolved.

481. Gilligan, James, M.D.: VIOLENCE; REFLECTIONS ON A NATIONAL EPIDEMIC, 306, 94; Vintage Books, A division of Random House, Inc., New
York, New York, United States of America, 1996.

482. Beck, Aaron: Ibid, 126-127.

483. Davies, Norman: Europe: A History 1st Edition, 1392; Oxford University Press,
Oxford, England, United Kingdom, 1996.

484. Tower of London: https://www.historic-uk.com/HistoryUK/HistoryofEngland?Torture-in-the-Tower-of-London.

485. Guillotine: https://en.wikipedia.org/wiki/Guillotine.

486. DEATH PENALTY INFORMATION CENTER: Statistics: https://www.deathpenaltyinfo.org/states-and-without-death-penalty.

487. DEATH PENALTY INFORMATION CENTER: is the death penalty a deterrent: Ibid.

488. DEATH PENALTY INFORMATION CENTER: Does the Death Penalty

Deter Murder, Statistics, Ibid.

489. Capital Punishment in the United States: https://en.wikipedia.org/wiki/ Capital punishment in the United States.

490. Robespierre: https://www.historytoday.com/marisalimton/robespierre -and-terror

491. Davies, Norman: Ibid.

492. King Louis XVI: https://www.history.com/this-day-in-history/King-louis-xvi-executed.

493. Marie Antoinette: https://www.history.com/topics/marie-antoinette.

494. PROCON.ORG: UNDERSTAND THE ISSUES. UNDERSTAND EACH OTHER: Does the Death Penalty Deter Crime? https://www.deathpenalty .procon.org/view.answers.000983.

495. Bessette, Joseph M.: The Pope Makes a Fatal Error: https://www.wsj. com/2018/08/08/the-pope-makes-a-fatal-error-15.html.

496. Wise, Jeff: EXTREME FEAR; THE SCIENCE OF YOUR MIND IN DANGER, 246, 176; PALGRAVE MACMILLAN, a division of St. Martin's Press, LLC, New York, New York, United States of America, 2009.

497. Wise, Jeff: Ibid, 30.

498. Davies, Norman" EUROPE: A HISTORY, 1392; Oxford University Press, New York, New York, United States of America, 1996.

499. Dudley, Steven and Bargent, James: The Prison Dilemma: Latin America's Incubators of Organized Crime: January 19, 2017: https://www.insightcrime.org/investigations/prison-dilemma-latin-america-incubators-organized-crime.

500. Dudley, Steven and Bargent, James: Ibid, 2.

501. Dreisinger, Baz: INCARCERATION NATIONS: A Journey to Justice In Prisons Around the World, 326, 289; Other Press, LLC, New York, New York, United States of America, 2016.

502. Rochefoucauld, Duc de La: MAXIMS, 126, 39; Penguin Books, London, England, UK, 1959.

503. Augustine, Norman R., Chairman and Chief Executive Officer, Martin Marietta Corporation, Bethesda, Maryland, At the Minnesota Meeting on April 3, 1992, Carried om KSJN National Public Radio; in Marrella, Len: IN SEARCH OF ETHICS: Conversations with Men and Women of Character, 368, 39; DC Press, A Division of the Diogenes Consortium, Sanford, Florida, United States of America, 2009.

504. Ermer, E., Kahn, R.E., Salovey, P, & Kiehl, K. A. (2012). Emotional intelligence in incarcerated men with psychopathic traits. Journal of Personality & Social Psychology 105 (1), 194-204, in Kiehl, Kent A., PhD: PSYCHOPATHIC WISPERER: THE SCIENCE OF THOSE WITHOUT CONSCIENCE, 294,235; Broadway Books an imprint of Crown Publishing; New York, New York, United States of America, 2014.

505. Kiehl, Kent A., PhD: PSYCHOPATH WISPERER: THE SCIENCE OF THOSE WITHOUT CONSCIENCE, 294,235; Broadway Books, an imprint of Crown Publishing; New York, New York, United States of America, 2014.

506. Gilligan, James, M.D.: VIOLENCE: REFLECTIONS ON A NATIONAL EPIDEMIC, 306, 163; Vintage Books, A Division of Random House, Inc., New York, New York, United States of America, 1996.

507. Gilligan, James, M.D.: Ibid, 163.

508. Gilligan, James, M.D.: Ibid, 164.

509. Gilligan, James, M.D.: Ibid, 166

510. Kiehl, Kent A., PhD: Ibid, Chapter 11.

511. Amen, Daniel, M.D.: CHANGE YOUR BRAIN CHANGE YOUR LIFE: The Breakthrough Program for Conquering Anxiety, Depression, Obsessiveness, Anger, and Impulsiveness, 337, 16-36; Times Books, a division of Random House, Inc., New York, New York, United States of America, 1998.

512. Kiehl, Kent A., PhD: Ibid, 1.

513. Kiehl, Kent A., PhD: Ibid, 35.

514. Kiehl, Kent A., PhD: Ibid, 50.

515. Kiehl, Kent A.' PhD: Ibid, 46-47.

516. Kiehl, Kent A.., PhD: Ibid, 38.

517. Kiehl, Kent A., PhD: Ibid, 42.

518. Alport, G. (1956). Becoming. New Haven, CT: Yale University Press. In Kiehl,

Kent A.: PSYCHOPATH WHISPERER: THE SCIENCE OF THOSE WITHOUT CONSCIENCE, 294, 273; Broadway Books, an imprint of Crown Publishing, New York, New York, United States of America, 2014.

519.http://www.clintools.com/victims/resources/assessment/personality/psychopathy checklist.html 29.

520.https://learningenglish.voanews.com/a/outcasts-of-poker-flat-american-stories/3261888.html

521. Newton, Isaac: laws: inertia and motion: https://www.physicsclassroom.com/newtlaws/Lesson 1/Inertia-and-Mass.

522. Corley, Cheryl, host; and, Martin, Rachel, Byline: Chicago Battles Its Image as Murder Capital of The Nation: NPR Interview; https://www.npr.org/2018/08/10/637410426/chicago-nattles-its-image-as-murder-capital-ofthe-nation; August 10, 2018.

523. Morales, Gabriel C.: La Familia-The Family: Prison Gangs in America, 178; CreateSpace, Parker, Colorado, United States of America; 2015, 4th Edition.

524. Gottschalk, Marie: THE PRISON AND THE GALLOWS: THE POLITICS OF MASS INCARCERATION IN AMERICA, 451, 263; Cambridge University Press, New York, New York, Unite States of America, 2006.

525. Gilligan, James, M.D.: VIOLENCE: REFLECTIONS ON A NATIONAL EPIDEMIC: 306, 94-95; Vintage Books, A Division of Random House, Inc., New

York, New York, United States of America, 1996.

526. Kiehl, Kent A., PhD: Ibid 38, 42.

527. Samenow, Stanton E., Ph.D.: INSIDE the CRIMINAL MIND, 349, 186; Broadway Books, an imprint of the Crown Publishing Group, a division of Random House, LLC, New York, New York, United States of America, 2014.

528. Barrows, S.J., Commissioner for The United States in behalf of THE INTERNATIONAL PRISON COMMISION, REPORTS; THE REFORMATORY SYSTEM
IN THE UNITED STATES, 240, 10; Government Printing Office, Washington,
D.D., United States of America, 1900.

529. Proteus: in Greek Mythology: prophetic old man of the sea and shepherd
of the sea's seals dwelling at the head of the Nile Delta: kept waters calm
for return after the Trojan War.
https://www.britannica.com/topic/Proteus-Greek-Mytholgy.

530. Triton: in Greek Mythology, son of Poseidon and Amphitrite, merman
(demigod of the sea): According to Homer Triton guided Argonauts to safety:
https://www.brittanica.com/topic/Triton-Greek-mythology.

531. Wordsworth, William: The World Is Too Much with Us, Poetry Foundation:
https://www.poetryfoundation.org/poems/45564/the-world-is-too-muchwith-us.

532. Canard: a false or absurd story, origin: https://www.hoaxes.org/weblog/ comments/origin of canard.

533. Fish story: an exaggerated, unlikely story: https;//www.idioms.the freedictionary.com/fish/story.

534. Sophistry: a false, or, clever argument to deceive: https://en.oxforddictionaries.com/definition/sophist.

535. Alexander, Michelle: The New Jim Crow: Mass Incarceration in the Age of Colorblindness, 290; The New Press, New York, New York, United States of America, 2010.

536. Barrows, S.J.: THE INTERNATIONAL PRISON COMMISSION: THE REFORMATORY SYSTEM IN THE UNITED STATES, 240, 10; Washington Government
Printing Office, Washington, D.C., United States of America, 1900.

537. PREA (Prison Rape Elimination Act, 2003): https://www.prearesourcecenter.org/about/prison-rape-elimination-act-prea.

538. O'Grady, Mary Anastasia: The U.S. Funds Guatemalan Abuse: https://www.wsj.com/2018/08/20/article-mary-anastasia-o'grady-the-u.s.-funds-guatemalan -abuse.

539. Wilber, Del Quentin: MS-13 Gang Tries to Organize an Unruly Young Membership: https;//www.wsj.com/report/del-quentin-wilber-ms-13-Gang-Tries-toOrganize-An-Unruly-Young-Membership.

540. Geller, Pamela: STOP the ISLAMIZATION of AMERICA: A PRACTICAL GUIDE TO THE RSISTANCE, 198; WND Books, Washington, D.C., United States of America, 2011

541. Kirby, Stephen M.: The Lure of Fantasy Islam: EXPOSING THE MYTHS AND MYTH MAKERS, 269; CreateSpace, Charleston, South Carolina, 2017.

542. Addicott, Jeffrey F.: RADICAL ISLAM WHY: CONFRONTING JIHAD at HOME & ABROAD, 202; Lawyers & Judges Publishing Company, Inc., Tucson, AZ, 2016.

543. Haney, Philip & Moore, Art: SEE SOMETHING SAY SOMETHING: A HOMELAND SECURITY OFICER EXPOSES THE GOVERNMENTS'S SUBMISSION TO JIHAD, 237; WND Books, Washington, D.C., United States of America, 2016.

544. Morales, Gabriel Morales: La Familia---The Family; Prison Gangs in America, CreateSpace, Parker, Colorado, United States of America, 4th Edition, 2015; no pages for two quotes; first: introduction; second: closing.

545. Zoukis, Christopher: FEDERAL PRISON HANDBOOK: THE DEFINITIVE GUIDE TO SURVIVING THE FEDERAL BUREAU OF PRISONS, 491; Middle Street Publishing, Charleston, South Carolina, United States of America, 2017.

546. Boothe, Demico: WHY ARE SO MANY BLACK MEN IN PRISON: A COMPREHENSIVE ACCOUNT OF HOW AND WHY THE PRISON INDUSTRY HAS BECOME A PREDATORY ENTITY IN THE LIVES OF AFRICAN-AMERICAN MEN, AND HOW MASS TARGETING, CRIMINALIZATION, AND INCARCERATION OF BLACK MALE YOUTH HAS GONE TOWARD CREATING THE LARGEST PRISON SYSTEM IN THE WORLD, 155; Full Surface Publishing, Memphis,
Tennessee, United States of America, 2007.

547. Quammen, David: Bacteria Strike Back, 17-20, in National Geographic, September, 2018 issue, Vol. 234, No. 3.

548. Keats, John: Ode on a Grecian Urn: https://poetryfoundation.org/poems/44477/ode-on-a-grecian-urn.

549. Shaw, George Bernard: THE CRIME OF IMPRISONMENT, 125, 115; Greenwood Press, Publishers, Westport, Connecticut, United States of America,1946 (Copyright by the Philosophical Library, Inc.); Illustrated by William
Gropper.

550. Rochefoucauld, Duc de La: MAXIMS, 126, 58; Penguin Group, Penguin Books Ltd, London, England, UK, 1959.

551. Shaw, George Bernard: Ibid, Preface (no page number).

552. https://www.britannica.com/topic/Pygmalion-play-by-Shaw

553. Remnick, David: THE NEW YORKER: article, 7-10-2006: William Safire and
the "Nattering Nabobs of Negativism:
https://www.newyorker.com/magazine/2006/07/10/nattering-nabobs.

554. Brainy Quote: unattributed:
https://www.brainyquote.com/quotes/unknown 133991.

555. Bozelko, Chandra: WSJ Article:
https://www.wsj.com/2018/24/24/article/
don't-lock-ex-prisoners-out-of-jobs.

556. PUBLIC LAW 96-157---DEC. 27, 1979; 96th Congress:
https.ncjrs.gov/pdffiles1/Digitization/64236NCJRS.pdf.

557. The Constitution of the United States: The Heritage Foundation Pamphlet:
pages 18 and 21.

558. Federation for American Immigration Reform:
http://www.fairus.org/issue/societal-impact/criminal-aliens

559. Comparative race numbers:
https://www.prisonpolicy.org/graphs/Racial
Geography Black binned.html.

560. Racial and ethnic disparities in prisons and jails:
https://www.prisonpolicy.
org/graphs/pie2016 race.html.

561. Rochefoucauld, Duc de La: Ibid: 58.

BIBLIOGRAPHY

1. "The Art and Science of Supervision"; Columns Levenstein, The Nurse as Manager. New York: Nursing Management Books.

2. 10.com, V. L. (2013, May 29). Gosnell's Wife Sentenced, Apologizes for Husband's Actions. Philadelphia.

3. In J. Hilton, Lost Horizon (Harper Perennial Reissue Edition ed., p. 272). Harper Perennial. Retrieved 2012, from www.
amazon.com (1933, 2012).

4. In M. Twain, The Autobiography of Mark Twain. New York, New York, USA: Harper Perrenial Modern Classics, 2000.

5. 2011 National Gang Threat Assessment. (2011). Retrieved April 19, 2018, from; https://www.fbi.gov/stateservices/publications/2011-national-gang-threat-assessment

6. Aaron T. Beck, M. (August 22, 2000). Prisoners of Hate: The Cognitive Basis of Anger, Hostility. and Violence. New York, New York, USA: Harper Perennial.

7. abc7chicago.com/weekend-violence-10-killed-53-wounded-weekend-august-4-and-5-2018. (n.d.). Retrieved 8 6, 2018, from: https://www.abc7chicago.com/10-killed-53-wounded-in-chicago-weekend-shootings/3892234.

8. Adams, C. (2004, December 31). straightdope.com/slow-as-molasses-in-January.

Retrieved July 10, 2008, from
https://www.straightdope.com/
columns/read/2577/was-boston-once-literally-flooded-
with-molasses

9. Addicott, J. F. (2016). Radical Islam Why?:
Confronting Jihad at Home & Abroad. Tucson, Arizona,
USA: Lawyers & Judges Publishing Company, Inc.
AESOP. (1999).

10. The Classic Treasury of AESOP'S FABLES. In
AESOP, The Classic Treasury of AESOP'S FABLES
(p. 56). New York, NewYork, United States of
America: Running Press Kids, Hachette Book Group.
Retrieved 10 11, 2017.

11. Alexander, M. (2010). The New Jim Crow: Mass
Incarceration in the Age of Colorblindness. New York,
New York, USA: The New Press.

12. Ali, A. H. (2008). Infidel. New York, New York,
United States of America: Atria Books, an Imprint of
Simon & Schuster. Retrieved 10 11, 2017.

13. Alighieri, D. (2003). The Divine Comedy: The
Inferno, The Purgatorio and The Paradiso. In D.
Alighieri, The Divine Comedy: The Inferno, The
Purgatorio and The Paradiso (J. Ciardi, Trans., 1st
Edition ed., p. 928). London, England, United
Kingdom: Berkley, 1st Edition. Retrieved 10 11, 2010.

14. Alinsky, S. D. (1989). "Rules For Radicals." In S. D.
Alinsky, Rules for Radicals (p. 224). New York, New
York, United States of America:
Vintage Books, An Imprint of Knopf Doubleday
Publishing Group.

15. aljazeera.com/the-iraqi-baath-party. (2005, June 23). Retrieved May 31, 2018. From http://www. aljazeera.com/archive/2005/06/23/2008 4101213442336996.html.

16. Allie Malloy, C. (2013, December Tuesday). Philadelphia abortion doctor Kermit Gosnell gets 30 years for pillmill. Philadelphia.

17. Amatulli, J. (2018, April 24). yahoo.com. Retrieved April 25, 2018, from https://www.yahoo.com/news/meek-mill-reportedly-slated-release-200804672.html...

18. Amen, D. G. (1998). Change Your Brain, Change Your Life: The Breakthrough Program for Conquering Anxiety, Depresion, Obsessiveness, Anger, and Impulsiveness, (p. 337). New York, New York, United States of America: Times Books, Random House.

19. america.aljazeera.com/supreme-court-examining-obama-over-regulating-of -epa. (2014, February 24). Retrieved June 4, 2018, from https:// www.america.aljazeer.com/articles/2014/2/23/epa-carbonregulationrulescomeundersupremecourtscrutiny.html.

20.americanaddictioncenters.org/race-and addiction. (n.d.). Retrieved 8 3, 2018, Fromhttps://www.americanaddictioncenters.org/race-and-addiction/#the Asher, S. E. (2016).

21. Hauntings of the Kentucky State Penitentiary. In S.E. Asher, Hauntings of the Kentucky State Penitentiary (p. 224). Brentwood, Tennessee, United States of America: Permuted Press. Retrieved July 9, 2018, from https://www.permutedpress.com.

22. Balko, R. a. (2018).
The Cadaver King and the Country Dentist. In R. a. Balko, The Cadaver King and the Country Dentist (p. 391). New York, New York, United States of America: Public Affairs: Hachette Book Group.

23. Ball, W. D. (2014). digitalcommons.law.yale.edu/w-david-ball-why-state-prisons. Retrieved May 28, 2018, from https://www.digitalcommons.law.yale.edu/ylpr/vol33/iss1/3

24. Ball, W. D. (2014). Yale Law & Policy Review. Why State Prisons, 33(3). Retrieved April 5, 2018, from https://www.digitalcommons.law.yale.edu/ylpr/vol33/iss1/3

25. BaltimoreSun.com. (2016, October 5). Retrieved April 25, 2018, from https://www.baltimoresun.com/news/maryland/crime/bs-mdprison-corruption-20161005-story/html.

26. Baron-Cohen, S. (2011). The Science of Evil: on Empathy and the Origins of Cruelty. In S. Baron-Cohen, The Science of Evil: on Empathy and the Origins of Cruelty (p. 256). New York, New York, United States of America: Basic Books: A Member of the Perseus Book Group.

27. Baron-Cohen, S. (September 4, 2012). The Science of Evil: On Empathy and the Origins of Cruelty. New York, New York, USA: Basic Books.

28. Barrows, S. C. (1900). The Reformatory System in The United States. in S. Barrows, The Reformatory System in The United States (p. 240).

Washington, D.C., District of Columbia, United States of America:United States Government.

29. Baumeister, R. F. (March 19, 1999). Evil: Inside Human Violence and Cruelty. In R. F. Baumeister, Evil: Inside human Violence and Cruelty (p. 431). New York, New York, United States of America: Holt Paperbacks: Henry Holt and Company, LLC.

30. bbc.com/obama-noble prize-regretted-by retiring-nobel-secretary. (2015, September 17). Retrieved June 4, 2018, from https://www.bbc.com/news/world-europe-34277960.

31. Beck, A. T. (1999). Prisoners of Hate: The Cognitive Basis of Anger, Hostility, and Violence. In A. T. Beck, Prisoners of Hate: The Cognitive Basis of Anger, Hostility, and Violence (p. 354). New York, New York, United States of America: HarperCollins Publishers.

32. berkely.edu/effect-of-education-on-crime-lochner-&-moretti. (2003, October). Retrieved July 20, 2018, from https://www.eml.berkely.edu/-moretti/lm46.pdf

33. Berlitz, C. (1974). The Bermuda Triangle: an incredible saga of unexplained disappearances. In C. Berlitz, The Bermuda triangle: an incredible saga of unexplained disappearances (p. 203). Garden City,New York, United States of America: Doubleday & Company, Inc.

34. Berra, Y. (1998). The Yogi Book: I Really Didn't Say Everything I Said (p. 127). New York, New York, United States of America: Workman Publishing, L.T.D. Enterprises.

35. Bhattacharjee, Y. (2018, January). "The Science of Good and Evil." (E.-i.-C. Susan Goldberg, Ed.) National Geographic, pp. 116-143.

36. bjs.gov. (2016, December 29). Retrieved April 25, 2018, from:

https://www.bjs.gov/index.pbdetail&iid=5870.

37. bjs.gov/caroline-wolf-harrow-compares-educational-attainment-of-state-&-federal-prisoners-to-normal population. (2003, January 1). Retrieved July20, 2018, from

38.https://www.bjs.gov/index.cfm?ty=bdetail&id=814

39. bjs.gov/probation-and-parole-in-u.s.-2016-report-summary. (2018, April 26).

Retrieved June 21, 2018, from:

40. https://www.bjs.gov/index.6188

41. bjs.gov/recidivism-patterns-2005-2010. (n.d.). Retrieved July 30, 2018, from

https://www.bjs.gov/content/pub/pdf//rprts05p0510,pdf.

42. bjs.gov/recidivism-rates-and-prison-reentries-releases. (n.d.). Retrieved 6-22-2018 from:

https://www.bjs.gov/content/reentry/releases.cfm

43. bjs.gov/sentencing-states. (n.d.). Retrieved June 20, 2018, from:

https://www.bjs.gov/index,cfm?ty=tp&tid=2214

44. bjs.gov/sentencing-states-by-race. (n.d.). Retrieved June 20, 2018, from:

https://www.bjs.gov/indec.cfm?ty=pbdetail&iid=1572.

45. bjs.gov/state-prison-expenditures. (n.d.). Retrieved July 30, 2018, from

https://www.bjs.gov/State-prison-expenditures-2001-statistics

46. bjs.gov/state-prison-expenditures-2001-stastistics. (n.d.). Retrieved July 11,
2018, from:
https;//www.bjs.gov/content/pub/pdf/spe01.pdf

47. Blake, W. (n.d.). brainyquote.com/prisons-brothels. Retrieved June 28, 2018,

48. https://www.brainyquote.com/quotes/william blake165313.

49. Blankschaen, K. B. (2017). Drain the Swamp. Washington, D.C., Washington, D.C., USA: Regnery Publishing.

50. bls.gov/current-labor-staitistics-unemployment-rate-4-%-etc. (n.d.). Retrieved July 25, 2018.

51.https://www.bls.gov/news.release/pdf/empsit.pdf bls.gov/employment-statistics. (n.d.). Retrieved June 22, 2018, from:
https://www/bls.gov/web/empsit/cesprog.htm#Data Available.

52. Boothe, D. (2007). Why Are So Many Black Men In Prison? (p. 155). Memphis, Tennessee, United States of America: Full Surface Publishing, LLC. Retrieved July 11, 2018, from https://www.fullsurfacepublishing.com.

53. bop.gov. (n.d.). Retrieved April 26, 2018, from https://www.bop.gov/about/statistics/statistics inmate offenses.jsp.

54. bop.gov/bureau-of-prisons-statistics-race-ethnicity-etc. (n.d.). Retrieved June
20, 2018, from:
https://www.bop.gov/about/statistics/statistics inmate sentences.jsp.

55. bop.gov/federal-bureau-of-prisons-website. (n.d.). Retrieved March 11, 2018,

56. https://www.bop.gov: bop.gov/offenses-recidivism-breakdown. (n.d.). Retrieved July 3, 2018, from

57.http://www.bop.gov/statistics/statistics/recidivism/in mateoffenses.jsp.

58. Boston.com. (n.d.). Retrieved April 12, 2018, from http://www.boston.com/sports/new-england-patriots/2018/.../robert-kraft-meel-mill brainyquote.com/charles-dudley-warner-politics-make-strange-bedfellows.

59.(n.d.). Retrieved 8 6, 2018, from https://www.brainyquote.com/ quotes/charlesdudleywarner 379741.

60. brainyquote.com/thomasponeill-politics-local. (n.d.). Retrieved June 25, 2018, from https://www.brainyquote.com/quotes/thomas p oneill-212119

61. brainyquote.com/unknown-insanity-doing-the-same-thing-over-and-overand-expecting-different-results. (n.d.). Retrieved 8-24-2018, from https://www.brainyquote.com/quotes/unknown 133991

62. Brignull, Harry. (2010). 90 Percent of Everything. self. Retrieved September 2010, from www.brignull.com britannica.com/-

63. kabuki-theater. (n.d.). Retrieved July 17, 2018, from: https://www.britannica.com/art/Kabuki

64. britannica.com/proteus-the-oracular-old-man-of-the-sea-dwelled-on-islandof-Pharos-at-head-of Nile Delta-subject-of-poseidon-god-of-sea. (2018, 8 20). Retrieved 8 20, 2018, from https://www.britannica.com/topic.

65. Proteus-Greek-mythologybritannica.com/second-persian-gulf-war-george-w-bush-2003-2011. (n.d.).

66. Retrieved May 25, 20018, from https://www.britannica.com/print/article/870845.

67. britannica.com/tower-of-babel. (n.d.). Retrieved July 5, 2018, from https://www.britannica.com/print/article/47421 brittanica.com/triton-greek-mythology-merman-demigod-of-sea-son-of-poseidin-and-amphitrite. (2018, 8 20).

68. brookings.edu/crime-and-incarceration-statistics. (n.d.). Retrieved 8 24, 2018, from https://www.brookings.edu/research/ten-economic-factsabout-crime-and-incarceration-in-the-united-states

69. brookings.edu/more-prisoners-versus-more-crime. (n.d.). Retrieved July 30, 2018, from https://www.brookings.edu/.../more-prisoners-versusmore-crime.

70. brookings.edu/prison-costs-more-v.-more-crime-n0. (n.d.). Retrieved July 30, 2018, from https://www.brookings.edu/.../more-prisoners-versusmore-crime-is-the-wrong-question...

71. browardpalmbeach.com/rick-scott-corruption. (2011, September 11). Retrieved July 17, 2018, from https://www.browardpalmbach.com/news/owner-of-greyhound-adoption-agency-details-abuses-ofdogs-at-palm-beach-kennel-club-9679146 Brown, A. (2017, April 20). Post and Courier Newspaper. Retrieved 25 2018, April, from https://postandcourier.com/news/south-carolina-department-of-corrections-director-discusses-officer-shortages-silent-article.

72. bsj.gov/staistics-parolees-jail-inmates-probationers-total-adult-correctional-population-1980-2016. (2018, 8 16). Retrieved 8 16, 2018, from: https://www.bjs.gov/index.cfm.

73. Bunyan, J. (2015). Pilgrim's Progress (Illustrated): Updated, Modern English.
More than 100 illustrations.

74. In J. Bunyan, Pilgrim's Progress (Illustrated): Updated, Modern English. More than 100 illustrations (p. 384). Abbotsford,
Wisconsin, United States of America: Aneko Press, 2nd Edition. Retrieved 10 11, 2017.

75. Bureau of Alcohol, Tobacco, Firearms and Explosives: ATF Homepage. (2018).
Retrieved March 18, 2018, from htpps://www.atf.gov

76. Bureau of Justice. (n.d.). Retrieved March 13, 2018, from https://www.bjs.gov.

77. Butt, Y. (2015, January 20). huffingtonpost.com/saudiwahhabism. Retrieved June 14, 2018, from:

https://www.huffingtonpost.com/dryousaf-butt-/saudi-wahhabism-islam-terrorism b 6501916.html

78. Byrnes, J. F. (n.d.). just-one-liners.com/byrnes-james-f-bureaucracy-quote. Retrieved July 9, 2018, from https://www.just-one-liners.com/ppl/james-f-byrnes.

79. Carr, H. (2006). The Brothers Bulger: How They Terrorized and Corrupted Boston For A Quarter Century. In H. Carr, The Brothers Bulger: (p. 342). New York, New York, United States of America: Warner Books, Time Warner
Book group.

80. Carr, H. (2011). HITMAN: THE UNTOLD STORY OF JOHNNY MARTORANO: Whitey Bulger's Enforcer and the Most Feared Gangster in the Underworld. In H. Carr, JOHNNY MARTORANO: Whitey Bulger's Enforcer and the Most Feared Gangster in the Underworld (p. 464). New York, New York, United States of America: Tom Doherty Associates, A Forge Book.

81. Census Bureau. (2017). Retrieved March 12, 2018, from https://www.census.gov census.gov/bishaw-and-benson-poverty-2015-&-2016. (2017, September).

82, Retrieved July 20, 2018, from https://www.census.gov/content/dam/census/library/publications/2017/acs/acsbr16-01.pdf-census.gov/black-population-statistics-2010. (n.d.). Retrieved: Juky:24,2018; census.gov/educational-attaicnment-races-black-white-hispanics-asians.

(n.d.). Retrieved 8 24, 2018, from https://www.census.gov/content/dam/Census/library/publications/2016/demo/p20-578.pdf;

census.gov/poverty-2015-2016-statistics-levels-and-rates. (n.d.). Retrieved July 13, 2018, from https://www.census.gov/content/dam/Census/library/publications/2017/acs/acsbr16-01.pdf

census.gov/quick-facts-for-all-ethnicities-all-categories-like-housing-education-etc. (n.d.). Retrieved July 24, 2018, from https://www.census.gov/quick-facts/fact/table/US/RH1225217.

83. Centers for Disease Control and Prevention. (n.d.). Retrieved March 30, 2018, from https://www.cdc.gov Centers for Disease Control and Prevention. (2018). Retrieved March 16, 2018, from: https://www.cdc.gov.

84. Chan, M. (2016, June 20). People.com. Retrieved April 6, 2018, from https://www.people.com/andrea yates-15years-after-drowning-five-children-in-a-texas-mental...

chicago.suntimes.com/chicago-gang-culture. (n.d.). Retrieved 8-6-2018:

from https://chicago.suntimes.com/news/social-media-street-chicago-gang-culture-fueling-violence

columbia.edu/kathy-boudin-columbia-university-center-for-justice. (n.d.). Retrieved July 30, 2018, from https://www.centerforjustice.columbia.

85. edu/about/staff (2017). Congress and the Public. Gallup. Retrieved October 9, 2017, from www.news.gallup.com.

86. congress.gov/congress-house-bill. (n.d.). Retrieved July 16, 2018, from https://www.congress.gov/bill/115th-congress/house-bill/3356.

87. congress.gov/H.R.3356/prison-reform-and-redemptio-act. (2017, September 6). Retrieved May 24, 2018, from https://www.congress.gov/bill/115th-congress/house-bill/3356 congress.gov/h.r.3356-115th-congress-2017-2018-prison-reform-and-redemtionact. (n.d.). Retrieved July 16, 2018, from https://www.congress.gov/bill/115th-congress/house-bill/3356.

88. Corsi, J. P. (Corsi, JeromeR., Ph.D). Killing the Deep State: The Fight to Save President Trump. In J. P. Corsi, Killing the Deep State: The Fight to Save President Trump (p. 228). West Palm Beach, Florida, United States of America: Humanix Books. Retrieved March 30, 2018.

89. http://www.humanixbooks.com courses.lumenlearning.com/south-after-reconstruction. (n.d.). Retrieved July 2, 2018, from https://www.courses.lumenlearning.com/boundless-ushistory/chapter/the-south-after-reconstruction Cousins, N. (2017, September Wednesday).

90. Brainy Quotes of Norman Cousins. Retrieved from Famous Quotes at BrainyQuote: http://www.brainyquote.com.

91. credit, n. (Producer), Robinson, L. (Writer), & Hill, G. W., Director (1930). The Big House [Motion Picture]. USA.

92. Criminal Victimization, 2016. (2017, December). Retrieved March 13, 2018, from https://www.bjs.gov.

93. csmonitor.com. (2009). Retrieved May 20, 2018, from: https://www.csmonitor.com/USA/2009/1019

94. csmonitor.com/prison-radicals. (n.d.). Retrieved May 23, 2018, from: https://www.csmonitor/USA/2009/1019/p21s01-usgn.html

95. dailycaller.com/radicalization of inmates. (2014, November 21). Retrieved May 23, 2018, from https://www.dailycaller.com/2014/11/21/u-sprisons-churning-out-thousands-of-radicalized-inmates/

96. Dantes, E. (2018). Surviving and Thriving in Prison: A How-To Manual for Federal Inmates. In E. Dantes, Surviving and Thriving in Prison: A How-To Manual for Federal Inmates (p. 147). Columbia, South Carolina, United States of America: Independently Published. Retrieved March 30, 2018, from: http://SurviveNThriveBook.com

97. Davies, N. (1996). Europe: A History. In N. Davies, Europe: A History (p. 1392). New York, New York, United States of America: Oxford University Press. Retrieved 10 11, 2017.

98. Davis, R. S. (1954). Ghosts and Shadows of ANDERSONVILLE: Essays on the Secret Social Histories of America's Deadliest Prison. Macon, Georgia, USA: Mercer University Press. Davis, R. S. (2006). Andersonville: Essays on the Social Histories of America's Deadliest Prison.

99. deathpenalty.org/facts-about-deterrence-and-the-death-penalty. (n.d.). Retrieved 8 9, 2018, from https://www.deathpenaltyino.org/factsabout-deterrence-and-death-penalty.

100. Dennett, D. (1995). Darwin's dangerous idea. In D. Dennett, Darvin's dangerous idea. New York, New York, United States of America: Simon and Schuster. Retrieved April 25, 1995.

101. Dhume, S. (2018, June 1). wsj.com/desperate-religious-muslims-india-rejection. Retrieved June 1, 2018, from https://www.wsj.com/2018/06/01/fear-of-islam-leads-india-to-snub-refugees Dhume, S. (2018, June 15).

102. wsj.com/pakistan's-pashtuns. Retrieved June 15, 2018, from: https://www.wsj.com/2018/06/15/pakistan's-pashtuns-take-on-army---and-terrorists

103. Dillon, S. (2009, April 22). The New York Times. Retrieved March 14, 2018, from: https://www.nytimes.com/2009/04/22/education discoverthenetworks.org/michellemalkin and robertspencer-radicalization. (2009, May 22(Malkin) and 28(Spencer)). Retrieved May 23, 2018.

104. Diversion Control Division. (2018). Retrieved March 16, 2018, from: https://www.deadiversion.usdoj.gov.

105. doccs.ny.gov/parole-board-12-appointed -by-governor. (n.d.). Retrieved July 31, 2018, from https://www.doccs.ny.gov?ParoleBoard.html

doj.gov. (n.d.). Retrieved April 26, 2018, from https://www.doj.gov.

106. The-department-of-justice's-reliance-on-private-contractors-for-prison-services doj.gov/office-of-justice-programs-for-child-and-youth-victims-of-opioid-crisis. (2018, June 5). Retrieved June 5, 2018, from https://www.content-govdelivery/accounts/USDOJOJP?bulletins/1f4f0c6 doj.gov/violent-crime-statistics. (n.d.). Retrieved July 3, 2018, from https:// www.doj.gov/statistics/statistics inmate violent crime.

107. Downing, M. P. (2011, June 15). homeland.house.gov. Retrieved May 20, 2018, from: https://www.homeland.house.gov/files/Testimony-9620Downing.pdf

108. Dreisinger, B. (2016). Incarceration Nations: A Journey to Justice in Prisons Around the World. In B. Dreisinger, Incarceration Nation: A Journey to Justice in Prisons Around the World (p. 325). New York, New York, United States of America: Other Press. Retrieved March 30, 2018.

109. Drug Trafficking-United Nations Office on Drugs and Crime. (2018). Retrieved March 13, 2018 from: https://www.unodc.org/unodc/en/drug-trafficking/Index.html

110. duihua.org/parole-in-usa-people-and policies-in-transition. (n.d.). Retrieved July 31, 2018, from https://www.duihua.org/wp/2704

111. Dukakis, M. S. (1988, July 31). https://nyti.ms/29syMxn. (R. Toner, Producer)

Retrieved April 16, 2018, from NewYorkTimes.com: https://www.nytimes.com/1988/07/31/dukakis-focuses-on-reagan-ethics.html.

112. E. Ann Carson, P. (2014). Prisoners in 2014. Washington,D.C: http://www.bjs.gov.

113. ed.gov. (2015, March 16). Retrieved May 3, 2018, from https://www.ed.gov/news/press-releases/achievement-gap-narrows-high-school-greaduation-rates-minority-students-improve-faster-rest-nation.

114. ed.gov. (2015, December 15). Retrieved May 3, 2018, from https://www.ed.gov/news/press-releases/us-high-school-graduation-rate-hitsnew-record-high-0 ed.gov/effect-of-education-on-crime-lochner-&-moretti-2001. (2001, December). Retrieved July 20, 2018, from https://files.eric.ed.gov/fulltext/ED463346.pdf

115. Einstein, A. (n.d.). wiseoldsayings.com/einstein-albert-corruption. Retrieved July 9, 2018, from: https://www.wiseoldsayings.com/corruption-quotes/page-2.

116. Elinson, Z. a. (2018, April 26). wsj.com. Retrieved April 26, 2018, from: https://www.wsj.com/zusha-elinson/erich-schwartzel/2018/26/04/suspected-serial-killer-captured.

117. Ellis, J. J. (2000). Founding Brothers: The Revolutionary Generation; In J. J. Ellis, Founding Brothers: The Revolutionary Generation (p. 288). New York, New York, United States of America: Vintage

Books: A Division of Random House, Inc. Retrieved July 3, 2018.

118. Emerson, R. W. (1940). The Selected Writings of Ralph Waldo Emerson, New York, New York, USA: Random House, Inc.

119. Emerson, S. (n.d.). investigativeproject.org. Retrieved May 20, 2018 from: https://www.investigativeproject.org/1041/radicals-in-our-prisons.

<u>120</u>. Factcheck.com/donald-trump-lies. (2017, April 29). Retrieved June 26, 2018, from: https://www.factcheck.org/2017/04/29/100-days-whoppers.

121. Factcheck.org/Benghazi-timeline. (2012, October 26). Retrieved June 4, 2018, from: https://www.factcheck.org/2012/10/26/benghazi-timeline.

122. Fairus.org/criminal-aliens-population-outside-inside-prison=percentages-compared-very-dangerous. (n.d.). Retrieved 8 26, 2018.

123. FBI National Press Office. (2016, September 26). Retrieved March 13, 2018 from: https:''www.fbi.gov

124. FBI.gov. (n.d.). Retrieved April 2018, 2018, from: https://www.fbi.gov/investigate/public-corruption.

125. fec.gov/electronicfilings/donaldtrump. (n.d.). Retrieved May 24, 2018, from: https:/www.docquery.fec.gov/cgi-bin/forms/C00580100/

126. fec.gov/electronicfilings/obama'selection. (n.d.). Retrieved May 24, 2018, from https://www.docquery.fec.gov/cgi-bin/forms/C00431445/

127. Federal Bureau of Investigation. (2012). Retrieved March 12, 2018, from https://www.fbi.gov.

128. FITSNEWS.com. (2014, 12 01). Retrieved April 25, 2018, from https://www. fitsnews.com/2014/01/12/south-carolina-prison-system-blasted.

129. FITSNEWS.com. (2017, July 13). Retrieved April 25, 2018, from http://www. fitsnews.com/2017/07/13/henry-mcmaster-must-fire-corrections-czar.

130. forbes.com/obama's-benghazi-shameful-dereliction-of-duty. (2012, October 25). Retrieved May 2, 2018, from https://www.forbes.com/sites/ peterferrara/2012/10/25/benghazi-obama-actions-amount-to-ashameful-dereliction-of-duty/#16c66ce1359c

131. forbes.com/obama'sbillionaires. (2009, January 15). Retrieved May 24, 2018, from https:///.forbes.com/2009/01/15/obama-backers-billionaires-biz-billies-inauguration09-cz co 0115funding.html#170365a2671c.

132. forbes.com/obama's-weaponization-of-government. (2014, January 31). (T. B.--. forbes.com, Producer) Retrieved June 4, 2018, from: https://www.forbes.com/sites/thomasbasile/2014/01/31/ obama-weaponization-of-government/

forbes.com/Obama's-weaponization-of-government. (2014, January 31). Retrieved June 4, 2018.

133. forum.wordreference.com/paese-che-vai-usanza-che-trovi. (n.d.). Retrieved
8 9, 2018, from
https://www.forum.wordreference.com/threads/
paese-che-vai-usanza-che-trovi.1442235.

134. foxnews.com/radicalization-federal-prisons. (2016, January 5). Retrieved May 23,
2018, from:
https://www.foxnews.com/us/2016/01/05/ripe-for-radicalization-federal-prisons-breeding-ground-for-terrorists-say-experts.html.

135. Frontline. (2001). pbs.org/madrassas. Retrieved June 14, 2018, from:
https://www.pbs.org/wgbh/pages/frontline/shows/saudi/
analyses/madrassas.html.

136. Furman, J. (2018, July 10). wsj.com/gross-domestic-product-and gross-domestic-income-reporting-by-bea. Retrieved July 10, 2018, from
https://www.wsj.com/2018/07/10/the-economy-is-growing-faster-than-the-government-says.

137. Gabbidon, Shaun L., and, Greene, Helen Taylor: Race, Crime, and Justice: A Reader, 379; Routledge Publishing, 711 Third Avenue, New
York, NY 10017, 2005.

138. gatestoneinstitute.org. (n.d.). Retrieved May 20, 2018, from:
https://www.gatestoneinstitute.org/8873/prisons-radical-islam; (n.d.). Retrieved May 23, 2018.

139. Geiger, A. (2017, April 11). pewresearch.org. Retrieved April 26, 2018, from: https://www.pewresearch.org/abigail-geiger/2017/11/04/u.s.-private-prison-population-has-declined-in-recent-years.

140. Geller, P. (2011). Stop the Islamization of America, Washington, D.C., USA: WND Books.

141. Geller, P. (2010). The Post American Presidency: The Obama Administration's War on America. New York, New York, USA: Threshold Editions, A Division of Simon & Schuster.

142. Geographic, Y. B. (2018, January). THE SCIENCE OF GOOD and EVIL. (S. Goldberg, Ed.) National Geographic (January 2018), p. 144. Retrieved January 28, 2018, from: https://www.nationalgeographic.com Gertz, B. (2017).

143. War and Peace in the Information Age. New York, New York, USA: Threshold Editions. Getting MAD: Nuclear Mutual Assured Destruction. (n.d.). Retrieved April 11, 2018, from: https://www.strategicinstitutestudies.army.mil//pdf files/PUB585.pdf.

144. Gilligan, J. (April 29, 1997). Violence: Reflections on a National Epidemic, New York, New York, United States of America: Vintage Books, Retrieved March 30, 2018.

145. Glaeser, E. (2018, July 10). wsj.com/cure-for-poverty-? Retrieved July 10, 2018, from: https://www.wsj.com/the-cure-for-poverty-column Gleason, R. (2017).

146. And into The Fire. In R. Gleason, And into The Fire:(p. 366). New York, New York, United States of America: FORGE: A Tom Doherty Associates Book. Retrieved March 30, 2018.

147. Goldberg, J. (2000-6-25): nytimes.com/goldbery-jeffrey-jihad-u. Retrieved 6-14-2018, from: https://www.nytimes.com/2000/06/25/magazine/inside-jihad-u-yhe-education-of-a-holy-warrior.html.

148. goodreads.com/carl-sandburg-facts-law-neither-pound-the table-yell-like-hell. (n.d.). Retrieved July 16, 2018, from https://www.goodreads.com/quotes918291-if-the-facts-are-against-you-argue-the-law-if...

149. Goodwin, D. K. (2005). Team of Rivals: The Political Genius of Abraham Lincoln. In D. K. Goodwin, Team of Rivals: The Political Genius of Abraham Lincoln (p. 916). New York, New York, United States of America: Simon & Schuster. Retrieved March 30, 2018.

150. Gopnik, A.: April10, 2017: newyorker.com/review-of-john-pfaff-book-locked-in. Retrieved June 28, 2018, from: https://www.newyorker.com/magazine/2017/04/10/how-we-misunderstand-mass-incarceration

151. Gottschalk, M. (2006). The Prison and The Gallows: The Politics of Mass Incarceration in America. New York: Cambridge University Press, 2006.

152. Gramlich, J. (2018, January 14). pewresearch.org/black-white-prison-ratios.

Retrieved June 20, 2018, from
https://www.pewresearch.org/facttank/2018/10/12/shrin
king-gap--between-number-of-blacks-and-whites-in-
prison.

153. Grant, M. (1985). The Roman Emperors: A
biographical Guide to the Rulers of Imperial Rome, 31
BC-AD 476. In M. Grant, The Roman
Emperors: A biographical Guide to the Rulers of
Imperial Rome, 31 BC-AD 476 (p. 367). New York,
New York, United States of America: Charles
Scribner's Sons. Retrieved March 30, 2018.

154. Green, M. (2018, June 14). wsj.com/middle-
eastern-christians. Retrieved June 18, 2018, from
https://www.wsj.com/2018/06/14/help-is-onthe-
wayformiddleeasternchristiansgreenvillenews.com.
(n.d.).

155. Retrieved April 27, 2018, from https://www.
greenvilleonline.com/story/news/crime/2018/04/24/lee-
correctional-inmates-cause-death-south-carolina-
prisoneriot/547751002/
greenvilleonline.com. (n.d.).

156. Retrieved April 27, 2018; why-deaths-and-
violence-continue-lee-correctional/532430002/
greenvilleonline.com. (n.d.). Retrieved April 27, 2018,
from:
https://www.greenvilleonline.com/story/news/local/sout
h-carolina/2018/04/25/south-carolia-correctional-
employees-chargedcontraband-ring/549028002/
greenvilleonline.com. (n.d.). Retrieved April 27, 2018,
from:
https://www.greenvilleonline.com/story/news/2018/04/2

3/deadly-prison-killings-complete-coverage-violence-lee-correctional-institution/541764002.

157. Hamilton, E. (2017). Mythology: Timeless Tales of Gods and Heroes, 75h Anniversary Edition. In E. Hamilton, Mythology: Timeless Tales
of Gods and Heroes, 75h Anniversary Edition (p. 384). New York, New York, United States of American: Black Dog & Leventhal; Deluxe,
Illustrated, Anniversary edition. Retrieved January 11, 2018

158. Hang "Em High (1968). (n.d.). Retrieved April 5, 2018, from:
https://www.imdb.com/title?tt0061747/fullcredits
Harris, S. H. (1994).

159. Factories of Death: Japanese Biological Warfare, 1932-45, and, The American Cover-Up. In S. H. Harris, Factories of Death:
Japanese Biological Warfare, 1932-45, and, The American Cover-Up (p. 297).
London, England, G.B.: Routledge. Retrieved March 15, 2018.

160. hatch.senate.gov/orrin-hatch-utah-senator-website. (n.d.). Retrieved 8 6,
2018, from https://www.hatch.senate.gov
healthcare.gov/affordable-care-act-march-2010. (n.d.). Retrieved 10-11-2017 from:
https://www.healthcare.gov/glossary/affordable-care-act.

161. Helling, S. (2017, September 26). People.com. Retrieved April 6, 2018, from:
https://www.people.com/crime susan-smith.

162. historic-uk.com/the-tower-of-london-the-rack-and-skeffington's-irons-bodystetcher-and-compressor. (n.d.).

163. Retrieved 8-9-2018, from: England/Torture-in-the-tower of-London; history.com/all-history-topics-marie-antoinette-and-louis-xvi-and-others.

(n.d.). from: https://www.history.com/topics

164. history.com/black-death. (n.d.). Retrieved 8-3-2018, from https://www.history.com/topics/black-death/print history.com/brown-board-of-education-1954. (n.d.).

165. Retrieved March 17, 2018, from: https://www.history.com/topics/black-history/brownv-board-of-education-of-topeka history.com/brown-v.-board-of-education. (1954). **166.** Retrieved July 2, 2018, from: https://www.history.com/this-day-in-history/brown-v-board-of-ed-is decided history.com/brown-v-board-of-education. (n.d.).

167. Retrieved July 2, 2018 from: https://www.history.com/this-day-in-history/brown--board-of-ed-is-decided history.com/civil-rights-act-1964. (n.d.).

168. Retrieved March 17, 2018, from https://www.history.com/topics/black-history/civil-rights-act history.com/Feb-26-1993-world-trade-center-bombed. (n.d.).

169. Retrieved May25, 2018, from: https://www.history.com/this-day-in history/world-trade-center-bombed.

170. history.com/king-louis-xvi-guillotined-January-1793. (n.d.). Retrieved 8-9-2018, from: https://www.history.com/this-day-in-history/King-louis-xvi-executed.

171. history.com/voting-rights-act-1965. (1965). Retrieved July 2, 2018, from https:// www.history.com/topics/black-history/voting-rights-act-1965.

172. historytoday.com. (2006, 8). Retrieved 8-6- 2018, from: https://www.historytoday.com/marisa-linton/robespierre-and-terror.

173. hoaxes.org/the-origin-of-the-word-canard. (2018, 8 20). Retrieved 8-20-2018 from: https://www.hoaxes.org/weblog/comments/origin of canard.

174. Hobbes, T. (2010). Leviathan: Or the Matter, For men, and Power of a Commonwealth Ecclesiastical and Civil' ed. by Ian Shapiro. New Haven, Connecticut: Yale University Press.

175. homeland.house.gov/testimony-downing-terrorism. (2011, June 15). Retrieved May 23, 2018, from https://www.homeland.house.gov/ files/Testimony9620Downing.pdf

176. Homicide in the U.S. Known to Law Enforcement, 2011. (2013, December).

Retrieved March 13, 2018, from:
https://www.bjs.gov/index

177. Hong, N. (2018, April 26). wsj.com. Retrieved April 26, 2018, from:
https://www.wsj.com/nicole-hong/2018/26/04/terrorists'-life-after-jail-in-focus/

178. Hornblower, M., Reid, T., & and, W. P. (1981, April 26). washingtonpost.com/boll-weevils. Retrieved July 2, 2018, from https://www.washingtonpost.com/archive/politics/1981/04/26/after-decadesthe-boll-weevis-are-back-and-whistling-dixie.

179. Horowitz, M. E. (2013, December 11). oig.justice.gov. Retrieved April 26, 2018, from: https://oig.justice.gov/challenges/2013.htm

180. Hoss, R. (1992). Death Dealer: The Memoirs of the SS Kommandant at Auschwitz. (S. P. Pollinger), Ed.) Buffalo, New York, USA: Prometheus Books (DA CAPO PRESS of the Perseus Books Group-1966).

181. huffingtonpost.com/high-school-dropout-rate. (n.d.). Retrieved 8 24, 2018, from: https://www.huffingtonpost.com/matthew-lynch-edd/highschool-dropout-rate b 5421778.html

182. Huxley, A. (2013). Brave New World (Original Copyright: 1932; Again in 1946. ed.). New York, New York, USA: Alfred A. Knopf.

183. imdb.com/Jimmy-stewart-mr-smith-goes-to-washington-to-fight-corruptionmovie-1939. (n.d.). Retrieved June 25, 2018, from https://www.imdb.com/title/tt0031679

184. Ina Jaffe for NPR, S. C. (2009, October 30). Cases Show Disparity of California's 3 Strikes Law. Columbia, South Carolina.

185. insightcrime.org/latin-american-prisons-incubators-of-organized-crime. (2017, January 17). Retrieved August 9, 2018, from https://www.insightcrime.org/investigations/prison-dilemma-latin-america-incubators-organized-crime investigativeproject.org/american-islamists-celebrate-anti-semitism. (2018, May 16).

186. Retrieved June 5, 2018, from https://www.investigativeproject.org/7455/american-islamists-celebrate-an-avowed-anti-semite

187. investigativeproject.org/prison-radicalization-belgium-deadly-terror-attack. (2018, May 31). Retrieved June 5, 2018, from https://www.investigativeproject.org/7471/belgium-terror-attack-mirrors-an-all-toofamiliar-pattern investigativeproject.org/southern-poverty-law-center-indifferent-to-muslim-antisemitism. (2018, June 5).

188. Retrieved June 6, 2018, from https://www.investigativeproject.org/7473/the-split-is-indifferent-to-muslim-anti-semitism.

189. investigativeproject.org/steven-emerson-radicals-in-our-prisons. (2009, May 24). Retrieved May 21, 2018, from https://www.investigativeproject.org/1041/radicals-in-our-prisons

investigativeproject.org/terrorist-sues-bureau-of-prisons. (2018, June 6).

190. Retrieved June 6, 2018, from https://www.investigativeproject. org/7474/another-terrorist-sues-the bureau-of prisons.

191. investigativeproject.org/u.s.-imam-advocates-violence. (2018, April 20).

192. Retrieved June 5, 2018, from https://www.investigativeproject. org/2018/04/20/7409/ipt-exclusive-us-based-imam-advocates-violence

193. investopedia.com/dodd-rank-regulatory-reform-bill. (n.d.). Retrieved 10-11-2017 from https://www.investopedia.com/terms/dodd-frank-financial-regulatory-reform-bill.asp.

194. James Gilligan, M. (1997). Violence: Reflections on A National Epidemic. In M. James Gilligan, Violence: Reflections on A National Epidemic (p. 306). New York: Vintage Books, A Division of Random House, Inc.

195. Jasser, D. M. (2012). A Battle for the Soul of Islam. New York, New York, USA: Threshold Editions, An Imprint of Simon & Schuster.

196. Jewishmag.com/dhimmis-christians-and-jews-living-in Islamic-conquered-lands. (2002, July). Retrieved May 25, 2018, from: https://www.jewishmag.com/57mag/dhimmi/dhimmi.htm.

197. John R. Lott, J. (2010). More Guns Less Crime: Understanding Crime and Gun-Control Laws (Third

Edition ed.). Chicago, Illinois, USA: The University of Chicago Press.

John R. Lott, J. P. (2016). The War on Guns:

198. Arming Yourself Against Gun Control Lies. Washington, D.C., District of Columbia, USA: Regnery Publishing. Johnson, M. E. (1900).

199. The Reformatory System in the United States. Reports prepared for the International Prison Commission. (I. P. Commission, Ed.) Washington, D.C., United States of America: The Reformatory System in the United States Justice, B. O. (Ed.). (2017, December 8).

200. National Crime Victimization Survey. National Crime Victimization Survey, Technical Documentation, 2016, p. 61. Retrieved April 5, 2018, from: https:/www.bjs.gov/indexcfm?ty=dcdetail&iid=245 justice.gov. (2017, December 21).

201. Retrieved May 3, 2018, from: https://www.justice.gov/opa/prdepartments-justice-and-homeland-security-release-data-incarcerated-aliens-94-percent-all.

202. justice.gov/history-of-the-federal-parole-system. (n.d.). Retrieved July 31, 2018, from https://www.justice.gov/sites/default/files/uspc/legacy/2009/10/07/history.pdf.

203, just-one-liners.com/oxymoron-government-organization. (n.d.). Retrieved July 9, 2018, from https://www.just-one-linets.com/misc/oxymoron.

204. Kantor, M. (1955). Andersonville. In M. Kantor, Andersonville (p. 767), Cleveland and New York, Ohio and New York, United States of
America: The World Publishing Company. Retrieved March 30, 2018.

205. Kassam, R. (2017). No Go Zones.Washington, D.C., Washington, D.C., USA: Regnery Publishing.

206. Kiehl, K. A. (2014). PSYCHOPATH WHISPERER: THE SCIENCE OF
THOSE WITHOUT CONSCIENCE. In K. A. Kiehl, PSYCHOPATH WHISPERER: THE SCIENCE OF THOSE WITHOUT CONSCIENCE (p.294), New York, New York, United States of America: Broadway Books, an imprint of Crown Publishing Company. Retrieved 10 11, 2017.

207. Kipling, R. (1973 the Limited Edition). Tales of East and West, Avon, Connecticut, USA: Limited Edition Club.

208. Kipling, R. (n.d.). The Ballad of East and West. Retrieved 1 11, 2018, from:
https://www.bartleby.com/246/1129.html;
Kiplingsociety.co.uk. (n.d.). Retrieved May 17, 2018, from: https://www.Kiplingsociety.co.uk/poems eastwest.htm.

209. Kirby, D. S. (2017). The Lure of Fantasy Islam: Exposing the Myths and Myth Makers. Charleston, South Carolina, USA: CreateSpace.

210. Kirk, G. (1974). The Nature of Myths. New York, New York, USA: 2009 Edition Published by Barnes & Noble, Inc. by Arrangement with The Overlook Press.

211. Kushner, J. (2018, April 25). wsj.com. Retrieved April 25, 2018, from https://www.wsj.com/jared-kushner-trump's-forgotten-men-and-women-include-prisoners/ latimes.com/from-death-row-ft.-hood-shooter-asks-to-join-islamic-state.

212. (2014, August 30). Retrieved June 4, 2018, from https://www.latimes.com/nation/nationnow/la-nn-fort-hood-shooter-islamic-state-20140830-story.html.

213. latimes.com/san-bernadino-attack-terror. (2015, December 14). Retrieved June 6, 2018, from: https://www.latimes.com/local/california/ la-me-san-bernadino-shooting-terror-investigation-htmlstory.html.

214. Laurence J. Peter, a. R. (1969). The Peter principle: Why Things Always Go Wrong. New York: William Morrow and Company.

215. Law.Columbia.com. (n.d.). Retrieved April 25, 2018, from: https://www.law.Columbia.edu/.../prison-corruption contribution...law.columbia.edu/prison-corruption.

216. Retrieved July 17, 2018, from: https://www.law.columbia.edu/.../prison corruption-community contribution

217. Leonard Tancock. (1959). In D. d. Rochefoucauld, & L. Tancock (Ed.), MAXIMS (L. Tancock, Trans.). London, England: The Penguin Group.

218. Lepore, Jill: These Truths: A History of the United States, 932; W.W. Norton & Company, Inc., 500 Fifth Avenue, New York, NY 10010, 2018.

219. Levenstein, A. (n.d.). goodreads.com/stistics-are-like-bikinis-what-they-revealis-suggestive-but-what-they-conceal-is-vital. Retrieved June 28, 2018, from: https://www.goodreads.com/quotes/130178

220. Levin, Marc. (1996). "The Prisoners of the War on Drugs." New York: Home Box Office. Retrieved January 8, 1996.

221. Levy, P. S. (2018, June 11). wsj.com/university-boardrooms. Retrieved June

18, 2018, from:
https://www.wsj.com/2018/06/11/university-boardrooms-need-reform.

222. livescience.com/geographic-and-magnetice-poles-changing-relationships. (n.d.). Retrieved 8-6-2018, from https://www.livescience.com/41955-north-pole.html

223. Lowrey, A. (2018). Give People Money: How a Universal Basic Income Would End Poverty, Revolutionize Work, and Remake the World.
In A. Lowery, Give People Money: How a Universal Basic income Would End Poverty, Revolutionize Work, and Remake the World (p. 272). New York, New York, United States of America: Crown Publishing.

224. Retrieved July 10, 2018 from: lumenlearning.com/south-reconstruction. (1865 (after end of Civil War)).
Retrieved July 2, 2018, from:
https://www.courses.lumenlearning.com/boundless-ushistory/chapter/the-south-after-reconstruction.

225. MacDonald, H. (2017). The False 'Science" of Implicit Bias. New York: Dow Jones & Company. Retrieved October 11th, 2017, from https://www.wsj.commainehealth.org.

226. memorial.hospital/doctor-george-h-shedd. (n.d.). Retrieved March 17, 2018, from: https://www.mainehealth.org/-/media/memorial-hospital/11-3-memorial-100th-supplement-final.

227. Malkin, Michelle: Open Borders Inc., Who's Funding America's Destruction? 468; Gegnery Publishing, A Division of Salem Media Group, Washington, D.C. 20001, United States of America, 2019.

228. Marrella, L. (2009). In Search of Ethics: Conversations with Men and Women of Character. In L. Marrella, In Search of Ethics: Conversations with Men and Women of Character (Third Edition ed., p. 368). Sanford, Florida, United States of America: DC Press: A Divison of the Diogenes Consortium. Retrieved April 12, 2018.

229. Martin, M. (2004, June 21). sfgate.com/califonia-new-state-director-rehabilitation-not-recycling-inmates. Retrieved July 13, 2018, from: https://www.sfgate.com/news/article/New-director-of-state-prisons-believes-in-2747530.php.

230. Mauldin, J. (2017, 10 10). Forbes.com. Retrieved April 23, 2018, from: https://www.forbes.com/.../your-pension-is-a-lie-theres-210-trillion-of-liabilities-ou-government-can't-fulfill.

231. McFarlane, R. a. (2018, June 8). wsj.com/iraqi-christians. Retrieved June

18, 2018, from: https://www.wsj.com/2018/06/08/iraqi-christiansare-still-waiting-mr-pence

232. Mencken, H. (2015, September 19). tdayinquotes.com/h.l.mencken-broke-underestimate-intelligence. Retrieved June 21, 2018, from https://www. thisdayinquotes.com/2011/09/no-one-ever-went-broke-underestimating.html.

233. mentalhealthdaily.com/age-of-complete-brain-development-mid-20's-influences(n.d.). Retrieved July 31, 2018, from https://www.mentalhealthdaily. com/2015/02/18/at-what-age-is-the-brain-fully-developed.

234. Merriam-Webster Dictionary. (n.d.). Retrieved 4 11, 2018, from https://www.merriam-webster.com/dictionary/corruption.

235. Merriam-Webster Dictionary. (n.d.). Retrieved April 11, 2018, from https://www.merriam-webster.com/dictionary/gang.

236. Meyer, I. H., Flores, A. R., Stemple, L. J., Romero, A. P., Bianca, D. W. and, H. J. (2017, February). williamsinstitute.law.ucla.edu, and, ajph. apha.publications.org. Retrieved May 5, 2018, from https://www.williamsinstitute.law.ucla.edu/wp-content/uploads/Meyer Final Proofs.LGB.ln.pdf

237. Miller, F. T. (1945, 1948). The Complete History of World War II. In F. T. Miller, The Complete History of World War II (p. 999). New York, New York, United States of America: The Publishers Guild. Retrieved March 30, 2018.

238. Moore, P. H. (2016). See Something Say Something. Washington, D.C., Washington, D.C., USA: WND Books.

239. Morales, G. C. (2015; 4th Edition). La Familia-The Family: Prison Gangs in America (Vol. 4th edition; 2015). Parker, Colorado, USA: CreateSpace. Retrieved 10 11, 2017.

240. motherjones.com/french-prisons-radicalization. (2015, August 1). Retrieved May 23, 2018, from: https://www.motherjones.com/politics/2015/08/01/frenc h-prisons-terrorists-radical-islam.

241. Munoz-Santos, M. E. (2017, September). TERROR ON THE LOW "LOW SEAS": The Naumachiae of Rome.

242. (A. E. Briggs, Ed.) NATIONAL GEOGRAPHIC: HISTORY, Volume 3(Number 4), 50-53. Retrieved October 9, 2017, from www.nationalgeographic.com.

243. musicmatch.com-mitzi-gaynor-cockeyed-optimist-musical-south-pacific(n.d.). Retrieved June 25, 2018, from https://www.musicmatch. com/lyrics/Mitzi-Gaynor/Cockeyed-Optimist-South-Pacific National Gang Center. (2012).

244. Retrieved March 12, 2018, from http:// www.nationalgangcenter.gov

245. nationalgeographic.com/the-plague. (n.d.). Retrieved 8 3, 2018, from: https//www.nationalgeographic.com/science/health-and-human-body/human-diseases/the-plague nationalstudentclearinghouseresearchcenter.org/content. (2017).

246. Retrieved May 24, 2018, from:
https://www.nscresearchcenter.org/wp-content/uploads/2017HSBenchmarksReport-1.pdf
nbcnews.com. (n.d.).

247. Retrieved May 5, 2018, from
https://www.nbcnews.com/feature/nbc-out/overwhelming-number-lesbians-bisexual-women-incarcerated-n728666.

248. nces.ed.gov/graduation-rates-white-black-hispanic-asian-american-indian(n.d.). Retrieved 8- 24-2018,
from: https://www.nces.ed.gov/programs/coe/indicator coi.asp.

249. nces.ed.gov/percentage-of-high-school-dropouts. (n.d.). Retrieved 8-24-2018,
from https://www.nces.ed.gov/progrms/digest/dt16 219.70.

250. newyorker.com/nattering-nabobs-of-negativism-william-safire-7-10-2007-david-remnick-article. (7-10-2007). Retrieved 8-23-2018, from:
https://www.newyorker.com/2007/07/10/nattering-nabobs.

251. nih.gov/blacks-and-hispanics-less-likely-than-whites-to-complete-addictionrx-due-to socioeconomics. (n.d.). Retrieved 8-3-2018, from
https://www.ncbi.nlm.nih.gov/pmc/articles/PMC237740 8.

252. nij.gov/prisonerradicalization. (October 27, 2008). Retrieved May 24, 2018,
From: https://www.nij.gov/journals/261/pages/prisoner-radicalization.aspx.

253. nobelprize.org-obama gets-nobel-prize-for-peace-2009. (2009, October 9). Retrieved June 4, 2018, from https://www.nobelprize.org/nobel prizes/peace/laureates/2009/press.html.

254. npr.org/chicago-battles-murder-murder-capital-of-the-country. (8-10-2018). Retrieved 8-18- 2018, from: https://www.npr.org/2018/08/10/chicago-battles-its-image-as-murder-capital-of-the-nation

255. npr.org/fact-check-trump-low-unemployment-for-african-americans-responsible-? (2018, January 8). Retrieved July 25, 2018, from https://www. npr.org/2018/01/08/576552028/fact-check-trump-touts-low-unemployment-rates-for-african-americans-hispanics.

256. npr.org/unemployment-rates-african-americans-hispanics-whites. (January 8, 2018). Retrieved June 22, 2018, from https://www.npr. org/2018/01/08/576552028/fact-check-trump-touts-low-unemployment-rates-for-african-americans-hispanics

257. NYPD News. (n.d.). Retrieved April 13, 2018, from https://www.nypdnews.com/2018/04/truth-herman-bell.

258. nypost.com. (n.d.). Retrieved April 13, 2018, from https://www.nypost.com/2018/04/11/how-infamous-cop-killer-herman-bell-convincedparole-board-he=should-be-a-free-man.

259. nypost.com/steve.emerson/radicals-in-our-prisons/. (2009, May 24). Retrieved May 23, 2018, from https://www.nypost.com/2009/5/23/radicals-in-our-prisons.

260. nypost.cpm. (n.d.). Retrieved April 13, 2018, from https://www.nypost.com/2018/04/10/cuomo-parole-board-appointee-married-to-convicted-murderer.

261. nytimes.com/ford-hood-wrestling-with-label-terrorism. (2014, April 8). Retrieved June 4, 2018, from https://www.nytimes.com/2014/04/09/us/at-fort-hood-wrestling-with-label-of-terrorism.html.

262. nytimes.com/thomas-p-oneill-second-obituary. (1994, January 6). Retrieved June 25, 2018, from https://www.nytimes.com/1994/01/06/obituaries/thomas-p-oneill-jr-dies-at-81-a-power-in-the-house-for-decades.html.

263. Occam's razor. (n.d.). Retrieved April 5, 2018, from https:///www.brittanica.com/topic/Occam's razor.

264. Odeku, N. (2015, June 15). Wicked Horror. Retrieved April 6, 2018, from: htpps://www.wickedhorror.com

265. Office, F. N. (2018, January 23). FBI Press Office. Retrieved April 3, 2018, from Federal Bureau of Investigation: https://www.fbi.gov/news/pressrel/press-releases/fbi-releases-preliminary-semiannual-crime-statistics-for-2017.

266. ojp.gov (office of justice programs). (n.d.). Retrieved April 27, 2018, from: https://www.ojp.gov

267. opensecrets.org/contributions-to-Trumps-election. (n.d.). Retrieved May 24, 2018, from https://www.opensecrets.org/pres16/geography?id=N00023864.

268. Orwell, George (1945), Animal Farm, New York: Harcourt, Inc.

269. Ostrowski, J. (2014). Progressivism: A Primer on the Idea Destroying America. Buffalo, New York, USA: Cazenovia Books.

270. ourdocuments.gov/brown-v.-board-of-education. (1954). Retrieved July 2, 2018, from https://www.ourcoduments.gov/doc.

271. ourducuments.gov/brown-vs.-board-of education-1954. (n.d.). Retrieved July

2, 2018, from: https://www.ourdocuments.gov/doc.php-87

272. Patel, J. K. (2018, February 15). nytimes.com. Retrieved May 5, 2018, from: https://www.nytimes.com/interactive/2018/02/15/us/schoolshootings-sandy-hook-parkland.html.

273. Peale, N. V. (2003). The Power of Positive Thinking: A Touchtone Book, Simon & Schuster, 2015, 219 pages.

274. Peter, D. L. (2011). The Peter Principle: Why Things Always Go Wrong. In D. L. Peter, The Peter Principle: Why Things Always Go Wrong (p. 161). New York, New York, United States of America: Harper Business: Reprint Edition. Retrieved May 9, 2018.

275. Peoples, Edward E.: Basic Criminal Procedures, 4th Ed., 245; Meadow Crest Publishing, Forestville, CA, United States of America, 2017

276. Pew Research Center. (2018). Retrieved March 16, 2018, from https://www.pewresearch.org
Pew Research Center: Millennials: Confident. Connected. Open to Change. (2011).

277. Retrieved March 14, 2018, from: https://www.pewsocialtrends.org/files/2010/10/millenials-confident-connected-open-to-change.pdf

278. pewforum.org/barack-obama-reverend-jeremiah-wright-united-church-ofChrist-Chicago. (n.d.). Retrieved May 8, 2018, from https://www.pewforum.org/2008/11/04/religion-and-politics-08-barack-obama

279. pewresearch.com/john-gramlich-most-violent-and-property-crimes-in-us-gunsolved. (3-1-2017).

280. Retrieved 8 16, 2018, from https://www.pewre search.org/fact-tank/2017/03/01/most-violent-and-property-crimesin-the-u-s-go-unsolved pewresearch.org/john-gramlich-violent-and-property-crimes-unreported-unsolved.

281. Retrieved 8 16, 2018, from: https://www.pewresearch.org/fact-tank/2017/03/01/most-violent-and-property-crimesin-the-u-s-go-unsolved.

282. pewresearch.org/u.s.-dropout-rate-reaches-record-low-driven-by-blacks-and hispanics (n.d.).

283. Retrieved 8-24-2018, from: https://www.pewresearch.org/fact-tank/2014/10/02/u-s-high-school-dropout-ratereaches-record-low-driven-by-improvements-among-hispanicsblacks.

284. Pfaff, J. F. (2017). Locked In. New York: Basic Books.

285. Pfaff, J. F. (2017). LOCKED IN: THE TRUE CAUSES OF MASS INCARCERATION AND HOW TO ACHIEVE REAL REFORM. In J. F. Pfaff, LOCKED IN: THE TRUE CAUSES OF MASS INCARCERATION AND HOW TO ACHIEVE REAL REFORM (p. 311). New York, New York, United States of America: Basic Books, an imprint of Perseus Books. Retrieved January 11, 2018.

286. phrases.org/lies-damn-lies-and-statistics-leonard-h-courtney-lord-courtney (1895). Retrieved June 29, 2018, from https://www.phrases.org.uk/meanings/lies-damned-lies-and-staistics.html physicsclassroom.com/newton/inertia/and/motion. (n.d.).

287. Retrieved 8-14-2018, from https;//www.physicsclassrom.com/newtlaws/Lesson 1/Inertia-and-Mass.

288. poetryfoundation.org/william-wordsworth-the-world-is-too-much-with-uspoem. (8-20-2018); https://www.poetryfoundation.org/poems/45564/the-world-is-too-much-with-us-poets.org/william-wordsworth-the-world-is-too-much-with-us; also: https:/www.poets.org/poetsorg/poet/william-wordsworth (8-20-2018).

289. political.com/prison-reform-bill-commentary. (5-22-2018). Retrieved 5-24-2018 from https://www.politico.com/story/2018/05/22/house-easily-passes-prison-reform-bill-backed-by-white-house-603333.

290. politifact.com/ben-shapiro/muslims-radicals-numbers. (11-5-2014)

291. Retrieved May 23, 2018, from https://www.politifact.com/pun ditfact/statements/2014/11/05/ben-shapiro/shapiro-says-majority-muslims-are-radicals.

292. politifact.com/obamas-lies-all. (n.d.). Retrieved June 26, 2018, from: https://www.politifact.com/personalities/barack-obama/statements/byruling/false popcultureaddictlifeguide.blogspot.com/days-of-our-lives. (9-26-2011).

293. Retrieved July 5, 2018, from: https://www.popcultureaddictlifeguide.blogspot. com/2011/09/like-sands-through-hourglass-so-are.html.

294. prearesoucecenter.org/prison-rape-elimination-act-prea-2003. Retrieved 8 20, 2018, from https://www.prearesourcescenter.org/ about/prison-rape-elimination-act-prea.

295. Press, A. (May 15, 2013). Philadelphia abortion doctor sentence to three life terms in jail, Philadelphia. Press, F. N. (May 13, 2013). Doctor Kermit Gosnell found guilty of murdering infants in late-term abortions. Philadelphia. prisonpolicy.org/executions-awaiting-execution. (n.d.).

296. Retrieved July 3, 2018, from: https://www.prisonpolicy.org/graphics/cjrace death executions.html.

297. prisonpolicy.org/global-incarceration-rates-country-by-country. (n.d.). Retrieved 8-16- 2018 from https://www.prisonpolicy.org/statistics/ global-incarceration-rates-country-by-country prisonpolicy.org/incarceration-numbers. (n.d.).

298. Retrieved July 12, 2018 from:
https://www.prisonpolicy.org/reports/pie.html
prisonpolicy.org/incarceration-rates-south-carolina-compared-to-founding-nato-countries. (n.d.).

299. Retrieved 8 16, 2018, from:
https://www.prisonpolicy.org/global/2018-incarceration-rates-south-carolina-compared-to-founding-nato-countries.

300. prisonpolicy.org/whole pie-2018. (n.d.). Retrieved July 26, 2018, from:
https://prisonpolicy.org/reports/pie2018,html--disproportionately-higher-black-population-in-prison.(n.d.).

301. Retrieved 8-26-2018, from:
https://www.prisonpolicy.org/
graphs/Racial Geography Black binned.html

302. Pro Football Hall of Fame. (n.d.). Retrieved April 5, 2018, from:
https://www.profootbalhof.com/players/bill-parcells
procon.org/statements-pro-and-con-about-death-penalty-as-deterrent. (n.d.).

303. Retrieved 8-9-2018, from
https://www.deathpenalty.procon.org/
view.answers.php?questionID=000983.

304. Profile of Nonviolent Offenders Exiting State Prisons. (2004, October). Retrieved March 13, 2018, from https://www.bjs.gov.

305. prsonpolicy.org/statistics-numbers. (n.d.). Retrieved 8-28-2018, from:
https://www.prisonpolicy.org

306. Quandt, K. R. (2016). outline.com/norman-brown-parole-versus-don-ruzicka-missouri-board-of-probation-and-parole. Retrieved June 21, 2018
from: https://www.theoutline.com/post/3625/the-false-hope-of-parole-pushhwm

307. quora.com/snopes-politifact-factcheck-right-or-left-leaning-accuracy-? (November 18, 2016).

308. Retrieved June 26, 2018, from:
https://www.quora.com/is-snopes-biased-why-do-some-people-believe-snopes-is-biased
realclearpolitics.com/congressional-job-approval-july-2018-low-6-high-15-percent. (n.d.).

309. Retrieved July 26, 2018, from:
https://www.realclearpoliticss.com/epolls/other/congres sional job approval-903.html.

310. Reisig, M. D., D., B. W., Hay, C., & and Wang, X. (2007, September); doi.org/the-effect-of-racial-inequality-on-black-male-recidivism-2007. Retrieved June 22, 2018, from https://www.doi.org/the-effect-of-racial-inequality-on-black-male-recidivism.

311. Riley, J. L. (2018, June 13). wsj.com. Retrieved June 18, 2018, from:
https://www.wsj.com/2018/06/13/the-attack-on-educational-excellence.

312. Robert H. Lustig, M. M. (2017). The Hacking of the American Mind. New York, New York, USA: Avery.

313. Robey, J. P. (March 1, 2017):
robinainstitute.umn.edu/parole-boards-described-qualifications-univ-of-minnesota. Retrieved June 21, 2018 from: https://www.robinainstitute.umn.edu/news-

views/paroleboard-members-statutory-requirements-educational-achievements-and-institutional.

314. Rochefoucauld, L. D. (1959). MAXIMS. (L. Tancock, Trans.) London, England: Penguin Group.

315. rochester.edu/full-brain-development-u-rochester-med-ctr-25-yrs-about. (n.d.).
Retrieved July 20, 2018, from:
https://www.urmc.rochester.edu/encyclopedia/3051

316. Rodgers, M. E. (2005). MENCKEN: THE AMERICAN ICONOCLAST:
In M. E. Rodgers, MENCKEN: THE AMERICAN ICONOCLAST (p.662). New York, New York, United States of America: Oxford University Press. Retrieved October 11, 2017.

317. Romanyshyn, Y. (2017, September 26). chicagotribune.com. Retrieved May 3, 2018, from:
https:/www.chicagotribune.com/news/data/ct-homicide-spikes-comparison-htmlstory.html.

318. Roosevelt, T. (n.d.). goodreads.com/senators-roll-call-present-not-guilty. Retrieved June 28, 2018, from https://www.goodreads.com/quotes/tag/senate.

319. Russell, C. (2007). Incarceration Around the World. In c. Russell, Incarceration Around the World (p. 112). Philadelphia, Pennsylvania, United States of America: Mason Crest Publishers.

320. Safire, W. (n.d.). Safire's New Political Dictionary. April 2, 2006. Retrieved 2006, from:
https://www.santacruzpl.org/readyref/files.

321. Samenow, S. E. (2014). INSIDE the CRIMINAL MIND. In S. P. Samenow, INSIDE the CRIMINAL MIND (p. 349). New York, New York, United States of America: Broadway Books, an imprint of the Crown Publishing Group. Retrieved 10-11-2017.

322. Samuel Johnson (1709-1784), J. M. (August 3, 2009). The Lives of the Poets: A Selection (Oxford World's Classics). Oxford, England, UK: Oxford University Press; Televised ed. edition.

323. Santayana, G. (n.d.). brainyquote,com/george-santayana. Retrieved April 4, 2018 from: https://www.brainyquote.com/quotes/george santayana 101521.

324. Retrieved April 25, 2018 from: https://www.prisonpolicy.org/reports/pie2018/html; prison population percentages.

325. Schinto, J. (1997). Murder on Tick Tock Lane. Yankee magazine.

326. School, C. L. (2016, September). Center For The Advancement Of Public Integrity. Retrieved May 14, 2018 from https://www.law.columbia. edu/sites/default/files/microsites/public-integrity/files/prison corruption - capi community contribution - september 2016.pdf.

327. Schweizer, P. (2010). Architects of Ruin (Paperback Edition; Hardcover Edition, New York, New York, USA: HarperCollins Publishers, 2009.

328. Scott, J.: A Singular Woman: The Untold Story of Barack Obama's Mother. In J. Scott, A Singular Woman: (p. 386). New York: Penguin Books, 2011.

329. sentencingproject.org. (n.d.). Retrieved April 25, 2018, prison populations, from:
https://www.sentencingproject.org,

330. Shakespeare. (1948, 1952). Shakespeare: The Complete Works. In Shakespeare, & G. Harrison (Ed.), Shakespeare; The Complete Works (p. 1668). New York, New York, United States of America: Harcourt, Brace and Company, Inc.; Retrieved July 3, 2018

331. shakespeare.org.uk/much-ado-about-nothing. (n.d.). Retrieved July 16, 2018, from:
https://www.shakespeare.org.uk/explore-shakespeare/shakespedia/shakespeares-plays/much-ado-about-nothing.

332. Shapiro, B.: politifact.com.../ben-shapiro; November 5, 2014; Retrieved May 05, 2018, from:
https://www.politifact.com/punditfact/statements/2014/Nov/05/ben-shapiro/shapiro-says-majority-muslims-are-radicals.

333. Shaw, G. B. (1969). The Crime Of Imprisonment. In G. B. Shaw, The Crime of Imprisonment (p. 125). Westport, Connecticut, United States of America: Greenwood Press, Inc.; Retrieved July 26, 2018

334. Sherwood, B. (2009). The Survivors Club: The Secrets and Science That Could Save Your Life. In B. Sherwood, The Survivors Club: The Secrets and Science That Could Save Your Life (p. 383). New York, New York, United States: Grand Central Publishing, Hachette Book Group.

335. Sides, H. (2001). Ghost Soldiers: The Forgotten Epic Story of World War
II's Most Dramatic Mission, (p. 342). New York, New York, United States of America: Doubleday: A Division of Random House, Inc. Retrieved March 30, 2018.

336. simplypsychology.org/maslow's-pyramid. (n.d.). Retrieved August 1, 2018,
from: https://www.simplypsychology.org/maslow.html

337. Skarbek, D.: The Social Order of the Underworld: How Prison Gangs Govern the American Penal System, New York, New York, USA: Oxford University Press. 2014.

338. Slater, L. (2006, February). LOVE: The Chemical Reaction. (C. Johns,Ed.) National Geographic, pp. 32-49.

339. Smith, C. (n.d.). brainyquote.com/prison-learning. Retrieved June 28, 2018,
from https://www.brainyquote/quotes/clint smith 893473.

340. Smith, S. (n.d.). izquotes.com. Retrieved Aril 15, 2018, from iz-quotes:
https://www.izquotes.com/quote/287383

341. snopes.com/obamas-50-lies-evaluation. (n.d.). Retrieved June 26, 2018, from:
https://www.snopes.com/fact-check/obams-50-lies

342. snopes.com/robert-byrd-wv-senator-in-kkk-garb. (n.d.). Retrieved 8 6, 2018 from:
https://www.snopes.com/fact-check/robert-byrd-kkk-photo.

343. Solzhenitsyn, A. I. (1973). The Gulag Archipelago: 1918-1956: An Experiment in Literary Investigation. In A. I. Solzhenitsyn, The Gulag Archipelago: 1918-1956: An experiment in literary Investigation (T. P.English), Trans., p. 660). New York, New York, United States of America: Harper & Row Publishers, Inc. Retrieved March 30, 2018.

344. Spencer, R. (2009). The Complete Infidel's Guide to the Koran. Washington, D.C., District of Columbia, USA: Regnery Publishing, Inc.

345. Springfield, D. (1964, August 21st). Retrieved Uploaded August 21, 2008 by blumentopf443, from You Tube: https://www.youtube.com.

346, staistica.com/number-of-households-1960-to-2017-but-in-2017-126.22-million. (n.d.). Retrieved 8-16-2018, from: https://www.stistica.com/statistics/183635/number-of-households-in-the-us.

347. The Assassination of Abraham Lincoln: A Tribute of the Nations.The Assassination of Abraham Lincoln: A Tribute of the Nations (p. 837). Old Saybrook, Connecticut, United States of America: Konecky & Konecky. Retrieved March 30, 2018.

348. Stephen M. Kirby, PhD: The Lure of Fantasy Islam, Exposing the Myths and Myth Makers, Published by Create Space, 2017, 270 pages.

349. Stephen M. Kirby, PhD: Islam and Barack Hussein Obama: A Handbook on Islam, Published by Stephen M. Kirby, PhD, 210; 45 pages.

350. Stratton, R.: Kingpin: Prisoner of the War on Drugs. New York, New York, USA: Arcade Publishing an imprint of Skyhorse Publishing, Inc 2017.

351. sutherland-careers.com/irresistable-force-meets-immovable-object-paradox. (n.d.). Retrieved May 4, 2018, from https://www.sutherland-careers. com/blog/paradox-puzzle-friday.

352. Taranto, J. (2018, May 5-6). wsj.com. (W. E. Baker, Editor) Retrieved May 5, 2018, from https://www.wsj.com/2018/05-06/May/taranto-themaking-and-unmaking-of-a-jihadist.

353. Taranto, J.: wsj.com/obama-red-lie. June 9-10, 2018; Retrieved June 18, 2018 from: https://www.wsj.com/2018/06/09.

354. obama's-red-linedebacle-from-the-inside-ben-rhodes-book-taybafoundation.org. (2016); from: https://www.taybafoundation.org/2016/islam-and-muslims-in-the-u-s-prisonsystem-by-rami-nsour taybafoundation.org/2016/islam-in-u-s-prison-system. (n.d.). Retrieved May 21, 2018.

355. The Constitution of the United States. (n.d.). (S. 1. The Emoluments Clauses, Compiler) The Heritage Foundation. Retrieved 8-24-2018.

356. The Economist. (2017, February 7); from: https://www.economist.com: The Golden Age of Drug Trafficking: How Meth, Cocaine, and Heroine Move Around the World/Vice News. (2016, April 25). Retrieved March 13, 2018.

357. https://www.news.vive.com/.../drug-trafficking-methcocaine-heroin-global-drug-smuggling.

358. The National Registry of Exonerations. (n.d.):
from:
https://www.law.umich.edu/special/exoneration/Pages/c
asedetail.aspx-3684. Retrieved April 23, 2018,
from University of Michigan Law School:
https://www.law.umich.

359. The National Rifle Association. (2018). Retrieved
March 12, 2018, from
https://www.nra.org.

360. The Qur'an. (2015). In the Qur'an (M. A. Haleem,
Trans., p. 464). New York, New York, United States of
America: Oxford University Press,
Inc. Retrieved May 22, 2018.

361. The Trace-A Nonprofit Newsroom Covering Gun
Violence in America. (n.d.). Retrieved March 30, 2018,
from:
https://www.the trace.org/features/gun-violence-2017.

362. theathlantic.com/least-trusted jobs-congress-with-
car-salespeople. (n.d.). Retrieved July 26, 2018, from:
 https://www.theatlantic.com/business/
archive/2012/12/the-least-trusted-jobs-in-america-
congress-members-and-car-salespeople/265843

363. thehill.com/trump-approves-of-kushner's-private-
prison-reform-joke! Retrieved 8-3-2018

364. https://www.thehill.com/homenews/senate/400176-
trumps-gives-thumbs-up-to-prison-sentencing-reform-
bill-at pivotal-meeting.

365. thoughtco.com/dan-quayle-malapropi from:
https://www.thoughtco.com/dan-quayle-quotes-
2733512sms; Retrieved July 27, 2018.

366. thoughtco.com/grain-alcohol. (2017, September 02). Retrieved May 24, 2018,
from https://www.thoughtco.com/what-is-grain-alcohol-3987580

367. time.com/epa-regulations-obama-pruitt-deregulaltion. (n.d.). Retrieved June
4, 2018, from:
https://www.time.com/4983904/epa-regulationsrules-lawsuits-scott-pruitt/

368. time.com/weather-underground-ayers-and-dohrn. (n.d.). Retrieved May 8,2018
from:
https://www.time.com/4549409/the-weather-underground-bad-moon-rising

369. townhall.com/bush-did-not-lie-weapons-of-mass-destruction. (2016, February 21). Retrieved May 25, 2018, from https://www.townhall.com/columnists/johnhawkins/2016/02/21/show-this-column-to-anyone-who-claims-bush-lied-about-wmds-in-Iraq-n2122278

370. THE QUR'AN (Fourth Edition; Others: 2004,2005, and 2011 ed.). (M. A. Haleem, Trans.) New York, New York, USA: Oxford University Press, Inc.

371. transmioonsmedia.com/worldview-warfare-weltanschauungskrieg-science-of-coercion. (2018, 8 20). Retrieved 8 20, 2018, from:
https://www.trnasmissionsmedia.com/weltanschauungskrieg-worldview-warfare-and-the=science-of-coercion.

372. Treadgold, W. (2018). THE UNIVERSITY WE NEED: Reforming American Higher Education. In W. Treadgold: THE UNIVERSITY

WE NEED: Reforming American Higher Education (p. 184). New York, New York, United States of America: Encounter Books. Retrieved July 27, 2018.

373. Turow, S. (2010). One L. In S. Turow, One L (p. 304). New York, New York, United States of America: Penguin Books, 1977.
Retrieved October 11, 2017

374. TZU, S. (1983). THE ART OF WAR. In S. Tzu, & J. Clavell (Ed.), THE ART OF WAR (Unknown, Trans., p. 82). New York, New York,
United States of America: Delacorte Press. Retrieved April 23, 2018.

375. U.S. Department of Commerce: 2010 Census Report. Washington, D.C.: https://www.census.gov.

376. U.S. Department of Justice, Office of Justice Programs, National Institute of Justice. (n.d.). Retrieved March 30, 2018, from:
https://www.nij.gov/topics/gunviolence/pages.

377. U.S. Poverty Statistics. (2017, September). Retrieved March 12, 2018, from:
https://www.federalsafetynet.com/us-poverty-statistics.html.

378. Uniform Crime Reporting Statistics. (n.d.). Retrieved April 2, 2018, from:
https://www.ucrdatatool.gov/Search/Crime/State/RunCrimeStatebyState.cfm

379. usdoj.gov/military-prisons-59. (n.d.). Retrieved 8 16, 2018, from:
https://usdoj.gov/searchnumber+of+military+and+number=of+prisoners-BJS-OJS.

380. usgovernmentspending.com/federal-deficit-debt. (n.d.). Retrieved July 11, 2018 from: https://www.usgovernmentspending.com/federal deficit-debt chart.html.

381. ussc.gov/criminal-history-of-federal-offenders-important data. (May 17, 2018). Retrieved June 5, 2018, from https://www.ussc.gov/research/research-reports/criminal-history-federal-offenders-utm medium-email&utm source-govdelivery.

382. Velleman, P. F. (August 29,2017): phrases.org/courtney-leonard-h-lies-damned-lies-and-statistics. Retrieved June 28, 2018, from: https://www.tandfonline.com/doi.

383. vera.org/price-of-prisons-2015. (2017, May). Retrieved July 11, 2018, from: https://www.vera.org/publications/price-of-prisons-2015-state spending-trends/price-of-prisons-2015; Retrieved July 30 30, 2018 from: https://www.vera.org/newsroom/press-releases/new-verareport-the-price-of-prisons-what-incarceration-costs-taxpayer.

384. Violence Policy Center: Research, Investigation, Analysis & Advocacy for a Safer America. (2018). Retrieved March 18, 2018, from: https://www.vpc.org/regulating-the-run-industry/gun-trafficking.

385. Volokh, A. (2011). "Prison Vouchers." University of Pennsylvania Law Review, 160(3), 779-864.

386. Voltaire. (2016). Candide. In Voltaire, Candide (p. 122). Overland Park, Kansas, United States of America: Digireads.com, a subsidiary of
Neeland Media, LLC Digireads Publishing. Retrieved July 24, 2018.

387. Voltaire. (n.d.). brainyquote.com. Retrieved May 5, 2018, from Brainy Quotes:
https://www.brainyquote.com/quotes/voltaire 106180;
accessedMay3,2018

388. Voltaire. (n.d.). shmoop.com/voltaire-candide-el-dorado. Retrieved July 24, 2018 from:
https://www.shmoop.com/candide/el-dorado-symbol.html.

389. vox.com. (2017, August 8). Retrieved May 23, 2018, from:
https://www.vox.com/first-person/2017/8/8/16112864/recidivism-rate-jail-prostitution-break-cycle.

390. vox.com/george-w-bush-lies-wmds-iraq-war. (2016, July 9). Retrieved May 25, 2018 from:
https://www.vox.com/2016/7/9/12123022/george-w-bushlies-iraq-war.

391. vox.com/jared-kushner-prison-reform-federal-v-state-prisons. (2018, May 22).

392. Vronsky, P. (2004). SERIAL KILLERS: THE METHOD AND MAD NESS OF MONSTERS. In P. Vronsky, SETIAL KILLERS: THE
METHOD AND MADNESS OF MOMSTERS (p. 412). New York, New York, United States of America: The Berkley Publishing Group.
Retrieved 10-11-2017.

393. Wagner, P. a. (n.d.). Prison Policy Initiative Updates. (P. Wagmer, Editor)
Retrieved April 3, 2018, from Prison Policy Initiative: https://www. prisonpolicy.org

394. Warner, B. P. (2010). SHARIA Law for Non-Muslims. Center for the Study of Political Islam; CSPI PUBLISHING, Nashville, TN 2010.

395. washingtonexaminer.com/new-prison-bill-hatch-and-cotton-armed-careercriminal-act-8-6-2018. (2018, 8 6). Retrieved 8-9-2018; from:
https://www.washingtonexaminer.com/opinion/op-eds/sens-tom-cottonorrin-hatch-close-loophole-that-letting-violent-criminals-go-free 2018. (n.d.). Retrieved 8-7-2018.

396. https://www.washingtonexaminer.com/opinion/op-eds/sens-tom-cotton-orrin-hatch--close-
-the-loophole-thats-letting-violent-criminals-go-free
washingtonpost.com. (2018, April 23). Retrieved May 5, 2018.

397. https://www.wahingtonpost.com/graphics/2018/loc al/school-shootings-database

398. washingtonpost.com/boll-weevil-democrats. (n.d.). Retrieved July 2, 2018, from:
https//www.wasgingtonpost.com/archive/politics/1981/0 4/26/after-two-decades-the-bolloweevis-are-back-whistling-dixie.

399. washingtonpost.com/IRS-under-Obama-admits-to-targeting-conservatives; May 10, 2013). Retrieved June 4, 2018, from:
https://www.washingtonpost.com/busines/economy/irs-admits-targeting-consrvatives-for-tax-scrutiny-in-2012.

400. washingtonpost.com/obama-claim-no-foreign-terror-organization-attacked-homelandsuccessfully; December 8. 2016). (G. Kessler-contributor, Producer) Retrieved June 4, 2018, from: https://www.washingtonpost.com/news/fact-checker/wp/2016/12/06/obamasclaims-that-no-foreign-terror-organization-successfully-attackedthe-homeland-on-his-watch.

401. washingtonpost.com/reynaldo-rodriguez-michigan-judge-advice-parole-board-avoidance; July 11. 2015 from: https://www.washingtonpost.com/national/the powerandpoliticsofparoleboards/2015/07/10/.html. Retrieved July 31, 2018.

402. Weiss, M. (2003). The Man Who Warned America: The Life and Death of (Feb. 6, 1952) John O'Neill (Sept. 11, 2001): The FBI's Embattled Counterterror Warrior. In M. Weiss, The Man Who Warned America: The Life and Death of (Feb. 6, 1952) John O'Neill (Sept. 11, 2001): (p. 450). New York, New York, United States of America: Regan Books: An Imprint of HarperCollins Publishers. Retrieved March 31, 2018.

403. wikipedia.com/crusades. (n.d.). Retrieved May 16, 2018, from: https://en.wikipedia.org/wiki/Crusades.

404. wikipedia.org/andrea-yates. (n.d.). Retrieved 2018 6, 2018, from: https://en.wikipedia.org/wiki/Andrea Yates.

405. wikipedia.org/bedford-hills-correctional-facility-for-women. (n.d.). Retrieved July 30, 2018

from:
https://en.wikipedia.org/wiki/Bedford Hills
Correctional Facility for Women
406. wikipedia.org/boll-weevil. (n.d.). Retrieved July 2, 2018, from:
https://en.wikipedia.org/wiki/Boll weevil (politics);
wikipedia.org/boll-weevil-democrats. (n.d.). Retrieved July 2, 2018,
407. wikipedia.org/capital-punishment. (n.d.). Retrieved 8-9-2018, from:
https://www.wikipedia.org/wiki/Capital punishment in the United States.
408.wikipedia.org/caryl-chessman. (n.d.). Retrieved July 5, 2018, from:
https://www.wikipedia.org/wiki/Caryl Chessman.
409.wikipedia.org/charles-kushner-imprisonment-14-month-sentence-jared's-father. (n.d.). Retrieved July 16, 2018, from https://en.wikipedia.org/
wiki/Charles Kushner
410.wikipedia.org/civil-rights-act-1964. (n.d.).
Retrieved July 2, 2018, from:
https://en.wikipedia.org/wiki/Civil Rights Act of 1964.
Retrieved July 2, 2018, from
https://en.wikipedia.org/wiki/civil rights act 1964
411. wikipedia.org/cognitve-dissonance. (n.d.).
Retrieved July 13, 2018, from:
https://en.wikipedia.org/wiki/Cognitive Dissonance
412. wikipedia.org/conversion-to-Islam. (2018, March 15). Retrieved May 23,

2018, from:
https://en.wikipedia.org/w/index.Conversion to Islam in U.S. prison-830487977
Retrieved June 11, 2018.

413. wikipedia.org/guillotine. (n.d.). Retrieved 8-9-2018, from:
https://en.wikipedia.org/wiki/Guillotine
wikipedia.org/guillotine-last-used-september-10-1977-last-used-abolished-in-1981-when-france-abolished-capital-punishment. (n.d.). Retrieved 8-9-2018, from: https://en.wikipedia.org/wiki/Guillotine-history

414. wikipedia.org/jean-baptiste-alphonse-karr-more-things-change-expression(n.d.). Retrieved July 27, 2018, from https://en.wikipedia.org/wiki/Jean-Baptiste Alphonse Karr.

415. wikipedia.org/kathy-boudin. (n.d.). Retrieved July 30, 2018, from:
https://en.wikipwedia.org/wiki/Kathy Boudin
wikipedia.org/list-of-us-military-prisons. (n.d.). Retrieved 8 16, 2018, from:
https://www.wikipedia.org/wiki/List of U.S. military prisons.

416. wikipedia.org/michael-gerson-expressions. (n.d.). Retrieved May 31, 2018, from:
https://www.wikipedia.org/wiki/Michael Gerson

417.wikipedia.org/national-debt-deficit. (n.d.). Retrieved July 11, 2018, from:
https://en.wikipedia.org/wiki/National debt deficit of the United States.

418. wikipedia.org/pamela-smart. (n.d.). Retrieved July 30, 2018, from:
https://en.wikipedia.org/wiki/Pamela Smart.

419.wikipedia.org/pee-wee-gaskins. (n.d.). Retrieved April 6, 2018, from:
https://en.wikipedia.org/wiki/Donald Henry Gaskins.

420. wikipedia.org/plessy-v.-ferguson. (n.d.). Retrieved July 2, 2018, from:
https://en.wikipedia.org/wiki/plessy v. ferguson
wikipedia.org/plessy-vs.-ferguson-1896. (n.d.). retrieved July 7, 2018.

421. wikipedia.org/professor-irwin-corey. (n.d.). Retrieved July 27, 2018, from:
https://en.wikipedia/wiki/Irwin Corey.

422. wikipedia.org/robert-stroud. (n.d.).; retrieved July 5, 2018, from:h
tpps://en.wikipedia.org/wiki/Robert Stroud

423. wikipedia.org/susan-smith. (n.d.). Retrieved April 6, 2018, from:
https://en.wikipedia.org/wiki/Susan Smith.

424. wikipedia.org/trinitarios-gang-violent-new-york-based. (n.d.).; retrieved July 30, 2018, from:
https://en.wikipedia.org/wiki/Trinitarios

425. wikipedia.org/u.s.-cities-with-large-african-american-populations. (n.d.); retrieved July 24, 2018, from:
https://en.wikipedia.org/wiki/List of U.S. cities with large African-American populations.

426. wikipredia.com/2009-fort-hood-shooting. (n.d.). retrieved June 4, 2018 from:
https://en.wikipedia.org/wiki/2009 Fort Hood shooting.

427. wiktionary.org/semordnilap. (n.d.); retrieved 4-14-2018 from:
https://en.wiktionary.org/wiki/semordnilap

428. Wise, J.: Extreme Fear, The Science of Your Mind in Danger; Palgrave Macmillan. St. Martin's Press, New York, New York; 246 pages; 2009.

429. World Drug Report (United Nations). (2015). Retrieved March 13, 2018 from
https://www.unodc.org/documents/wdr2015/World Drug Report 2015.pdf.

430. Wright, W. (2012, March 29-31). Semantic Scholar. Retrieved March 14, 2018 from:
https://www.pdfs.semanticscholar.org.

431. Wright, W. (2012, March 29-31). The Disparities between Urban and Suburban American Education Systems: A comparative Analysis
Using Social Closure Theory. Proceedings of The National Conference on Undergraduate Research (NCUR), pp. 1612-1619. Retrieved April 5, 2018, from:
https://www.pdfs.semanticscholar.org.

432, wsj.com; retrieved 8-9-2018 from:
https://www.wsj.com/2018/08/09/the-pope-makes-a-fatl-error-death-penalty-a-stain.

433. wsj.com. (2018, May 29); retrieved May 29, 2018, from:
htps://www.wsj.com/2018/05/29/i'm-in-prison-for-practicing-politics.

434. wsj.com. (2018, June 5); retrieved June 5, 2018 from:

https://www.wsj.com/2018/06/05/gulag's-shadow-flls-on-korean-summit.

435. wsj.com/andy-pudzer-working-multiple-jobs (n.d.); retrieved July 25, 2018 from: https://www.wsj.com/2018/07/25/andy-pudzer/does-everyone-have-two-jobs.html.

436. wsj.com/BringBackThe Asylum; May 19-20, 2018; retrieved May 19, 2018, from: http://. wsj.com/c-boyden-gray-andrew-cuomo-coercion; June 7, 2018; retrieved June 7, 2018 from: https://www.wsj/andrew-cuomo's-extralegal-coercion.

437. wsj.com/Islamist-countries-struggle-to-keep-maritime-sea-channels-power-struggle; June 2-3, 2018; retrieved from: https://www.wsj.com/2018/06/02-03/mideast-power-struggle-plays-out-on-new-stage.

438. wsj.com/jason-riley-airport-control-tower-race-relations-hiring-Obamaenough-minorities; Wednesday, June 6, 2018; retrieved from: https://www.wsj.com/jason-l-riley/the-airport-control-tower-is-noplace-for-racial-redress.

439. wsj.com/kimberley-a-strassel-deep-state-article, May 25, 2017; retrieved June 10, 2018, from: https://www.wsj.com/articles/anatomy-of-adeep-state-1495753640.

440. wsj.com/mary-anastasia-o'grady-u.s.-funds-guatemalan-abuse; 8-20-2018; retrieved from: https://www.wsj.com/2018/08/20/the-u.s.-funds-guatemalan-abuse.

441. wsj.com/massachusetts-mentally-ill-in-prisons-reestablish-asylums; May 19-20, 2018; from: https://www.wsj.com/bring-back-the-asylum-take-mentally-ill-out-of-prisons-massachustts.

442. wsj.com/ms-13-mara-salvatrucha-ms-13-gang-tries-to-organie-an-unrulyyoung-membership; 8-20-2018; retrieved from: https://wsj.com/2018/08/20/ms-13-gang-tries-to-organize-an-unruly-young-membership.

443. wsj.com/religious-Islam-celebration-of-ramadan; June 1, 2018; retrieved from: https://www.wsj/2018/06/01/how-america-makes-ramadan-easier

444. wsj.com/sean-m-bigley-deep-state-vetting-of-trump; May 1, 2018; retrieved June 10, 2018, from https://www.wsj.com/articles/the-deep-state-weaponizes-vetting-of-trump-appointees-1525215143.

445. wsj.com/tom-cotton-reform-the-prisons-without-going-soft-on-crime; 8-16-2018); retrieved from: https://www.wsj.org/2018/08/16-reform-the-prisons-without-going-soft-on-crime.

446. wsj.com/tom-cotton-senator-repub-arkansas-reform-prisons-without-goingsoft-on-crime; 8-16-2018; retrieved from: https://https. wsj.com/2018/08/16/reform-the-Prisons-Without-Going-Soft-on-Crime.

447. Yang, A. (2018). The War on Normal People: The truth About America's Disappearing Jobs and Why Universal Basic Income is Our Future.

In A. Yang, The War on Normal People: The Truth About America's Disappearing Jobs and Why Universal Basic Income is Our Future (p. 304).
New York, New York, United States of America:
448. Zoukis, C.; April 15, 2001: prisonlegalnews.org. Retrieved April 25. 2018 from:
https://www.prisonlegalnews.org/news/2001/apr/15/south-carolina-rapes-exposed.
449. Zoukis, Christopher: Federal Prison Handbook: The Definitive Guide to Surviving the Federal Bureau of Prisons; Middle Street Publishing, South Carolina, 492 pages; 2017.

Robert Allyn Goldman grew up in Newton, Massachusetts. He received a BA in History from the University of Pennsylvania, a Doctor of Dental Medicine from Case Western Reserve University School of Dental Medicine, and a Doctor of Science from the Henry M. Goldman School of Dental Medicine at Boston University in addition to specialty training in Periodontology, Oral Medicine, and Oral/General Pathology at Boston University Medical Center (now part of Boston Medical Center), Boston, Massachusetts. He currently lives in Palm Beach Gardens, Florida.

www.ingramcontent.com/pod-product-compliance
Lightning Source LLC
Chambersburg PA
CBHW030232030426
42336CB00009B/74